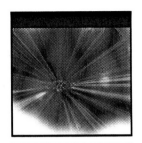

Enterprise Integration

An Architecture for Enterprise Application
and Systems Integration

Fred A. Cummins

Wiley Computer Publishing

John Wiley & Sons, Inc.

NEW YORK · CHICHESTER · WEINHEIM · BRISBANE · SINGAPORE · TORONTO

Publisher: Robert Ipsen

Editor: Robert Elliott

Assistant Editor: Emilie Herman

Managing Editor: John Atkins

New Media Editor: Brian Snapp

Text Design & Composition: MacAllister Publishing Services, LLC

Library of Congress Cataloging-in-Publication Data

Cummins, Fred.
    Enterprise integration : an architecture for enterprise application and systems integration / Fred A. Cummins
        p. cm.
    ISBN: 0-471-40010-6 (PAPER/WEBSITE : alk. paper)
    1. Computer architecture. 2. Systems engineering. I. Title.

QA76.9.A73 C86 2002
004.2'2--dc21   2001008394

10 9 8 7 6 5 4 3 2 1

Advance Praise for
Enterprise Integration

"Fred Cummins has written a thorough and up-to-date guide to system and application integration. This book shows, step-by-step, how to develop and execute a program to combine business systems into a coordinated whole.

This is also an excellent reference handbook for the software architect. In one volume Cummins provides an encyclopedic coverage of the whole range of integration issues and technologies."

Joaquin Miller
Chief Architect, Financial Systems Architects

"*Enterprise Integration* gives companies an architecture for developing distributed and secured global systems using current standards and Internet-based approaches, based on the author's own experiences in the workplace."

Hideshige Hasegawa
Director of Software Alliance, Hitachi, Ltd.

2001 OMG Press
Advisory Board

Karen D. Boucher
Executive Vice President
The Standish Group

Carol C. Burt
President and Chief Executive Officer
2AB, Inc.

Sridhar Iyengar
Unisys Fellow
Unisys Corporation

Cris Kobryn
Chief Technologist
Telelogic

Nilo Mitra, Ph.D.
Principal System Engineer
Ericsson

Jon Siegel, Ph.D.
Director, Technology Transfer
Object Management Group, Inc.

Richard Mark Soley, Ph.D.
Chairman and Chief Executive Officer
Object Management Group, Inc.

Sheldon C. Sutton
Principal Information Systems
   Engineer
The MITRE Corporation

Ron Zahavi
Chief Technology Officer
MedContrax, Inc.

OMG Press Books in Print

- *Java Programming with CORBA, Third Edition* by Gerald Brose, Andreas Vogel, and Keith Duddy, ISBN: 0-471-24765-0.

- *The Object Technology Casebook: Lessons from Award-Winning Business Applications* by Paul Harmon and William Morrisey, ISBN: 0-471-14717-6.

- *The Object Technology Revolution* by Michael Guttman and Jason Matthews, ISBN: 0-471-60679-0.

- *Programming with Enterprise JavaBeans, JTS and OTS: Building Distributed Transactions with Java and C++* by Andreas Vogel and Madhavan Rangarao, ISBN: 0-471-31972-4.

- *Programming with Java IDL* by Geoffrey Lewis, Steven Barber, and Ellen Siegel, ISBN: 0-471-24797-9.

- *Quick CORBA 3* by Jon Siegel, ISBN: 0-471-38935-8.

- *UML Toolkit* by Hans-Erik Eriksson and Magnus Penker, ISBN: 0-471-19161-2.

About the OMG

The Object Management Group (OMG) was chartered to create and foster a component-based software marketplace through the standardization and promotion of object-oriented software. To achieve this goal, the OMG specifies open standards for every aspect of distributed object computing from analysis and design, through infrastructure, to application objects and components.

The well-established Common Object Request Broker Architecture (CORBA) standardizes a platform- and programming-language-independent distributed object computing environment. It is based on OMG/ISO Interface Definition Language (OMG IDL) and the Internet Inter-ORB Protocol (IIOP). Now recognized as a mature technology, CORBA is represented on the marketplace by well over 70 Object Request Brokers (ORBs) plus hundreds of other products. Although most of these ORBs are tuned for general use, others are specialized for real-time or embedded applications, or built into transaction processing systems where they provide scalability, high throughput, and reliability. Of the thousands of live, mission-critical CORBA applications in use today around the world, over 300 are documented on the OMG's success-story Web pages at *www.corba.org*.

CORBA 3, the OMG's latest release, adds a Component Model, quality-of-service control, a messaging invocation model, and tightened integration with the Internet, Enterprise Java Beans, and the Java programming language. Widely anticipated by the industry, CORBA 3 keeps this established architecture in the forefront of distributed computing, as will a new OMG specification integrating CORBA with XML. Well-known for its ability to integrate legacy systems into your network, along with the wide variety of heterogeneous hardware and software on the market today, CORBA enters the new millennium prepared to integrate the technologies on the horizon.

Augmenting this core infrastructure are the CORBA services, which standardize naming and directory services, event handling, transaction processing, security, and other functions. Building on this firm foundation, OMG Domain Facilities standardize common objects throughout the supply and service chains in industries such as Telecommunications, Healthcare, Manufacturing, Transportation, Finance/Insurance, Electronic Commerce, Life Science, and Utilities.

The OMG standards extend beyond programming. OMG Specifications for analysis and design include the Unified Modeling Language (UML), the repository standard Meta-Object Facility (MOF), and XML-based Metadata Interchange (XMI). The UML is a result of fusing the concepts of the world's most prominent methodologists. Adopted as an OMG specification in 1997, it represents a collection of best engineering practices that have proven successful in the modeling of large and complex systems and is a well-defined, widely accepted response to these business needs. The MOF is OMG's standard for metamodeling and meta data repositories. Fully integrated with UML, it uses the UML notation to describe repository metamodels. Extending this work, the XMI standard enables the exchange of objects defined using UML and the MOF. XMI can generate XML Data Type Definitions for any service specification that includes a normative, MOF-based metamodel.

In summary, the OMG provides the computing industry with an open, vendor-neutral, proven process for establishing and promoting standards. OMG makes all of its specifications available without charge from its Web site, *www.omg.org*. With over a decade of standard-making and consensus-building experience, OMG now counts about 800 companies as members. Delegates from these companies convene at week-long meetings held five times each year at varying sites around the world, to advance OMG technologies. The OMG welcomes guests to their meetings; for an invitation, send your e-mail request to *info@omg.org*.

Membership in the OMG is open to end users, government organizations, academia, and technology vendors. For more information on the OMG, contact OMG headquarters by phone at 1-508-820-4300, by fax at 1-508-820-4303, by e-mail at info@omg.org, or on the Web at *www.omg.org*.

Contents

Foreword

The IT practitioner faces a continual high-wire balancing act. The goal of IT activity is of course to automate the processes of a business. Occasionally this means implanting in that business a new process, impossible without automation that garners fame or fortune for the enterprise. The goal is not the further use of emerging technologies. In fact, these goals seem often at odds. The reality is, however, that new and emerging technologies (and particularly new and emerging standards) often offer significant opportunities for new revenue sources or expense savings. Both of these opportunities smile gently on the business' bottom line.

The Chief Information Officer has an immediate goal of smoothly and invisibly (to the rest of the company) integrating the information assets of the corporation. Various integration solutions strive to support this immediate goal; unfortunately, integration solutions change constantly as the underlying (emerging) technologies change. Keeping up with the pace of change is not an easy job in the IT industry.

Since its introduction, OMG's open, platform-neutral CORBA technology—covered extensively in this book-has revolutionized systems integration by allowing smooth, portable, straightforward interoperability between application systems; from the small, embedded, and real-time markets, through desktops and minicomputers, all the way to large enterprise-system "big iron." After over a decade of shipments of over a hundred implementations of the standard, CORBA is deeply embedded in tens of thousands of applications and literally tens of millions of computers. CORBA has succeeded, in part, because it is an industry standard, not a proprietary solution designed to exclude other solution providers.

The CORBA success story, however, has not deterred generation after generation of other integration "backbone" technologies, from the proprietary (Microsoft's COM), to the semi-proprietary (Sun's Java RMI), to the open (the various XML RPC mechanisms). The CIO is now faced with a choice of integration technologies; and who integrates the integrators?

To my mind, the complete and detailed treatment in this reference of the many integration technologies in the marketplace, and how they may be applied to the systems problem, leads me to the belief that a central modeling technique is the essential, long-term solution to management of enterprise information assets. At OMG, we strongly believe that a Model Driven Architecture (MDA) approach, based on detailed modeling of systems and automatic generation of platform-specific implementations (from CORBA to COM to XML to Java) is the only way forward that finally fulfills the promise of "divorcing the problem from the solution."

At the same time, the CIO must assure that these model-based solutions can be deployed in a technology environment that supports integration within a diversity of implementations. This book describes an enterprise architecture that supports flexible integration and provides a target environment for MDA solutions. This is not the only possible architecture, but it is based on industry standards and trends. These are not all the available technologies, but the book focuses on a set of industry-standard technologies that can work together to achieve integration at all levels and accommodate diversity in the implementation of specific applications and integration of legacy systems.

In essence, this is what the CIO needs to fulfill his or her mission of integrating assets: technologies that comprise a target architecture and supporting infrastructure, and a way to characterize information assets such that they may be reused and repurposed as the underlying technology (and more importantly, the business need) changes. As you read through this comprehensive work, don't let the trees blind you from the forest: the problem is managing, integrating, and deploying information assets, and the implementation and integration technologies must be chosen to further that goal.

Richard Mark Soley, PhD
Chairman and CEO
Object Management Group, Inc.
Over the Atlantic Ocean
December 2, 2001

Introduction

This book is about transforming an enterprise to exploit emerging technologies and a changing marketplace while at the same time streamlining and harmonizing the enterprise to realize reduced cost, improved quality, and the ability to respond faster to business problems and opportunities.

After many years of developing computer applications in an evolving technological landscape, most enterprises are burdened with a vast array of computers and applications that are linked together through a variety of ad hoc mechanisms. The diversity of application architectures and technology, along with the local focus of application functionality, have fragmented the enterprise, creating major barriers to the capture, communication, and integration of management information necessary for the effective operation and improvement of the business. The maze of connections between applications conceals the intricacies of the business operation, locks the enterprise into outdated business practices and organization structures, and presents a major challenge for access to needed data and to the introduction of new applications. Skilled knowledge workers are unable to access needed data and collaborate to develop enterprise solutions to key problems. As a result of their dependence on computer systems, enterprises have become encumbered by fragmented and fragile systems that obscure the business operation and frustrate attempts to respond to changing business needs and opportunities.

Now a new wave of technology, driven largely by the Internet, has created additional business challenges and greatly increased the role and importance of information systems to the survival of most businesses. Electronic marketplaces have changed the relationships of customers and suppliers and raised expectations for access to information, personalization, and responsiveness. Businesses must now operate in "Internet time," and compete in a global marketplace. Global competition demands increased efficiency, quality, and responsiveness. To meet these demands, the enterprise must make information technology work to its advantage to become more streamlined, constantly improve its business processes, and respond quickly to resolve problems and pursue opportunities. Knowledge workers must be able to use the technology to access information and work together more effectively, collaborating to achieve enterprise objectives. This cannot be achieved by developing the integrated enterprise one application at a time. It requires an enterprise perspective and a technical architecture that achieves economies and synergy across the enterprise and extends to business partner and customer relationships.

The next wave of technology will be driven by the Object Management Group (OMG), Model Driven Architecture (MDA), and Unified Modeling Language (UML). Specifications for standards and applications will be expressed as technology-independent models, and tools will provide the ability to transform these models into executable code on specific platforms. This will allow application and standards developers to focus more attention on the solution of business problems, and it will enable specifications of standards and applications to survive changes in technology. In addition, it will enable the concise specification and integration of commercial application components. While this technology is still evolving, tools are currently available to transform specifications to code. Standards for the transformations are required to achieve interoperability between independently developed components and applications. This book provides a foundation for deployment of the MDA.

The Purpose of This Book

The purpose of this book is to bring together business and technical perspectives on enterprise integration and provide an enterprise integration architecture that will position an enterprise to excel in this new business and technological environment. Many managers recognize the need to change but don't fully understand the opportunities or how to employ the technology effectively. Many technical people understand the details of various technologies but don't have the enterprise perspective or authority to provide consistent, integrated solutions. This book builds a bridge from business needs and opportunities to technical architecture, infrastructure, and standards so that managers and developers can share a vision and communicate more effectively to transform the enterprise for this new electronic era.

One of the major challenges facing enterprise managers is the overwhelming array of products, technologies, and services, all promising easy solutions to the new business challenges. In many cases, managers are drawn in by promises of quick solutions provided by a single vendor. The complexities of implementing and integrating different products, both the business and technical implications, can be enormous-particularly when each product is considered on its own merits. The age of the Internet is taking us out of this free-for-all development of new solutions because the Internet demands that products work together. Technical standards are now becoming important to vendors as well as consumers of the technology. Standards provide benchmarks against which products can be evaluated—they eliminate many of the variables that result in incompatibilities. Standards are essential to enterprise integration because an enterprise must be supported by products from many vendors, both for flexibility in the choice of solutions and to enable implementation of new technologies and business solutions as they become available. An important aspect of this book is to show how a number of standards fit together to provide detailed specifications for the enterprise integration architecture.

Who Should Read This Book

This book is written for managers, enterprise architects, and system designers as a guide to enterprise integration and the implementation of an enterprise architecture. It recognizes the need to:

- Integrate many of today's stove-pipe applications
- Incorporate commercial, off-the-shelf (COTS) solutions
- Rapidly develop new, flexible applications for competitive advantage
- Exploit new technologies and business solutions
- Participate in the world of electronic commerce
- Enable the enterprise to exploit its intellectual capital
- Promote solutions that are optimized for the enterprise

At the same time, it recognizes that the technology will continue to change, and that the architecture must enable incremental and local improvements in business functions and technology with minimal disruption of business operations.

While the manager, architect, and designer do not come with the same needs for understanding, this book should provide a common point of reference. It should enable the manager to envision a strategic transformation of the enterprise to exploit technology and to gain an understanding of the factors to be considered and the problems to be solved when selecting products and making investments in new technology. For the architect, it should provide a basic framework from which to devise an architecture tailored to the needs of the particular enterprise and it should provide the basis for communication with managers regarding the nature and importance of the architecture. For the designer, it should provide guidance on solving application problems in a way that will support the strategic enterprise goals for integration, economies of scale, and optimization of business processes, and it should provide an appreciation of how individual applications and services can better serve the needs of the enterprise as a whole.

How This Book is Organized

The approach of this book is to take the reader from business objectives to technical solutions in order to illustrate how the technologies fit together to support an integrated enterprise. The enterprise integration architecture provides the basic framework into which particular technologies provide key integration solutions. It incorporates concepts of enterprise application integration (EAI) but extends this technology to include Internet access, business process automation, and distributed objects technology. This provides a basis for unification of emerging trends and reveals how an enterprise can manage the transformation of its business systems in an orderly, incremental manner based on business priorities.

The book begins with a discussion of the changing business and technical environment and the business needs and opportunities created by this environment. It presents a general architecture followed by a description of the necessary shared facilities and services-the information systems infrastructure. Next we characterize the business systems that rely on this infrastructure, the "business system domains," which may take the form of legacy applications, commercial enterprise applications, or component-based distributed applications. We then explore several key technologies in greater detail to link the architecture to specific industry standards and generally accepted solutions. Finally, we will examine the potential to extend this foundation to build an intelligent enterprise. We conclude with a management roadmap for implementing the architecture.

The appendixes include a list of references that were used in the development of this book. More extensive references to relevant Web sites.

What's on the Web Site

The companion Web site, *www.wiley.com/compbooks/cummins*, provides standards documents. This Web site will provide on-going support for enterprise integration with relevant references as they become available.

Acknowledgments

The technologies and standards discussed in this book are products of the efforts of many people throughout the industry. The enterprise integration architecture, which brings these technologies together, is a result of insights I have gained over the years from many colleagues, primarily at EDS and the Object Management Group (OMG), where I have had the pleasure of working with many talented and dedicated people. While I cannot name them all, I want to specifically recognize a few who have had particular influence on my ideas and have had the patience to debate issues, particularly in the development of technical solutions and proposals for OMG specifications. They are Bill Bejcek, Arne Berre, Cory Casanave, David Frankel, Mamdouh Ibrahim, John Lewis, Dan Matheson, Joaquin Miller, Karsten Riemer, Waqar Sadiq, Marc Thomas Schmidt, Oliver Sims, Bill Swift, Bryan Wood, and David Zenie.

On this particular effort, I want to thank Waqar Sadiq for getting me started; Joaquin Miller for his review of the manuscript; Richard Soley for the Foreword; the OMG staff for supporting an environment of learning, creativity, and debate; Bob Elliott, Emilie Herman, and John Atkins at John Wiley & Sons for their patience and support; and my wife Hope, for tolerating the time and attention I devoted to this work and for her continued support of my varied pursuits.

CHAPTER

1

Assessing the Technology Landscape

In the last decade, major changes have occurred in information technology. Microcomputer technology drove the transition from large, centralized computing systems to client-server and personal computing. The Internet and Web technology eliminated communication barriers and gave individuals immediate access to information from anywhere in the world. New businesses sprang up to exploit new business opportunities created by the global electronic marketplace. Old businesses were shaken by new competitive pressures and the need to reexamine basic operating assumptions.

Information technology is driving a revolution in business. The core drivers are microcomputer and Internet technologies, but these have spawned a wide range of new, related technologies and capabilities that must be integrated in a consistent enterprise architecture for the enterprise to remain competitive and exploit the business opportunities of this new era.

This chapter examines the technology landscape to establish a context for the rest of this book. We will look at the following list of key technologies and assess their implications for the enterprise of the future:

- Legacy systems
- Data warehousing
- Enterprise application integration

- Electronic commerce
- Web-enabled applications
- Extensible Markup Language (XML)
- Workflow management
- Distributed objects
- Components
- Java
- Unified Modeling Language (UML)
- Public key infrastructure
- Digital signatures
- Wireless interface devices
- Knowledge management
- Agent technology
- Interactive voice
- Model Driven Architecture (MDA)

Understanding these technologies provides the basis for Chapter 2, where we will consider the implications for strategic business change.

Legacy Systems

We cannot understand the impact of new technology without considering it with respect to legacy systems. The current enterprise landscape is littered with systems that are the result of the evolution of business and technology over many years. Systems have been developed to solve specific high-priority problems or achieve specific productivity improvements. Paths have been forged to connect systems to each other to avoid manual intervention and improve response time. In some cases, databases are shared by several systems to achieve consistency and streamline communication. However, these databases generally are not the sole repositories for the data they contain, and equivalent but inconsistent data often are stored in other systems.

The evolution of technology also has contributed to the fragmentation of systems. When new systems are developed, the latest technology is employed. Systems built with older technology cannot simply be redeployed using the new technology, but rather require substantial reworking or redevelopment to port them to the new technology. If the current business functionality of a system is adequate, there often is no clear incentive to perform the rework. As time goes on, the old systems become more out of date and difficult to operate or integrate because of both changes in the technology and changes in business operations that are reflected in the newer system.

In large corporations, local units develop many of the business solutions. The isolation of similar organizations, difficulties reaching consensus, and competition between business units discourage the sharing of ideas and the development of common solutions. The solutions that are developed typically are inconsistent from a business standpoint as well as technically. Business data are captured in different forms, given different names, and computed in different ways. Sources and uses of the data will vary. When corporate management seeks information on the associated business operations, the data available from different units will not support summaries and comparisons.

Client-server technology in many cases made this fragmentation of the enterprise worse. Systems that used to run in the same data centers, sharing some of the same data and technology, have been off-loaded to local servers where the applications are optimized for the local business unit, but isolated from the rest of the enterprise. The move to client-server technology was the beginning of a wave of technology proliferation. The rapid evolution of technology and products resulted in the definition of a new architecture for each new client-server system. Although this exploited the latest technology, it sub-optimized the solution, overlooking the impact on the enterprise as a whole. Enterprise-level analysis, planning, and decision making must gather data from many independent local systems. These cross-enterprise functions often face both technical challenges and inconsistencies in the data.

Major business restructuring often has further complicated the system's landscape. Restructuring may come in a variety of forms such as outsourcing, acquisitions, consolidations, or the creation of new business units to pursue business opportunities. When restructuring occurs, system changes are pursued in the most expedient manner possible. Systems that were independent previously now must be connected. In some cases, systems are eliminated, but then the systems that replace them must be linked in their place. Incompatibilities, when they are understood, are resolved either through system revisions or by placing adapters in the links between systems. In the end, the landscape has been further complicated by more links, more systems, and more inconsistencies.

Top managers of major corporations are frustrated by their information systems. They have difficulty getting information about how the business is running, as well as difficulty getting information to analyze the causes of major problems in order to develop solutions. When needs arise to change the business, the information systems are a major barrier to the implementation of change.

In addition, the Internet and electronic commerce are changing the way business is conducted and have increased the need to improve the operation of the enterprise as a whole. The Internet has created a global marketplace. Even small businesses must prepare for global competition. Large enterprises must be able to integrate globally distributed operating units. There is new demand for access to information from across the enterprise to respond more quickly to problems and opportunities. Customer expectations for Internet-speed responsiveness are driving the need for more responsive internal systems. Batch systems are being replaced by transactional systems, where inputs are processed as they occur.

Businessesneed to exploit commercial-off-the-shelf (COTS) applications where custom solutions no longer provide a competitive advantage. COTS applications can reduce maintenance costs and put the burden of incorporating technological advances on the COTS vendor. At the same time, business processes must be streamlined and improved continuously. It must be possible to incorporate new technology for competitive advantage without undertaking long, expensive, and risky projects. Change must be rapid and incremental, supported by a flexible integration framework.

The following sections examine a number of technologies that are changing enterprise information systems. The enterprise integration architecture must provide a framework in which effective legacy systems can continue to function as these new technologies and the corresponding business changes are integrated into the operation of the business.

Data Warehousing

Data warehousing emerged some years ago to address needs for decision support. Mainstream business systems contain the day-to-day operating information, but it is often difficult to access such information in a form that is appropriate for analysis of business problems. Where the scope of problems spans multiple business functions, access to consistent information is more difficult. In addition, mainstream systems seldom retain the data needed for analysis of trends and correlation for long periods of time. Figure 1.1 depicts the sales history for three different products over a one-year period. Most operational systems would not have these data available because they are no longer relevant to current operations. In addition, most systems for current operations would not have the tools available to obtain such information on an ad hoc basis. Online analytical processing (OLAP) tools provide much more sophisticated analyses of relationships and trends.

Data warehouses typically establish an operational data store (ODS) to capture and integrate operational data where mainstream systems do not support operational queries and reporting. The ODS then may be the source of data on current business transactions to be passed to a data warehouse for the accumulation of historical data. Data "cleansing" and transformation operations often are performed to improve the consistency and integrity of the data going

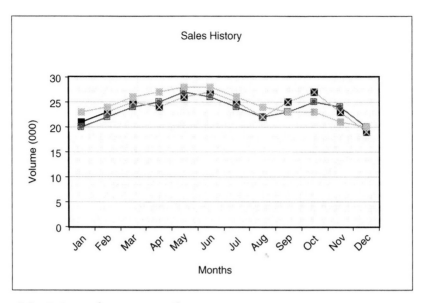

Figure 1.1 Data warehouse perspective.

to the data warehouse. Frequently, this involves the reconciliation of data on the same business transaction coming from different sources. The data warehouse may accumulate data for years. The storage requirements for data warehouses are extremely large. The data warehouse technology typically is tuned for the addition and retrieval of data, but not for updates to existing data. *Data marts* provide the actual data-analysis support. A data mart is designed to optimize the analysis of specific business data for specific purposes. The required data are extracted periodically from the source data warehouse and loaded into the data mart. Analysts and managers then use specialized tools to analyze the data for trends and correlation.

The need for data warehouses and data marts will continue. Mainstream systems will not retain historical data for years, nor support specialized analytical tools. On the other hand, operational data stores duplicate the data found in mainstream systems and lag in timeliness. As mainstream systems are redeveloped, it is reasonable to expect that they will meet the need for operational decision support, and the ODS will be phased out.

Data warehousing has driven the development of special tools for the capture, transformation, and integration of data from multiple sources. Typically, these tools operate on batch files extracted from mainstream systems. When data must be merged from multiple sources, these tools provide for holding the data from some sources, pending receipt of matching data from other sources. When the records are matched, there may be inconsistencies to reconcile. These types of operations likely will continue, although batch processing may be less common in the future.

A key challenge for data warehousing efforts is to determine the scope and representation of the data to be captured. If data are not captured today, then they will not be available to support analyses in the future. However, it is expensive to develop consistent data models and implement the cleansing and transformation processes. If the data-capture decisions are driven exclusively by current needs for analysis, then when current problems are resolved, data may not be available to address new or more sophisticated problems.

Enterprise Application Integration

Enterprise application integration (EAI) also involves the capture and transformation of data, but for a different purpose. EAI was driven by the need to integrate COTS applications. In the mid-1990s, a number of commercial applications emerged to support specific business functions, particularly manufacturing, personnel, and accounting functions. The installation of these products required integration with related legacy systems. EAI is the practice of linking COTS and legacy systems, and a number of products have emerged to support this practice.

The basic approach is the store-and-forward transfer of data between systems. Although this may be accomplished with batch files, the need for more timely data transfers led to the use of message-queue technology typified by IBM's MQ Series. In its basic form, a sender places a message (a record) in a queue for transmission, a queue manager forwards the message to a destination queue, and the destination queue holds the message until the recipient is ready to process it. This provides a loose coupling connection because the recipient need not be ready to process the message when the sender originates it. Further independence of the sender and recipient is achieved by providing a transformation facility that converts the sender's data format to the recipient's format requirement.

Where data are exchanged between many sources and many destinations, it becomes inefficient for every source to have a connection to every destination. This is addressed by a message-broker facility that receives messages from many sources and selectively redirects them to many destinations (see Figure 1.2). This improves the flexibility of communications and reduces the overall number of links.

EAI products may incorporate some or all of these facilities. In addition, they may provide adapters for a number of commercial applications. These adapters provide the connection to the message queues and may perform some local data transformation. EAI products also may provide tools and components to facilitate the implementation of adapters to legacy systems.

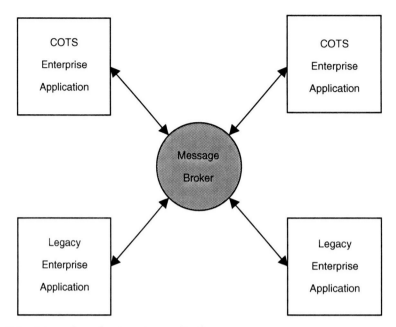

Figure 1.2   Integration of enterprise applications.

Although EAI technology originated to support interfaces to legacy systems, it has a long-term role. As new systems are purchased or developed, there will always be legacy systems to integrate. EAI technology provides for the exchange of information as events occur, rather than the periodic transfer of batch files. It streamlines the associated business processes and provides additional flexibility for the routing of messages to meet new requirements for information, including operations monitoring and the initiation of corrective action on a timely basis.

Electronic Commerce

The Internet and the World Wide Web have opened the door for enterprises to communicate directly with their end customers, exchange data in a more timely fashion with business partners, and establish new business relationships more quickly. The Internet, as depicted in Figure 1.3, is the new marketplace, and it is global. Buyer-seller relationships can be established where they were not even considered in the past. New relationships can be established quickly, and the cost of establishing new relationships is going down.

Enterprises want to make information available to customers to promote products and services. They want to make it faster and easier for customers to

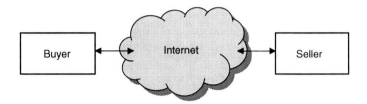

Figure 1.3   Commerce over the Internet.

obtain those products and services. Finally, they want to establish a continuing relationship with customers to promote sales and customer loyalty. This business-to-customer (B2C) electronic commerce requires the exchange of data between customers and enterprise systems in new, more effective, and personalized ways.

B2C electronic commerce requires Web servers and supporting applications to present information to the customer and accept the customer's input using standard Web browser facilities. These applications must then be integrated with legacy systems to obtain current information for customer displays and accept customer inputs to obtain products and services. Direct interaction with the customer also creates opportunities to learn more about the customer and expose the customer to related products and services.

Direct communication with customers enables the business to be more responsive. It also presents opportunities to streamline distribution channels and potentially eliminate wholesalers. Inventories may be reduced, and the business can be more sensitive to changes in the marketplace.

The Internet also has opened the door to closer communication between business partners—business-to-business (B2B) electronic commerce. Business operations can be streamlined by replacing Electronic Data Interchange (EDI) batch-file transfers with the exchange of information at the level of individual business transactions as they occur. Through the Internet, an enterprise can integrate with its suppliers to streamline the purchase, shipment, and payment for component products. It can integrate with its distribution channels to streamline the sales and distribution operations. Streamlining these processes can contribute to reductions in inventories and the capability to respond more quickly to customer orders and changes in market demand.

The electronic marketplace has engendered the development of electronic auctions. Customers from around the world can bid on products and services. Similarly, suppliers can bid in so-called reverse auctions to supply products and services. These marketplaces drive the creation of many new business relationships.

The potential for new and rapidly changing business relationships requires the ability to establish data communications quickly. As a result, service providers have emerged to support certain *marketplaces*. A marketplace supports the exchange of data between buyers and sellers of a particular class of products. The service provider defines standards for information exchanged in the marketplace, supports interfaces to the marketplace for individual enterprises, and provides for the routing of messages from sources to destinations. New standards developed by the United Nations' Center for Trade Facilitation and Electronic Business (CEFACT) have set the stage for enterprises to establish electronic commerce relationships quickly without the need for an intermediary to broker the exchange.

Web-Enabled Applications

Early efforts to provide Web access to applications were driven by the need to provide access to customers. However, Web browsers provide a universally available form of interface to any user with a workstation or personal computer. This means that a system that is Web-enabled can be accessed by just about anybody without any special preparation of the client system. This is a valuable capability within the enterprise as well as outside.

Making applications Web-enabled, as depicted in Figure 1.4, resolves a significant portion of the difficulties involved in accessing information across the

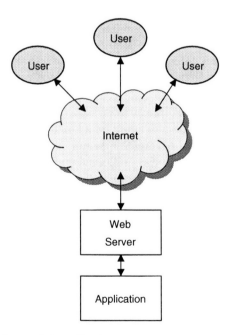

Figure 1.4 Typical Web-enabled application.

enterprise. Although the data may not be in a compatible form, at least an authorized user can access them. In addition, users of a system are not confined to accessing data from particular devices located in a particular office, but they can potentially access many systems from anywhere in the world over the Internet.

In addition to Web access by personal computers, wireless hand-held devices such as personal digital assistants and cell phones are being used for Web access. This provides user access in many situations where a personal computer is not a practical user device. Because of the small displays on these devices, special consideration must be given to page formatting. Applications may be required to provide alternative displays depending on the user's client device.

Extensible Markup Language (XML)

The Extensible Markup Language (XML) is a language for free-form expression of data structures in a universal character set. It is a a refinement of the basic syntax of HyperText Markup Language (HTML), the language of data exchange for Web browsers. It is a specification established by the World Wide Web Consortium (W3C). For a number of reasons, it has become the preferred medium for the exchange of data both between enterprises and between systems within an enterprise.

Fundamentally, XML provides a tagged data format. An XML document contains a number of elements, each with a descriptive tag and an associated value, all expressed as characters. Special characters delimit the elements so that the documents and their element names and values are of variable length. An element value may contain a group of subordinate elements or references to another XML document or Internet resource.

An XML document may be described by a Document Type Definition (DTD) or XML Schema document. An XML Schema document is also expressed in XML. An XML parser may use the DTD or schema to validate an XML document. XML Stylesheet Language (XSL) may be used to specify a transformation of an XML document. The Document Object Model (DOM) defines an object interface protocol for accessing the content of an XML document through an object-oriented interface. A number of other standards and facilities have been developed around XML.

The key strengths of XML include the following:

- It carries with it descriptive tags that provide meaning to the content.
- The format allows for the interpretation of the content, even though items may be omitted or new items may be added.

- It facilitates transformation.

- It is compatible with the HyperText Transfer Protocol (HTTP) and can pass through firewalls.

XML has become the preferred syntax for the exchange of data in an EAI environment because of XML's format flexibility and support for transformation. Various groups, such as the Open Application Group (OAG), have defined document standards for specific types of messages exchanged by enterprise applications. XML also has become the preferred syntax for B2B exchanges for the same reason it is used in EAI and for its capability to pass through firewalls. It has been incorporated in the Simple Object Access Protocol (SOAP) for performing remote procedure calls over the Internet; XML documents are used to express a message to invoke a process or method and to return a result. There are many other applications, some with merit and some of questionable value.

XML is replacing Electronic Document Interchange (EDI). EDI defines fixed-field documents for communication in batch files. XML is associated with flexible, self-documenting documents communicated as they occur. Although XML is inherently less efficient due to the addition of tags and delimiters, the interest in flexibility and timeliness of delivery overshadows the additional cost.

Workflow Management

Workflow management systems (sometimes called business process management systems) have been around for many years. For the most part, they have been applied in small organizations for managing the flow of documents between activities performed by humans. They are now gaining attention for the automation of business processes on a larger scale and for coordinating the activities of humans and computers, as depicted in Figure 1.5.

A workflow process manages the execution of activities. Activities may perform limited operations directly, they may invoke applications, and they may delegate tasks to humans by posting them on individuals' work lists.

Workflow management fits in with the move from batch processing to event-based processing, where business transactions are processed as they occur. Each business transaction receives individualized attention. Transactions can be handled with different priorities, authorized based on different criteria, and serviced with different specialized skills.

Workflow management provides the means to formalize processes, enforce compliance, monitor performance, and quickly introduce process improvements. It also provides the means to coordinate distributed and concurrent activities.

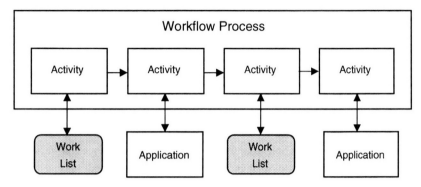

Figure 1.5   Workflow between people and applications.

One of the barriers to the expanded scope of applications is the need for the interoperation of different workflow systems. Business processes often link the activities of different business units in an enterprise. If different units implement different workflow management systems, then they may be unable to link to each other's business processes. The first step in providing interoperability has been addressed by the Object Management Group (OMG) with runtime interface specifications. Unfortunately, workflow product vendors have been slow to implement these interfaces.

Workflow management and EAI technologies are beginning to converge. Workflow techniques are being integrated with EAI message-routing tools. This makes the business processes implicit in the flow of data between enterprise applications more visible. At the same time, enterprise application vendors are incorporating workflow technology in their products to make them more adaptable to the individual needs of their customers.

The availability of workflow management affects the design and scope of applications. Workflow management allows the business processes to be moved out of the application code and into a facility where they can be tailored to customer needs. Large, monolithic applications can be divided into more discrete business functions that are linked together and managed through workflow. When business processes change, workflow processes can be adapted, and smaller application functions become easier to replace with less risk and a smaller impact on the rest of the business.

Distributed Objects

Distributed objects technology supports the development of systems with distributed components that interact as objects exchanging messages over a network. The objects may be shared services or objects of a business application.

Distributed objects systems often take the form depicted in Figure 1.6. The Web server manages the user interface. The objects on application servers (Order, Invoice, and so on) implement application functionality. A database server manages the persistent state of the objects.

There are three primary distributed object technologies:

- Common Object Request Broker Architecture (CORBA) from the OMG
- Component Object Model (COM+) from Microsoft
- Enterprise JavaBeans (EJB) from Sun Microsystems

Although these three technologies are supported by different products, they are all very similar. This suggests that the basic approach is sound, but for various business reasons, they have not yet converged.

CORBA offers three particular benefits:

1. It enables a robust, scalable solution.
2. It supports messaging between objects implemented in different languages.
3. It is the product of an industry consortium and enables interoperability between products from different vendors.

COM+, on the other hand, is provided by the world's leading software vendor and is supported by its products and operating systems. As a proprietary solution, the Microsoft implementation is the de facto reference implementation.

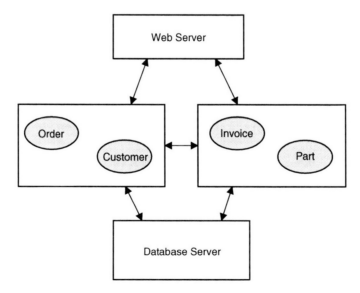

Figure 1.6 Typical distributed cbjects application.

EJB is focused on the implementation of distributed objects using the Java language. Although there are a number of vendors involved in the development of specifications for EJB and related components, Sun Microsystems has the dominant role. Specifications related to EJB are somewhat aligned to CORBA, but Sun Microsystems puts CORBA compatibility second to achieving competitive advantage with Java technologies. Java technologies have the advantage of being the product of efforts by multiple vendors while preserving the capability to respond quickly to market opportunities through the decision-making authority of a single vendor.

The development of large-scale distributed objects systems requires considerable skill. Some CORBA products are not fully compliant and fail to achieve interoperability. Even with a stable infrastructure, applications must be designed carefully to avoid performance pitfalls, and application programmers must have considerable understanding of the technology.

Nevertheless, these technologies will continue to evolve and improve their ease of use and their similarity.

Components

Object technology for many years has held the promise of enabling the development of reusable components. Within individual applications or development teams, considerable reuse has been achieved. However, the vision of constructing applications from purchased application components has not been realized. There are a number of reasons; for example, sharable components require a standard environment in which to operate, they require consistent protocols by which they interoperate with other components, and their behavior either must meet specific business needs or must be adapted easily.

At the same time, considerable progress has been made in the development of components that perform computational functions for user interfaces, communications, and operating environments. Such products have greatly enhanced the ability of application developers to implement sophisticated systems.

In addition, very large components in the form of enterprise applications have been developed and marketed successfully. Nevertheless, the development of finer-grained components for the assembly of applications has not yet been successful.

The development of the CORBA Component Model (CCM) and EJB specifications may yet enable the development of finer-grained application components. These two specifications are very similar due to the joint efforts of many of the same vendors. The CCM is intended to accept EJB components while also defining an infrastructure to support similar components in other languages. In both cases, an application component is installed in a container, that

is, a runtime framework, which provides the integration of a number of supporting services. This achieves consistency in the computing environment and
relieves the application developer of many of the computational details.

The CCM and EJB components are network-visible objects. They may be
comprised of a number of finer-grained objects. For the most part, these may
be too fine grained to become independently marketable components. Associated assembly and deployment specifications provide a mechanism for defining composite, deployable units that can be larger-grained components. A
specification under development by the OMG will provide a more robust
expression of component interfaces and compositions so that systems may be
defined as nested compositions of components, as depicted in Figure 1.7. This
will improve system flexibility and may foster the development of application
component products so that business systems can be composed of a mix of
selected components that best meet the needs of the enterprise.

Java

The Java language has had a major impact on the industry. Its primary
strength is portability achieved through execution in the Java Virtual Machine
(JVM). Sun Microsystems has complemented the JVM with the Java Development Kit (JDK), which provides a number of user-interface and computing-
environment objects to support Java applications and encapsulate platform
differences. Applications can be developed to execute without modification on
multiple platforms. Java applets can be downloaded to Web browsers to provide active content to Web pages. Web browsers provide a JVM that restricts

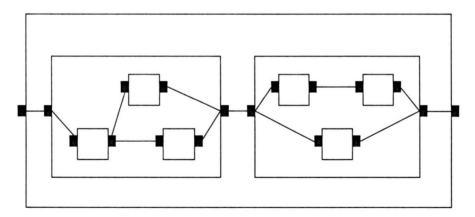

Figure 1.7 Component composition.

the execution of Java to prevent corruption of the client computer by ill-behaved applets.

In addition to portability, Java has some other important features. The JVM provides memory management so that developers do not need to explicitly destroy no-longer-used objects. It provides a degree of reflective capability, enabling a program to modify itself at run time. New objects can be introduced to an active environment so that a program can by extended dynamically.

Java initially executed within a single computer, and applications involved a single user. Sharable components, dubbed *JavaBeans*, were developed, particularly for the construction of user interfaces. Remote Message Invocation (RMI) provided the basic mechanism for distributed object computing with Java. The EJB specification introduced the concept of distributed Java components. Sun Microsystems, working with other vendors, has developed specifications for a number of related services to support EJB computing including Java Transaction API (JTA), Java Messaging Service (JMS), Java Naming and Directory Interface (JNDI), and Java Database Connectivity (JDBC).

Sun Microsystems has issued a specification for Java 2 Enterprise Edition (J2EE), which is being implemented by several vendors. This may be the primary distributed object architecture of the future.

Unified Modeling Language

Unified Modeling Language (UML) is a specification language adopted by the OMG. It was based on a specification developed by Rational Software, but experts of the OMG specification represent the combined efforts of 21 tool vendors and industry experts. It has gained wide acceptance in the industry, and efforts continue to expand its scope.

UML provides a number of visualizations and diagramming techniques. The visualization encountered most commonly is the *class diagram*, depicted in Figure 1.8.

At this writing, UML has been extended to define a Common Warehouse Metamodel (CWM) for specifications related to data warehousing systems. Specifications are under development to address specific requirements for modeling Enterprise Distributed Object Computing (EDOC), EAI, and action semantics, that is, application logic. Specifications are anticipated for workflow process definition.

UML is complemented by XML Model Interchange (XMI) specifications that provide for the exchange of UML models in XML syntax. This enables models to be stored in shared repositories and imported by different tools.

Some UML tools provide for generating skeleton, class code from specifications. As UML becomes more robust and application frameworks such as J2EE provide consistent, vendor-independent environments, it will be possible to

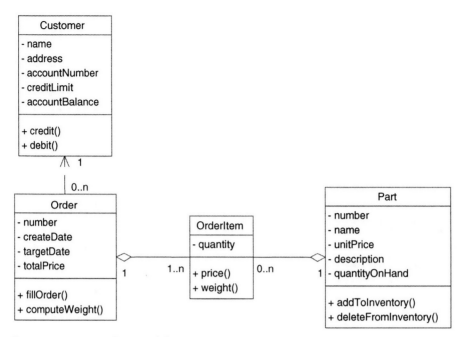

Figure 1.8 A UML class model.

generate nearly complete large-scale applications from UML specifications. Not only will this reduce the effort required to program applications, but it will also provide increased portability of applications by enabling code to be generated from the same application specifications for different implementation technologies.

OMG has adopted a Model Driven Architecture (MDA) strategy for specification of software standards. Under this strategy, standards will be specified using UML to define technology-independent models that can be mapped to specific technologies. This will provide standard specifications for services, applications, and components that can be implemented in different technologies and still interoperate in a distributed-computing environment.

Public Key Infrastructure (PKI)

Security has become an increasingly critical element of enterprise systems. First of all, enterprise systems are becoming increasingly accessible. Second, systems are interacting with customers and business partners who may be personally unknown to the enterprise and who may be accessing the systems from insecure environments. Traditionally, users are given an identifier and password for each system they must access. A typical user is burdened with many identifiers and passwords. Schemes that provide a single sign-on with passwords increase the risk by storing passwords in more places or by using one identifier and password for access to everything. A more effective security approach is provided by a public key infrastructure (PKI).

Public key technology involves the use of two complementary keys: one public and the other private. The private key (the password) is never shared, so only the owner can expose it. If a message is encrypted with the private key, it can only be decrypted with the associated public key, and if a message is encrypted with the public key, it can only be decrypted with the associated private key. One use of these key pairs is with digital certificates for user identification. Digital certificates are issued by a trusted certification authority and are encrypted with the authority's private key. The authority's public key is generally known, so a certificate is determined to be valid if it can be decrypted with the certification authority's public key. The systems and services for issuing and using certificates are called the PKI. The PKI provides a mechanism by which users can obtain certified identification from a trusted authority for use on the Internet, and they can then be identified to systems without previously being identified explicitly to each system.

This technology is used by Secure Sockets Layer (SSL) communications over the Internet to provide security. Both the sender and the receiver can authenticate each other with their digital certificates.

Public key technology also can be used to authenticate a message received from a specified source. If the message is encrypted by the source with its private key, then it can be decrypted only with the known public key of the same source. Although the public key may be generally available, the private key remains only in the possession of its owner.

Until recently, the export of public key encryption technology from the United States was restricted as a threat to national security. Since this restriction has been eased, it is likely that public key technology will be used more extensively, particularly for international commerce and enterprises with international locations.

Digital Signatures

A digital signature, when attached to an electronic document, functions essentially the same as a handwritten signature on a paper document. Digital signatures employ public key technology. The signature authenticates the document by validating the signer's identity, and it prevents the signer from repudiating the document because only the signer's public key can decrypt the signature.

To attach a digital signature to a document, the document is first processed by a digest function that produces a unique value. It is impossible to create a different document that would produce the same value. The digest value, along with other identifying information, is then encrypted with the signer's private key and attached to the digital document. The recipient of such a document can execute the same digest function on the document and decrypt the signature with the originator's public key to obtain a digest value, and if the two digest values are equal, the signature verifies that the originator signed the document and that the document has not been changed.

Federal legislation was adopted recently giving digital signatures the same legal effect as signatures on paper documents. This opens the door to widespread replacement of paper legal documents. The consequence is that the scope of business transactions conducted over the Internet will be expanded greatly.

Wireless Interface Devices

Cellular phones have become commonplace. Some cellular phone services already provide Internet access. Personal digital assistants also can have wireless Internet access. This enables a user to have Internet access from virtually anywhere. It enables new forms of Internet purchases, and it frees employees to conduct business anywhere and at any time. It also enables communication in countries where the communications infrastructure is of poor quality or limited in availability.

Of course, the Web pages accessed by these devices cannot be formatted the same as Web pages for conventional Web browser displays. Web sites accessed by these devices must recognize device limitations and provide an appropriately formatted display.

Knowledge Management

Knowledge management involves the capture, cataloging, retrieval, and application of enterprise knowledge, as depicted in Figure 1.9. In product design in particular, lessons are learned over the years that contribute to the quality of the product, including its ease of use, maintainability, reliability, efficiency, and so on. When employees leave or transfer to other activities, this knowledge may be lost. In addition, the circumstances under which such knowledge is needed may not be recognized.

Technical support for knowledge management is still in the early stages. Typically, knowledge will be captured and cataloged as text and retrieved based on key words or text searches. However, humans still must perform the final filtering and application of such knowledge.

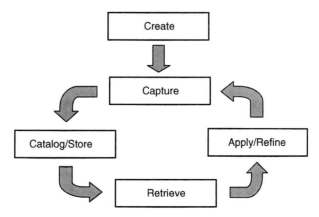

Figure 1.9 Knowledge management process.

Knowledge management is a second-order business function. It relies on links to business systems and to users at key points in their activities to both capture knowledge and identify points where it should be applied. It is difficult to implement and sustain such systems when mainstream systems involve inconsistent data, diverse technologies, and constant change. As enterprises implement consistent architectures, we can expect to see a growth in knowledge management facilities linked to business processes and applications.

We will return to a more detailed discussion of knowledge management, the process, and architectural support in Chapter 12.

Agent Technology

A *software agent* is an autonomous program that senses and reacts to its environment according to its own internal rules of operation. Its environment may include information about the actions of other agents. Unlike a conventional application, the agent itself will determine if, when, and how it will perform its function.

A simple agent might be employed to monitor some activity and raise an alarm when indicators suggest that the process is out of control. More sophisticated agents may be employed to direct the flow of work through the cells in an automated manufacturing facility. Such agents are effective when desired results can be achieved without overall control of the activities.

Agents also might be employed for knowledge management (discussed in the preceding section). Agents might detect situations where knowledge should be captured and interact with systems and people to capture that knowledge. Other agents might be employed to determine where relevant knowledge should be applied and present the information to an appropriate user.

Agent technology is still in its infancy. Like knowledge management, agent functions tend to be second-order business functions, depending on interfaces to other mainstream systems. As long as the mainstream systems are isolated and continue to employ diverse technologies, it is difficult to justify investment in second-order functions. Consistent enterprise architecture will be a key enabler for such technology.

Interactive Voice

Few applications make use of voice input or output. This is because most systems are accessed with devices that have keyboards and displays. Voice input and output require additional functionality and increase the risk of errors.

The widespread use of hand-held devices, particularly cell phones, is likely to change this. Users do not want to carry around keyboards and large displays. Voice input and output also enable hands- and eyes-free operation in activities and environments that are not conducive to conventional terminal interaction.

Like the character-based interfaces of wireless devices (discussed in the "Wireless Interface Devices" section), interactive voice communication will require yet another form of message formatting. Enterprise applications will need to anticipate these requirements when they prepare and accept message content.

Model Driven Architecture

The Model Driven Architecture strategy of the OMG provides the ability to specify applications and standards as Platform Independent Models (PIM) that can be mapped to evolving technical platforms. Tools provide the ability to transform a PIM specification to executable code. Standard mappings will enable independently developed applications and components to be interoperable. The UML Profile for Enterprise Distributed Object Computing (EDOC) provides the modeling elements for the platform-independent specification of component-based, large-scale systems. The technology to implement MDA exists, the standards and tools for composing large-scale applications are under development.

Summary

The technology trends discussed in this chapter have significant implications for enterprise integration and the design of an enterprise architecture. Several observations can be made regarding the impact of these trends on enterprise integration:

- Technology continues to change so that today's advanced systems are tomorrow's legacy systems.

- Business changes will continue at a rapid rate, driven in part by changes in technology and the need to exploit the technology to remain competitive.

- Exploiting the Web is a major driver in business and technology changes and will continue to be so for some time as related technologies and business opportunities emerge and evolve.

- In order to remain competitive, enterprises must be able to respond to global markets and exploit global operations, either their own international operations or those of business partners.

- Applications should be more limited in scope and loosely coupled to enable the selective purchase of COTS applications and the development of custom applications where they can achieve a competitive advantage.

- Close attention should be given to the impact of widely accepted standards such as CORBA, Java, XML, and UML.

- Industry standards and model-based solutions for the interoperability of services and supporting software should be exploited to avoid dependence on a single vendor as products evolve and incorporate new technologies.

- The architecture should enable the integration of second-order business functionality such as knowledge management and agents.

- Public key technology, including digital signatures, should be anticipated as an integral part of the architecture and the key to the security and integrity of future business transactions.

- User interfaces will continue to evolve, employing a number of devices and technologies.

These and other factors will be considered in the development of enterprise integration design objectives in the next chapter.

<image name="CHAPTER 2">CHAPTER

2</image>

Setting Enterprise Integration Design Objectives

Chapter 1 described technology trends and emerging capabilities that have set the stage for enterprise integration. However, enterprise integration will not just happen by adopting new technology. It must be managed with clear objectives and strategies. Figure 2.1 depicts enterprise integration from a management viewpoint. We will examine this business systems hierarchy in greater detail in Chapter 3. The management challenge is to provide the direction, manage the change, and improve the overall operation of the business.

Enterprise integration is a rather sweeping concept that could mean different things to different people. The strategic objectives of most business enterprises are to reduce costs, improve quality, and respond quickly to business problems and opportunities. Enterprise integration contributes to each of these objectives in a variety of ways. In this chapter we will consider the following design objectives to put enterprise integration into perspective, guide the efforts, and link the elements of enterprise integration to business objectives:

- Adaptable systems and processes
- Streamlined business processes
- Management information
- Support for electronic commerce

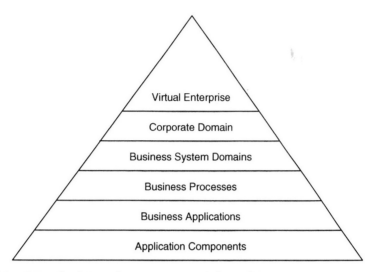

Figure 2.1   Enterprise integration: management viewpoint.

- Integrated security
- Replaceable components
- Reliable and recoverable systems
- Economies of scale

These objectives form the business basis for the approach to enterprise integration presented in the rest of this book. In Chapter 13 we will examine strategic business objectives that are enabled by the enterprise integration architecture as a basis for implementing the architecture.

Adaptable Systems and Processes

Today's business environment involves constant change. Changes are being driven by technology, by globalization of business activities, by rapidly changing markets, and by intense competition, as well as by reorganizations such as consolidations, divestitures, and mergers. Enterprise systems and processes must support these changes.

In most cases, business processes are tightly coupled to computer applications. Although humans manage much of the work, computer systems are designed to support the existing processes and organization structure. When attempts are made to change business processes, the computer applications usually require associated changes. These changes are often more complex and difficult to implement than they appear on the surface.

System changes are further complicated by the fact that the businesspeople responsible for the processes do not understand what is implemented in the business applications and the technical people who once understood the details of the design are no longer available.

The result is that changes in business processes require a long and tedious implementation that involves many people, considerable time, and usually trial-and-error solutions.

In general, changes to systems and processes should not require starting from scratch. It is seldom that the business has changed so much that there is no longer any relevant functionality in current systems. Unfortunately, business functions often are so intertwined with computational mechanisms that it is difficult to isolate what can be preserved from that which must be changed.

In order for systems and processes to be adaptable, they must be structured so that

- Responsibility and control over each business function is defined and assigned.

- Each business function is defined once, to be performed in a consistent manner.

- Coupling and dependencies between business functions are minimized.

Business functions, as described here, are comprised of both systems and people. Typically, we define business functions in terms of organization structure and associate various computer applications that support their activities. However, responsibility for computer applications is not always aligned with the organization that has the business function responsibility.

If responsibility and control for a business function are not aligned, then there likely will be definition and implementation difficulties. The current role of system developers undermines the control of businesspersons responsible for automated business functions. The businessperson often is unable to understand the implementation of the function in the computer and must depend on the developer to interpret the functional requirements properly and reconcile the details of integration with related business functions. Business-level specifications must enable business people to understand and control their business systems.

If the same business function is defined in different ways for different locations or organizations, then when changes are needed, they may be difficult to define, and the results may be unpredictable. Generally, to manage an enterprise effectively and achieve quality results, it is necessary for business functions to be performed in a reasonably consistent fashion. This does not mean that each business function must be performed by one organization and one system, but that the same processes should be employed throughout the enterprise, as much as possible, even if the executions are distributed.

Coupling between business functions will increase the complexity and often the scope of change. Coupling may take the form of the need to share information or resources, or the need to coordinate activities. In addition to creating risks of delays or rework, coupling causes changes in one business function to have ripple effects in related business functions. Often these ripple effects are not well understood, and inefficiencies persist long into the future.

The adaptability of systems and processes is key to reducing costs and delays and improving quality. Major changes in the way of doing business may require a significant redevelopment of systems and processes. In the long term, the reduction of costs and delays, as well as quality improvement, requires continuous process improvement, in other words, continuous change. If systems and processes are difficult to change or change brings excessive risk of introducing new problems, then continuous improvement will not occur.

Management Information

Enterprise integration should enable managers to monitor the operation of the business, identify problems and opportunities, define desired changes and improvements, and measure results. Although the automation of business systems and processes has improved business operations, it often has left managers with inadequate information to manage the business effectively. Operating data are difficult to find, retrieve, and understand and may be inconsistent when measures involve data from multiple systems.

Five key elements are required for effective management information:

- Data consistency
- Data accessibility
- Process consistency
- Exception reporting
- Historical data analysis

Generally, management information will span multiple segments of the organization. Data from different departments may be compared or used together in computations. These comparisons and computations are meaningless if the data codes, units of measure, and points of reference are not the same. For example, if different identifiers are used for customers, or if volumes of paint are sometimes measured in gallons and other times in liters, or if some sales figures are weekly and others are monthly, then management comparisons and computations will be meaningless unless transformations can be and are applied.

Data from various sources must be accessible to managers in a manner that is consistent. The simplest form of access is where the data are compiled and presented in a predefined report. However, many questions of concern to managers are not those that have been anticipated. It is too late to investigate sources, forms, and meanings and then implement conversions when a manager needs information to make a decision. The sources of information must be harmonized as they are developed if the enterprise is to be managed effectively.

In the harmonized enterprise, basic operational data are accessible using a consistent, browser-based interface. It is possible to import data from different sources into a spreadsheet or other form to perform computations and present the data in easily interpreted ways such as graphic displays.

A significant aspect of management evaluation and control is based on the measurement of processes. Processes will be measured in terms of timeliness, backlogs, defects, resource requirements, throughput, and so on. If the systems are not harmonized, that is, well defined and consistent, these measures will be of questionable value. In the harmonized enterprise, process measures are consistent from day to day and from department to department.

Managers cannot be expected to monitor everything that is going on continuously. Instead, management attention and supporting information should be focused on exceptions. An exception may be a process deviation, a production variable exceeding a threshold, an unacceptable delay, or any other variation from normal operation. Business processes should be designed to identify exceptions and raise the visibility of each exception for prompt resolution and action to prevent recurrence. The level of escalation of an exception must be appropriate to the business impact of the exception and the authority required to resolve it.

Finally, the recognition and understanding of problems and opportunities often require a historical or statistical perspective. Trends in business variables may provide early warning of an impending problem. Market trends may suggest business opportunities. Consequently, it is important not only to provide management access to current operational data, but also to provide historical data along with the means for analysis. The data must be consistent both across the enterprise and over time, or results may be misleading. For higher-level managers, trends and statistical analyses are of primary interest because day-to-day operational problems should be resolved at lower levels in the organization.

Support for Electronic Commerce

The Internet and the World Wide Web have made electronic commerce a critical aspect of integration for many enterprises. Electronic commerce is essentially enterprise integration that extends to customers and business partners.

Electronic commerce requires compatibility with the systems and applications of customers and business partners, as well as the mechanisms for timely and reliable communication of information. It also creates new security and accountability risks. Many unknown people in unknown environments will have access to enterprise data and resources. Personnel of business partners will have authorized access, and the Web facilities are exposed to many potential intruders on the public Internet.

Electronic commerce is accomplished through the exchange of data between trading partners. The data exchanged must have the same meaning to the sender and the receiver. This requires an agreement on standards for data elements and structures. Acceptance of Extensible Markup Language (XML) as a basis for formatting business-to-business (B2B) data has been hailed as a solution to many of these problems because it appears to be self-documenting. However, for reliable conduct of business, the meanings of tags and values must be defined much more precisely. The data exchanged likely will have an operational and financial impact as each enterprise relies on the accuracy of the data and the commitment it implies from the partner.

Whether or not data is exchanged as XML, communications will occur over the Internet, usually with the HyperText Transport Protocol (HTTP). Web servers are the portals through which these exchanges occur. Retail customers will use standard Web browsers to communicate with enterprise systems. The customer will search for information, select products to purchase, and make arrangements for payment through the Web server. Communications with business partners will occur between Web servers, generally operating for specific exchanges under rules established by contractual agreements. In the future, at least some B2B exchanges will occur on an ad hoc basis between enterprises that do not have prior contractual agreements.

Unlike exchanges of data within the enterprise, the exchanges in electronic commerce are between independent legal entities. Their objectives are not aligned like communicating departments within the enterprise. If they are not operating under a contractual agreement, the data exchanged will be part of a protocol to reach agreements; some degree of negotiation even may occur between partners operating under an umbrella agreement. These negotiations will have legal and financial effects on the enterprise.

The enterprise must adapt both technically and organizationally while participating in electronic commerce exchanges around the clock, establishing relationships with new customers and business partners, streamlining internal processes to respond more quickly to customers and partners, and providing current status information on orders for products and services.

Integrated Security

Electronic exchanges raise new concerns about security. Web servers are connected to the Internet to be accessible by anyone. They open up the enterprise to new risks not present in the old systems with a defined set of users accessing terminals in a controlled office space. Certain people on the Internet aspire to break into enterprise Web servers to make their mark on the enterprise—sometimes for the challenge and sometimes for personal gain.

Security must be an integral part of the integrated enterprise. The following key elements must be addressed:

- Firewalls
- Authentication
- Authorization
- Integrity
- Confidentiality
- Nonrepudiation

Firewalls are the first line of defense against intruders. A *firewall* is a control point for access to Web servers, the enterprise intranet, and enterprise systems. The firewall must restrict access by intruders while at the same time providing easy access to authorized users and business partners. This is accomplished by careful restriction of the messages that can be exchanged through the firewall.

The enterprise must be assured that the exchanges with financial or legal effect are with known customers or partners. This requires *authentication*. Traditionally, this is accomplished with some form of password for proof of identity. In the future, it will be accomplished by the exchange of digital certificates. In an exchange, each participant should be assured of the identity of the other. The enterprise also will need further information about the individual in order to respond appropriately. Directories will contain information about employees and business partners to enable their business activities. Information about customers may be captured when a customer makes an initial inquiry and is updated as business is conducted. As the transition to digital certificates emerges, the enterprise will need to develop or subscribe to the services of a certificate authority to issue certificates for the reliable identification of individuals and Internet services.

The system must restrict user access to data and functions appropriate for the role of each user. The determination of what a user can access is called *authorization*. Once a user is authenticated, so that his or her identity is assured, then authorization for access must be determined. Authorization may be defined in terms of the role of the user, that is, activities the user is expected to perform, and authorization may be defined in terms of the user's relationship to particular data, such as an employee's access to his or her personnel records.

If data are communicated over dedicated lines in controlled environments, the risk of access by an intruder may be controlled by restriction of physical access. When data are communicated over the Internet, the sender and receiver will have little or no idea of the path the data may follow. The data could go around the world just to get next door. There must be protection of the *integrity* of the data to ensure that the message received is the same as the message that originated from the authenticated source.

Intruders may not be interested in changing the data, but only in listening to obtain data the enterprise does not intend to share. If the data are confidential, then there must be mechanisms to ensure that an intercepted copy will be meaningless to the intruder. This is accomplished with some form of encryption.

System inputs, from individuals or other enterprises, can have significant effects on business operations, transfers of assets, and business decisions. At least for key inputs, it should be possible to reliably establish the content and source of input. The ability to prove the content and source of information is called *nonrepudiation*. The input cannot be repudiated by the source. In traditional business activities, nonrepudiation is established with signatures on paper documents. In electronic commerce, digital signatures are needed on electronic documents.

The enterprise security strategy must recognize not only the risks of access from the public Internet, but also the risks from within. A disgruntled employee may not need to worry about getting past a firewall to corrupt a system; the employee is inside the enterprise. The only difference between a disgruntled employee and an outside intruder may be the extent to which the enterprise can make employees accountable for their actions. Unfortunately, accountability may come into play only after the damage is done.

Replaceable Components

During the 1990s, enterprise applications were developed as commercial products: commercial-off-the-shelf (COTS) software. These applications provided highly integrated and comprehensive functionality. The cost and risk associated with the implementation of these applications were much higher than most customers anticipated. As the industry evolved, the need to adapt these applications to the needs of individual enterprises became a critical success factor. This adaptation is not acceptable if it undermines vendor support, so adaptation necessarily became part of the application design. Much of this was accommodated through configuration options and parameters.

However, it also became obvious that some customers only wanted certain functionality, not an integrated solution that imposed major changes on their businesses. Instead of a complete financial package, they might only want an accounts payable system. This caused vendors to start breaking their systems into smaller products. Not only did smaller products give customers more choices for individual business functions, but they also limited the scope of effort to install new systems. The cost, duration, and risk were reduced. The trend will continue.

As the enterprise application marketplace evolved, so did technology supporting the integration of these systems. Enterprise application integration (EAI) has become a discipline supported by numerous integration products. These products provide a common infrastructure by which enterprise applications and legacy systems can be loosely coupled to minimize interdependence. The infrastructure provides for the communication and transformation of data exchanged between systems.

The responsive, integrated enterprise must anticipate change. The enterprise cannot afford to develop major, new systems every time change occurs. Change must be addressed by replacing components of the enterprise systems either through the purchase of new components or the development of custom components. This requires a system architecture that facilitates the replacement of components to change functionality or extend capabilities. The cost and risk of replacing a component are related to the scope of functionality of the component. Larger components involve greater risk of adverse impact on the business and consequential adverse effects on related business functions. The custom development of larger replacement components carries the additional cost and risk associated with new application development.

The granularity of marketed components will continue to become smaller. Component architectures and supporting frameworks now exist for constructing applications from relatively small components. The industry is not yet ready to support the development and marketing of fine-grained components for the composition of enterprise applications. However, the technology and necessary standards are emerging. With interoperability standards, it will be possible to replace components of enterprise systems like components are replaced in a manufacturing facility—when a new capability is needed, the associated machine or tool is changed, not the entire production line.

The enterprise architecture should build on this trend toward the loose coupling of finer-grained components. It should support the composition of systems from components that provide limited units of business functionality even though most of the components may be custom developed in the short term. Vendor-developed components should be integrated where they provide stable, appropriate, and limited-scope functionality for noncompetitive business functions. Applications should be designed with a component architecture that reflects a logical partitioning of functionality associated with business process activities. These functional units should be loosely coupled. This architecture will enhance system flexibility in the short term and position the systems for the integration of replacement components when they become available in the future.

Reliable System Operation

Enterprise integration will increase the enterprise dependence on its computer systems because people will come to rely on the automated processes, the streamlined business functions, the coordination of activities, and the accessibility of information. At the same time that integration is streamlining enterprise operations, it may be making it impossible for humans to function effectively if systems fail. Consequently, the need for system reliability increases.

In addition, the enterprise will become more closely coordinated with trading partners, and it will expose its public systems and Web pages to the outside world. Many of these systems will be expected to be operational 24 hours a day, 7 days a week. If systems falter or fail, the world will know, and the activities of customers, suppliers, and investors may be affected immediately.

Systems exposed to the Internet, as well as the systems on which they depend, must be much more reliable than in the past. There are three basic techniques to improve system reliability:

- Minimize the risk that the system will fail.
- Detect malfunctions early.
- Limit the impact of failure.

The basic mechanisms to minimize risks of failure are (1) a safe environment with reliable power, (2) the testing of equipment and software prior to production operation, and (3) change control. A safe environment with reliable power will protect the system from outside causes of failure. Testing provides assurance that the system is not inherently flawed and incapable of reliable operation. Change control provides assurance that changes are screened and orderly and that if a malfunction is discovered, the change can be withdrawn to revert to a proven version of the system—of course, this may require backward compatibility. These mechanisms are primarily business practices, not technical requirements.

The early detection of malfunctions usually is accomplished with both business practices and technical solutions. Of course, good system design, development, and testing practices are preventive measures. Once the system is in production, malfunctions can occur that do not cause the system to come to a halt. These may be malfunctions in computations, lost records, timing conflicts, and so on. The basic mechanism of malfunction detection is redundancy. Computations can be performed twice, in different ways, to ensure that the same result is produced. Records can be counted as inputs and corresponding outputs. Hash values may be computed and later computed again for comparison. Business variables such as total receipts and disbursements may be cross-checked. Double-entry bookkeeping is the classic form of redundancy checking for financial systems. Other business variables may be monitored for unusual variance, suggesting that something is out of the ordinary.

The degree of redundancy built into the system or management practices again will depend on the cost of malfunction and the likelihood that the malfunction will not be detected by other human means such as a customer complaint or the attempt to attach the wrong part to an assembly.

Limitation of the impact of failure is primarily a technical issue. Systems fail for various reasons. When they fail, it may be necessary to redo some work, but the fundamental requirement is that lost work will be repeated reliably, and no information will be lost.

Most information systems employ transactional processing to minimize the impact of failure. As each unit of work is completed, the result is committed by updating a database and a log file. If the system fails, operation may be resumed at the point where the last transaction committed. If the database fails, the log file can be used to reconstruct the result. Any unit of work that is in process at the time of the failure will need to be redone. If the durations of units of work are small, this may be of little consequence. If they are long, involving users working perhaps for hours, the impact could be very large. For long-duration units of work, other forms of checkpoint and recovery may be appropriate; for example, users may save their work periodically or the system may create a checkpoint copy automatically. In any case, user business practices must complement the system recovery procedures so that users know which work is not committed when a failure occurs and can reconstruct that work.

The impact of failure also may be a function of the nature of the failure. If a data-processing center is destroyed, the enterprise must not go out of business. Backup copies of databases and files must be stored in a remote location. Alternate sites must be identified to restore operational capabilities. The mitigation mechanism consists of contingency plans—plans for recovery under all forms of failure.

In summary, reliable systems require both technical and procedural solutions. The solutions must be built into both the system and the associated day-to-day business practices.

Economies of Scale

The enterprise integration strategy must include a consideration of economies of scale. It is not enough simply to connect all the systems together. The strategy should move the enterprise toward greater efficiency, leveraging solutions, eliminating duplicated effort, reducing complexity, and making the best use of skilled personnel. In general, a well-integrated enterprise should cost less to operate and to adapt to changing business needs.

Several important opportunities must be considered to achieve economies of scale:

- Standards
- Software reuse
- Common infrastructure
- Consolidated systems operations

We will examine each of these in the following sections.

Standards

The key enabler of economies of scale is standards. Economies of scale result from sharing resources. Resources may be materials, people, equipment, systems, or facilities. Sharing will not be efficient if there is no consistency. Standards for enterprise integration should focus on data, interfaces, and practices. Industry standards should be applied unless there is competitive advantage in being different. Industry standards enable the use of commercial products in a competitive marketplace, and they facilitate interfaces with business partners. Where industry standards do not exist, enterprise standards must be considered.

Data are exchanged between systems and used for information to manage the enterprise. If standards are not established for these data, then they will not be readily usable for ad hoc purposes; incompatibilities may go unnoticed, producing erroneous results; and constant effort will be required to develop and maintain conversion programs.

The development of EAI tools and practices has resulted in the development of a number of products to facilitate the transformation of data. These tools are important for enterprise integration and will continue to be used as the enterprise evolves. As the business and the systems change, the data exchanged will change, and such tools will facilitate the integration of new solutions.

However, the enterprise needs a formal definition of the content and format of data being exchanged. The EAI transformations should convert to common data specifications for communication and to application specifications, where necessary, for each application. This allows new applications and management information systems to tap into the data being exchanged and obtain consistent results.

The goal should *not* be to develop standards for all data in the enterprise. Many data exist only within a single application or a single business function. Data standards efforts that attempt to address all such data are overwhelming, and efforts to implement such standards have only limited success. Considerable effort has been invested in the development of industry standards for data exchanged with COTS enterprise applications. The Open Applications

Group (OAG) has been a key forum in this effort. An enterprise should leverage these industry efforts and extend or complement them with local standards where necessary.

Interface standards focus on interfaces to applications and services. Applications and services should be described in terms of what they do from an external perspective, as opposed to how they do it, that is, a design perspective. A focus on interfaces, as with the data standards, limits the scope of standards efforts and limits the scope and effort of change as new solutions are developed or alternative products are introduced.

Often enterprise standards efforts focus on the selection of compatible products—frequently the selection of a single vendor to provide a set of compatible products. This is a shortsighted approach. When product compatibility is the focus, the result is dependence on particular products and interdependence between the products. The enterprise will not realize the benefits of a competitive marketplace, and new advances in technology or business solutions may not be available from the incumbent vendors.

Interface standards incorporate data specifications and include:

- The mode of communication (synchronous or asynchronous)
- The communications protocol
- The sequence and form of information exchange
- The format and meanings of the inputs and outputs

Where possible, data and interface standards should be industry standards. Many industry interface standards and associated data standards are *de facto standards*, adopted by the marketplace when a particular product receives widespread acceptance. These standards can be illusory. They often reflect a limited capability, and they may be changed by the vendor with the introduction of a new release of the dominant product. The preferred standards are *de jure standards*, adopted by a standards organization through a formal process that involves a variety of interested parties. The Object Management Group (OMG) has produced a number of specifications for application and service interfaces based on the Common Object Request Broker Architecture (CORBA) technology. Java standards are the result of participation by a number of companies, but the process and the product are still owned and controlled by Sun Microsystems. Consequently, Java standards are less risky than de facto standards defined by products, but they are still subject to the proprietary interests of Sun Microsystems.

Standard practices should be defined for the development, maintenance, and management of systems and the business operations they support. Here *practices* refer to the way things are done.

In the development of systems, standard practices provide control over the cost and timeliness of development efforts and the completeness and consistency of the results. A consistent process will define well-understood milestones, well-defined work products, and controls to resolve problems in a timely manner. Consistent results will ensure the maintainability of the system and the operational efficiency and reliability of its execution. Standard practices also should provide the mechanisms by which applicable standards are identified and applied during system development.

Standard practices in business activities enable the implementation of common systems, ensure consistency in the meaning of shared data, and support the comparative evaluation of similar operating units. Standard practices in any activity enable the use of common tools, terminology, and procedures, reducing the cost of tools and training for individual projects and allowing resources to be shared and workloads to be balanced more effectively.

Software Reuse

Software reuse involves using a software system or component to solve the same problem in different contexts. The basic premise is that using a software artifact more than once will yield economies of scale. Although this can be true, the costs of reuse offset some of the benefits, so the costs and benefits must be weighed to ensure that reuse yields a net gain.

Reuse may occur in a number of ways:

- Purchase of a commercial product
- Use of the same system in different organizations
- Provision of shared services
- Use of shared components
- Use of shared specifications

Purchase of a Commercial Product

The ultimate in software reuse is the implementation of a commercial product (a COTS solution). The enterprise shares the cost of development and support with other customers of the same product. This is ideal if the product is compatible with related systems and performs its function in a way that meets the needs of the particular enterprise. A number of business functions should be supported in this way in most enterprises. For example, accounting and personnel functions should be quite consistent for all enterprises of similar scale. If, on the other hand, the business function is a source of competitive advantage, then a COTS solution probably is not appropriate.

Problems occur with COTS software when it is necessary to adapt it for a particular enterprise, when the enterprise expects to maintain unique ways of performing its business function, or when interfaces with other systems require special adaptations. As soon as the application is modified for the enterprise, it begins to lose value as a shared application. Whenever problems occur, the vendor may be unable or unwilling to resolve them in a nonstandard implementation. When new versions of the application are issued, the enterprise will need to implement the same adaptations again; this requires retaining people who understand the application and the unique requirements of the enterprise. In addition, each time changes are made, the quality, reliability, and performance of the application will be at risk. There is also the risk that when something goes wrong or a change is required to meet a new business need, there may be nobody with sufficient knowledge to provide a timely resolution.

Use of the Same System in Different Organizations

The development of a system for operation at multiple sites carries similar concerns, but the economy of scale is smaller. These may be systems for branch offices, manufacturing systems for multiple plants, sales systems for multiple divisions, and so on. Such systems enable the enterprise to implement unique capabilities for a competitive advantage while sharing the development and maintenance efforts among multiple implementations. In addition, the use of a common system ensures data consistency, common interfaces, and common practices, at least to the extent that the system determines business practices. At the same time, implementation at multiple sites requires that the operating environment be reasonably consistent across all sites. Implementing common practices and computing environments may be very difficult in a decentralized organization.

Provision of Shared Services

Consequently, it is often preferable to implement a common solution in one place and share the implementation. This is the common service model. This approach can be applied to COTS applications as well as applications unique to the enterprise. Different systems or users may invoke the service at different sites, but it actually executes as one system at one site. This achieves a good economy of scale for development, maintenance, and operation of the system. On the other hand, there is little flexibility for the needs of different environments or related systems. Furthermore, communications must be managed centrally for interfaces with remote systems and for user access. Upgrades to the system may require the coordination of changes for a simultaneous upgrade of interfaces with other systems. The system also puts all the eggs in one basket so that a failure suspends the particular business function for the entire enterprise.

Use of Shared Components

Up to this point, we have been talking about software that implements substantial business functions or services. There is also an opportunity for the reuse of more fine-grained components. In contrast with large-scale systems that usually are integrated with asynchronous, store-and-forward file or message communications, fine-grained components usually are integrated with synchronous messages equivalent to function calls or remote procedure calls in which the caller waits for a response. These components generally require a common application architecture and supporting infrastructure in order to interoperate with other components of the same application.

The ability to compose systems from predeveloped, fine-grained components has been an industry goal for many years. Much has been achieved in the development of components for system services and user interfaces, but little has been achieved in the development of components that implement business logic. To achieve interoperability, the components must comply with standards for functionality, interfaces, and architecture. With compliance to appropriate standards, different implementations of the same component type can be substituted to change not what is done, but how it is done. This engenders competition among component providers and enables elements of a system to be upgraded without replacing the whole system.

The development of shared components within an enterprise is not simply a matter of picking components from existing systems and reusing them in other systems. Shared components require special analysis and design disciplines to enable them to function effectively in different contexts. Component providers must work with component users to develop a consensus on upgrades so that the impact on hosting applications will be acceptable, if not desirable. There must be a commitment to provide continued support for the components so that applications that incorporate them are not at risk due to the absence of knowledgeable people or responsive support. In addition, each new application must be designed with the compatibility of architecture and components in mind. The interoperability of components may be very expensive or impossible to achieve if the approach is to add it on later.

The development of fine-grained components as products may be on the threshold of possibility. Component technologies such as the CORBA Component Model (CCM) and Enterprise JavaBeans (EJB) provide standard environments and communication protocols for the deployment of sharable components, and they define a degree of consistency in the interfaces and supporting services. What remains is the need for consistent interfaces and protocols at a business function level.

Use of Shared Specifications

Sharing specifications is another way to achieve reuse and thus economies of scale. Under its Model-Driven Architecture strategy, the OMG is redirecting its efforts from the development of specifications for CORBA technology to the development of specifications that are independent of technology and map to alternative implementations such as CCM and EJB. If components can be generated from platform-independent specifications, then the market economies of scale for these components could be increased greatly. At the same time, technology-independent specifications could be used to generate technology-specific implementations.

The capability to generate application code from specifications has been demonstrated with prototype tools and will be better supported by the next generation of system metamodels and tools. Unified Modeling Language (UML) has become widely accepted as the language for system modeling. Efforts to define a UML profile for Enterprise Distributed Object Computing (EDOC) will provide more robust specifications along with support for the composition of systems from fine-grained components.

The combination of standard component environments (CCM and EJB), a common modeling language, and standard technology mappings will lead to the development of successful tools for generating applications from specifications. This will allow the enterprise to model a system incorporating commodity components and proprietary components for which code would be generated for a target environment. As the technology changes, the code will be regenerated for the new technology. As business logic needs change, system changes will be implemented at the specification level, potentially better understood by users of the applications, and quality code will be generated for the revised system.

In all these variations on the theme of reuse, it must be remembered that reuse is only partly a technical problem; unless the business challenges are well understood and addressed, attempts at reuse will be disappointing at best, and they could be very expensive.

Common Infrastructure

A *common infrastructure* is the complex of computers, networks, software, and associated services that supports the operation and interconnection of many systems. A common infrastructure provides connectivity, an operating environment, and shared resources to reduce the burden and promote synergy between systems. A common infrastructure is not necessarily monolithic or managed centrally. It simply provides consistent application-independent services and support. Such an infrastructure can yield substantial economies of scale in several ways:

- EAI support
- Web services
- Personal computing services
- System management facilities

A *common infrastructure* is defined here as the implementation of consistent facilities and services that comply with a full complement of standards and employ consistent hardware and software components. The primary source of an economy of scale is the sharing of human resources for implementation, operation, and support of the infrastructure, along with the benefits of being able to coordinate changes, resolve problems, and provide shared backup facilities more effectively and efficiently.

EAI Support

EAI support involves facilities for store-and-forward message queuing, routing, and transformation. In the early stages of EAI, it will be most economical for messaging to be point to point; messages from one application are communicated directly to the input queues of each application that uses its output. As the scale of EAI grows, there will be more and more point-to-point links between applications. Many applications will be receiving messages from multiple applications and sending the same messages to multiple applications. Implementation of a message broker service then will reduce the number of links dramatically—each application then communicates only with the message broker, and control and flexibility of the exchange will be improved.

Transformation facilities will be needed regardless of the use of a message broker. In fact, use of a message broker may encourage reworking transformation facilities to adopt standard message formats so that the same message can be routed to multiple applications and to ensure proper routing of the messages. However, the work associated with implementing transformations will be reduced in the long term by both the implementation of fewer transformations and the improved proficiency of the developers if data standards and a common set of tools are employed.

Web Services

The enterprise may have many Web applications and Web interfaces with enterprise applications. Although the Web and enterprise applications may be quite diverse, it generally is unnecessary to have diverse firewall and Web server technologies. The key is to limit the implementation of Web server components to standard technologies. The implementation of HTML Web pages will be relatively consistent. Implementations of dynamically created Web pages [Common Gateway Interface (CGI) scripts] may involve different languages and supporting services, but this diversity is seldom necessary to provide the desired functionality.

As long as the enterprise continues to allow diversity in the selection of firewall and Web server technologies, the adoption of common facilities will become increasingly difficult. The body of Web pages to be converted will only become greater. The management of firewalls and Web servers requires special skills, and the technology continues to evolve. At the same time, the reliance of the enterprise on the effective operation of its Web service facilities will continue to increase. The adoption of standards and the selection of consistent products to meet those standards will achieve economies of scale in operations, ongoing implementations of new applications, the resolution of problems, the implementation of enhancements for performance and security, and the availability of skilled personnel.

Personal Computing Services

Economies of scale in personal computing services are becoming increasingly important. Traditionally, each user was connected to one primary application that supported his or her job function. As the enterprise becomes more integrated and applications become Web-enabled, users are no longer confined to accessing single systems, but may reach across the enterprise to interact with a number of systems through browser-based access. In addition, users share information through e-mail and shared file servers. The ability to access information and collaborate with others depends on the consistency of their tools and desktop applications. These common tools and desktop applications, as well as the personal computers on which they run, should be part of a consistent infrastructure.

In addition, by adopting consistent tools and applications, the enterprise will be able to achieve economies of scale in acquisition and support. Hardware and software can be purchased as volume discounts. Support personnel can be trained in fewer products and will be able to apply the same solutions for problems experienced by many users, often before many of the users encounter them. In addition, economies of scale can be achieved in other support activities such as security administration and application upgrade testing and implementation.

System Management Facilities

System management is greatly simplified and consequently more efficient if the infrastructure is consistent. One of the most fragile elements of the infrastructure is the communications network. Network problems occur frequently and interfere with the reliable and efficient operation of the business. The simpler the network, the better is the level of service. Skilled people and adequate preventive measures can detect problems early, can resolve failures more quickly, can make adjustments to minimize or avoid performance problems, and can reduce the risk of future problems.

System management also involves the management of change. Changes to the infrastructure or applications bear a much greater degree of risk if the infrastructure is inconsistent. Changes will be more difficult to validate, the implementation will be more complex, the consequences may be more difficult to explain to users, and problems may require tailoring solutions to many different circumstances.

Finally, a consistent infrastructure is easier to support with backup facilities. If a major failure or natural disaster occurs, system operations may need to be relocated. If the infrastructure is consistent, then common alternate facilities of limited scale may meet the need. If the infrastructure is inconsistent, then arrangements may be required to provide different backup facilities for different applications.

Consolidated System Operations

The consolidation of system operations can achieve significant economies of scale. Traditionally, enterprise applications were executed in centralized data centers. The data center enabled the sharing of expensive computer equipment to achieve high utilization. Microprocessor technology provided a less expensive alternative, and systems developers were able to implement new, more user-friendly systems more quickly on desktop computers and local servers. The focus of much enterprise computing shifted from the data-processing center to a client-server architecture using local servers and desktop computers. Unfortunately, while the costs were reduced, so were supporting services that were essential to the secure and reliable operation of systems.

The Internet, the need for enterprise integration, and the promise of electronic commerce have reversed this trend. Enterprise applications must be interconnected. Some systems must be operational 24 hours a day, 7 days a week. Security is a major concern. Computing systems and networks have become much more sophisticated, requiring highly skilled people to ensure reliable operation. Individual departments have been challenged to manage client-server applications effectively, but they cannot hope to manage this technology adequately, and there are now greater economies of scale:

Personnel.   System operations once again involve 24-hour operations not to achieve higher computer utilization, but to provide services 24 hours a day. Now the key is personnel utilization and the availability of highly skilled people to manage the technology and resolve problems.

Physical facilities.   The facilities supporting computer operations must be highly secure, they must have uninterruptible power, and they must provide high-speed connectivity to the Internet. Specialized equipment and software provide monitoring, control, and reconfiguration capabilities.

Licenses.   Many software products are licensed for each computer. If the enterprise computing infrastructure is scattered over many sites with many computers, more licenses will be required. Consolidation reduces the number of licenses, often with considerable cost savings.

Backup capacity.   Individual computers will fail occasionally. In a large data center with many computers, it can be acceptable simply to redistribute the workload until the failed computer comes back online. In other cases, a single reserve computer can back up a number of other computers. Consequently, the overall backup capacity can be minimized while ensuring an acceptable level of service.

Change control.   Reliable system operation requires effective change control. Change control is much more difficult if changes must be coordinated across multiple sites, probably operating with different system software versions and hardware configurations and being managed by separate organizations.

These economies of scale do not require that systems be executed on large, shared computers. Although fewer computers may be needed, many will have special functions such as database servers, directory servers, security servers, Web servers, and so on. The economies come from the consolidation of services, both system services and operations services. The services can be provided more effectively and efficiently by sharing resources and enabling the specialization of both computers and people.

Although consolidation offers economies of scale, the degree of consolidation must be balanced against the risks and diseconomies of scale. Consolidation puts all the eggs in one basket. A failure or breach of security could endanger the entire enterprise. Some of the economies of scale will be achieved at the expense of flexibility. Adherence to accepted standards and systems' software product selections may become more important than the selection of an appropriate COTS application; changes or extensions to computing services may be difficult to obtain due to the priority given to operational stability and the time required to evaluate the potential impact on the rest of the systems.

Summary

Enterprise integration requires a management vision, commitment, and leadership that gets beyond short-term suboptimal solutions to position the enterprise to remain competitive long into the future. In Chapter 3 we will begin the journey into the enterprise integration architecture and the technologies that will implement it. In subsequent chapters we will establish the supporting infrastructure and explore key technologies in greater depth. In Chapter 13 we will return to the management perspective to examine the many factors that must be managed to make enterprise integration a success.

CHAPTER

3

Defining the Enterprise Architecture

In the preceding chapters we examined the technical landscape that sets the stage for enterprise integration, and we considered the design objectives for enterprise integration. In this chapter we will define the enterprise integration architecture. This architecture is based on current technology, existing or emerging standards, and industry trends. Using industry standards minimizes the architecture's dependence on a particular vendor and enhances its flexibility. Considering industry trends allows the architecture to adapt to new products and solutions as they become available.

The primary goal of this architecture is to address the needs of the enterprise as a whole for streamlined and flexible systems, rather than only the suboptimal needs of individual applications and business functions. This chapter will describe the general framework of the enterprise architecture. Subsequent chapters will examine particular aspects of the architecture in greater detail.

In the sections that follow, this chapter will examine the characteristics of the enterprise architecture from the following viewpoints:

- General characteristics
- Business system hierarchy
- Integration infrastructure model

- Network model
- Workflow process model
- Business system domain model
- Enterprise data storage model
- Knowledge access model
- An enterprise integration scenario

Except for the last one, these viewpoints represent abstractions on the enterprise integration architecture to address different interests and examine different relationships between the architectural components. The last viewpoint is a use-case example showing how systems of an enterprise can work together to perform overall business functions. These viewpoints, taken together, will provide an overall picture of the enterprise integration architecture.

General Characteristics of the Enterprise Architecture

This section describes the following general characteristics of the enterprise integration architecture:

- Distributed computing
- Component-based applications
- Event-driven processes
- Loose coupling of business functions
- Decision support information
- Workflow management
- Internet access
- Personalization of interfaces

This section thus will provide a high-level view of the nature of the architecture as a foundation for more detailed discussions in subsequent sections.

Distributed Computing

The architecture employs distributed computing. The value of distributed computing is scalability, alignment to geographic distribution of the enterprise, and support for diverse application technologies.

Systems can be scalable in several ways. For example, it should be possible to accommodate increased numbers of users, to include increased numbers of records about relevant entities, to process an increased number of transactions, or to expand the scope of functionality. Generally, in a distributed system it should be possible to accommodate such expansions by the addition of more or larger servers but without changes to the basic design of the architecture or the applications. Scalability also may be achieved by the addition of more sites, such as where an application is replicated at different plants or field offices.

Systems can provide a higher level of performance if they execute on servers that are geographically clustered. At the same time, applications for distinct business functions should not be integrated tightly nor be restricted to execution in a homogeneous computing environment because this would limit flexibility and constrain the choice of application solutions. At the enterprise level, systems should be loosely coupled to allow business functions to operate and improve their systems relatively independently. When system operations are decentralized and loosely coupled, system changes are more localized and easier to manage, the operation of the business is less dependent on the reliability of networks, and failure of a single system does not have an immediate impact on the rest of the enterprise.

Distributed computing also accommodates a diversity of computing platforms. With appropriate interoperability standards and middleware, applications can interoperate even though they are executing on different platforms, using different database managers, and written in different languages.

Component-Based Applications

Although the architecture should host a diversity of applications and application technologies, it should specifically support component-based applications. This means that it should be possible to construct and adapt applications by incorporating replaceable, shareable building blocks. This is essential for the business to be able to adapt quickly to changing business needs and technical opportunities at reasonable cost and with reliable results.

Components must be defined at different levels of functional scope and for different degrees of coupling depending on their scope. Consequently, basic building blocks should compose larger components, which, in turn, may be composed into still larger components. This facilitates the composition of systems with larger components while preserving the flexibility of replacing components at different levels of scope to introduce new business solutions or technology.

Event-Driven Processes

Business is driven by events: an order is placed, a shipment is received, a machine fails, a person is hired. Conventional systems are driven by file transfers and input queues. Orders are processed from the day's input through a batch process. Funds are transferred in batch Electronic Data Interchange (EDI) files and posted in a batch process. Reports are prepared on the third shift so that managers can review the status of production the first thing in the morning.

To meet current business demands, processes must be streamlined. Product design must be streamlined to respond to the marketplace. Customer order processing must be streamlined to respond quickly to customer demand. Production material ordering must be streamlined so that inventories can be minimized while ensuring continuous production.

Future business systems should be event-driven. When a customer places an order, action should be taken on the order as soon as available resources permit. The order should not be waiting for a computer system to process it with other accumulated orders. When a problem requiring management attention occurs in production, the appropriate manager should be notified immediately. This requires a change in the design of systems and the way they interoperate.

Loose Coupling

Traditionally, the drive to achieve speed, consistency, and reliability has fostered the development of large, monolithic solutions. Many business functions may share the same database in order to avoid delays in communication and inconsistencies caused by the timing of updates. To maintain this consistency, all updates occur in a transactional environment. This synchronous mode of operation means that bottlenecks can occur as a result of competition for the same computing resources. It also means, in most cases, that processing for the participating applications must be centralized to minimize communication delays and ensure recoverability.

Loose coupling refers to linking applications through the transfer of business transactions in an asynchronous mode of communication. Applications process input from a queue of records received from other applications and produce output to queues of records needed by other applications. The form and distribution of these records can be managed outside the applications to provide compatibility between independently developed applications and greater flexibility in the selection, configuration, and replacement of applications. Loose coupling minimizes interdependence among systems in terms of time, information format, and technology.

Decision Support Information

The enterprise integration architecture must support knowledge worker access to timely, consistent, and accurate information. Knowledge workers require four basic types of information:

- Current status
- Exceptions
- Historical records
- Relevant knowledge

Current status information generally exists within mainstream business application systems, but it may not be accessible, and related data from different systems may not be consistent to enable summaries and comparisons.

Today, business exceptions generally are not recognized by systems, but rather by humans. Events requiring human intervention, shifts in key business indicators, violations of policies, or deviations in variables that exceed defined limits should be treated as business exceptions. Automated business processes and rules should determine immediately who should take action and with what priority.

Historical records provide the basis for recognizing trends, correlations, or recurring problems and opportunities. In many cases, these insights cannot be realized by observing day-to-day operations. In addition, the insights may involve relationships across multiple operations or product lines. This is sometimes called *business intelligence* and can be supported by data warehousing technology.

Relevant knowledge may be business or technical insights regarding potential problems and opportunities. Knowledge should be available through access to the right people, through access to relevant documents, and through systems that apply encoded knowledge to specific problems, such as knowledge-based diagnostic or planning systems.

Business Process Automation

Early computer systems automated specific manual business functions. Documents typically were the source of inputs, and reports were produced as outputs. As more functions were automated, systems were enhanced to exchange data directly. This eliminated the human effort and errors that resulted from the reentry of data. As we move toward event-driven systems, the movement of data between systems will be further streamlined. However, many business activities still involve interactions between humans as well as interactions between humans and computers.

Business process automation—traditionally called *workflow management*—streamlines the communications and coordination among systems and people. When an action by a person is required, the system will post the action item immediately in the person's work list. Alarms can be used to bring the person's attention to priority items. Delays can be monitored, and when they exceed specified thresholds, the action item can be brought to the attention of a coworker or manager. Strict controls can be applied to ensure that events receive proper attention and actions receive proper authorization. In addition, processes can be changed quickly under manager control, either ad hoc or permanently, to reflect personnel changes, absences, reorganizations, and business process improvement.

Internet Access

The Internet has had a major impact on computer systems architecture by providing a ubiquitous communications service that is inexpensive and enables communication from anywhere to anywhere on an ad hoc basis. Internet technology is used for communications within the enterprise, as well as with people and business partners outside the enterprise.

  With browser-based user interfaces, employees can interact with systems at work, at home, or on the road. Customers with diverse computer platforms can access information and place orders even if they have never had contact with the enterprise before. Business transactions can be exchanged with business partners without special facilities or arrangements except for agreement on data-exchange protocols, formats, and semantics. In addition to providing greatly enhanced flexibility, the Internet has opened the door to widespread electronic commerce, now a competitive necessity for commercial enterprises. The architecture must exploit the flexibility, accessibility, and economy of the Internet and the associated technology.

Personalization of Interfaces

E-mail has created a new relationship between the user and the computing environment. When the user signs on, his or her personal mailbox is presented, with the status of messages as they were at the end of the previous session and, usually, with new messages added. The system knows the user, and the status of relevant information is preserved even though the user is disconnected.

  Similarly, work assigned to an individual through automated business processes, a *work list*, should be presented to the user in a way that suits his or her needs. This includes requests not yet accepted as well as work in process. All workflow processes should present their work items for an individual in the same, integrated work list, regardless of the product used to implement the business process.

  Applications should be designed to be adapted to the needs of specific users. This has become expected practice with personal computer applications. The user can specify the content of menus and default settings for various options as well as supporting functions such as automatic spell checking in word-processing or spreadsheet applications, and similar functionality should be provided in other applications.

In the enterprise integration architecture, the applications are not running on the user's personal computer, but instead are part of the distributed enterprise computing system. The user views the enterprise systems through an Internet browser. The systems are designed to maintain an ongoing relationship with the user in order to quickly provide the user with needed information and optimize the user interaction to improve ease of use and productivity.

This concept is extended to customers as well as employees. Enterprise managers are concerned about developing and maintaining customer relationships. In this case, a customer relationship may begin with an ad hoc query about products or services. When the customer has established an identity, the system should retain information about interests expressed in products or services in order to provide additional relevant information and potentially promote new business. For example, for an automobile owner, the system might provide service reminders and promote the purchase of a replacement vehicle at an appropriate time. The system might send e-mail messages to prompt a customer to link to his or her personal workspace and find out more.

Summary

The preceding characteristics are not meant to provide a complete discussion of the target architecture, but rather to provide a perspective on key changes in the nature of systems, the relationships between systems, and the relationships between systems and users. The following sections will explore the nature of the enterprise integration architecture in more depth.

Business Systems Hierarchy

The systems of an enterprise can be viewed at a number of different levels of detail (see Figure 3.1). As we move up the hierarchy, the scope of business functionality increases, and the level of detail exposed decreases. These levels have implications for both the structure of the systems and the design of interfaces. We will examine each of these levels in the sections that follow, starting from the bottom of the hierarchy.

Application Components

At the bottom of the hierarchy are application components. Components are units of application software that can be combined to produce larger units of functionality. Basic components are application objects that are implemented with programming languages. These will be grouped into object structures that provide functionality representing a service or business entity (a customer or a production schedule). In a distributed computing environment, these or

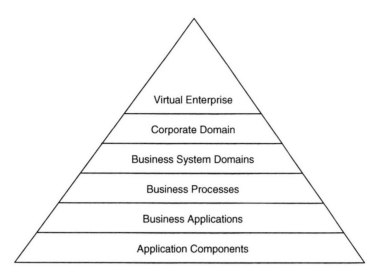

Figure 3.1   Business systems hierarchy.

larger compositions of components are accessible over the network as distributed components. Such components might be implemented as Enterprise JavaBeans (EJB). A component at run time may support a number of instances of the concept it implements; for example, a customer component may support object structures representing many customers, each accessible over the local network. Distributed components representing business entities have been called *business objects*.

There are three dominant specifications for the implementation of distributed components. The EJB specification defines a component container that provides an environment for an EJB component written in Java. The Object Management Group (OMG) has extended this functionality with the Common Object Request Broker Architecture (CORBA) Component Model (CCM) specification to comprehend implementations with different languages. Microsoft has defined the Component Object Model (COM+) components for the Microsoft operating environment. In this book we will focus on EJB components because these are receiving widespread acceptance and are available on a variety of computing platforms.

The EJB or CCM container provides integration with the computing environment and implements functionality that is common to all components. This enables the component developer to focus on the application functionality of the component instead of on the computational aspects of implementing the component. It also allows a component to be installed in different computing environments because the containers in different environments will provide the same interfaces and functionality to support the component.

The components are expected to be designed to interoperate, but the composition does not define the linkages between them. The Unified Modeling Language (UML) Profile for the Enterprise Distributed Object Computing (EDOC) specification describes a recursive component model. This specification provides for the assembly of distributed components into larger units of functionality. Components are integrated in a container that determines the connections between them and the connections to the outside world. These, in turn, can be components within larger compositions. Tools and frameworks to implement this technology are emerging.

The goal of this technology is to provide the basis for both a component structure for applications and a marketplace for the purchase of components to be incorporated into applications. Marketed components will provide well-defined and widely used functionality in order to realize return on investment. Applications that are designed with a component structure that parallels the functional structure of the business solution will be in a better position to incorporate purchased components in the future.

Of course, not all applications will be constructed using components—there will continue to be legacy applications, and some solutions may be unique, highly integrated, and optimized. Nevertheless, applications should evolve to a component structure, even though some components could be interfaces for large, complex, monolithic solutions.

Business Applications

The concept of business applications is changing. A business application traditionally is an integrated system that executes relatively independently, provides the functionality required by a group of users, and has an associated database and user interface. A business application in the future may manage some of the same information, but the business-specific functionality will be incorporated into business processes that are separated from the subject matter objects. The application will manage the model of that particular segment of the business but not the business processes. Multiple applications may share a database, common services, and a Web server. Consequently, an *application* will be defined in this context as a unit of software that provides a set of closely related business functions.

For example, a personnel application may manage information about employees. A number of different users may access the personnel system to obtain employee data and update records. However, the personnel application does not determine the business processes by which an employee is hired, given a raise, reassigned, promoted, or retired. The personnel system will be incorporated in a number of tasks of these different processes, but the processes are defined for the particular corporation and can be observed, analyzed, and improved independent of the personnel application.

Of course, any existing enterprise will have legacy systems that are broad in scope and incorporate business processes or segments of business processes. Current commercial enterprise applications have similar characteristics, but some have incorporated workflow management into the product to expose the business processes. The architecture will accommodate these applications as well, but their rigidity and concealment of encapsulated business processes constrain enterprise flexibility and control, particularly with respect to the business function supported by the monolithic application.

Business Processes

As noted earlier, most automated business processes currently are embedded in application code. These processes may determine the order in which activities occur, the participation of users, and the actions to be taken to resolve exceptions. When there is a need to change these business processes, users and programmers must work together to determine the changes required, and programmers then must modify program code to implement the changes. Often the business processes are not easily observed before or after the changes.

The goal of the enterprise integration architecture is to manage business processes with workflow management facilities so that the processes are visible and manageable. Monitoring tools will provide the capability to observe the status and progress of business processes, and process definition tools will enable authorized users to analyze, specify, and change business processes—in some cases on an ad hoc basis for the resolution of exceptional situations.

In this environment, the personnel application will maintain the personnel records and provide appropriate reporting and analysis as required. Workflow processes will direct the participation of people and applications to perform the appropriate functions and update appropriate records. Here the processes will capture and communicate changes and approvals to employee salaries and status. Certain events such as hiring, firing, and salary changes also will be communicated to other business processes, such as a payroll update process that must take further action in another department of the enterprise.

Workflow processes will drive the operation of the enterprise. Organizational units will implement workflow processes to define how their business functions are performed. Some of these business processes represent services that are available to other parts of the organization. A personnel department will provide processes to hire, fire, and promote employees. These services are accessible to managers of the employees, so managers outside the personnel department participate in the initiation and approval activities, but the process belongs to the personnel department.

Business System Domains

Business processes, applications, and their components must be managed to meet the needs of a particular organization. The organization will coordinate and control changes to the systems it uses. It will have primary responsibility for the integrity and security of the information, including the ability to recover the system from failures.

In the target architecture, a *business system domain* (BSD) is the set of business processes and applications that share components and maintain consistency among the state of those components, including the capability to roll back a computational transaction that cannot complete successfully and to recover to a consistent state in the event of a system failure.

Within the scope of a BSD, the state of a business entity (a customer or part record) is shared. All applications that operate on a business entity update the same state data. The updates occur in a computational transaction context so that attempts by multiple applications to update the same entity are resolved for a consistent result. The scope of applications does not extend beyond the scope of the associated BSD.

A BSD generally will be implemented at a single geographic site. It may include a number of computers connected by a local area network (LAN). In general, the scope is a function of management control, system performance, and technology integration. If multiple sites are included within a single BSD, then performance would be affected adversely by communication delays and failures, and the coordination of changes and the resolution of problems would be more complex. Conversely, it may be necessary to operate multiple BSDs at a single site or for a single organization because the technologies or applications cannot be integrated tightly or integration would not yield added benefit.

Replicated BSDs may be used independently at multiple, widely distributed sites. Each of these sites then becomes an independently operating BSD. Although they may share the same applications, each must control the operation and integrity of those applications at its own site. This may mean that at a given point in time different sites may be operating with different versions of the applications. It also means that some of the business processes can be tailored to address local needs.

The scope of a business process is also confined to a BSD. A business process must be managed and controlled by a specific organization. Changes to the process must be consistent, and they must be coordinated with changes to related processes. Nevertheless, business processes can coordinate the activities of multiple organizations; this is accomplished, as we will see later, by a process in one organization invoking processes in other organizations to achieve the desired result. Thus, a BSD may manage a business process that drives many related activities across the enterprise.

A BSD is also a security domain. Users of the functionality of a BSD must be authenticated. The LAN(s) of a BSD should be isolated from the enterprise intranet. Communications with other systems should be through secure, controlled asynchronous messaging, and the BSD should execute in a physically secure environment.

Corporate Domain

A corporation can incorporate a number of BSDs, just as the corporation may incorporate a number of organizational units. The corporation integrates these BSDs through infrastructure services and protocols that support communication and coordination between the business functions.

Coordination is accomplished primarily by the communication of business process requests and events. Processes in one BSD may invoke processes in other BSDs. Events in one BSD may cause processes to be performed or altered in other BSDs. In some cases, BSD might be outside the corporation—outsourced.

For example, the personnel department, discussed earlier, may invoke a payroll update process in accounting to reflect changes in the employee status. The payroll process is a service offered by the accounting department. Termination of an employee may produce an event of interest to various systems: A security process may cause an employee certification to be revoked, and a work-list process may cause the employee's outstanding assignments to be canceled or reassigned.

BSD integration is accomplished through the *loose coupling* of systems. This means that processing requests and information about events are forwarded in a store-and-forward asynchronous mode so that the sender does not suspend operations waiting for the receiver to take action. In addition, the communication mechanism may provide for transformation of the messages communicated to meet the recipients' requirements, and it will accommodate ad hoc requests to subscribe to (become a recipient of) events of specified types. This minimizes the dependencies between systems in terms of both timing and information format. Consequently, changes or disruptions in one BSD are less likely to have an adverse impact on applications and processes in other BSDs, and loose coupling limits the potential scope of security exposures.

Virtual Enterprise

Up to this point in our discussion, the systems and their users are contained within the single managing entity of a corporation. The virtual enterprise level integrates customers and business partners. The difference from intra-enterprise-level integration is the level of isolation between the corporation and its customers and partners and the use of the Internet to provide communications connectivity. The corporation must be protected from adverse actions of customers, business partners, or persons posing as customers or business partners and at the same time exploit the economy and flexibility of the Internet and close working relationships. This integration includes electronic commerce and outsourcing.

Electronic commerce will be conducted through controlled communication channels, where the identity of customers and business partners is authenticated, participants are accountable for their actions (nonrepudiation), and communications are conducted in a manner that prevents monitoring or the alteration of exchanges by outsiders (encryption). Although the same concerns exist with actions by employees within the corporation, exchanges with customers and business partners involve the exchange of goods for money. These exchanges generally occur in less secure environments, they are conducted over the public Internet, and the behavior of outside persons and organizations is more difficult to control than that of employees.

Electronic commerce likely may be conducted through one or more *portals*. The portal provides a single point of contact [a single Uniform Resource Locator (URL)] for a customer or business partner to conduct business. The portal performs security functions and redirects inputs to appropriate applications. In terms of the business system hierarchy being discussed here, the portal can be viewed as the access point of a BSD. There may be different portals for conducting different types of business, but, in most cases, the portals will be loosely coupled with other enterprise systems to prevent actions of outsiders from having a direct impact on the internal operation of the business.

In some cases, the customer or business partner is simply seeking information. In other cases, the input is a request that will be resolved by the execution of a business process. In order to provide information, a portal BSD may maintain a database that is updated from appropriate information sources from within the corporation. A request for action should be validated by the portal and then transformed into a request for execution of an internal business process appropriate to resolve the request.

Exchanges with systems of other corporations are through asynchronous messages, but uses the HyperText Transfer Protocol (HTTP) to be compatible with generally available Web service facilities and firewalls. Most exchanges between corporations are with established business partners, so the exchange protocols will be stable. Ad hoc exchanges with new business partners require the negotiation of common protocols. Web protocol registries will support this approach and also may provide services for locating appropriate product or service offerings on the Web. In the sections that follow we will emphasize particular aspects of the overall enterprise architecture.

Integration Infrastructure Model

The *integration infrastructure* is the collection of shared facilities that allow the various business systems to work together. The enterprise will incorporate many systems. These systems will come in various shapes and sizes. Some will be legacy applications, some will be purchased commercial-off-the-shelf (COTS) applications, and some will be custom applications developed to meet specific business needs. Although these systems may be developed independently, there is an opportunity to provide common facilities to support their integration and achieve economies of scale. These common facilities will provide flexibility in the overall operation of the business, reduce the cost of development and implementation of new applications, and enable the use of diverse technologies for the solution of specific business problems.

Figure 3.2 depicts the role of the integration infrastructure supporting a variety of business systems. These business systems are characterized as BSDs, and the different types derive different values from the infrastructure. The greatest value will be realized from the distributed component-based BSD. The components of a distributed computing BSD will be discussed briefly later in this chapter and in detail in Chapter 5.

We will examine the details of the integration infrastructure in Chapter 4. Following is a brief summary of the infrastructure elements. These are elements that are shared by multiple systems, provide the means by which systems are integrated, enable economies of scale, and are implemented and supported for the enterprise as a whole.

Intranet facilities.   The communication and computing facilities that link the internal systems and support basic services such as routing, file transfers, e-mail, and so on.

Personal computers.   The desktop and portable computers and workstations used by individuals for personal computing and access to Internet and intranet resources.

Messaging service.   A service for store-and-forward, guaranteed delivery of messages.

System management.   Services to operate, maintain, and configure the infrastructure and related services as well as to resolve problems.

Security services.   Management of digital certificates and infrastructure security controls.

Organization directory.   A directory defining the enterprise organization structure and the people in it.

Archiving.   A service for the long-term retention of electronic business documents.

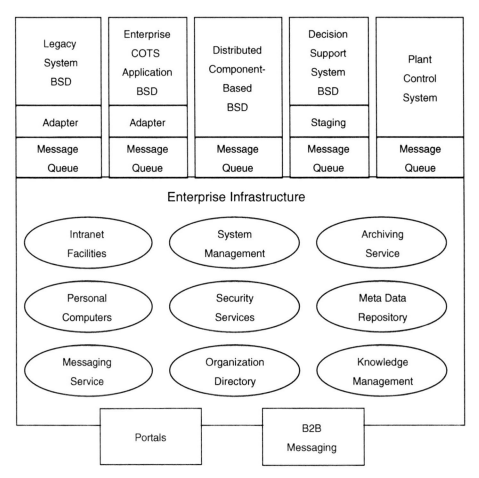

Figure 3.2   Integration infrastructure model.

Meta data repository.   A repository of data specifications used in a variety of contexts.

Knowledge management.   Services for the capture and retrieval of knowledge from across the enterprise.

Portals.   Web servers that provide access to applications intended to provide information and conduct business with humans on the public Internet.

Business-to-business (B2B) messaging.   A Web server that provides reliable store-and-forward messaging on the public Internet using HTTP.

Network Model

The elements of enterprise systems must be linked through networks. The networking model is illustrated in Figure 3.3. There are three primary domains:

- Internal systems
- Public Web applications
- The public Internet

We will discuss the details of each of these domains in the subsections that follow.

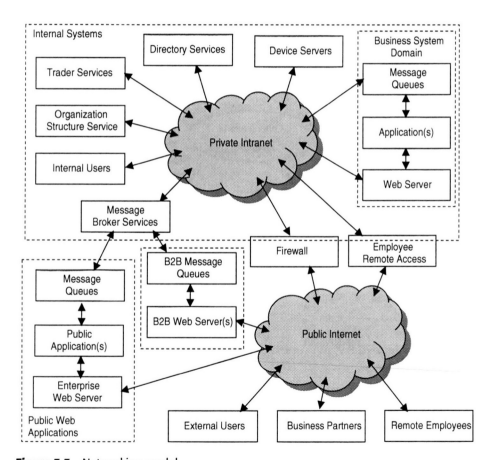

Figure 3.3 Networking model.

Internal Systems

From a network perspective, internal systems fall into the following categories:

- Intranet facilities
- Messaging services
- Local file, mail, and work-list services
- Device servers
- Organization directory
- Message queues
- BSD servers
- Web servers
- Security services

We will characterize these in the following subsections. The HTTP message exchange, firewalls, and remote-access components depicted in Figure 3.3 will be discussed as public Internet facilities.

Intranet Facilities

Intranet facilities include network directories, communication links on various media, routers, gateways, LANs, and private links over common-carrier facilities. Communications are isolated from the public Internet. The intranet may be global in scope. The intranet, like the public Internet, is expected to be heterogeneous, except that it will operate with the Transmission Control Protocol/Internet Protocol (TCP/IP) communication protocols.

Messaging Services

Messaging services include a message broker, message transformation services, and publish/subscribe notification services, as discussed earlier. Messages are communicated in a store-and-forward asynchronous mode. The messaging service provides a degree of isolation between systems for security and buffering of the workload. The message broker and message queues will hold messages until the recipient is ready to process them. The messaging service also can restrict message routing and must deny access to events where the subscriber is not authorized. Messaging services are discussed in detail in Chapter 6.

The isolation provided by the messaging service is particularly important for the connection to public applications (discussed later). This isolates internal systems from potential corruption through a publicly accessible application.

Internal Users

Internal users have personal computers that are connected directly to the private network, usually through a LAN. Their primary interface to enterprise applications is through their Web browsers. Typically, they also will have access to a local file server for file sharing, for receiving and sending e-mail, and for their work lists, that is, assignments from a workflow management facility. Many of these are the same users that will, from time-to-time, access enterprise systems as remote employees using their laptop computers.

Internal users can be given authorized access to network resources anywhere within the enterprise intranet. They also can access the public Internet through the firewall that separates the private intranet from the public Internet. The user's Web browser also may have various plug-ins for processing special Web-access data types or for implementing client-level functionality of certain applications.

Personal computers should have their own firewalls to protect them from a potential intruder who gains access to the private intranet and from intruders on the Internet in case they frequently access the public Internet from outside the enterprise.

Local File, Mail, and Work-List Servers

Local file servers will provide shared access to files and services within a local office environment, typically a particular organizational unit. Access to file servers should require user authentication.

Each employee requires a single location where mail and work assignments are received. The mail program on the employee's personal computer will retrieve mail from the file server mailbox and put outgoing mail in an outbox for distribution. Similarly, the employee will access his or her business process workflow work list on an assigned server. The mechanism and server location may depend on the particular workflow product. In general, however, the work list should be accessed using the personal computer Web browser. The mail and work-list facilities will be accessed in a similar manner if the employee connects to these servers from outside the enterprise.

Device Servers

Device servers provide access to input-output devices such as printers and scanners. Shared devices are located for convenient access by communities of users. Appropriate devices are selected based on user requirements and/or preferences. Personal computer access to device servers is a well-established intranet capability.

Organization Directory

Information about the organization must be available to applications and users across the enterprise. The directory should provide information on the structure of the organization, assignments of employees to positions, relationships between different positions, and enterprise-level roles of employees and/or positions for purposes of determining general authority.

It is expected that replicas of the organization directory will be distributed for high performance of local access by each BSD. At the same time, at least one copy of the directory should be available for browser-based access and query by employees.

Message Queues

Messages are exchanged by applications through message queues and the message broker. The message broker accepts messages from output queues and delivers messages to the appropriate destination queues. A message queue not only provides for buffering inputs and outputs, but it also provides a controlled point of access to prevent the intrusion and input of fraudulent messages.

Guaranteed delivery is accomplished by a transactional update of message queues. A message placed in the queue is not available for forwarding until the associated transaction commits. A message removed from the queue is not deleted from the queue until the transaction consuming the message commits.

BSD Servers

A BSD typically will include a number of servers for the execution of business applications. This may include application servers, database servers, a security server, and an organization directory server. These may be legacy applications, COTS enterprise applications, component-based applications, or decision support applications, as discussed earlier. A BSD has local network connections between servers of the BSD, but most of the communications between the BSD and the outside world go through either the associated message queues and the message broker or the BSD Web server(s). Additional communications may occur for accessing and updating the directories, but these communications must be highly restricted.

Web Servers

Internal users will interact with applications primarily through BSD Web servers. In some cases, the Web server simply will support access to HTML Web pages. The Web server will execute Web server components to accept user input and prepare user displays. The Web server components communicate with the business application to obtain Web page content or enter data.

Because the private intranet provides limited security, the Web server could be vulnerable to unauthorized intrusion. Consequently, depending on the nature of the business function and the vulnerability of the Web server, it may be appropriate to isolate the Web server from the private intranet with a firewall.

Security Services

From a network perspective, most security services are distributed. Each server or BSD on the intranet authenticates users or other servers with which it communicates and determines authority locally. The authentication of servers and users will be performed with digital certificates that allow users to sign on once and be authenticated automatically for access to each system. A digital certificate is like an electronic identification badge. However, there is a need to determine if a certificate has been revoked. This information must be available to all authentication functions. Digital certificates are discussed further in Chapter 11.

Public Web Applications

The enterprise must provide Web services to the outside world to provide information about the enterprise and its products and services and to conduct business, particularly with customers. As we will see later, B2B exchanges will occur in a somewhat different manner.

Direct access to applications on the private intranet would present a substantial security risk to enterprise applications, services, and personal computers. The security risk is reduced substantially if these public applications are isolated from the private network. This isolation is accomplished by exchanging data between internal systems as messages through the message broker. Each public Web service may be a specialized BSD. We will now discuss the following major components for public Internet integration:

- Message queues
- Application servers
- Web servers

Message Queues

The message queues for the public application send and receive messages with the associated internal BSD systems. The messages accepted from the message queues must be restricted to specific types and destinations as appropriate to the function of the public application.

Although messaging is asynchronous, it is possible to implement solutions that operate in a synchronous mode. The public application can direct a request to an internal system and wait for the response before responding to the user. This introduces inherent delays due to the store-and-forward mode of communication. For example, a user may ask for information that is more current if obtained from the associated business application, or it may be appropriate to perform certain internal processing before acknowledging an input, such as a customer order. Delays for some operations may be acceptable. However, as a general rule, it is appropriate for the public application to perform all immediate processing. If it is necessary to respond to a user after further processing, the use of e-mail is more appropriate. In this way, the customer does not need to wait, and an appropriate result is delivered later.

Public Applications

The public Web applications provide the specific functionality required for the external user. In general, a public application will have a database that replicates relevant information from internal sources. Interactions with external users then rely only on data local to the public application. If the public application becomes corrupted or overloaded, the impact is limited to the public application and does not spread to mainstream business applications.

At the same time, because the database does not always reflect the current state of internal systems, inconsistencies can occur, and an input transaction may be rejected when communicated to the internal system as a result of circumstances that were not apparent when the input was accepted. These potential inconsistencies and recovery from them must be considered in the design of the public application and associated business processes.

Often an external user will need to inquire about the status of an internal business process. For example, a customer may be interested in the status of an order, or a supplier may need to know the forecast requirements for a particular part. The application designer must determine how current the information provided must be. In general, this depends on the consequences of providing stale information. Even the state of the internal system will not reflect the state of the real world immediately. If current information is critical, then it may be appropriate to send a message to the internal application and wait for the response.

Public Web Servers

The public Web server functions much the same as an internal BSD Web server, except that the security controls are different. We will examine the general functionality of Web servers in detail in Chapter 8. Many of the public Web services provide only public information and therefore require no authentication. However, where authentication is required, the typical public user will not have a suitable digital certificate for authentication. Digital certificates can be issued to employees and some business partner personnel, but they cannot be issued to every potential customer. The issue of certificates to members of the general public by financial institutions is now only in the early stages. Consequently, some other form of identification will be needed.

In addition, the public Web server is more vulnerable to attack than the internal Web server. Consequently, it is appropriate to control access with a firewall tailored to allow only exchanges that are appropriate to the particular application.

It also may be appropriate to provide a single Internet Protocol (IP) address as a single point of contact for a number of public applications, that is, an *enterprise portal*. A portal provides a single point for authentication, when required, and can redirect requests to different application-specific Web servers. If the user accessed the different applications directly, then authentication would be required for each server, and this would add overhead. In addition, the portal enables the enterprise to perform workload balancing, get information on the browsing patterns of users to evaluate interests and the effectiveness of the Web services, and perform address translation for network security and address management.

Public Network Access

Integration with the public network involves three types of links to the private network:

- HTTP message exchange
- Firewall
- Remote access server

We will examine each of these and their relationship to remote employees, business partners, and Web resources. Relationships with other external users will be either through public applications, as discussed earlier, or as known users, equivalent to employees.

HTTP Message Exchange

B2B communications involve messaging between business processes of the enterprise and those of business partners. These exchanges use HTTP because it is readily supported by Web server facilities, and it can pass through standard firewalls the same as normal Web browser interactions. In addition, HTTP servers have been made less vulnerable through years of refinement.

Where there is an established relationship, the message content is similar to that exchanged between internal applications. This is particularly characteristic of exchanges with outsourced business functions.

Where the relationship is more ad hoc, it may be necessary to first reach agreement on a common process for exchange. In the past, this might have required human negotiation. However, automated protocols for selection of a common process have been defined by standards activities, and industry groups and standards bodies are establishing common processes. Once a common process is established between business partners, the business processes drive the exchange.

For B2B message exchanges, the HTTP message exchange server functions as a bridge between the internal message broker and the Internet exchange. An HTTP interaction protocol has been defined for guaranteed once-and-only-once delivery of messages. The HTTP message server will receive messages in its message queue and wrap and format them properly for delivery through HTTP. Conversely, messages received through HTTP will be placed in a message queue to be delivered to the appropriate application. The exchanges can be conducted with appropriate security and with digital signatures to establish the authenticity of the messages. HTTP is discussed more in Chapter 8, and Extensible Markup Language (XML) document formats and reliable messaging are discussed in Chapter 9.

Firewall

A firewall provides the connection for internal users to access Web resources on the public Internet while restricting access to the private network by external systems and users. Generally, interactions through such a firewall can be initiated only from the private network, and communications to the private network from outside sources can only be in response to internal requests. The firewall also may restrict the URLs that internal users can access on the Internet, perform address translation to hide intranet addresses from Internet access, and filter incoming responses to deny entry to prevent spoofing where a response comes from an imposter.

Remote Access Server

When employees of the enterprise want to access enterprise systems through the public network, the firewall will prevent access. Employee access from the public Internet and through dial-up connections can be important for employee productivity and may be essential for some jobs. The remote access server provides the necessary connection. It will authenticate the remote employee sign-on and maintain a secure link for employee access. Except for a possible performance degradation, the employee should be able to perform the same operations in the same way whether connected to the private network or connected through the remote access server.

Typically, a remote access server will be accessed through a virtual private network (VPN) connection. A public Internet service provider provides dial-up access to employees of the enterprise. When the employee signs onto the Internet service provider, the provider establishes a secure link to the enterprise remote access server. This provides the employee with a VPN direct connection to the enterprise intranet.

Alternatively, the employee may connect directly to the Internet through a cable service or other digital link. This allows the employee's personal computer to establish a direct Internet connection to the remote access server. This connection may be very fast, but it also creates additional risk. The employee's personal computer is now exposed to potential intrusion by Internet hackers. Consequently, it is essential that the employee's personal computer have firewall software to intercept such intrusions. This is the same protection that was suggested earlier for using personal computers on the intranets of a large enterprise.

Workflow Process Model

Business processes drive the operation of the business. Some business processes perform enterprise-level actions, such as filling a customer order, and some processes automate relatively trivial operations, such as obtaining approval of a package pass. In all cases the automation of business processes should be performed by workflow management systems. These systems have a common model, depicted in Figure 3.4. In the following subsections we will describe each of the components of this model, their relationships, and, in general terms, their implementation. Workflow management systems are discussed in more depth in Chapter 7.

- Process definition
- Process instance
- Activity

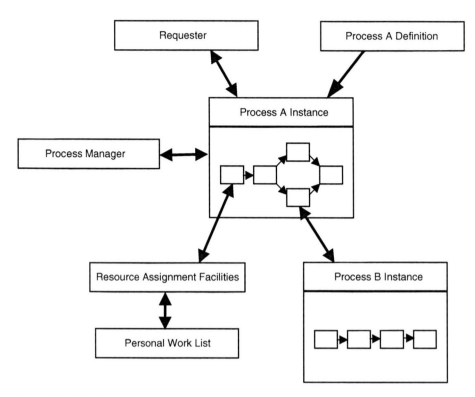

Figure 3.4   Workflow process model.

- Requester
- Personal work list
- Resource assignment facility
- Process manager
- Process interoperability

Process Definition

The *process definition* specifies how a process is to be performed. The process definition generally is created offline and references people, places, and things in abstract ways so that the definition can be applied to many specific requests. For example, a person to perform a task might be identified as somebody within a particular organizational unit who possesses certain skills. The specific person will be determined when the process is actually executed.

The process definition exists at run time in some form as the basis for the execution of process instances. Process definitions should be visible at run time and in some systems may be modifiable at run time. Access to the definition allows people to understand the manner in which activities are expected to occur and may facilitate the estimation of the time the process will take.

Typically, a workflow management product will include both a process definition tool and a runtime execution engine. The process definition tool presents the process definition in a form that can be understood by the process designer. Presentation of the process should be available in a similar form at run time so that the process designer, the organization manager or supervisor, and the persons participating in the process can understand and talk about what is happening.

Process Instance

When execution of a process is requested, an instance of a process is created. The *process instance* carries the specific values of variables specified in the process definition. Variables may include such things as identifiers for the request and its source, the persons assigned to perform certain tasks, the product or purchase involved, and so on.

A process consists of a number of activities, indicated by the small boxes in Figure 3.4. The activities may be performed sequentially, or some activities may be performed concurrently, as determined by the process definition. Depending on the circumstances of a particular request, a process execution may involve different activities or a different ordering of activities; that is, the process may have conditional flow control.

A process instance exists to respond only to a single request. It is started to act on a request, and it is completed with a response to the request. Activities within a process cannot be started until the process is started, and the process cannot be completed if any activities remain active. If an exception occurs, the process can terminate all activities internal and external, and a response should then be returned to the requester, indicating an abnormal completion.

A process instance executes within a BSD. It is the responsibility of a single organization. The organization accepts a request and is expected to respond to the request. At the same time, actions required to complete certain activities may be delegated to processes in other BSDs. Figure 3.2 depicts two process instances, *process instance A* and *process instance B*. Process A is shown as invoking process B. These processes may be in the same or different BSDs.

Activity

An *activity* is a component of a process. A process is comprised of its activities. An activity may perform an operation directly, it may invoke an application or another process, or it may request an action by a human.

When an activity invokes an application, the activity may need to establish mechanisms by which it can determine when the application is completed (or otherwise terminates) so that the activity can be terminated. When an activity invokes another process, it functions as a requester (as discussed later), and the process will notify the activity when it is completed. When an activity delegates to a human, it generally will post a request for the action, and the person will respond to the request when the action is completed. In most of these cases, the activity will capture some result data.

Activities may execute sequentially, one at a time, but typically workflow systems will allow more than one activity to be active in a process instance. This supports streamlining, where some activities, particularly human activities, can be performed concurrently.

Requester

A *requester* is the source of a process request. A requester may be a person, a computer system, or an activity within a process. Typically, the requester is represented within a computer system by an object that is intended to receive notice of the completion of the process.

In essence, a requester is like the caller of a function in a conventional program. The function call requests the execution of a function and passes relevant parameters. When the function is completed, it will return results, or it may return an exception indicating that the function did not complete successfully.

In general, the requester of a process should be loosely coupled with the process being requested. The requester should not keep a transaction uncommitted while waiting for a requested process to complete. The requester's action of requesting the process should be committed, and the requester should be notified, asynchronously, when the process is completed.

Personal Work List

A *personal work list* provides a user with a list of current and potential assignments. This reflects the individual's current and potential involvement in business processes. Often a request for a type of person will be presented on work lists for one or more people. When one person accepts responsibility for the assignment, the request will be removed from the work lists of others.

The work list will display activities that one of several individuals may accept as well as activities to which the individual currently is assigned. The individual is expected to indicate when an activity is accepted or completed, possibly providing relevant data, so that the business process can proceed. The process may cause corrective action to be taken if the activity remains open for an excessive period of time.

Resource Assignment Facility

A resource assignment facility provides a mechanism for the selection of a resource to meet the needs of a process. Facilities could be designed for a variety of assignment mechanisms for different kinds of resources. A process may request a resource of a particular type with certain qualifying parameters. A resource assignment facility, in fact, may be another process involving activities to acquire a needed resource. Of particular interest is the assignment of people to perform process activities.

In conventional workflow management systems, the assignment of resources typically is an integral part of the workflow system. This means that the same resource-assignment mechanism cannot be employed by business processes implemented with different workflow management systems. For example, a person would be required to have a different work list for each workflow management system from which he or she could receive assignments. The definition of the resource-assignment facility as a distinct mechanism enables each resource to be assigned by a single facility for participation in processes managed by different workflow products. It also means that the assignment of people is loosely coupled with the processes in which they participate. Standards for resource-assignment facilities are under development.

Process Manager

The process manager represents another type of user, the person who has the ability to observe and alter process instances. Not all workflow systems provide this capability, but it can be very valuable, particularly for complex and long-running processes.

A change to a process instance may be as simple as changing the assignment of a person. On the other hand, it could involve the addition or the repeat execution of activities where a request has unusual requirements or exceptions have arisen in the performance of the activities.

Process Interoperability

Business processes will be implemented by workflow management systems. In the near term, workflow management systems will include the definition of processes as well as the assignment of resources. OMG specifications currently define interfaces for the interoperability of workflow management systems, at least from the standpoint of a process implemented in one system invoking a process implemented in another system.

In the future, the definition of processes will employ a common model so that processes defined in one tool can be deployed in different runtime workflow systems. Independent resource-assignment facilities will be available to be shared by different workflow systems. Consequently, it will be possible to define common processes to be deployed to different organizations that may or may not be using the same workflow management product.

However, the execution of a business process should continue to be within the scope of a single workflow management system as well as a single BSD. Definition and control of the process are the responsibility of a single organization. When a request is received, it is the responsibility of that organization to see that the request is completed, successfully or unsuccessfully, and that a response is returned to the requester. This does not preclude the delegation of actions to other organizations, but the primary organization does not avoid responsibility for completion of the activities by delegation to another organization.

In general, this means that the process activities can be coupled tightly to the execution of applications in the BSD. In addition, a BSD may have a single workflow management system if that system meets its needs for all types of processes performed by that organization—some workflow systems may offer more effective or easier-to-use capabilities for specific types of processes.

BSD Model

Although the enterprise architecture will accommodate a number of application models, the component-based application model will be preferred for new applications. This model is consistent with the Java 2 Enterprise Edition (J2EE) specification, which incorporates EJB components. J2EE and EJB are considered preferred technologies in this book because of the widespread popularity of the technology and the commitment of a number of vendors to providing products compliant with these specifications. CORBA components technology provides similar capabilities and allows for implementation in other languages. J2EE can interoperate with CORBA components.

Figure 3.5 depicts the implementation of a component-based distributed computing BSD. Each of the components is described briefly in the following list. The BSD architecture is discussed in detail in Chapter 5.

Web server.   The Web server manages interactions with the user with, in most cases, a standard Web browser. Web-based access is discussed in detail in Chapter 8.

Business document archive.   Data exchanged with users or systems of business partners often represent transactions with legal effect or personal responsibility. These documents may be signed with digital signatures. For a signature to be valid, the document must be saved exactly as signed. The repository preserves these documents for future reference, equivalent to the preservation of paper documents in the past. Digital signatures are discussed further in Chapters 9 and 11.

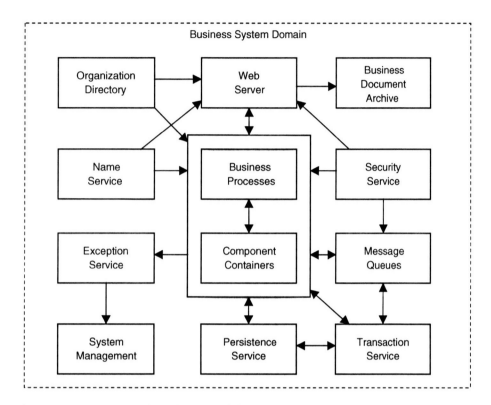

Figure 3.5   Component-based BSD model.

Business processes.   Business processes will manage the flow of work. This is to be separated from application functionality so that business processes can be observed and changed more easily. The general nature of workflow management was discussed earlier. If a user is requesting some action from the enterprise, such as placing an order or requesting a quote, the Web access will capture information and initiate a process. On the other hand, the user may be an employee who is participating in the business process. In this case, the employee accesses a work list to receive and post the completion of assignments. During an assignment, the user likely will interact directly with an application.

Component containers.   Component containers provide the environment for application components. Containers incorporate a number of services to minimize the complexity of the application component. The container makes the component transactional, it resolves concurrent access conflicts, it provides for event management, it provides persistence of the component state, and it implements life-cycle operations. Components, and particularly EJBs, are discussed in detail in Chapter 10.

Persistence service. The state of components that represent information about the business or the state of the systems must be preserved to survive system failure or shutdown. The persistence service provides a common interface to data storage facilities, typically databases, for the storage of component states.

Organization directory. The organization directory provides information on people, their authorized enterprise-level roles, and their relationships with the organization structure. This information is the basis for business process assignments and for ad hoc access to enterprise systems where the person does not have a specific role with respect to the system.

Name service. The name service provides the mechanism by which the identifier associated with a business entity in the real world can be associated with the internal reference to the component that represents that entity in an application.

Exception service. The exception service is invoked by an application when it recognizes an error that prevents further execution of the current operation, that is, an *exception*. This service provides for the consistent capture and presentation of exception information. For certain exceptions, the service initiates business processes for a follow-up to address immediate problems and to prevent future occurrences.

Security service. The security service supports the authentication and authorization activities of the Web server and applications. The security service will provide specifications for the authorized roles of individuals and the authority represented by each role. Each role may be associated with an *access control list*. Security is discussed in greater detail in Chapter 11.

Transaction service. The transaction service provides a transactional context for processing. This context is the basis of control of conflicting accesses to resources by multiple processes, and it is the basis for the commit or rollback of updates. It is key to maintaining the consistent state of the BSD and for the reliable exchange of asynchronous messages.

Message queues. Message queues provide for the exchange of asynchronous (store-and-forward) messages. Messages may be directed to the same or other applications, or they may be issued through a publish-and-subscribe mode of distribution. Similarly, messages may be received from other applications directly or by subscription. The most common uses of message queues will be for the communication of events and for the initiation and completion of processes. Messaging facilities are discussed in detail in Chapter 6.

Enterprise Data Storage Model

The enterprise data storage model, depicted in Figure 3.6, is the basis for observing the current state of the enterprise as well as historical activity. It is key to providing management information to support monitoring, planning, and decision making.

The integrity of this model and the information derived from it depend on the consistent definition of data and the consistent coordination of data changes in the different components of the data storage model. The components are discussed in the subsections that follow:

- Business operation applications
- Document management
- Operational data store
- Enterprise master databases
- Business document archives
- Meta data
- Data warehouses
- Data marts

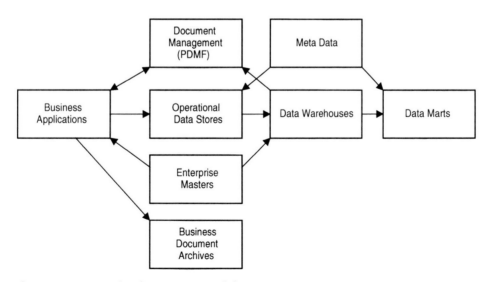

Figure 3.6 Enterprise data storage model.

Business Operation Applications

Business operation applications are the computer software that run the business. These contain the most current information about the state of the business, and they may involve large volumes of data and large numbers of transactions. Much of the data processed by these applications are only of concern for the particular activity being performed. Some applications will provide direct, widespread access to the operational data, but others may limit access due to the potential performance impact. The data that are of broader interest must be communicated to the operational data store or data warehouse (discussed later) to be combined with related data from other applications.

Document Management

Document management keeps track of files containing documents or other complex structures such as product specifications or models. Documents are checked into or out of the document management service. These documents typically are created or modified as a unit. When a document is changed, the changed copy may be stored as a new version.

In order to prevent conflicting updates, a document is checked out (flagged as in use) and checked in when it is no longer in use. This mode of conflict resolution is used instead of transactions because a document may be in use for an extended period of time and intermediate changes may be saved so that the user's work will not be lost if the system fails. The updates are committed when the revised document is checked in. In the long term, the document management system may manage historical documents as well as current documents. Robust document management systems occur primarily in engineering and manufacturing organizations to manage product specifications. These systems, often called *product data management facilities* (PDMFs), provide mechanisms for defining relationships between documents and attributes for finding documents. They also incorporate versioning and configuration capabilities to determine which versions of documents go together. The OMG has adopted specifications for interfaces to such systems. These specifications are called *PDM Enablers*. Similar systems have been developed for the management of information system development artifacts, but generally they are less robust.

Enterprise integration requires much more disciplined and automated control of all types of documents in the future. Workflow management and electronic data interchange will eliminate the flow of paper. The document management system provides an electronic file cabinet in which documents can be stored for future reference or sharing with others. The use of PDMFs will expand well beyond engineering and manufacturing organizations in the future.

Generally, the files in the document management system will be referenced by the business databases where they are relevant. Consequently, updates to the operational data store and the data warehouse may carry references to these documents.

Operational Data Store

The operational data store provides access to reasonably current data about the state of business operations in lieu of this data being accessible directly from the applications. An operational data store also may be used to bring together data from multiple applications to provide an integrated view of the current state of the business. This may require translations and cleansing of the data to resolve inconsistencies.

Communications from applications to the operational data store may be accomplished through batch file transfers. However, this means there will be a significant delay between the occurrence of operational events and the availability of the corresponding information in the operational data store. Alternatively, events may be communicated as they occur through asynchronous messaging. This will be more costly because processing individual events is not as efficient as processing batches of events. The timeliness-versus-cost tradeoff must be considered for the particular business operations.

Enterprise Master Databases

Certain relatively stable data may be shared by many parts of the organization and replicated at various sites to reduce communications overhead and the risk of failure. In such cases, one database will be defined as the enterprise master. Changes to the data will be made in the master database, and updates will be distributed to the dependent databases using batch file transfers or asynchronous messaging. Master databases typically contain customer data, business partner data, and product and service classifications and identifiers.

Business Document Archives

With electronic commerce, as well as some internal transactions, legally enforceable documents will be created electronically with digital signatures. These documents will be expressed in XML and must be preserved in the same form in which they were signed for the signatures to be valid. A business document archive is a common storage facility for the long-term retention and occasional retrieval of these documents.

Meta Data (data about data)

Meta data in this context are of two types: technical meta data and business meta data. The technical meta data define the data types and structures of stored data. The purpose is to manage the data. Business meta data provide information about the source, accuracy, and reliability of the data. This information is incorporated in some data warehousing and datamart tools so that when analysis is done, a user can investigate the basis for results by examining the nature of the data used as input to the analysis.

Data Warehouses

A data warehouse stores an accumulation of historical data. Typically, shortly after business transactions are completed in the application or operational data store, they are transferred to the data warehouse. There may be some period of overlap; consequently, transactions may be in the operational systems and at the same time in the data warehouse, so care must be taken to avoid double-counting by combining operational summaries with data warehouse summaries. Generally, in order to minimize the overhead and to structure the data warehouse for efficient queries, the data communicated to the data warehouse are expected to remain unchanged once they are written.

Because the data warehouse may contain data for many years, the size of the data warehouse storage may be very large. The data warehouse schema and database technology are designed to provide efficient retrieval of selected data to support analysis.

Data Marts

Since analysis of historical data may involve examining and restructuring the data in various ways, analysis usually is not done from the data warehouse directly. Online analytical processing (OLAP) usually is done with a data mart. Selected data are extracted periodically from a data warehouse for different data marts. The data mart database schema is designed for rapid access to the specific data of interest for particular types of analysis. Special tools are then used to analyze the data, looking for trends and correlations that are obscured by the volume or complexity of the data and relationships.

Knowledge Access Model

Knowledge is information about the business and its technologies. Typically, it is not stored in operational databases or data warehouses, but often it is stored in less structured ways or retained in the memories of knowledge workers. Knowledge management involves capturing and preserving enterprise knowledge so that it is accessible and is not lost when memories fade or people leave the enterprise.

Figure 3.7 depicts the forms of knowledge to be accessed by the knowledge worker:

- Other people
- Web resources
- Encoded knowledge
- Meta knowledge

We will discuss each of these briefly in the subsections that follow. Knowledge management is discussed in greater detail in Chapter 12.

Other People

Other people always will be an important source of knowledge. In general, people are the primary source of knowledge, and they always will have knowledge that has not been captured by a system.

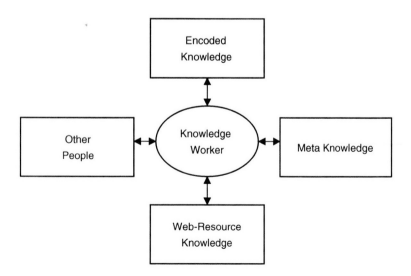

Figure 3.7 Knowledge resources.

The key to getting knowledge from other people is identifying the right people. Consequently, this form of knowledge access involves identification of appropriate experts and support for the exchange of knowledge.

Web Resources

Web resources are various forms of documents or files containing knowledge for human consumption. Most often these will be traditional documents, but they also may include multimedia presentations of information. The knowledge worker will access this knowledge through a Web browser. Again, an essential element of accessing this knowledge is finding it.

Encoded Knowledge

Encoded knowledge is knowledge used by expert systems. Generally, these systems apply knowledge in the form of rules to well-defined models of problem situations. The expert system will then advise the knowledge worker to help identify a problem, diagnose a problem, or configure a solution.

Meta Knowledge

Meta knowledge is information about knowledge. This means defining attributes of knowledge that can be used to search for relevant knowledge. Meta knowledge in the form of attribute values has been incorporated in Web pages as a basis for Web searches. Similar knowledge must be attached to the Web resources (discussed earlier) and Web pages about people who have certain valued expertise. A Web search engine can then be used to find the relevant knowledge and knowledgeable people.

An Enterprise Integration Scenario

Up to this point, the discussion of enterprise integration has been abstract. In order to link these concepts to the real world and provide a basis for the illustration of issues throughout this book, we have created the hypothetical business scenario depicted in Figure 3.8. We will discuss the operation of this example enterprise and then make some observations about the integration aspects.

Hypothetical Operation

Figure 3.8 depicts an enterprise engaged in retail sales. A customer accesses the enterprise sales portal and selects a product, such as a modem, for purchase.

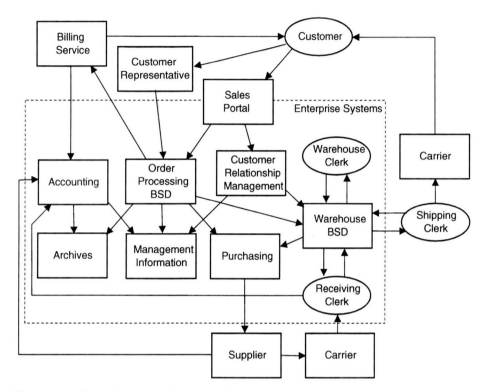

Figure 3.8   Enterprise integration scenario.

The sales portal is a publicly accessible application that has information on products and prices and accepts customer orders. The portal is not linked directly to other enterprise applications because of the risk that intruders might compromise the security of enterprise systems through the portal.

The customer's completed order is communicated in store-and-forward mode to the order-processing BSD. This BSD is internal to the enterprise. The communication is controlled to ensure that only customer orders, changes, and status requests are accepted from the sales portal. The order-processing BSD validates the order and sends a request to the warehouse BSD to ship it.

When an order is received from the customer, it represents a purchase agreement. Other transactions with external entities, such as the supplier purchase, are also legal documents. These records are captured in the archive for future reference in a form that ensures nonrepudiation.

The warehouse BSD checks the inventory and posts a shipping request to the work list of the warehouse clerk. The warehouse BSD returns a notice to the order-processing BSD that the modem is available and will be shipped. Later, the clerk checks his or her work list and selects the modem order request to prepare the shipment. He or she gets the modem from inventory, prepares the package, and marks the task as completed. The shipping clerk then gets a task in his or her work list to turn the package over to a carrier for transportation. During this process and the ensuing transportation process, events may be communicated back to the order-processing system to update the status of the order. The carrier ultimately delivers the modem to the customer. When the order-processing BSD receives notice of the shipment, it sends a request to the external billing service to issue the customer a bill. The billing service is outside the enterprise, so messaging must be over the public Internet. The billing service issues the invoice and notifies accounting of the receivable, again over the public Internet.

During processing of the order, the customer might contact his or her traveling customer sales representative and ask about the status of the order. The customer representative can connect remotely to check the status of the order process for the customer's order. If the order appears delayed, the representative might trace the request to the warehouse process to see where the order stands in greater detail.

This illustrates the order cycle when the product is in the warehouse. On the other hand, when the inventory is depleted, the product must be reordered from the supplier. In this case, the warehouse BSD initiates a purchasing request. Purchasing issues a purchase order to the appropriate supplier. The supplier ships the product and sends an invoice to accounting. The carrier delivers the product to the receiving clerk. The receiving clerk updates the inventory and notifies accounting that the product was received to match the supplier's invoice. When the inventory is available, the shipping clerk's task is restored to prepare the order for shipment.

After the customer receives the product, he or she may return it, or at any time during the process, the customer may register a complaint. These occurrences are handled by customer relationship management and are reported to the management information system. Returned items will be returned to the warehouse. Information about the customer and the customer history will be used to establish a customer profile to personalize the customer's future interactions.

When the order processing is complete, the order-processing BSD sends a record of the completed transaction to the management information system. A historical record of each transaction is kept in a data warehouse for future analysis. Operational information on the current status of active orders and warehouse inventory is also available to managers through intranet access to the order-processing and warehouse BSDs.

Observations

Implicit in this example are many requirements for enterprise integration as well as potential requirements for an integration infrastructure. We will discuss each of the following observations:

- Messages between BSDs
- Events and requests
- Reliable communications
- Coordinated activity
- Potential outsourcing
- Supply-chain integration
- Customer relationship management
- Management information
- Legal records

Messages between BSDs

As systems have been developed over the years, links between them have been developed as needed. Typically, the links come in different forms and may use different technologies and facilities. This example shows how each BSD may communicate with several other BSDs. A common infrastructure facility can reduce the complexity of these communications, improve the management for more reliable operation, and realize economies of scale in the sharing of resources.

Requests and Events

The communications in this example are of two basic forms, requests and events. For example, the mainstream process for order fulfillment involves the portal requesting order processing and order processing requesting shipment from the warehouse. Each of these requests requires a response. Events, on the other hand, are sent to provide information on relevant changes of state. For example, accounting receives events for the issue of the invoice and for the arrival of a shipment from the supplier to enable payment of the supplier's invoice. The request message form implies that the requester has a continuing interest and needs to receive notice of the result. The event message form implies that the recipient needs to know about an occurrence, but the sender is not dependent on completion of the receiver's action.

Reliable Communications

Whether communications are in the form of requests or events, they must be reliable. The overall operation of the enterprise depends on it. If requests are lost, the requester eventually may recognize that there has been no response, so the system will not fail completely, but the responsiveness of the enterprise will be degraded seriously. If events such as those in the example are lost, then the customer may not be billed, supplier invoices may not be paid, management information will be unreliable, and important documents may not be archived. This could seriously undermine the viability of the business.

Coordinated Activity

This example, particularly in the warehouse and shipping operations, illustrates the integration of people and processes needed for smooth operation of the business. Each employee has access to pending and active tasks on his or her work list. This clearly defines who is responsible both to the employee and to somebody trying to learn why an order is delayed. When tasks are completed, the event is communicated quickly to the next activity.

The customer representative role illustrates the need for employees to access information regardless of where they are. In this case, the employee is remote. In other situations, the employee may be at an enterprise site but not at his or her normal workstation. This location of the employee should not affect his or her ability to interact with the system, with the possible constraint that remote access may not provide the best performance.

Potential Outsourcing

The billing service represents the outsourcing of a traditionally internal business function. With the advent of application service providers (ASPs), this may happen more and more. Other internal enterprise systems that interact with the outsourced billing system should see no difference whether the billing system is internal or external. At the same time, since the enterprise does not control the security of the outsourced system, security precautions should be taken to ensure that communications with the outsourced functions do not create an opportunity for outsiders to infiltrate enterprise systems.

Supply-Chain Integration

This example also illustrates the need to include suppliers and carriers in the design of enterprise integration. In many cases, suppliers and carriers are critical links in enterprise performance, as they are here, when adequate inventory has not been maintained. In fact, close coordination with suppliers and carriers will enable such an enterprise to reduce inventories and, in the case of low-demand products, potentially carry no inventory.

Customer Relationship Management (crm)

The interface to the customer is also a critical element in customer satisfaction. A good interface will guide the customer through the ordering process. However, customers are going to expect more. The system should recognize a repeat customer and respond appropriately to make the customer welcome and expedite the process. A customer should be able to easily check the status of outstanding orders and possibly the status of his or her account. This requires having ready access to internal systems or timely, ongoing updates to the customer relationship management database. The latter is preferred because it preserves protection for internal systems and ensures customer access to information regardless of the operational status of the internal systems.

Management Information

A number of systems provide information to the management information activity. It is necessary, for effective management of the enterprise, to have an integrated viewpoint. This includes both the current operating status and, maybe more important, historical data to support analysis of performance, trends, and relationships over time. This integration of information requires a consistent definition of data so that managers are not computing and comparing incompatible data. The integration also must consider that data from different sources may become available at different times, so the information system should provide warnings or prevent premature aggregations and comparisons from being misleading.

Legal Records

Finally, exchanges of records with external entities, in many cases, represent legal documents. The customer order and the supplier purchase order, in this example, represent agreements on product and price and possibly other terms. These documents could become the subject of litigation. Electronic signatures are required to establish the validity of these documents. For the signatures to be effective, they must be preserved with the document in the original form. The archive should provide long-term retention along with the physical and access security to ensure the availability of these records.

Summary

The enterprise architecture includes a number of parts and a variety of interactions between these parts. This chapter helped you familiarize yourself with the parts and roles. Unfortunately, current technology is still evolving, and industry standards still have gaps. In the short term, implementation of the enterprise architecture may require some proprietary or custom solutions to fill these gaps.

Additionally, a real-world architecture must account for legacy systems using inconsistent technology. Consequently, enterprise integration requires selecting a complementary set of technologies and standards along with design and development efforts to fill in the gaps.

The remainder of this book will examine the implementation of the enterprise integration architecture in greater detail, showing the functionality of the pieces and how they fit together. Chapter 4 will illustrate the application of the enterprise architecture through applying it to a hypothetical enterprise. Subsequent chapters will examine in greater detail the specific technologies employed in the enterprise architecture.

CHAPTER

4

Establishing the Enterprise Infrastructure

Integration of the enterprise relies on an enterprise-wide infrastructure to support communications and shared services. Infrastructure facilities should achieve substantial economies of scale, improve sharing and access to information, and provide the backbone management and communications that link the business system domains (BSDs) to each other and to the outside world.

This chapter will establish the general design of the enterprise integration infrastructure. This infrastructure unifies the various systems while allowing diversity in their functionality and implementation technology. It reflects a balance between the scope of consistency achieved by the enterprise infrastructure and the flexibility and diversity achieved through the autonomy of BSDs.

Figure 4.1 depicts the enterprise integration infrastructure as a collection of facilities and services that link the BSDs, management information services, and portals for customers, partners, and employees.

The integration infrastructure supports a number of other systems designed for particular business functions. In Figure 4.1 we have characterized them as BSDs, decision support facilities, and plant control systems.

There will be many BSDs, potentially implemented with a variety of technologies. They will interface with other BSDs and employees through the integration infrastructure and will use various infrastructure services to achieve

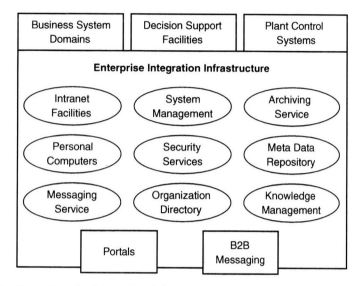

Figure 4.1 The enterprise integration infrastructure.

security, consistency, and economies of scale. A BSD may be a custom application, a legacy system, or a commercial-off-the-shelf (COTS) application. It also could be a composition of integrated applications or components. Each of the business functions defined in the retail sales example in Chapter 3 may be an independent BSD communicating with the other BSDs through the integration infrastructure. The nature of BSDs will be examined in detail in Chapter 5.

The decision support facilities represent systems that provide information for planning and decision support from an enterprise perspective. They typically include a data warehouse and data marts for the capture and analysis of historical data. These systems may be characterized as BSD systems from an infrastructure perspective because they exchange data with other BSDs and may leverage other infrastructure services. Decision support facilities are discussed further in Chapter 12.

Plant control systems are those that control the production operation. This applies to a wide range of enterprises, including manufacturing, utilities, telecommunications, petrochemicals, pharmaceuticals, transportation, and information services. The plant is the production facility, which may take various forms. The plant control systems are generally real-time systems that direct and monitor production activities and respond directly to events and exceptions to alter the process. These systems also may be characterized as BSD systems from an infrastructure perspective because they will exchange messages with other BSDs and decision support systems and may use some other infrastructure services. We will not examine plant systems in any greater depth in this book because of the special considerations of real-time systems and the distinct technologies involved in real-time process control.

The remaining components in Figure 4.1, including the portals, comprise the basic infrastructure for integration. We will discuss each in greater detail in this chapter.

This basic infrastructure includes the least common denominator of application support facilities, plus services that may be shared by a number of systems for economies of scale. As BSDs are developed with shared technology, aspects of the BSD architecture should be consolidated operationally to achieve further economies of scale and reduce risks. At the same time, the basic separation of BSDs and the infrastructure should be preserved to maintain BSD autonomy and the ability to replace a BSD with minimal impact on the rest of the enterprise.

Intranet Facilities

The intranet is the primary vehicle for providing internal user access to applications and for the exchange of messages and files between applications. The enterprise landscape consists of a number of local-area networks (LANs) for work groups linked by a wide-area network, as depicted in Figure 4.2. In addition, each BSD should have its own LAN with restricted physical and network

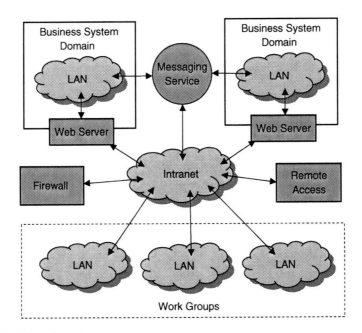

Figure 4.2 Intranet strategy.

access. The BSD LAN is intended to provide connectivity only between servers within the BSD. Since the BSD LAN is isolated, it might use an entirely different network technology to address specific needs of the associated business function.

The corporate intranet provides communications throughout the corporation. Messages must be transported over various facilities—telephone lines, satellites, microwaves, or optical fibers—to reach various corporate locations, but like the public Internet, the intranet uses the Transmission Control Protocol/Internet Protocol (TCP/IP) as the standard communications protocol, so the different media may only affect performance. Intranet facilities include e-mail services, search services, and possibly a bulletin board service (such as news). These are long-standing Internet services that have demonstrated value over the years. E-mail has become essential.

The intranet is isolated from the public Internet for security purposes. It includes LANs for departmental and personal computers, printers, file servers, and mail servers. At the same time, it may extend around the world to link every Web server, messaging interface, and user client. Virtual private network (VPN) services may be acquired from Internet service providers to allow the enterprise intranet to have a global reach without the corporation owning or maintaining exclusive control of the network facilities. Users on the intranet may access the public Internet through a firewall that restricts access to the private intranet from the public Internet. Conversely, employees not connected to the intranet can access the internal systems through a remote access server.

Each work group has a LAN for access to shared servers and devices. Each employee in a work group will have a mailbox and a workflow work list. The intranet enables employees with portable computers to plug into the intranet anywhere and access applications as well as e-mail, work lists, and file servers. With dynamic IP addressing, the portable computer can be incorporated quickly in the local network domain and then access the employees' home servers through the intranet.

The intranet provides similar flexibility for messaging between applications. New message destinations can be defined to message brokers, and messages can be communicated without any physical network reconfiguration.

The intranet also includes directory services. We will discuss security and organization directory services as separate infrastructure facilities later. The intranet incorporates directory services for network routing, resolving domain names and email addresses to Internet Protocol (IP) addresses. We will consider these directories to be part of the intranet infrastructure because they support the entire enterprise and the intranet will not function without them. Routing data provide the basis for routing a message through various network nodes from a source to a destination with the possibility of using alternate routes if certain links become overloaded or defective. A domain name server supports translation of a symbolic Universal Resource Identifier (URI) such as eds.com to a numeric IP address so that it can be routed properly. An e-mail directory provides the translation of a person's e-mail address to his or her mailbox location.

Directory technology enables directory information to be replicated on multiple, distributed directory servers. Directory content is expected to be relatively stable, so directories are tuned for rapid retrieval. Updates, when they occur, are propagated automatically to the directory replicas—sometimes they are propagated on a demand basis.

Personal Computers

Personal computers are part of the infrastructure because business applications depend on them for user access, and many personal computer applications should be common across the enterprise. In addition, they represent a substantial investment and potential source of risk to the enterprise.

Personal computers execute the Web browsers that are the primary user-interface facility for the enterprise architecture. In addition, personal computers handle e-mail and provide a number of personal computing applications for documents, spreadsheets, presentations, distributed conference displays, and plug-ins for the Web browser. There is certainly an opportunity for economy of scale in the purchasing and support of these common applications as well as the computers and operating systems on which they run. In addition, it is desirable that many of the applications are common throughout the enterprise to reduce incompatibilities in the sharing of information.

Personal computers may come in a variety of forms depending on the needs of the individual for computing resources. Some employees may only require access to basic services; others may require workstations with powerful computing capacity for design and analysis applications; still others may require laptop computers for mobility.

Personal computers are a particular source of security risk because of the diverse environments in which they may be used, because they can expose proprietary data, and because they can host and propagate computer viruses. In addition, the personal computer may carry a substantial investment in work product of the individual user; this work product may be lost if the computer malfunctions or is stolen.

For all these reasons, the purchase, configuration, operational support, and security of personal computers should not be left to the discretion of individuals or separate departments of the corporation. The differences in personal computers should be viewed as differences in level-of-service requirements. Nonstandard applications should be viewed as local usage to meet business function requirements. Infrastructure specifications should define appropriate criteria for the acceptance of local applications to preserve system integrity and ensure future flexibility in the upgrading of personal computers.

Messaging Services

Messaging services, sometimes called message-oriented middleware (MOM), provide communication of messages between BSDs and their applications in a store-and-forward, that is, asynchronous, mode of communication. An application posts messages to a queue for later delivery. The messages are forwarded to one or more destination queues. A receiving application removes a message from its queue when it is prepared to process the message. The use of queues allows messages to accumulate between the sender and receiver. The mechanism of updating the queues and the communication of messages provides guaranteed once-and-only-once delivery.

In order to provide flexibility and reduce the number of connections between applications, a message broker service is used to receive messages from many applications and forward them to many applications. The message broker must maintain a directory of destination queues as part of the service in order to distribute the messages properly.

An additional capability, a publish-and-subscribe service, enables applications to *publish* the occurrence of events to other applications that have *subscribed* to the receipt of those events if and when subscriptions exist. The event messages may be filtered by rules so that only messages with certain characteristics are forwarded. The publish-and-subscribe service is a key element of a plug-and-play capability. New functions can be installed and obtain their inputs by subscribing without the need to change source applications.

Message transformation is another service associated with asynchronous messaging. Transformation specifications are used to transform the structure and format of message data in order to resolve incompatibilities between the source and destination. These transformations must be coordinated with changes to the source and destination applications.

As a general rule, messages should be communicated in Extensible Markup Language (XML) format. This enables the use of a common transformation specification and execution engine using XML Stylesheet Language Transformation (XSLT). It also improves compatibility as message content is extended. These and other aspects of XML are discussed in detail in Chapter 9.

The store-and-forward mode of communication achieves loose coupling to minimize dependence between the sending and the receiving systems. As long as a system has needed inputs, its operations can be performed independent of other systems. It can process inputs as they become available or later, and it can produce outputs without waiting for receiving systems to accept them. In addition, messages are communicated as circumstances occur rather than being batched into files for periodic transfer. This business transaction level of communication improves the ability of the enterprise to respond to events as they happen. The publish-and-subscribe service further decouples the sender and receiver by making it unnecessary for the sender to be aware of where the messages are to be delivered.

The messaging service is examined in detail in Chapter 6. This mode of messaging has gained great popularity for enterprise application integration (EAI), the practice of integrating large-scale COTS applications with legacy applications. A variety of products and associated tools are available in the marketplace.

System Management

Infrastructure system management services support operation, configuration, and problem resolution for the infrastructure. Exceptions, hardware failures, and performance problems must be recognized. Action must be taken to resolve infrastructure problems quickly and reliably. Upgrades to components and changes in workload must be anticipated, coordinated, and managed to avoid disruption of service. Network facilities must be configured and updated to accommodate new systems and users.

The following are key aspects of infrastructure system management:

Operations.   System management involves the day-to-day operation of the infrastructure. This includes management of the execution of services, the routine addition and removal of applications and devices from the network, monitoring of performance to identify malfunctions and redistribute workload, and execution of contingency plans when failures occur.

Configuration.   The enterprise infrastructure consists of many components, including hardware, software, and network facilities. The configuration of these components, including consideration of different versions, must meet the needs of users and applications, and information about the configuration must be available to support other system management activities.

Change management.   Changes to the infrastructure must be managed carefully. As new components are installed or existing components are upgraded, attention must be given to potential incompatibilities and the process by which a change will be propagated across the enterprise. This will include both technical and business changes—changes to hardware, software, and network facilities as well as changes in operating procedures and the training of users if they are affected. The propagation of change is particularly challenging when it involves changes to personal computers.

Problem resolution.   Problems will be reported from various sources, particularly users and system operators. These problems must be recorded, investigated, and resolved systematically while providing status information to persons affected.

Performance monitoring, tuning, and load balancing.   Infrastructure management must be constantly aware of the level of performance of the network and services. Performance of the systems, services, and networks must be evaluated for quality, stability, and trends. Adjustments may be required to the network configuration and allocation of work. Performance problems also may indicate BSD problems or overloads that may escalate if action is not taken to mitigate the effects.

Cost allocation/accounting.   Depending on the enterprise management policies, use of the infrastructure services may be tracked for cost allocation. Even if costs are not to be rebilled, tracking is useful for the justification of expenses and expansions to be able to identify where costs are incurred.

Directory management.   The infrastructure directories mentioned earlier —routing directories, domain name directories, and e-mail directories— must be kept up to date on a continuing basis.

Infrastructure systems management should be viewed as a specialized BSD. It focuses on a particular domain of responsibility and has common data and functions. Well-defined business processes must direct the activities of employees, and these activities must be supported by various tools and information. The system management organization receives requests for services, including installation, removal, problem resolution, and repair of infrastructure facilities and services. As such, information on performance and problems should be communicated to the systems management business processes through asynchronous messages or Web access, and corrective actions taken as a result should be communicated to the affected BSDs and users via asynchronous messaging (including e-mail). The status of facilities, services, and requests should be available through Web page access.

Security Services

Security is primarily the responsibility of each BSD. The BSD should execute in a physically secure environment. Users must be authenticated and then authorized to access particular BSD data and functionality. For communication between BSDs, participating servers should authenticate each other, and the communications between them should be encrypted.

Five basic security services should be provided as part of the infrastructure:

Infrastructure security administration.   Valid users must be authenticated and given appropriate authority for access to infrastructure services, such as e-mail, firewalls, system management information, messaging service routings, and archiving services. Attempts to obtain unauthorized access must be monitored.

Digital certificates. Digital certificates provide authentication without explicit user sign-on. They also provide the public-private key information needed for digital signatures. An enterprise *certificate authority* must issue digital certificates to every employee, the same as it would issue badges. Certificates also may be issued to contract personnel and selected employees of business partners when they require access to enterprise systems. The digital certificate is stored on the individual's personal computer and is used to identify the person whenever he or she accesses any system in the enterprise. The user signs onto the personal computer once, to enable access to the certificate. The security service also must provide a repository of certificates for terminated employees, revoked certificates, and certificates that are no longer secure. The facilities and services supporting the use of digital certificates is referred to as a public key infrastructure (PKI).

Firewalls. Firewalls protect the intranet from persons attempting to intrude from the outside Internet. This makes the intranet safer from hackers and denial-of-service (that is, request overload) attacks. At the same time, in a large enterprise, each BSD and each personal computer should have firewall protection. Personal computers are particularly vulnerable if they are connected, from time to time, to the public Internet. Since the intranet may be accessible from many locations throughout the corporation, it does not have the level of security appropriate to BSDs or personal computers. It would be beneficial for all BSD firewalls to be managed as part of the infrastructure so that they can be updated quickly in response to security threats. Personal computer firewalls should be managed the same as other personal computer applications and virus protection. The security service should manage the configuration and access restrictions of these firewalls.

Virus protection. Virus protection is a constant burden. Whenever a new virus emerges, there must be quick action to implement protection measures. Some measures should be implemented at firewalls and in e-mail servers to keep the virus out if possible. In addition, protection must be installed on every personal computer that could be affected. The security service should be the focal point for the recognition of virus threats and the installation of detection and repair software. This should not be left to individuals or departments, or it will not be accomplished as quickly or effectively as needed or at minimum cost.

Security assurance. The configuration of infrastructure facilities, operating practices, and the implementation of security measures should be reviewed as changes are made and audited periodically. This requires specialized expertise that should be part of the security services.

Organization Directory

Information about the employees and the corporate organization structure must be accessible anywhere in the corporation. While a digital certificate provides authentication of a user's identity, the organization directory defines who that person is in the organizational context. Valid, enterprise-level roles of employees should be defined in the organization directory as distinct from roles within individual organizations, which would be defined within the specific BSDs with respect to the local application data and functionality.

The directory should contain a model of the organization structure. Closely associated with the organization structure is the financial account structure that must be included in the directory. Attributes of organizational positions should include levels of authority with regard to certain business functions and financial amounts. Positions in the organization must be linked to information about the people who occupy the positions. This model of authority will have security implications and will provide the basis for work assignments and approval routings for workflow management.

The organization directory also may contain limited personalization information to enable user interfaces and application processing to be specialized to meet the needs of individual users. There may be minimal personalization information at the enterprise level, such as preferred language, a preferred system of measures (English or metric), and other personal data that might be of interest to a number of applications to communicate more effectively with the user. Most personalization information, however, is related to specific applications. This information should be held by the associated application within a BSD.

The organization directory should be implemented in technology similar to the intranet domain name servers so that the information is replicated and distributed for high-performance access. Each BSD may have its own copy of the organization directory for local access. The master organization directory must be managed by the enterprise financial or human resources management organization.

Archiving Service

An enterprise produces many types of documents. Some of them define agreements with customers and other enterprises. Others represent internal transactions. With the movement to electronic commerce and the elimination of paper, many documents that used to be on paper will now be digitally signed electronic documents. For performance and accessibility, it may be appropriate for individual BSDs to archive documents locally. Documents accumulated in a BSD might be batched periodically to the enterprise archiving service for long-term storage. In addition, some e-mail messages will take the form of signed documents. In the long term, documents will be generated in many contexts. Legally binding documents are relevant to the enterprise as a whole. Consequently, it is appropriate for the infrastructure to provide a shared service to save legal documents in order to achieve economies of scale and ensure reliable long-term preservation.

A signed business document usually is more than just a record of useful information; it carries implications of responsibility, authority, and commitment. When a customer orders a vehicle, that customer has made a commitment to pay for the vehicle when it arrives. Traditionally, this requires signatures of both the customer and the seller. Such documents must be captured and preserved in a form that will be acceptable as proof of the transaction.

Similarly, there are a number of internal documents that traditionally have required signatures to establish agreement and provide authentication. These include expense reports, purchase requisitions, and personnel transactions such as hiring, firing, performance evaluation, promotion, and compensation. These documents are important to the enterprise for accountability and control. To meet this goal, they must be available often years after the associated transaction was completed. Signed XML documents are discussed in Chapter 9, and Chapter 11 discusses security aspects of signatures and nonrepudiation in greater detail.

The archiving service must preserve documents and associated signatures for future reference and as legal evidence if it is needed. Documents for archiving are received by the archiving service as asynchronous message content. The preferred format of documents is an XML format so that they can be interpreted in the future when the content and structure of the document may have changed, but some documents, such as e-mail messages, will be in free-form text, and documents may include attachments in specialized formats.

Meta Data Repositories

A *meta data repository* is similar to what used to be called a *data dictionary*. It contains data about data but also data about systems and interfaces. The traditional data dictionary was used to provide common data models for programmers. These meta data repositories provide data for runtime operations. This should be distinguished from model repositories used to support application development. A runtime repository must represent the current state of system specifications. The development repository may represent one or more future states for future systems or future versions of existing systems.

A broader concept of repositories has been developed to retain Unified Modeling Language (UML) models. The Object Management Group (OMG) has defined specifications for this repository as the metaobject facility (MOF). These models are much more extensive in their representation of an application, the flow of processes and data, and the semantics of objects. The MOF is focused primarily on build-time models, but it eventually should be extended to provide access to the models at run time. This will provide support for interactive, configurable tools for debugging and performance tuning.

Six key categories of meta data are to be addressed. These likely will each have separate repositories, as depicted in Figure 4.3:

Database schema. Database schema typically are managed by the associated database management systems. These schema should support Web-based queries and enable computations and comparisons involving data from multiple sources.

Object interface specifications. In a distributed-objects environment using Internet Inter-ORB Protocol (IIOP) from OMG, the interface repository contains specifications for the interfaces of network-accessible

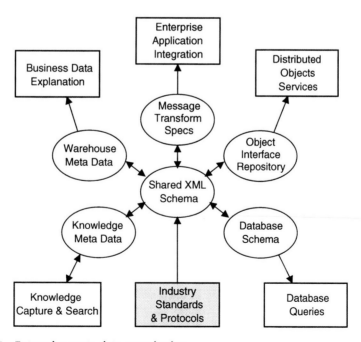

Figure 4.3 Enterprise meta data repositories.

objects. These interface specifications are used at run time by the message brokers and other facilities to communicate properly with objects over the network.

Message transform specifications. Transformation specifications are somewhat different from other meta data, but they are about data nevertheless. Transformation specifications are needed to transform messages from various sources to be compatible with recipient requirements. The nature of these specifications will vary depending on the messaging product, but the trend is to express them in XSLT. XSLT is discussed further in Chapter 9. Transformation specifications will change as the application changes or new versions are installed.

Data warehouse meta data. Certain data warehouse products incorporate another form of meta data. A data warehouse manages historical business data for the analysis of performance and trends over time. The meta data repository may include *technical meta data* and *business meta data*. The technical meta data define the data warehouse data model. The business meta data are used for explanations. Data from various sources may have different levels of accuracy, completeness, and reliability. When reports are generated or analyses performed, it is important for the user of the report or analysis to understand the basis of the result.

Knowledge meta data. Knowledge meta data are data about knowledge. Properties must be defined for different types of knowledge, and property values must be assigned for knowledge sources. The knowledge repository collects knowledge meta data to support searches. The actual knowledge may be stored on Web servers inside and outside the enterprise. Knowledge management is discussed in more detail in Chapter 12.

XML schema specifications. XML schema specifications define the structure of XML documents and document fragments. The source of many schema specifications may be outside the enterprise on the Internet. Documents defined within the enterprise need a reference source within the enterprise. This repository must be available for Web access to the XML schema files based on a URI. The same URI may be used to identify an associated XML name space. It may be convenient to make this repository accessible on the public Internet so that XML schema and name space specifications are available in the event that internal documents are used outside the enterprise.

In the current state of technology, these repositories are not integrated. Currently, that is not a particular problem because their scope of use differs. The interface repository applies within a BSD and generally will be used only by IIOP services involving synchronous messaging between objects. The warehouse business meta data apply primarily to the support of analyses of historical data. XML transformation specifications are used primarily by messaging transformation facilities. XML schema and name spaces apply to XML documents, and knowledge meta data apply only to classification and the search for knowledge.

However, the same data show up in many of these places. When the definition of a data element changes, there may be many places to be changed and coordinated for implementation. The warehouse meta data repository is of interest for management information that spans the enterprise. There is a need to have operational data in various mainstream business operations consistent with the enterprise management information so that enterprise managers can communicate effectively with operations managers.

It is not practical to develop a single enterprise data model as a common point of reference for all data in the enterprise. Instead, the strategy of an XML schema and name spaces should be adopted. Documents are created as required, and element names are qualified by name spaces where their context and meaning can be defined clearly. Similar elements from different business functions may be inconsistent, but the differences will be understood, and transformations can be applied when necessary. Over time, the definitions may converge. Consequently, the XML schema repository may become a central component in the definition and interpretation of enterprise data.

Knowledge Management

We discussed knowledge management briefly in Chapter 3 and will explore it in greater depth in Chapter 12. Knowledge is information about relationships, consequences, and priorities. Knowledge, along with relevant facts, provides the basis for decisions. Knowledge will exist throughout the enterprise, sometimes in documents or rules but more often in people's heads.

Knowledge is an enterprise asset and should be shared, where applicable, across the enterprise to achieve optimal performance. The key role of an infrastructure service is not to store knowledge but to help find it. The capture and classification of knowledge must be, for the most part, a responsibility of specific business functions. The infrastructure should provide for the storage and search of knowledge meta data to enable knowledge workers to find the knowledge they need.

Portals

Portals are windows on the enterprise from the public Internet. They provide points of contact and control for access to information and services provided by the enterprise. They are intended to let the outsider see only what the enterprise determines is appropriate so that risks to the enterprise are minimized while the benefits of Internet visibility are exploited. In addition, by routing accesses through a portal, the computing workload can be managed and the user's linking patterns can be studied. User linking patterns provide a basis for improving the effectiveness of the Web service and potentially identifying customers to be targeted for particular marketing efforts.

There are four primary categories of portals:

- Enterprise portal
- Employee portal
- Retail portal
- Customer service portal

There is a tendency to have a single enterprise portal, but there are significant differences in the user communities and in the nature of the capabilities to be supported. Since portals are windows on the enterprise, it is appropriate that they be provided as infrastructure facilities and be linked to various applications as appropriate. We will discuss each briefly.

Enterprise Portal

The enterprise portal is the public Internet face of the enterprise to the outside world. It should have Web pages that provide access to everything the enterprise wants generally known. Potential users include customers, current and potential shareholders, business partners, and even potential employees. The portal may function as an advertising and marketing tool to influence attitudes about the enterprise, promote political positions, and raise awareness and understanding of enterprise products and services.

From the user's point of view, the Web pages of the enterprise portal should provide an overall introduction, directory, and source of information about the enterprise. The enterprise portal should provide easy-to-follow links to Web pages, descriptions of products and services, and Web pages for making purchases (discussed later).

In general, the enterprise portal is display-only. There may be some pages that accept input to provide more selected information or to perform some helpful computations. For example, a stock brokerage may provide information and current quotations on selected securities, or a bank might provide computations of monthly payments based on a mortgage amount and interest rate.

In general, the role of the enterprise portal is to encourage users to do business with, invest in, or otherwise support the goals of the enterprise. This is a strategic investment and should be developed with the care and caution of a multimillion dollar advertising campaign. The consequences to the enterprise could be even more significant.

Employee Portal

The employee portal provides access to the private intranet Web sites from the public Internet. It is a reverse firewall that allows authorized persons to pass through to the intranet and blocks other requests. The employee digital certificate provides automatic authentication. This portal is appropriate for employees as well as other persons who are known to the enterprise, such as contractors and business partner employees.

The phrase *employee portal* has been used in reference to a collection of Web pages and services of interest to employees, which might be indexed from a home page for that purpose. We view such portals as simply information and services available on the intranet. The employee portal here provides external access to enterprise systems.

Access through the portal may be in several alternative modes:

Dial-up modem connection.   The user connects to a modem on the portal server through the telephone network and is authenticated for access to the intranet.

VPN.   The user connects a modem to an Internet service provider (ISP), the ISP authenticates the user, and the ISP establishes an encrypted connection to the portal server. This creates a VPN. The ISP likely will provide local telephone access to dial-up users in a large geographic area.

Digital service provider (DSP) or Integrated Services Digital Network (ISDN).   The user's computer is connected to the Internet so that the personal computer becomes a network node with no ISP address translation or firewall protection. The personal computer requires a firewall to protect it from intruders.

The first two alternatives provide slower access because they are limited by telephone service bandwidth. The third alternative can provide very high-speed access, but carries greater risk of intrusion. Once the connection is established, the user has the same access as he or she would if connected on the intranet.

Retail Portal

The retail portal is for conducting business with the general public. The business transactions typically are sales transactions with humans who are not previously known to the enterprise. The users must identify themselves because they do not have digital certificates recognized by the enterprise. In the future we can expect that there will be generally accepted certificate authorities, such as credit card companies or banks that will provide certificates to the general public. In the mean time, using identifiers such as credit card numbers, there is a significant risk of impersonation. Consequently, there must be other methods associated with the transaction that will prevent the impersonator from benefiting from a fraudulent transaction.

The retail portal should provide access to one or more BSDs that are isolated from the rest of the enterprise—public Web applications. This provides a layer of protection to internal systems both from direct intrusion and from request overloading. A direct connection of public Web servers to mainstream systems sometimes is required to ensure real-time consistency; in these cases, special controls must be incorporated in independent BSD firewalls to ensure security of the BSD and the intranet.

Customer Service Portal

When a customer becomes known to the enterprise, other services may be offered. This may occur when a customer establishes an account on a first encounter such as with a brokerage or a bank, or it may be a consequence of a successful sale. In these circumstances, the customer can be given a password for authentication. The customer can then conduct business and be held accountable. It is reasonable to provide services for account status, payment, purchases, and so on. This portal could be established the same as the employee portal, except that the issue of certificates to customers could get difficult to manage.

The customer service portal is an appropriate vehicle for customer relationship management. The enterprise can keep track of customer contacts and the activities performed. The enterprise may be able to tailor Web pages to draw the customer's attention to interesting opportunities. With an e-mail address, unsolicited information can be mailed to the customer based on account and Web access history.

Business-to-Business (B2B) Messaging

B2B exchanges typically will be conducted between computers of business partners rather than between a human and a computer. Business partners could be suppliers, financial institutions, outsourced business functions, or commercial customers. Each participant must authenticate the other, and each must agree on the protocol for the business it wishes to conduct. Electronic business XML (ebXML), a set of standards sponsored by the United Nations, provides for the specification of protocols and documents for such exchanges along with a protocol for a reliable messaging service to ensure once-and-only-once delivery of messages. We will examine these specifications in detail in Chapter 9.

The B2B messaging portal provides the reliable messaging service for these exchanges. Messages are routed to the B2B messaging portal through the infrastructure messaging service, that is, through a message broker. The B2B portal forwards the message using the HyperText Transport Protocol (HTTP), thus minimizing firewall interference and exploiting commonly available Web server facilities. Conversely, the B2B portal will receive messages from the business partner and route them to the appropriate application through the infrastructure messaging service.

The exchanges generally will be performed using HTTP with Secure Sockets Layer security (HTTPS) encrypted communications. The messages may be signed digitally, but the B2B portal simply will pass the signed documents through to the application. Messages accepted must be restricted by type and application so that an intruder cannot send fraudulent messages to other internal applications. For the compatibility of messages, the infrastructure messaging service may apply transformations in the same way as transformations are applied between internal applications.

Summary

The enterprise infrastructure is a key element in achieving the following goals:

Integration. Integration is achieved through internal Web services, the messaging facilities, and the intranet. Users can access any application for which they have access authority. Messages can be communicated from any BSD to any other BSD. Message transformation services associated with the messaging service will resolve incompatibilities between senders and receivers. Employees, customers, business partners, and others have appropriate ways to connect to the enterprise from the public Internet and access authorized applications and services.

Economies of scale. The enterprise infrastructure provides a shared network and a number of shared services. Messaging with a message broker reduces the number of network links and message queues. Services such as the portals, archiving, shared devices, and security administration avoid the duplication of facilities and services. The consistency of the infrastructure provides economies of scale in operations, technical support, and problem resolution. It reduces the overhead of introducing new applications.

Flexibility. The network can be reconfigured, facilities can be relocated, and new applications can be introduced with minimal impact on the overall network or existing applications. Much of this flexibility comes from loose coupling and transformation in the messaging facilities. Additional flexibility comes from the ability to access systems and devices over the Internet. Flexibility also derives from the sharing of facilities and information so that new applications need not be developed from scratch and changes to certain capabilities need only be implemented in one place instead of many.

Security. The infrastructure provides a separation between the private intranet and the public Internet to reduce the risk of intrusion. It also provides a certificate authority for the identification of known users. Digital certificates support digital signatures and the transparent authentication of users so that they need not repeatedly sign onto systems and manage multiple passwords. Digital certificates also reduce security risks in other ways.

In the next chapter we will examine how the architecture of a distributed computing BSD complements the enterprise infrastructure.

Creating a Business System Domain

Chapter 3 described the *business system domain* (BSD) as a central level of the business systems hierarchy. It participates in enterprise integration and electronic commerce, and it incorporates business processes, applications, and components. The enterprise infrastructure of Chapter 4 provides a common environment for the integration and support of BSDs. In this chapter we will establish the detailed requirements of a BSD and design considerations for creating a BSD.

While a BSD may embody legacy, commercial-off-the-shelf (COTS), or new business-function applications, the emphasis here will be on a robust distributed computing BSD that can support process automation with integrated component-based applications. A BSD that is consistent with the architecture defined here will support enterprise integration, will provide a flexible application environment, and will enable the streamlining and tailoring of processes and functions to better meet overall enterprise objectives. In addition, it will improve operational economies of scale and ease of use by leveraging infrastructure capabilities and providing consistent access to users from across the enterprise.

We will begin this chapter by defining the external characteristics and components of a typical BSD, and then we will discuss some of the application design issues to be considered in designing a BSD.

Characteristics of BSDs

This section will examine the following characteristics of a BSD:

- Scope
- Interfaces
- Supporting enterprise infrastructure
- Alternative types of BSDs
- Alternative technologies

These characteristics should apply to a variety of implementations and thus provide a basis for the relationships of BSDs to the enterprise infrastructure, other BSDs, and the outside world.

BSD Scope

BSDs are where the actual computational work of the enterprise gets done. Data are captured, computations are performed, records are updated, and results are produced. Many current enterprise applications may be characterized as BSDs. Enterprise applications typically perform primary business functions such as accounting, human resources management, or manufacturing planning, scheduling, and control. These systems typically are highly integrated and loosely coupled with other enterprise applications.

The key to determining BSD scope is not size or complexity, nor scope of the associated business function. Instead, it is the scope of a system that maintains a single, consistent representation of a segment of the business, supports a number of users, is the responsibility of a specific organization, and is bounded by loose coupling interfaces with other systems. This could be a relatively small application such as a tool inventory system, or it could be a very large production management system consisting of a cluster of applications with a shared database. In either case, the system manages a single, integrated, and consistent representation of the domain, and it receives and communicates relevant information with other systems through store-and-forward messaging.

A BSD may be a simple record-keeping system for ad hoc information sharing among a community of users. However, it is expected that a BSD will include business processes that coordinate the efforts of users and operations with the system. The business processes and the associated data and computations are the responsibility of a single organization. At the same time, the community of users may come from different segments of the enterprise. For example, a purchasing system is the responsibility of the purchasing organization. The purchasing organization defines the records to be kept, the business rules about purchase orders, and the business processes by which purchase orders are issued. The community of users of the purchasing system, however, has enterprise scope. People outside the purchasing organization will enter purchase order requests, check the status of in-process purchase orders, and possibly request revisions to purchase orders.

Consequently, a BSD may provide access to a large community of users that extends beyond its primary organization. At the same time, the BSD will communicate with other BSDs to share information and events. In the purchasing example, purchase orders may be communicated to the receiving dock for matching incoming shipments, and they may be communicated to accounts payable to be matched with supplier invoices.

BSD Interfaces

In the preceding subsection we identified two primary interfaces through which the business functionality of a BSD is expressed: the user interface and the messaging interface. The BSD is integrated with the enterprise infrastructure through several interfaces. We will examine these interfaces in three categories:

- User interface
- Messaging interface
- Infrastructure interfaces

User Interface

We expect the client user interface to use an Internet browser in most—if not all—cases. This gives the user a universal mechanism for access to information that imposes few, if any, restrictions on the user's client platform. In order to improve performance, some applications can download applets or, in some cases, plug-in applications. However, for most commercial information systems, a browser interface should be sufficient. In some cases, data will be downloaded to support user activities when the user's computer is disconnected from the network. This downloading and subsequent uploading of results still should be managed through a Web browser interface.

Web applications provide three basic forms of Web page content:

- Static content
- Dynamic content
- Transactional content

All three of these forms likely will be employed for a single BSD.

Static Content

Static content typically is provided with HyperText Markup Language (HTML) pages that are stored on the Web server. The Web server simply retrieves and sends a requested Web page. The page may have a number of embedded data types, such as graphics, video, and sound, but they are simply retrieved as is, and the browser or a plug-in provides the functionality to display them properly.

Applications should use static content to help the user understand the application and access appropriate application functionality. Static content should include appropriate application documentation along with help notes to resolve particular problems.

Dynamic Content

For dynamic content, the Web browser must obtain relevant data from an application or a database to respond appropriately to a user request. The Web server has a servlet that may need to interpret the user's request before requesting the appropriate data.

For simple applications, the servlet may retrieve data directly from a database. Where content must be computed, the servlet will send a message or messages to the application, requesting the appropriate information. The servlet must incorporate the data into an HTML Web page to be returned to the user.

When data are accessed directly from a database, the query result will be in the form provided by the database manager. When the content is returned by an application, it can be tailored more specifically to the needs of the servlet. In particular, it is recommended for more complex responses that the content be returned in Extensible Markup Language (XML) format. This will enable the use of XML Stylesheet Language for Transformation (XSLT) to create the appropriate HTML display.

Note that for the same content it may be appropriate to produce different displays. For example, displays may be designed for different countries or user roles.

Transactional Content

Transactional operations are an extension of the dynamic content mode discussed earlier. When users are entering data to update records or initiate processes, the actions must be performed in a transactional context for recoverability. When the data are communicated to the application, a transaction must be started. Depending on the technology (for example, Enterprise JavaBeans, discussed in Chapter 10), the start of a transaction may be performed automatically by the application environment (for example, a component container) based on the request and the absence of an existing transaction context.

When the update is complete, the transaction commits, causing the database to be updated appropriately. The successful return of the result to the servlet on the Web server should prompt an acknowledgment back to the user.

If the operation fails, the transaction will cause all changes performed in its context to be rolled back, restoring the system to its prior state with regard to that transaction. This should prompt the servlet to respond to the user with an error message. If the system fails, the user will get nothing back.

From the user's perspective, a transaction begins when the data are sent, and if the system does not acknowledge the acceptance, then the transaction may not have completed successfully. The application design must consider the appropriate action for the user to take when there is no response. The intuitive response of the user should be to inquire about the input to determine if it was accepted—the application should facilitate such inquiries.

Messaging Interface

Input and output queues support asynchronous messaging with other BSDs and external systems. An asynchronous message will be posted to an output queue to be removed later and delivered to a destination queue. Messages received by an input queue are removed and processed at a time appropriate for operations being performed by the receiving BSD. The enterprise infrastructure guarantees once-and-only-once delivery of messages. The message queues are recoverable so that messages waiting in a queue will not be lost or duplicated as a result of system failure.

We will examine the messaging service capabilities in greater depth in Chapter 6. Here we will briefly examine the two basic messaging modes as defined in Java Messaging Service (JMS):

- Point-to-point messages
- Publish-and-subscribe messages

Point-to-Point Messages

Point-to-point messages are delivered to a destination specified by the originator. These are the most reliable and secure because they will be held until accepted by the specified destination, and they will only be delivered to the specified destination.

These messages always should be used for a request to initiate a business process. They also should be used for most other enterprise application integration exchanges that drive the mainstream operations.

Publish-and-Subscribe Messages

Publish-and-subscribe messages are delivered to a *topic*. Applications that have an interest subscribe to a topic and receive messages directed to that topic. The messages are delivered to all subscribers. Messages that arrive before a subscription is submitted will not be delivered to that subscriber. Unless otherwise specified, messages will not be held for subscribers that are not active when a message is available for delivery.

Potential recipients of messages are not predefined but can be added and removed at any time. This raises concerns about reliable and secure delivery. Subscribers must be authenticated to ensure that they have legitimate access to the information. Message senders must be authenticated to ensure that they are legitimate sources. Subscribers that depend on reliable delivery must ensure that they are always subscribed and that their messages will be held if they are not active.

At the same time, the publish-and-subscribe mode provides great flexibility. New applications can be installed and then subscribe to receive relevant messages without affecting the source applications (assuming that the messages are being published). In particular, ad hoc applications can tap into message activity when there is a particular problem to be monitored and later can be removed without any changes to the rest of the system.

Applications should be designed to issue publish-and-subscribe messages for important business events so that the information is available for ad hoc monitoring and integration of new applications. At the same time, there is messaging overhead associated with these messages, even if there are no subscribers. The amount of overhead will depend somewhat on the design of the message service.

Infrastructure Interfaces

The user and messaging interfaces provide the linkage for business activity. At the same time, there are interfaces to the infrastructure to support the integrated operation of the BSD. We will briefly examine the following categories:

- Directories
- System management
- Archiving

Directories

Each BSD may incorporate several directories that replicate data shared across the enterprise. These include directories for security, organization structure, and meta data. These directories likely will be implemented in compliance with the Lightweight Directory Access Protocol (LDAP). They will be linked to enterprise directories for propagation of updates over the intranet. These communications will be transparent to the BSDs. In most cases, if not all, updates will originate with central directories under the control of specific organizations, and the updates will be replicated automatically to the BSD directories.

System Management

Infrastructure system management is a specialized BSD for managing the infrastructure and related services. BSD system management must be coordinated with infrastructure system management. Most of this should be through associated business processes, so communication should be through exchange of asynchronous messages. In particular, business processes should address change management and problem resolution.

For economies of scale, infrastructure system management may be integrated with BSD system management. In this case, system management would provide the same services and support functions for the application BSD as it provides for infrastructure. This is outlined in Chapter 4.

Business applications and system management are linked by the exception service. Appropriate exceptions should be communicated to system management through asynchronous messages for monitoring and to initiate processes for corrective action. System management is also linked to computing and communications facilities through the Simple Network Management Protocol (SNMP) for monitoring and control.

Archiving

Electronic documents with significant legal effect should be delivered to the infrastructure-archiving service for long-term retention. There are two possible modes of communication of documents for archiving: messaging and batch files. Messaging would deliver documents to be archived as they occur. Batch files would deliver accumulations of documents periodically. The transfer of batch files should be managed by messaging.

It is likely that the documents to be archived will originate with the Web server. These will be in the form received from the user and may be signed digitally. The application will not likely see the user document but will see relevant data needed for application processing as provided by the Web server.

Supporting Enterprise Infrastructure

In Chapter 4 we developed the requirements of the enterprise infrastructure and defined a number of components. We will briefly examine the following infrastructure components as they relate to the BSD:

Intranet.   The intranet is the primary medium for communication with a BSD, for users, for other BSDs, and for infrastructure services.

Personal computers.   Personal computers are a platform for BSD user interfaces, in most cases using a Web browser. In some cases, personal computers will host more complex functionality to provide higher interactive performance or to allow the user to develop a solution or accumulate input before communicating with the BSD.

Messaging.   Store-and-forward messages are received from a BSD message output queue and are delivered to appropriate destination queues, typically the input queues of other BSDs. Conversely, messages from other sources are delivered to the BSD input queue. The infrastructure messaging services provide message transformation as required and routes the messages based on point-to-point destinations or subscriptions.

System management.   Infrastructure system management must coordinate problem resolution and changes that affect BSDs or changes to a BSD that have effects outside the BSD. Specifically, any changes that affect BSD interfaces likely will require some level of change management. System management also must provide the infrastructure appropriate configuration of facilities to accommodate BSD resource requirements.

Security.   The BSD will use digital certificates managed by the infrastructure and verify certificate validity with the revoked-certificate directory. Legacy and COTS applications can be adapted to user digital certificates in order to support user single sign-on. A BSD may have a local directory that is coordinated with the infrastructure directory.

Organization.   The BSD will rely on the infrastructure organization directory for a current representation of the organization and the people in it. A BSD may maintain a replica organization directory because enterprise-wide access to one directory would be a performance bottleneck.

Archiving.   A BSD may not have electronic documents to archive or could archive documents locally. Where documents have significant legal consequences, the infrastructure archiving service should be used. Documents can be archived through the messaging service.

Meta data repository.   Not all BSDs will need meta data. Where it is used actively, such as for a data warehouse, the BSD may require a local copy for performance. Meta data should be managed for the enterprise to promote consistent representation.

Knowledge management.   A BSD should provide mechanisms for the capture of knowledge as part of its business processes and make it available on the Web server. Metaknowledge (data about the knowledge) must be communicated to the infrastructure knowledge management system to support enterprise-level searches.

Portals.   BSDs that provide Web access for outside users, for example, customers, investors, and so on, should be accessed through the appropriate portal so that accesses can be monitored and security controls ensured.

Business-to-business (B2B) messaging.   Messages to and from business partner systems will be communicated through the B2B messaging service via the infrastructure messaging service. The messages must be in XML for compatibility with HTTP communications and to enable the consistent use of XML tools and specifications.

Alternative Types of BSD

In Chapter 3 we identified the following alternative forms of BSDs:

- Distributed, component-based
- Legacy
- COTS
- Decision support
- Plant

The distributed, component-based BSD is the most robust form and represents the target architecture for future systems. We will first examine the intent of the distributed, component-based BSD model and then consider variances represented by the other forms to fit the BSD model.

Distributed, Component-Based BSD

In this chapter we develop the architecture for a distributed, component-based BSD. This is a model for developing scalable, flexible systems to provide competitive advantage for the enterprise. The enterprise should not develop such systems where COTS solutions meet reasonable standards for the target business functions and there is no opportunity for competitive advantage. Nevertheless, there will always be some business functions for which unique functionality will yield competitive advantage.

In the near term, a component-based architecture will provide a flexible, scalable solution. In the future, a component-based architecture will enable custom components to be combined with commercially available components to leverage both the competitive advantage of a custom solution and the economies of COTS solutions.

In the long term, a market in application components should emerge. Specifications such as Java 2 Enterprise Edition (J2EE) and Enterprise JavaBeans (EJB) are evolving a consistent environment available from multiple vendors. Specifications also are being developed under the Object Management Group (OMG) Model Driven Architecture (MDA) strategy for modeling components and for standard application interfaces. This should lead to economies of scale that would support the development of commercially available components, which will, in turn, enable the development of a BSD from a combination of commercial and custom components.

Components incorporated into flexible business processes enable continuous process improvement without replacement of major applications. This will become the dominant architecture in the future for both custom and COTS applications, allowing enterprises to integrate more finely grained components, both commercially available and custom, rather than being required to choose between large, one-solution-fits-all products or undertake major custom development efforts.

The BSD design developed here is appropriate for any distributed computing enterprise application, but it is particularly suited to a component-based application architecture. We will examine the design of application components in Chapter 10.

Legacy Systems

Legacy systems include any existing applications that need to be linked to other systems. They come in a wide variety of architectures and involve a wide variety of products and technologies. The requirements for integration of each will be somewhat unique.

Legacy systems may have mainstream interfaces to other legacy systems in the form of batch file transfers. These may remain until the sending or receiving legacy system is replaced. At that time, batch file transfers should be reviewed to determine if they should be replaced by the communication of messages as actions occur. At the same time, these batch files may contain data to be exchanged with new applications. Consequently, it may be appropriate to transform the batch files into messages for these new applications, and vice versa.

There also may be a need to accept or produce messages as transactions occur within the legacy system. For messages to be accepted, adapters will be needed to invoke legacy system operations and apply the incoming message content. For messages to be produced, more involved modifications may be required to the legacy application. In some cases this may take the form of database procedures that will invoke message-sending logic when changes of interest occur. Techniques for adaptation of legacy systems are discussed in various books focused on Enterprise Application Integration (EAI). In many cases, vendors of messaging software provide adapter components for particular technologies to facilitate integration of legacy applications.

The legacy system also should be Web-enabled if it has information of interest to a broader community. Providing a Web interface is fairly common. There are two primary forms: (1) interface to the interactive display facility to translate between the Web display and the legacy interface or (2) interface Web components directly to the legacy database. The second approach is preferred for display-only operations. It may be acceptable for update operations as well if the database manager provides locking and the legacy application logic can be bypassed and reprogrammed where necessary.

In summary, most legacy applications can be adapted for enterprise integration. However, they are not likely to exhibit the scalability and flexibility we expect from a system that implements a BSD architecture, and they are not likely to exploit the enterprise infrastructure beyond messaging services, Internet facilities, and personal computers.

COTS Applications

The development of EAI tools and techniques was driven by the challenges of integrating COTS enterprise applications such as those for human resources management, materials management, payroll, and accounting. The ease with which these applications can be integrated is an important factor in their success in the marketplace. Consequently, these applications have well-defined interfaces for sending and receiving store-and-forward messages. In most cases, the messages accepted and produced by these applications should conform to industry standards (for example, standards by the Open Application Group [OAG]). Vendors of messaging software often will provide adapters to interface the enterprise application to their particular messaging product.

At this point, most COTS applications already provide Web access. For those that do not, maybe the acceptability of the application should be reconsidered.

In general, COTS applications are designed for enterprise integration and scalability. However, like legacy applications, they each bring a predefined solution that may not meet current enterprise needs or adapt to future needs. Unless the necessary adaptations are anticipated in the design of the COTS application, it is not appropriate to implement changes or extensions to customize the vendor product. The value of vendor support is diminished, additional work will be required for each new release, and reliability will be at risk. If there are special requirements, then maybe a COTS application is not the right answer.

Consequently, we can expect, in general, that COTS applications will fit the external characteristics of the BSD model, but like legacy systems, they are not likely to exploit the enterprise infrastructure.

Decision Support Systems

Decision support systems include systems for reporting and analysis to support decision making and planning by managers and knowledge workers. Generally speaking, information about the operation of the business is communicated to these systems, but they do not communicate information in return. Data warehouse systems are a prime example. Data about the operation of the business must be communicated reliably in a compatible form so that the management information will be a true reflection of the business operation. Often the data are received in a staging facility for cleansing and reconciliation with data from other sources before being applied to the data warehouse.

The speed of communication generally is less critical than for systems supporting current operations. In addition, the information needed may change from time to time as managers focus attention on different aspects of the business. Consequently, the infrastructure must support evolving data input requirements.

These systems may use the meta data repository to provide insight on the nature of data used for analysis. They also use the organization directory and security service for access authorization. Beyond this, their use of the enterprise infrastructure may be minimal.

The online analytical processing (OLAP) tools used to analyze the data are specialized applications and may execute directly on the user's workstation. However, it is not unreasonable to expect that some time in the future, OLAP will be performed on a shared server, particularly analyses of broad interest, and users will specify and view outputs through a Web display.

Consequently, decision support systems will receive updates through the messaging service like other BSDs. They may provide Web access to data integrated from multiple sources, and they may incorporate security, organization, and meta data directories. However, they do not, in general, implement business processes nor a component architecture—rather, they are oriented toward database query.

Plant Control Systems

Plant control systems provide control, monitoring, and feedback for production operations. These occur in a variety of industries. In general, plant systems will operate in a real-time mode. The user interfaces typically will be specialized and local to the operations. However, plant systems should accept input from the commercial information systems regarding production requirements, customer orders, schedules, inventories, and so on. The plant systems should produce outputs to reflect events in the production process. These inputs and outputs should be exchanged through the infrastructure messaging service.

Consequently, plant control systems fit into the infrastructure for asynchronous messaging but otherwise are quite different from the distributed, component-based BSD model described here for business information systems.

Alternative Technologies

Distributed computing can be implemented with several alternative technologies such as the Object Management Group's (OMG) Common Object

Request Broker Architecture (CORBA), Microsoft's Component Object Model (COM+), or Sun Microsystems' J2EE and EJB. While the enterprise architecture will comprehend a variety of other technologies, the preferred technology for BSDs should support distributed objects for flexibility and scalability.

CORBA Component Model (CCM) and EJB provide containers for components that enable deployment to a variety of platforms. The J2EE specification defines an application architecture for EJB components that provides a more robust model for a BSD implementation.

The J2EE specification includes interfaces to a messaging service that complies with the JMS specification. This will provide a direct link between the application and the messaging service. The J2EE specification also includes a Web server for the user interface.

However, J2EE and EJB do not provide the complete answer. For example, they do not include workflow management for automation of business processes, nor do they define the infrastructure support for enterprise integration.

In this book we use Java technology as our benchmark because of its widespread acceptance, the relative completeness of the standard application architecture, and the availability of implementations from multiple vendors. At the same time, the BSD architecture discussed here is applicable to CORBA and COM+ technologies. Some CORBA technologies are incorporated into J2EE, and CORBA components can be integrated with a J2EE environment. COM+ components do not have the same degree of interoperability but can be used to implement a BSD as a distributed computing application. Generally, message-oriented middleware (MOM) products provide interfaces and message queues for Microsoft environments as well as CORBA and Java environments.

BSD Components

In Chapter 3 we introduced the distributed, component-based BSD model, which is shown again in Figure 5.1. In this section we will examine the components of this model, including:

- Computing environment
- Web server
- Business document archive
- Business processes
- Component containers
- Persistence service
- Organization directory
- Name service
- Exception service

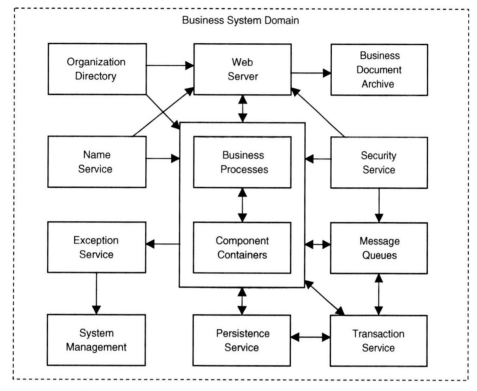

Figure 5.1   Distributed, component-based BSD model.

- Security service
- Transaction service
- Message queues

Computing Environment

The computing environment is not explicit in the diagram, but it is an essential component of a BSD. We will discuss these four basic aspects of the computing environment in order to characterize the environment in which the remaining components are integrated:

- Servers
- Local networking
- Request broker
- System management

Servers

The typical BSD will have four types of servers (see Figure 5.2):

Web server.   The Web server interfaces with the intranet and provides Web access to BSD information and services. The Web server is the point of authentication and applies authorization criteria for access to Web pages and Web resources. For Web pages with dynamic content, the content will be obtained from an application server or database server. There is logically a single Web server as a point of contact, but this may be implemented as multiple physical servers to accommodate high workloads.

Application servers.   Application servers execute the BSD business functions. These include workflow systems for business processes, application components, and associated computational services such as the name service, exception service, security service, and message queues. Some of these services may be implemented on separate servers for performance or to accommodate different technologies.

Database servers.   Database servers manage the persistent storage and execute the database management system(s). These servers may be tuned for high performance in processing queries and updates.

Directory servers.   Directory servers are specialized for providing rapid access to relatively static data. They also provide mechanisms for distributing updates so that the same data can be obtained from multiple, distributed directories. Directory servers should implement LDAP and be linked to the corresponding infrastructure directories. These include the organization directory, security directory, and meta data directory.

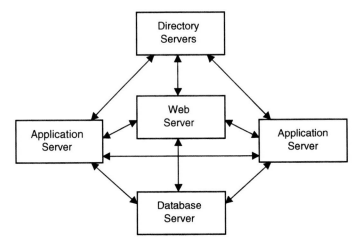

Figure 5.2   Local BSD networking.

Not all BSDs will have all these servers as separate physical devices, but they will all require support for these different categories of functionality.

Local Networking

The servers are networked as depicted in Figure 5.2. Because there is communication from many sources to many destinations, this networking likely will be implemented as a local-area network (LAN) for the BSD. This LAN should be isolated from the intranet so that there is no risk of direct intrusion. External connections are through the intranet access to the Web server, exchanges of messages with message queues on the application servers, and updates to directory servers.

In some environments, the database server could be shared with other systems through a storage-access network (SAN) for economies of scale. The storage server facilities must provide appropriate isolation of storage and network accesses for security.

Request Broker

A request broker provides the mechanism for invoking methods on remote objects. This remote, synchronous messaging is the primary mode of communication between components in the BSD environment, as depicted in Figure 5.3. For J2EE- and CORBA-based systems, these messages use the Internet Inter-ORB Protocol (IIOP) defined by the OMG.

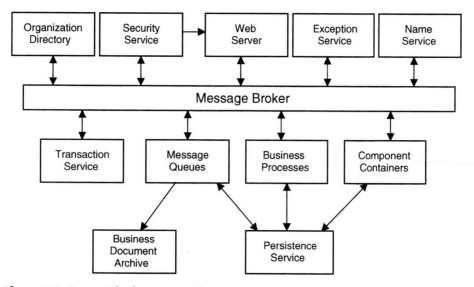

Figure 5.3 Request broker connectivity.

Each participating server hosts an Object Request Broker (ORB), as shown in Figure 5.4. The application sends a message to a local proxy object, and the message is relayed first to the local ORB, then the remote ORB, and finally to the target remote object. The reverse path returns results or exceptions.

IDL

The interfaces of network-accessible objects are defined with Interface Definition Language (IDL), a CORBA and International Standards Organization (ISO) international standard. The IDL specifies the object method signatures and attributes that are accessible over the network. Method signatures include parameter and exception specifications.

The IDL defines interfaces, not implementations. Different classes of objects can implement the same interface. An interface specification defines a *type*, which has a unique name. Types can inherit specifications from other types— subtypes inherit from supertypes. Generally, if an object supports a subtype, it also is referenced in terms of its supertype interface.

IDL is strongly typed. The parameters and return values in method signatures require type specifications, as do the values of attributes.

IDL has defined mappings to most common programming languages. For example, a message can be sent by a C++ object and received by a Java object. IDL and the ORB provide a basic mechanism for integration of components written in different languages. At the same time, this imposes some restrictions on the form of messages and interfaces in order to ensure interoperability.

IDL is the basis for generation of the proxy objects on the sending server (often called the *client*) and the skeleton objects that receive the messages in the target server. The ORB uses the IDL specifications to ensure compatibility

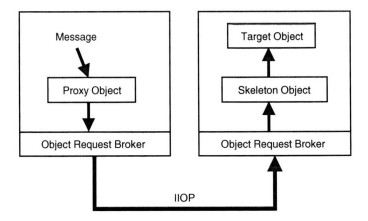

Figure 5.4 A message to a remote object.

between the proxy and the target object interfaces. IDL also provides types that are not network-accessible objects; these include data elements and objects passed by value, which are discussed in a later section.

Object Reference

A remote object is located by its *object reference*. In addition to providing information sufficient to locate the object, it contains information about the interface type. Object references are seldom accessed directly because a remote object is represented locally by a proxy object. In addition, the object reference as well as the proxy object cannot be used for identity comparisons because the same object may be referenced by different object references, depending on the circumstances under which the object reference was obtained.

The object reference is the value that is actually passed over the network in messages to locate the target object and provide references to objects passed as parameters or return values.

Objects that have object references generally are objects that have unique identity from the concepts they represent such as an employee, a customer order, or a department. When a server receives a message, the target object is not always active (in memory). An object identifier embedded in the object reference provides the basis for retrieving the object state from a database in order to activate the object.

Messages

Messages invoke operations according to the signatures specified in the IDL interface. When a message is sent to a proxy object, the proxy object implementation must translate the message parameters to forms appropriate for communication over the network using IIOP. These are synchronous messages, which means that the sender blocks until the response is received.

In addition to the target object reference, the message name, and the parameters, the message also may contain the transaction context and security credentials. While these could be passed as additional parameters, it is preferable to carry them implicitly to simplify programming and avoid programming errors.

Objects Passed by Value

Not all objects are network-accessible. Some objects, typically objects that do not have unique identities, are passed by value rather than by reference. Similarly, basic data types, such as integers and arrays, are passed by value. These objects also have been called *dependent types* because they will be persistent only if they are attribute values of identifiable objects so that they can be located on persistent storage. Because these types are passed by value, a value obtained in a message parameter or as a return value is a local copy of the state of the source object.

System Management Facilities

System management facilities must be provided to monitor the operation of applications, manage the workload distribution across servers, manage the startup and shutdown of the BSD or specific servers, monitor network activity for potential performance problems, and resolve server or network failures.

BSD system management facilities may be dedicated to the BSD, or they may be integrated with infrastructure system management facilities. Integration may provide economies of scale, particularly if a number of BSDs are colocated. The primary consolidation would occur in the business processes and personnel for operations, configuration management, change management, problem resolution, and performance monitoring. In addition, some facilities may be shared by multiple BSDs, such as storage management and Web services, such that these facilities become part of the local, shared infrastructure.

Web Server

The Web server manages the interaction with the user. Exchanges use HTTP, the protocol of the Web. The user uses a standard Web browser. The functionality used by the Web server depends on the nature of the Web page content and the input from the user. Much of the activity may be devoted simply to providing static information that is stored in HTML pages on the Web server. Some pages will require computations or may enable the user to enter data. Pages with input or computed content will be produced and processed by servlets or a special form of servlet called a *Java Server Page* (JSP).

Servlets may process input and compute pages independently, but in most cases, they will obtain content from other sources or capture data for an application. A servlet may interact directly with a database to retrieve content or update the database. This mode of operation can be used for small applications. Larger, more complex applications are implemented on application servers.

In J2EE, servlets use IIOP to communicate with application servers synchronously, invoking methods on application objects to obtain content and perform updates. The servlet is responsible for transforming the content received from the application into a form suitable for display as a Web page. Conversely, the servlet is responsible for transforming input parameters into messages to application objects to perform appropriate operations. The same operations may be performed by different servlets to provide different Web pages for users in different roles or for international differences.

The Web server also incorporates security measures for authentication and authorization supported by the associated security service. For exchanges with sensitive content, communications should use HTTPS, that is, HTTP along with the Secure Socket Layer (SSL) encryption protocol. When using

SSL, a user session can be maintained to perform a series of exchanges with the same user without the need for repeated authentication. Web services, including both remote client and Web server functionality, are discussed in detail in Chapter 8.

Business Document Archive

The business document archive captures documents that could have a legal effect in their source form. When an electronic document is signed, the signature is tied to the specific form of the document. Typically, a unique value (a *hash value*) is computed from the message content using a particular algorithm. In order to validate the signature, it must be possible to generate the same value again using the same algorithm. If anything in the message is changed, including the format, the algorithm will not generate the same value. Digital signatures are discussed in Chapter 11 from a security perspective and in Chapter 9 from the perspective of application to XML documents.

In order to ensure that documents along with their digital signatures are captured without change, the BSD diagram shows that such documents are sent directly from the Web server to the business document archive. These documents may never be used unless it becomes necessary to provide them as legal proof. Consequently, it may be simply a chronological file. It may be useful to provide some form of indexing for future reference.

Because of the legal nature of this information, it will be necessary to ensure its protection from loss or alteration.

Business Processes

In conventional systems, some business processes are managed manually, and some of them are embedded in computer applications. In an integrated enterprise, all business processes will be managed by workflow management systems. This makes all processes visible for tracking and analysis and provides a greater degree of flexibility in the definition and ad hoc alteration of processes.

Consequently, the workflow management facility keeps track of the state of all processes within the scope of the BSD; it has information on all work in process for each participating employee as well as work currently not assigned. A user can sign on and select an assigned activity to begin or resume. Typically, the state of a process is committed when each activity starts or completes and potentially at intermediate points as well. When the user signs off, the current, committed state of the process is preserved and available when the user returns.

Users may perform operations directly on application components to obtain information or perform updates. However, a user will, in many cases, be communicating with a business process in the workflow management system. If the user is requesting some action from the enterprise, such as placing an order or requesting a quote, the Web server will capture information and initiate a process. On the other hand, if the user is an employee, he or she may be participating in the business process. In this case, the employee accesses a work list to receive assignments and post their completion. During an activity assignment, the employee likely will interact directly with an application.

Business processes manage the flow of work. This is to be separated from application functionality so that business processes can be observed and changed more easily. The general nature of business processes was discussed earlier. Workflow management is discussed in detail in Chapter 7.

Component Containers

Component containers provide the environment for application components. Containers incorporate a number of services to minimize the complexity of the application component. The container makes the component transactional, it resolves concurrent access conflicts, it provides for event management, it provides persistence of the component state, and it implements life-cycle operations. A container manages objects of a particular type. A single container may manage many instances of a type.

EJB and CORBA component specifications include specifications for XML documents that define how components are to be assembled into composite components or complete systems. Currently, these specifications provide little assurance that the components being integrated are compatible. Specifications for a Unified Modeling Language (UML) Profile for Enterprise Distributed Object Computing (EDOC) developed by the OMG provide more robust specification of the components and the elements necessary to define the interactions between components.

Component containers provide two types of application interfaces:

- Instance interfaces
- Type interfaces

Instance interfaces accept messages and return responses on a particular instance of the type managed by the container. These messages may alter the state of the object or perform other computations, including sending messages to other objects, both local and remote.

Type interfaces deal with the object type generally. In EJB technology, the type interface is called a *home*. The type interface may provide the following categories of operations:

Instantiation.   The type manager provides a factory function to create a new instance of a type.

Query. A type manager can provide an interface for retrieval of objects of the type that meet specified selection criteria. This capability is not yet well defined in component specifications such as the CCM and EJB.

Event activation. When there is interest, a type manager should be able to activate a specific event type for all instances of an object type and deactivate the event when there is no longer interest. Current component containers do not provide this capability. It would avoid the overhead of generating events for which there is no interest.

There may be other functions associated with particular type interface such as application-specific methods or variables associated with all instances of a type. Components, and EJB in particular, are discussed in detail in Chapter 10.

Persistence Service

Recoverability of a system relies on persistent storage. Various elements of a BSD must be saved in persistent storage to ensure the integrity of the system. This includes the state of workflow processes, the content of message queues, information about users and security, and system configuration information, as well as the state of objects representing the business domain. Here we are concerned primarily with preserving the state of objects in support of the business applications. The persistent state service provides a consistent interface to storage facilities that would allow applications to employ different database management systems over time or in different installations.

The state of an object must be retrieved from persistent storage when it becomes active, and its state must be updated in persistent storage when it has been changed and the associated transaction commits. The component container can handle these operations, so the application programmer does not need to implement the capabilities or determine when database accesses are required.

Typically, persistent storage is managed by a database management system. However, in order to provide for interchangeability of database management systems and provide seamless integration with the distributed object environment, an additional level of abstraction is needed. This is provided by a persistent state service (PSS); the *state* refers to the data of the objects. The following subsections describe the basic functionality that should be provided by a persistent state service.

Object Mapping

The data structures of objects must be mapped to the physical storage structures of persistent storage. This may be quite straightforward if persistent storage is an object-oriented database, but most often it is a relational database. This mapping can be quite complex, particularly if the mapping is to a legacy database.

In some cases, the data for one object may be stored in multiple relational tables. In extreme cases, the data of one object could be stored in tables of more than one database. In addition, relationships between objects typically will be stored as foreign key references in a table corresponding to one or the other of the related objects. For many-to-many relationships, key pairs will be stored in a third table. As a result, when a transaction commits, individual tables may be affected by updates in more than one object. It may be necessary for the database manager to process updates in a particular order to comply with the database integrity constraints as well as the creation and use of system-generated keys. The ability of the persistence service to handle these complexities may constrain the design of the object-oriented application.

Create, Delete, and Update

Database entries must be created, deleted, and updated to correspond with the creation, deletion, and update of objects in the computing environment. However, the actual database create, delete, or update should not occur until the associated transaction commits.

The database should be read and objects instantiated whenever messages are sent to objects that are not currently active; this should be transparent to the application programmer. Likewise, the application programmer should not be concerned with writing updated objects to the database. The updated objects should be written to the PSS update operations when they receive a synchronize message from the transaction service commit operation. The relationships between objects and the tables they are stored in may create update-sequencing requirements that must be observed for successful completion.

When an identifiable object is created, it must be assigned a unique identifier. In some cases, the identifier is assigned by the database management system. Consequently, the PSS should provide a mechanism for the creation of the system-assigned key when the object is instantiated rather than deferring it until the creating transaction commits.

When an object is deleted, the deletion may propagate across relationships, such as where deletion of an order implicitly causes deletion of the order items. In addition, the object may participate in other relationships that must be removed, such as where an order item has a relationship to a part; the part is not deleted, but the relationship is.

The addition or removal of objects from relationships affects related objects and therefore the associated database tables. The PSS must manage the sequencing and propagation of updates to comply with database integrity constraints, or it may be necessary to remove the database integrity constraints and rely on the PSS to maintain the database integrity—this is probably not an option if the database is shared.

Queries

Queries are a fundamental aspect of application processing. Without knowing specific instances, an application would need to read or update all instances of type that comply with selection criteria.

Queries cannot be performed without reference to the system's persistent storage. First, not all objects of the specified type will be active when the query is requested; it would be an impractical and sometimes impossible burden to activate all objects of a particular type in order to evaluate each against selection criteria. Second, database management systems are designed to optimize queries, and this capability should be exploited.

The query expression that defines the selection criteria must be in terms of the object model, not the persistent storage data structure. Again, the application programmer should deal with the objects without being concerned with how they are stored. In addition, it should be possible to change the database schema without changing the programs that issue queries. Consequently, the PSS should accept a query expressed in terms of the object model and translate it to the appropriate database query based on the object mapping to the database schema.

When the query is satisfied, the selected objects should not be activated immediately—there could be thousands. Instead, the PSS should return an iterator that provides access to members of the result set as they are requested. It also should be possible to specify the order in which the members of the result set are returned.

While there are proprietary solutions for query support by persistent state services, there are no industry standards at this time.

Connection Management

Database management systems often define connections or paths for database operations associated with individual transactions. Each connection may allocate storage space and manage updates for one transaction at a time. The number of connections allocated also may be related to software licensing fees. The opening and closing of connections also will have associated system overhead and will affect performance.

Consequently, the PSS should manage the allocation of connections to transactions so that connections are pooled and used by one transaction after another. This will enhance performance and ensure compliance with licensing constraints.

Organization Directory

The organization directory provides information on people, their authorized enterprise-level roles, and their relationships to the organization structure. This information is the basis for business process assignments and ad hoc access to enterprise systems when the person does not have a specific role with respect to the system.

For workflow management, a person may be selected according to authority, location in the organization, relationship to others involved in the process, geographic location, or skills. The organization directory should support search/query capabilities for selecting appropriate people.

The roles defined for people in the organization directory are default roles that apply across the enterprise so that the basic authority of a person can be determined for access to any system, particularly one that the user does not access normally. Role assignments for a specific system should be managed within the BSD of the particular system because these are the responsibility of the associated business function organization.

Name Service

The name service provides the mechanism by which the persistent identifier associated with a business entity or application service can be associated with the internal reference to the component that represents that entity for communication of requests through an object request broker. The name service provides the capability to classify and organize entity identifiers in a manner similar to a file directory. This supports the creation of a hierarchy of *name spaces*. Basic name spaces can be used for the keys of each type of identifiable entity such as purchase orders, employees, internal part numbers, vendor part numbers, and so on. A name service specification has been adopted by the OMG.

The name service is a specialized database management system. While it could be used to associate all business object identifiers with their object references, this would be redundant and inefficient. Retrieval of a business object would then require first an access to the name service database and then an access to the database that contains the actual object state. In a large enterprise, there could be millions of such objects. Generally, the primary database containing the object state will contain the object identifier along with its other state, and the object can be activated on this basis.

The more appropriate role for the name service is to access system services and computational objects including type managers. This provides a separation between the logical name (the identifier) and the physical name (that is, the object reference). For example, the name service might provide access to business process managers, security services, the organization directory, and the exception service.

Exception Service

The exception service is invoked by an application when an exception occurs. The exception service may be implemented as a component application itself. This service provides for consistent capture and presentation of exception information. Web access should be provided to support monitoring and analysis of exceptions. Certain exceptions should initiate business processes for follow-up to address immediate problems with the system or the state of the application activity and to prevent future occurrences.

Exceptions can occur in a variety of ways. An application may encounter a business rule violation. An assignment or computation may cause an exception due to a type error or arithmetic overflow, an error may occur in the communication of messages, or a transaction may be terminated due to a deadlock.

Exceptions must be classified according to their severity for purposes of defining appropriate action by the exception service. System integrity exceptions indicate that an error has occurred that renders the system unreliable and that the operation should be terminated; these typically are hardware errors. Transaction errors are those which make operations within the current transaction invalid, and the current transaction will be terminated, causing a backout of operations performed in the transactional context. Correctable errors are those which are within the ability of the user or the application to resolve. Communication errors occur in user-interface communications, in the communication of asynchronous messages with other BSDs, or in communications between servers within the BSD. Communication errors normally are recoverable and are logged for future analysis because they may have a performance impact.

Exceptions are logged to support analysis of recurring conditions. Exceptions of interest to a user may be displayed directly to the user in response to the failing request, exceptions with system management implications are communicated to the system management facility, and some exceptions should initiate problem-resolution processes managed by workflow management.

Security Service

The BSD security service supports the authentication and authorization activities of the BSD, as depicted in Figure 5.5. When a message queue server connects to the messaging service, digital certificates should be used to authenticate the identity of each and to engage in secure communications using SSL. When the Web server establishes a connection, the certificate of the remote user should be available for authentication. For both the message queue and the Web server, certificates must be checked against the revoked certificates list provided locally by the security service.

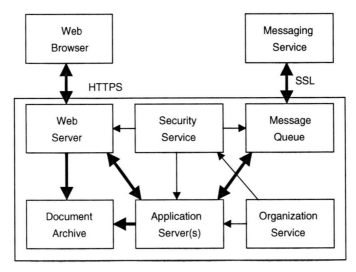

Figure 5.5 BSD security.

For Web accesses, the security service specifies the authority associated with user roles. User roles are determined by reference to known users identified in the local security directory, by reference to the organization directory, or by the context of user activities. Typically, each role will be associated with an *access control list*.

Generally, authentication facilities within the Web server will determine the identity of the user from the user's digital certificate, and the security service will use this identity to determine roles and access control lists. If the user is not specifically known to the BSD, then default enterprise roles will be obtained from the organization directory.

If digital certificates are not used, then an identifier and password will be required for authentication. In this case, the security service also will manage user identifiers and passwords. If specific users do not have user identifiers and passwords, then they will be denied access even though they may be identified in the organization directory because they cannot be authenticated.

Depending on the nature of the access being requested and the security requirements of the application, authorization may be implemented in the Web server or in the application or both. A user can be authorized to access certain Web pages and the content that comes with those Web pages. If authorization is more stringent or complex, it may be necessary to incorporate authorization decisions in the application itself. This may be implemented on the basis of access to object methods, which can be implemented without application component awareness, or on the basis of application logic potentially involving the user role, the access control list, the user's relationship to the specific information, or the activity in which the user is participating, that is, the business process context. In order to minimize the complexity of security management and the complexity of the application, it is desirable to manage authorization outside the application as much as possible.

Other aspects of security—confidential data, protection from data corruption, legally enforceable documents—must be implemented in exchanges through the Web server and messaging service. To ensure the integrity and confidentiality of data exchanged over the network, communications should employ the SSL protocol. This protocol relies on digital certificates (public-private key pairs) for encryption of communications. This applies both between servers communicating messages and between the Web server and browser where HTTPS incorporates SSL. Digitally signed documents may be received through either the Web server or the messaging service. Digital signatures also rely on digital certificates for signature encryption. In most cases, humans sign documents, so a remote client will apply a signature. Signed documents are in XML format and must be preserved in their original form for the signatures to be valid. It is appropriate for application components on the Web server to archive such documents when they are received. When they are delivered by the messaging service, it is up to the application to ensure that they are archived properly.

Security is a complex and critical aspect of information systems and enterprise integration, particularly with the expanded accessibility provided by the Internet. We have identified general requirements here. We will return to a more complete discussion of security issues in Chapter 11.

Transaction Service

In order to maintain a BSD in a consistent and recoverable state, operations must be performed in a transactional context. The transaction service establishes this context by providing a unique identifier for each transaction. A *transaction* (that is, a computational transaction as opposed to a business transaction) transitions a system from its current consistent state to a new consistent state. The changed state of the system is stored when the transaction is completed because this represents a new state to which the system can be restored if it later fails. If the system fails before a transaction completes, then the state of the system will be restored to the consistent state that existed prior to the start of the incomplete transaction, and the same or a different transaction can then proceed with system integrity preserved.

A number of factors must be considered when executing in a distributed transactional environment:

- Serialization
- Deadlocks
- Concurrency service

- Lock modes
- Transactional context
- Callback
- Transaction control operations
- Phased commits
- Recovery
- Nested transactions

We will now discuss each of these aspects in more detail.

Serialization

Large systems generally support the concurrent work of multiple users. Users will enter information and execute computations independently, usually involving information about different business entities. Each such operation is executed in a different transactional context; that is, it transitions the system from one consistent state to another consistent state. Each transaction assumes that it is operating on a system in a consistent state.

If two or more independent transactions involve some of the same entities, then while one transaction is operating on the assumption that the system is in one consistent state, another transaction may be changing the state of shared entities, rendering the results of the first transaction invalid.

Serialization is a mode of operation that causes transactions to execute as if they were executed one at a time, serially. This does not mean that only one transaction can be active at a time but rather that when one transaction changes the state of a shared element, the other transactions must wait to access that shared element until the updating transaction is completed. Similarly, if one transaction gets the state of an element to use in its computation, then other transactions cannot be allowed to change the state of that element until the first transaction is completed; otherwise, the first transaction could be acting on a state that is no longer consistent with other data used in its computation. Control over accesses to shared resources is called *concurrency control* and is achieved by *locking*.

Locking for concurrency control is applied to any system resource that can only accommodate one transaction at a time. This could apply to a customer object, for example. When an operation accesses a resource in a transactional context, that resource is locked to prevent other transactions from using it until the locking transaction is completed. At the same time, the transaction holding the lock may perform other operations that involve the locked resource, and these operations should be allowed to proceed. This distinction is accomplished by reference to the *transactional context*.

Deadlocks

When a transaction encounters a locked resource, it must either wait or be abandoned. In some cases, two transactions will lock multiple resources in such a way that each transaction is waiting for the other to proceed—they are in a *deadlock*. In such cases, one of the transactions must be abandoned so that the other can proceed.

Whenever concurrent transactions involve shared resources, deadlocks can occur, and the system must provide some mechanism for deadlock detection and resolution. The simplest form of deadlock detection is to use *timeouts*. The system will monitor the duration of transactions, and if a transaction does not complete within a specified period of time, it is assumed to be deadlocked. Of course, a transaction may exceed the allowed duration and not be deadlocked, and repeated attempts to perform the same transaction could be terminated in the same way.

On the other hand, reliable deadlock detection can be complex, particularly in a distributed computing environment. In order to detect a deadlock, the system must determine if transaction A is waiting on another transaction B that is, in turn, waiting directly or indirectly on transaction A. Transaction B may be waiting indirectly waiting on transaction A by waiting for another suspended transaction that is directly or indirectly waiting on transaction A. This form of deadlock detection can be fairly straightforward in a single-threaded environment, but when distributed computing activity is not suspended during deadlock detection, the detection cannot be entirely accurate. Consequently, deadlock detection sometimes will report a phantom deadlock when there actually is no deadlock rather than take the risk that a deadlock will go undetected.

Deadlock detection requires the participation of all servers in the computing environment (that is, the BSD). In order to detect a deadlock, the relationships of all transactions and locked resources must be accessible. Since there are no standards for deadlock detection, this may be difficult to achieve in a heterogeneous environment. Consequently, deadlock detection with timeouts is currently the most practical approach.

Concurrency Service

A concurrency service can be used to manage resource locking. The concurrency service maintains a list of locked resources. When a transaction requires access to a resource, it requests a lock from the concurrency service. The concurrency service looks for the resource in its list, and if the resource is not already locked, it will lock it for the requesting transaction. If the resource is locked, it will make an entry to indicate that the requesting transaction is waiting for the lock to be released.

If all resources are locked using the concurrency service, then the concurrency service has all the information necessary for deadlock detection, and reliable deadlock detection can be achieved in a single-threaded implementation. On the other hand, the concurrency service may then become a bottleneck to system operation. In a distributed object environment, every network-accessible object becomes a resource requiring concurrency control, and every time a message is received, a lock must be requested from the concurrency control service. The concurrency control service may be distributed to reduce the performance impact, but then it cannot perform reliable deadlock detection. For this reason, a concurrency control service has limited utility.

Another alternative is to defer to the database manager for locking of shared object states. The implications of this approach are addressed later in the discussion of object-sharing mode.

Lock Modes

Specialized modes of locking can be used to minimize the impact of locking on performance. For example, if a resource is locked for a read access, the locking transaction depends only on the state of the resource remaining unchanged. This need not prevent other transactions from accessing the same resource for read-only operations. On the other hand, transactions that would change the state of the resource must wait for the read-only transactions to release their locks.

Distinctions between lock modes can enhance performance by reducing the likelihood that transactions will be suspended for concurrent access to a resource. This is particularly relevant for objects that provide data to many transactions but seldom change. On the other hand, recognition of locking modes adds complexity.

If a transaction has accessed a resource for read-only and later attempts to access it for update, the update may be delayed because other transactions have the resource locked for read-only. If one of the other read-only transactions also attempts to perform an update, the two transactions will be in a deadlock. Each is waiting for the other to complete and remove its read lock. If, on the other hand, each had originally obtained a write (update) lock, there would be no deadlock because the second transaction simply would wait for the first to complete.

Transactional Context

Each transaction has a unique identifier. As operations are performed for a transaction, the program code must have access to the identifier of the transaction for which the code is being executed.

In a single-server environment, each process—and each thread within a process if it is multithreaded—must maintain its transactional context.

If transaction A is executing and initiates an input operation, it must wait for completion of the input, and the operating system will switch control to another thread of execution. The context of the new thread carries its transaction identifier so that operations for transaction B will execute in its transactional context.

In a distributed computing environment, a transaction may span multiple servers—while a transaction is only active on one server at a time, during its lifetime it may access objects on different servers. When a message goes from one server to another server, the identifier of the associated transaction must be passed along with it. This may be accomplished with a transaction identifier parameter on each method, but the preferred method is for the request broker to carry the transactional context implicitly. This eliminates a programming burden and a substantial risk that the wrong transaction identifier will be passed with the message. Implicit passing of the transactional context is supported by IIOP and used by both CORBA components and J2EE.

Callback

When a message is sent from a client or another server, the receiving object, directly or indirectly, may send a message that goes back to the object in the originating process. This is called *callback*. The originating process must recognize that the callback message is executing in the same transactional context. If it does not, then the message would be blocked because the originating object is already in use. This would cause the transaction to be deadlocked on itself.

Callback is not supported in all remote messaging environments. This is a serious constraint on the design of distributed object systems. The principle of encapsulation means that the user of an object should not know the manner in which the object implements its operations. An operation could involve collaborations with many other objects. If callback is prohibited, then either a server hierarchy must be defined so that message direction is constrained, or all collaborations must be known to a message sender in order to ensure that a callback will not occur.

Transaction Control Operations

A transaction service provides the mechanism for implementing transactional control. When an application begins to execute operations to perform some business function, it must *begin* a transaction. It begins a transaction by sending a request to the transaction service. This sets the transactional context for operations that follow.

When the application completes the operations required for the business function, it requests a *commit* from the transaction service. The commit operation signals the need to update the database (or multiple databases) to reflect the new state of the system. The transaction service will go through the commit process, causing each affected resource to commit its new state.

If a transaction fails for some reason, then a *rollback* must occur to return the system to its consistent state from before the transaction started. A rollback can be invoked automatically when an exception occurs, or it may be invoked by the application. This means that the state of every object that has been changed by the transaction is no longer valid. The transaction service will then notify each affected resource to restore its prior state.

Reverting to the state that is stored in the database restores the state of an object. In conventional, database-oriented systems, this is accomplished simply by abandoning the state that is in memory. In systems that share active objects or where the object represents a shared service, the active state of the object must be restored. This may be accomplished by caching the prior committed state when the object is updated or by retrieving the prior state from the database.

Phased Commits

When a system employs multiple databases, the commit process is a bit more complicated. The problem is that if one database commits but the other fails to commit, then the system is left in an inconsistent state. This can occur fairly easily where database management systems check the integrity of the data being stored, and any violation of integrity rules could cause the commit to fail.

The *two-phase commit* ensures that all databases involved commit the results of a transaction to ensure consistent system state. The two-phase commit involves, first, a *prepare phase* and, then, a *commit phase*.

In the prepare phase, the required updates are applied tentatively so that appropriate validity checks can be applied. Each prepare request returns an indication of the success or failure of the prepare operation. If any prepare request fails, then the transaction is aborted. If the prepare is successful, then the commit phase is performed. In the commit phase, each database manager finalizes the new state so that the system is then recoverable to the new consistent state.

When a commit occurs with objects that are actively shared, the state of each changed object must be written to the database. This could occur as part of the prepare phase, but a database manager should not accept additional updates to affected resources when it has completed a prepare phase but not a commit phase; otherwise, completion of the prepare phase may not correctly reflect the acceptability of the commit.

In order for shared object updates to be performed properly, the state of the affected objects must be sent to the database before the prepare phase so that the database has all update information when it performs its prepare phase. This additional phase is defined in the CORBA transaction service protocol as a *synchronize* phase that occurs before the prepare phase. This achieves a three-phase commit. The synchronize phase also provides the opportunity for changed objects to validate their new state by applying consistency rules. If the new state fails validation, then the transaction will be aborted in the synchronize phase. The synchronize phase is not supported by all transaction services.

In more sophisticated implementations, an additional phase is needed. Updates performed within a transaction may call for a propagation of effect. For example, the total cost for a purchase order may be recomputed automatically after changes have been made to line items. It is useful to defer the propagation of effect until all the direct changes are made so that the propagation is based on the net result of inputs. Such consequential changes should be made when the application direct-update logic is ready to commit so that all inputs have been applied. The consequential changes then must be completed before the start of the synchronize phase, or the state of the system conveyed to the database would be inconsistent. The transaction service must execute actions registered for a *propagation phase* before proceeding with the synchronize phase and two-phase commit. The propagation phase generally is not supported by transaction services.

Recovery

If a system fails, transactions will be in various states of completion at the time of the failure. Recovery will be to the state achieved by all committed transactions. Users who were waiting for transactions to complete must reenter the transaction information. The two-phase commit ensures that all databases can be restored to a consistent state that existed prior to the failure.

Note that recovery of a BSD to a consistent state, and therefore integrity of the system as a whole, depends on transaction serialization and updates to the database to commit the results of transactions. If a failure occurs, necessitating a recovery, then the entire BSD must be recovered—all objects and associated databases must be restored to a prior consistent state. The necessary scope of recovery is a factor to be considered when determining the scope of a BSD. Not only does the scope of a BSD define the scope of tightly coupled consistency of information and processes, but it also defines the scope of impact of failure and reentry of information associated with system failure.

Nested Transactions

Generally, serialization assumes that operations for each transaction are performed synchronously. Thus, when a message is sent to an object, the sender does not proceed with other operations but waits until the requested operation is complete and control is returned. In this way, a transaction is only performing one operation at a time, and the sequence of the operations is determined.

If, on the other hand, a message sender continued to execute while waiting for completion of a remote message, then the sender and the target object would both be performing operations on the system at the same time. In performing these operations, they could access and change some of the same elements, but the order in which they accessed the shared elements would be unpredictable, and each could be operating on the system in an inconsistent state from the perspective of those operations.

Consequently, if a transaction initiates concurrent operations, then each of the concurrent operations must be executed in a unique transactional context. These transactions may be called *nested transactions* or *daughter transactions*.

If a transaction has nested transactions, then the primary transaction cannot be committed until all its nested transactions have completed. Similarly, none of the nested transactions can be committed before the primary transaction commits because failure of the primary transaction would require rollback of all the nested transactions.

Generally, nested transactions are not supported because of the increased complexity of serialization and coordination of commits. When concurrency is necessary for performance in business systems, it can be achieved at the primary transaction level by spawning separate transactional processes through asynchronous messaging. For example, multiple request-response messages can be posted to the same or different processes. These processes can execute concurrently when they receive the messages. When all the requested processes have completed, then the result posting process can proceed. These concurrent activities would be executed in independent transaction contexts, so each would commit or roll back independently.

Message Queues

Message queues are the primary mechanism of communication with other BSDs and business partners in electronic commerce. Message queues support asynchronous, store-and-forward messaging. They support loose coupling because a message originated by one BSD is not required to receive immediate action by the destination BSD, and one BSD can continue to operate when another fails because the only requirement of consistency between them is that no messages be lost or duplicated. Additional flexibility is provided by the enterprise infrastructure through message routing and transformation capabilities.

Transactional Operations

Consistency between BSDs is maintained by updating the queues in transactional operations. When a message is posted to a queue, it is posted within a transactional context that maintains consistency with the state of the BSD that originated the message. The message is not committed to the queue until the transaction is committed. The queue, of course, uses persistent storage to ensure that its contents are recoverable.

Similarly, when a message is removed from a queue, it is removed in the context of an application transaction, and the application will perform appropriate processing to accept the message before committing both the application and queue updates. In other words, the message is not gone from the queue until the associated application transaction commits. This applies both when the message is communicated over the network and when it is removed from an input queue for processing within a BSD. These transactional operations ensure that a message is not lost or duplicated.

Message Types

Earlier we discussed two messaging modes from a messaging service perspective: point-to-point messages and publish-and-subscribe messages. Here we consider the types of information communicated by applications.

Event

An event indicates that a significant change of state has occurred. Events often are broadcast to be received by any interested recipient (subscriber). An application, usually a process but occasionally an object representing a business entity, will subscribe to receive specified events for a particular topic from the enterprise infrastructure messaging service. An application may generate events that are determined to be of interest to a particular topic.

Events are not always published for subscription. In some cases, events specifically drive other processes. The messages communicated between enterprise applications for enterprise application integration often represent the occurrence of events, but they are intended for input to specific applications.

An event may be used to initiate a process, alter the flow of an active process, or signal the completion of a process. The originator of the event may be unaware of the effect of the event on the recipients and is not dependent on any result being returned.

Process Request

An activity within a workflow process may request another process to accomplish its task. The requested process may be remote from the BSD. If initiation of the remote process were performed through synchronous messaging, the BSDs would become tightly coupled. Instead, the messaging is performed asynchronously through message queues. In this case, the messages are directed to a specific recipient in point-to-point mode, and the sender is dependent on appropriate action by the recipient. When the request is completed, a response will be returned to the requester. Publish-and-subscribe mode would not be appropriate here because the messages are directed to a specific process with the expectation of a response.

Remote Collaboration

Remote collaboration occurs when a business transaction is performed through a series of interchanges between a BSD and an independent participant. This collaboration is typical of the conduct of a B2B transaction. For example, the transaction could be to make a sale or negotiate a loan. Together the participants step through a process to either complete or abandon the business transaction. The function of these point-to-point messages is similar to the process request, except that each participant is stepping through a business process that receives a message and determines the business action to be taken and the next message to be sent.

Application Design Issues

The performance and flexibility of a BSD depend on the allocation of functionality and exchange of data between the Web sever, the supporting applications, and the database facilities. We are not going into details of application design here, but we will discuss a number of issues to be considered in designing a distributed computing BSD.

Application Server Interface

In order to incorporate an application into Web services, the Web server must be able to access data and functionality of the application. There are two primary modes of communication: synchronous messaging and asynchronous messaging.

Synchronous

Synchronous messaging involves communication of a request and response while the requesting process waits. This is often in a transactional context.

CORBA messaging using IIOP is an industry standard supported by multiple vendors. The Web server process sends a message to a proxy object, which is a local representation of an application server object. The message is forwarded, transparently, to the object on the application server through ORB middleware. The result of the request is then returned via the ORB middleware through the proxy object to the requester.

IIOP supports communication of a transaction context as well as security information. Consequently, the Web server can authenticate a user and then communicate the user information with requests to the application. Similarly, the Web server can initiate a transaction for interaction with the application, and the transaction is committed when the interaction is complete. This ensures that update operations are backed out if they do not complete successfully.

Asynchronous

Asynchronous messaging is sometimes used to separate the Web server from the supporting application for security purposes. Asynchronous messaging can reduce security risks but also may reduce responsiveness. The Web server program will post a message to an output queue. The messaging middleware then retrieves the message from the queue and forwards it to an application input queue. The application retrieves the message from the queue to perform a requested operation and posts its response in its output queue. The response is forwarded to the Web program queue, where it is then retrieved by the Web program to create the response to the Web client.

Asynchronous messaging generally is more secure because the format and routing of messages will be restricted. A corrupted Web server still will be limited in the types of messages it can send and the applications it can send to.

Asynchronous messaging also can control application overload. Each of the steps, that is, posting or retrieving messages from queues, is executed in a transactional context and committed. This provides guaranteed delivery. Since the message is held in a queue, it is removed at the convenience of the recipient. If the application is backlogged, then the message will wait its turn for processing.

Asynchronous messaging is not intended to be as fast as synchronous messaging. Each commit (typically four commits to deliver a message and return the result) will involve a database update. If a message broker is involved in routing messages, additional commits may be involved. This mode generally is not recommended.

Object-Sharing Mode

In a distributed objects environment, messages are sent to objects as active computational elements. Over time, many different users may perform operations on the same object. There are two fundamentally different modes of sharing objects:

- Database-oriented
- Object-oriented

The mode employed will have performance implications. Some operating environments may only support the database-oriented mode. In a robust environment, it is likely that different modes will be used for different object types, depending on the characteristics of their participation in applications. We will discuss each mode briefly.

Database-Oriented

Most conventional systems rely on a database for concurrency control. Each transaction retrieves the data it needs to perform its operations, and the database manager locks the data to keep other transactions from accessing them. The data are held in memory for the duration of the transaction, and when the transaction commits, the database is updated and the locks are released.

This form of locking requires each transaction to retrieve data from the database. Data that are in memory when a transaction completes cannot be used by another transaction because they would bypass the database manager concurrency control. This adds some level of overhead for repeated retrieval of data that are used by many transactions. This overhead may be mitigated if the database manager caches data to avoid physical reads of data written recently.

In addition, if concurrency control is to be optimized for lock modes, then the mode of each access must be specified; that is, the transaction must specify if it is accessing the data for update or for read-only operations. Consequently, the programmer must know the type of access intended when the data are retrieved so that the database manager can control access accordingly. Mode-based locking requires that database operations must be explicit in the application programs.

Some systems employ an alternative form of concurrency control called *optimistic locking*. This mode of control allows transactions to retrieve and operate on data freely, but when a transaction completes, the database manager checks to see if the data used by the transaction have been updated in the database after they were retrieved by the transaction. If the data have been changed in the database, the update fails, and the transaction fails. This mode of operation allows the application logic to ignore the possibility of concurrency conflicts, and thus, the programmer does not need to be concerned explicitly with database access. For some applications, where users seldom share the same data (for example, engineers working on different designs), this works quite well, but for other applications, it results in a high rate of transaction failure with associated loss of productivity and user satisfaction.

Object-Oriented

Database accesses can be reduced and programming can be simplified if concurrency control is implemented by each object. Each object (that is, its container) must keep track of its lock status, the transaction that holds the lock, and any transactions waiting on the lock.

When an object receives a message, it must check its lock status. If it is locked and the transaction of the message is not the transaction holding the lock, then the new transaction must be suspended pending release of the lock. If the object is not locked, then the object must record the transaction as the holder of the lock and register itself with the transaction service as an object in use by that transaction. If the transaction already holds the lock, then execution of the message simply can proceed.

When the transaction commits, the object will receive a synchronize message to cause it to write its changed state to the database. It will later receive a commit message indicating that the database has been updated and that it must release its lock. This will enable any suspended transaction to proceed. If the transaction fails, then the object will receive a rollback message indicating that it must restore its prior state. Once its state is restored, any suspended transaction can then proceed.

The use of shared, active objects with individual concurrency control relieves the application programmer of concerns about database accesses. When a message is sent to an object, the server can activate the object (that is, bring it into memory) if it is not already active. When the transaction is completed, the object will update the database automatically, and it can ignore the commit if its state has not changed. In addition, the programmer does not need to keep track of which objects need to be updated because objects affected by the transaction are registered automatically with the transaction service. Fewer database accesses are required because active objects will remain available for subsequent transactions.

Note that this method of concurrency control is required for uniquely identifiable objects that are shared by reference among multiple transactions. Some objects occur only as elements of an identifiable object but do not have independent identity. These dependent objects rely on the objects that contain them for persistence, and they are shared by value, that is, by passing copies, rather than by reference. Consequently, they do not require independent concurrency control.

Other objects that do have unique identity but are relatively fine-grained may be encapsulated in containing objects so that they do not require independent concurrency control. The containing, identifiable object is often characterized as a *business object*. As a result, the encapsulated object is not network-accessible, so all accesses go through the containing object. For example, the order items of a customer order can be uniquely identified by the order number and item numbers within the order. However, exposing the order items as network-accessible objects could increase the level of network activity to access the items, and they would require independent concurrency control. As encapsulated objects, they derive concurrency control from the order, and operations on the order perform necessary operations on the items.

Object-oriented sharing is particularly important for objects and services that are heavily accessed. Object-oriented sharing can reduce database accesses substantially, and if a high number of accesses are read-only, these require no database access once the object is activated.

Network Chatter

One of the most common performance problems with distributed computing applications is the excessive use of messaging for interactions between the client and application server(s). Particularly with synchronous messaging interfaces, the client developer is inclined to request individual attributes from remote objects in order to populate user displays. This network chatter, particularly when there are many concurrent users, can have a major performance impact.

The solution to this problem lies in providing application methods designed to gather a number of elements in response to a user-interface requirement. For example, a method might be provided to request a list of attribute values returned in a name-value pair list. In other cases, methods might be implemented to return commonly used collections of attribute values. If the application designer anticipates the user-interface needs, the Web page developers will be less likely to fall into the trap of creating network chatter.

A particularly flexible approach is to provide application methods that return XML structures. Methods can be defined to return different XML structures for different categories of user-interface requirements. Some structures may be quite shallow, whereas others may return more complete representations of desired aspects of an object structure. This then enables the Web page developer to use common functions for populating the Web page.

Page Content versus Format

In general, it is desirable to assign implementation of the Web page format to the Web server program and delegate preparation of the content, that is, the application data, to the application. This separation of responsibilities corresponds to the differing skill requirements of the developers and also improves flexibility.

This approach supports the design of Web pages to meet the needs of different users. For example, the same content may be used to design different Web pages for users in different countries. The layout and scope of content may differ for persons performing different job functions.

If the application provides content in the form of XML structures, then the job of the Web page developers will be simplified. The Web page developers can, for example, use XSLT to transform the XML data structure to an HTML Web page. Different transformations can be used for different job functions and nationalities, including filtering of content to meet the particular needs of the user's job function.

Security

Security is another common source of performance problems. It is also a potential source of application complexity and administrative overhead. The core issue is the granularity of control. If granularity of control is detailed, then authorization may be checked many times in responding to a user request. It is possible to check authority for access to every method on every object. For some applications, it also may be necessary for the application to apply rules to determine if the particular user is allowed to access the particular object. On the other hand, if authority can be checked once for the request, then the overhead and complexity will be minimized.

CORBA security provides application access control at the method and attribute levels. Each time a message is sent to an application object, the authority of the user can be checked without affecting application logic. While this provides very strict control, it also introduces considerable overhead.

Minimal intervention can be implemented at the Web page access level. The Web server can control which users have access to which pages at the Uniform Resource Locator (URL) level. This may be sufficient where a user's organizational role can be mapped easily to page access authority.

However, determination of authority often is more complex. The user's authority often is a function of a particular job assignment and his or her relationship with the data being accessed. For example, a project manager will have particular authority with respect to particular projects but not other projects. These decisions can still be implemented at the Web server level but require more support of the Web server component with relevant data from the application.

Multithreading

Some middleware products and some operating systems do not support multithreading. Multithreading is similar to multiprocessing. With multiprocessing, an operating system will manage the execution of multiple address spaces as logically concurrent, allocating time to each. With multithreading, multiple threads of control can be executing in the same address space. Without multithreading, an address space must complete execution of a request before beginning the execution of the next.

In a distributed objects system, this means that when a server receives a request, all other requests will be suspended until the first request is completed. A container on that server may manage many instances of a type of object, but only the object(s) that are the subject of a single request can be active at one time. If user actions frequently involve a particular object type, then all user requests that involve that type will be executed serially. This could have a major performance impact.

The impact may be reduced if objects of the same type can be instantiated on multiple servers. Then multiple server processes can be executed on the same computer, and these can be executed concurrently (assuming that the operating system can multiprocess). Not all container products or object request brokers will support execution of the same object type on multiple computers.

Sessions

HTTP is described as a stateless protocol. This means that under normal operation, each browser request is treated as an original request, even if it is a result of a previous request. The server does not remember the user actions from one request to the next. HTTP does not support a *session*, where a user is expected to perform a sequence of actions.

As a result, everything that is needed to perform an action must be included with the request. This typically is accomplished by including *parameters* or *cookies* in the request. Parameters are name-value pairs attached to the *get* or *post* request sent to the server. Cookies are sets of name-value pairs that are saved by the browser and associated with the URL from which the cookie was received. A cookie will be submitted with requests to the same server. In either case, the necessary state to guide a sequence of actions is included in a response to the browser to be returned by the Web page logic with the next request. Effectively, the browser retains the state of the server with respect to the particular user. In this way a session can be managed.

A session also can be managed by SSL in conjunction with HTTP, (expressed as HTTPS in the Web request). SSL requires several exchanges to accomplish authentication. This exchange requires the server to retain state; at a minimum, it must retain the session key used to encrypt exchanges for the particular session. In addition, due to the overhead of establishing SSL authentication, it would be a major performance burden if each new request required a new authentication. Consequently, an SSL session can be preserved through a series of exchanges.

Each of these modes of session management has different benefits. All three are supported by the EJB specification. The use of parameters is totally transient. Each response page must be the basis for the next request. A request need not be submitted immediately following the preceding page because all the necessary data are in the request. A user could fool the browser by submitting a request with parameters saved from some other session, even a session of a different user, and the server would interpret it as the continuation of a session. At the same time, the approach is very lightweight.

The cookie-based session is similar to the parameter-based session, except that the cookie can be retained automatically for an extended period of time. Whenever the user connects to the same server, the cookie will be activated. This allows a session to extend over days with other activities and requests to other servers interleaved. The cookie parameters are not as visible, and it will be more difficult for a user to steal a cookie to impersonate someone else.

For both parameters and cookies, it is possible to use encryption to encode a variable value that would be invalid for other users, assuming that the user is originally authenticated in some other way, but neither of these mechanisms per se supports digital signatures. Digital signatures require digital certificates.

The SSL session uses digital certificates—public-private key technology—to establish an encrypted exchange session. Only the server needs to have a certificate to establish an SSL session. However, the SSL protocol will enable authentication of the client if it has a digital certificate. Otherwise, the session is established regardless of authentication. The SSL session cannot be interrupted for other activities—the continuity of the session must be preserved. Consequently, the session cannot extend over days. Since a unique session key is used, the user cannot be impersonated. Using SSL with client digital certificates provides a more consistent security protocol. The certificate is used for authentication, then it is used for encryption, and then it can be used for digital signatures.

Personalization

Personalization involves tailoring the user interface and the functionality of the application to meet the needs of the individual user. The particular requirements will be specific to the application, but some common techniques may be employed.

Personalization relies on retention of settings of variable values that define the particular user's preferences. These preferences may be saved in a variety of places. For the ad hoc user, not normally known to the system, settings could be preserved in a cookie, saved by the browser.

For known users, preferences could be saved in the organization directory. It is preferable to restrict these preferences to those applicable across the enterprise. If the organization directory is used for application-specific preferences, then there will be more frequent changes to the organization directory schema, increasing risk of an error that could have an impact on much of the enterprise. The global preferences might be designations, for example, of native language and nationality.

Application-specific parameters can be retained by the application. The stored application preferences can be saved and retrieved based on the user's identity.

For application-specific personalization, the user should have access to a Web page for setting preferences. Just as in desktop applications, the user may wish to change the preferences as he or she becomes more proficient or uses the application in different ways.

Summary

The BSD defines the local system architecture and builds on the enterprise infrastructure to interoperate with other BSDs and share enterprise resources. While this chapter has gone into considerable depth in defining some of the system elements, others require more lengthy discussion. The following chapters will address key technologies in greater detail:

- Messaging (Chapter 6)
- Workflow management (Chapter 7)
- Web access (Chapter 8)
- XML documents (Chapter 9)
- Component architecture (Chapter 10)
- Security facilities (Chapter 11)

Providing the Messaging Infrastructure

In Chapter 5 the focus was on the implementation of business functions in a transactional environment. These business system domains (BSDs) represent large components in the overall operation of the business. They generally are organized around domains of responsibility, access to shared data and specialized expertise, or computations.

BSDs cannot operate in isolation. They must receive inputs either from other BSDs or external sources, and they must provide outputs to other BSDs and external recipients. The overall operation of a business relies on the appropriate communication of information to coordinate and drive the business function operations.

This chapter focuses on the messaging infrastructure that supports exchanges between BSDs as well as exchanges with business partners. While most of the interactions within a BSD are synchronous and occur within the scope of a computational transaction, interactions between BSDs, as well as business partners, should occur asynchronously. With asynchronous messaging, an originating domain is not suspended waiting for immediate action in another domain over which it has no control. The facilities that implement asynchronous messaging are sometimes called message-oriented middleware (MOM).

The basic messaging facilities needed have been implemented in a number of commercially available products. The Java Messaging Service (JMS) specification has been developed by Sun Microsystems along with a number of other vendors to provide a common interface to such products. It is recommended that enterprise integration be based on the JMS specification in order to achieve a reasonable degree of vendor independence. JMS defines an application programming interface (API) and certain expectations regarding the functionality of a compliant messaging service.

This chapter is organized in three parts:

■ Design objectives

■ Application of JMS

■ Design considerations

The design objectives will provide an overview of requirements for the messaging infrastructure. The section on the application of JMS will describe the functionality of JMS and requirements for implementation products as they apply to this enterprise integration architecture. The last section addresses additional considerations such as a transformation service, security, and messaging over the Internet to address the needs of enterprise integration.

Design Objectives

This section outlines a set of design objectives for the messaging infrastructure. This will provide an overview of the use of this technology in the enterprise integration architecture. The following objectives are discussed:

■ Store and forward

■ Message broker

■ Guaranteed delivery

■ Message sequence

■ Symbolic routing

■ Request-response

■ Event messages

■ Message transformation

■ Ad hoc destinations

■ Exception resolution

■ Standards

■ File transfers

- Business-to-business (B2B) communications
- Security

Store and Forward

A message must be accepted by the messaging infrastructure and held until the recipient or recipients are ready to accept the message. The sender must not be blocked once the message is accepted for delivery. This allows the sender to proceed without waiting for the recipient to be active or ready to accept the message. It is equivalent to the mode of communication used by e-mail.

Message Broker

Primitive messaging facilities provide direct communication from one sender to one receiver. This is acceptable for integration of very limited scope. Once several systems are communicating with several other systems, there is considerable economy of scale, as well as substantial improvement of flexibility, by providing a service where messages from any system can be routed to any other system.

Guaranteed Delivery

The mechanism for the delivery of messages between senders and receivers must be able to guarantee that each message will be delivered to each recipient once and only once. The operation of the sender must be able to proceed on the assumption that the message eventually will be received and processed by the recipient. If this cannot be ensured, then the operation of the business will be unreliable, or considerably more overhead will be incurred to verify delivery and repeat the request if delivery has failed.

Message Sequence

The sequence of messages from a single source should be preserved when received by a single recipient. Often messages reflect a sequence of events such that the last message received reflects a transition to the current state. If messages are received out of sequence, the current state may be misrepresented, and the path to the current state could be misunderstood, potentially resulting in erroneous computations. While the receiving application can be designed to compensate for out-of-sequence situations, the application likely will become much more complicated.

Symbolic Routing

If messages were directed explicitly by one system to another using physical addresses, such as Internet Protocol (IP) addresses, the operation of the enterprise would be very inflexible. Changes in system configurations and networks, as well as the implementation of new systems, could require changes to all related systems. Instead, the routing and delivery of messages must be based on symbolic recipient addresses defined in a directory.

Request-Response

Certain business or computing services will be shared by many applications. These common services may receive requests in the form of messages from many sources and provide results back to the message senders. It is important that these services need not be programmed explicitly for each potential source. Instead, each request should define the recipient of the response.

This is similar to messaging performed synchronously where the sender expects a response, except that here the message and the response are communicated asynchronously. While the sender could communicate a return address within the message, this puts an additional burden on the sending application to provide a valid return address because the requests may be fulfilled on different computers at different times, or the sending application may be executed at multiple sites.

Event Messages

Event messages communicate the occurrence of an event. An event message may come from an external source or may represent the occurrence of activity or a change of state within the system. Events may be used to initiate or alter system processes. The infrastructure must allow certain events to be monitored selectively on an ad hoc or continuing basis. Generally, the originator of these events is not specifically aware of the recipients, but only provides notice of the events when they occur.

Message Transformation

When independently developed systems are integrated, particularly when some are commercial-off-the-shelf (COTS) products, the format of messages that different systems accept or produce may be inconsistent. Furthermore, it is not possible to define fixed formats for all messages and never change them.

A message transformation service can accept a message in the sender's format and transform it to the format(s) required by each recipient. For large enterprises with diverse operations, it is essential that the infrastructure provide mechanisms for the transformation of messages so that as new systems are introduced and old systems are eliminated, the effects of changes in senders and receivers can be isolated and managed over time.

Ad Hoc Recipients

Some messages between business functions are part of the mainstream operation of the business and always must be communicated between certain business functions. On the other hand, some applications are outside the mainstream operation of the business or need information on business operations on a more ad hoc basis. It must be possible for these systems to obtain ad hoc subscriptions to the distribution of certain types of messages in order to monitor the business operation.

In some cases, the recipients will only be interested in current events that occur while the recipient is active. For example, a performance monitor might provide a display of current activity. When the recipient is terminated, it no longer exists for the receipt of messages.

On the other hand, some ad hoc recipients require guaranteed delivery that applies whether or not the recipient is currently active. This mode will be used when new applications are integrated using events to receive activity from other enterprise systems. When the recipient is inactive, the messages must be held until it is again active and can accept them.

Exception Resolution

The messaging infrastructure should resolve exceptions as much as possible to minimize the need for concern by the application developer while maintaining the integrity of the applications. The principal exception of concern to applications is where guaranteed delivery, once and only once, could be compromised.

Delivery failure could occur if the network or the receiving application were not available for an extended period of time. The list of messages to be delivered could become excessive and have an impact on system performance or exceed the capacity of the system to hold the messages for delivery. The messaging infrastructure must define an orderly approach to resolving this situation.

Delivery failure also could occur if the destination is invalid, the sender is not authorized, or the recipient cannot interpret the message content. Again, an orderly approach must be defined for resolution. Other exceptions, such as communications errors, should be resolved by the messaging infrastructure so that the messages are delivered with minimal delay under the circumstances.

Standards

The integration infrastructure should be comprised of shared facilities that achieve economies of scale in development, operation, and support and use purchased components to deliver solutions quickly and incorporate new technology as it becomes available. The application of industry standards will help ensure flexibility in the configuration of facilities as well as in the ability to incorporate new and different products to exploit technological improvements.

File Transfers

The general concept of the messaging infrastructure is to communicate information about business events and transactions as they occur. Typically, these messages are relatively small; large messages might be a few thousand bytes in length. Unfortunately, some systems will still operate in batch mode, and other systems that communicate events and transactions also must transfer large files of associated data, such as graphics or product design specifications. The messaging infrastructure must provide reliable transfer of files without a significant adverse impact on the performance of the rest of the system. The file transfers must have the same guarantee of delivery as the messages with which they are associated.

B2B Communications

Communications between business functions must extend to the business functions of business partners. This requires communication through firewalls, which place restrictions on the communications. At the same time, the communications must be in a nonproprietary mode so that the enterprise can communicate with a variety of external systems with few compatibility requirements.

Security

Security must be considered at two levels:

- Messaging within the enterprise
- Messaging with external systems

Within the enterprise, we will assume that the systems that participate in messaging are in environments that are appropriately secure for their business function. However, messaging often will occur between business systems over less secure communications facilities and possibly the public Internet. Communications facilities and protocols must ensure the privacy and integrity of communications between systems. In addition, since any source might send a message to any destination, an application must be assured that a message is being received from an authorized source, that the source is authorized to send to the specified destination, and that subscribers are authorized to receive the messages they are requesting.

B2B messaging raises additional security considerations. First, the external system must be authenticated for sending or receiving messages. Business partners may exchange messages with different machines over time, and the enterprise must be assured that it is not exchanging messages with an imposter. Also, the enterprise may need to prove the source and content of a message (nonrepudiation) if a legal dispute arises.

Application of JMS

This section will describe the core technology for the messaging infrastructure in terms of JMS. The goal is to achieve an understanding of the technology and how to use it, not how to implement it. This discussion will describe how a JMS-compliant product will be used to support enterprise integration, and it will identify product requirements that resolve relevant ambiguities allowed in the JMS specification. The discussion will cover the following facilities:

- Message queues
- Basic messaging facilities
- Point-to-point messages
- Publish-and-subscribe messages
- Message format abstraction
- API object model

Message Queues

The concept of message queues is fundamental to asynchronous messaging. A sender places a message in a queue for the service to deliver. The message is transmitted to a destination queue, where it is held until the recipient is ready to process it. This provides a pure point-to-point communication. This primitive form is used to link a specific source and a specific destination.

Recoverability and guaranteed delivery are achieved by making message queues persistent and transactional. When a message is submitted to a queue for sending, the submission is performed in a transactional context. The message is not logically accepted into the queue until the transaction is committed. At that time, both the message queue database and the database of the source application are updated. If the commit fails, both the application activity and the message queuing will be backed out.

Similarly, on the receiving side, the receiving application accepts a message from an input queue in a transactional context. The application performs operations to process the message, updating associated application data. When the operation is complete, the application commits the transaction, causing both the message queue and the application database updates to be committed. If the application or the commit fails, then the updates are backed out, and the message remains in the queue, waiting for the application to process it.

The concept of a message broker was introduced to allow many sources to communicate with many destinations. Figure 6.1 illustrates the economies of scale and flexibility provided by a message broker. Figure 6.1a illustrates direct-connect communications among four systems. This requires six communications links along with three sending and receiving connections in each system (three sending and three receiving queues). Figure 6.1b shows the impact of the message broker. It requires only one sending and receiving message connection for each system and only four communications links instead of six. The message broker becomes the source and destination for all systems. As more systems are added, the connections and links in the first configuration go up exponentially, whereas those in the second configuration go up linearly.

In addition to economy of scale, a message broker provides greater independence between the systems. The message broker determines where the destination system is located, rather than each system determining where its destinations are located. Thus, administration is centralized instead of being buried in each system.

These basic capabilities are provided by a number of messaging products. JMS incorporates these capabilities and defines product-independent interfaces.

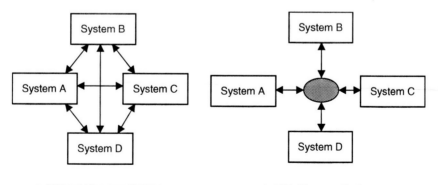

a. Without Message Broker   b. With Message Broker

Figure 6.1   Message routing alternatives.

Basic Messaging Facilities

JMS defines two modes of messaging: point-to-point and publish-and-subscribe. First we will examine the facilities that are common to both these styles, and then we will consider the styles individually. This will not be an exhaustive examination because details can be obtained from the JMS specification. Instead, we will examine the features and options that are particularly relevant to support enterprise integration.

Applications communicate with JMS through a *connection*. Messages may be sent and received (in other words, placed in and removed from queues) through a connection, and concurrent processes to consume or produce messages may operate through the same connection. The connection operations of each process thread are managed by a *session*.

A connection may accept messages for multiple destinations. The destination specifications, for the most part, will be predefined through administrative facilities in the implementation product. However, temporary destinations can be created that exist for the life of the connection. These typically are used as reply destinations when a message is sent as a request with a designated *ReplyTo* destination. This is particularly useful when a requester is executing multiple threads; the reply-to destination can provide the mechanism to link the response back to the requesting thread.

JMS sessions are optionally designated as *transacted*, and the session provides commit and rollback methods. However, this does not incorporate the facilities of a distributed transaction service, and JMS does not require that products implementing JMS support distributed transactions. While transacted sessions may be sufficient for some recipients of messages in the integrated enterprise, this does not provide reliable, once-and-only-once delivery of messages. Consequently, a JMS product used for enterprise integration must support distributed transactions. Furthermore, the originators of messages always should operate in a transactional context, leaving the option for less reliable delivery (presumably using fewer computing resources) to be determined by the recipient application. To operate in a distributed transaction mode, the application will use the commit and rollback methods of the Java Transaction Service (JTS) API and use specialized JMS objects.

JMS also provides an option of persistent or nonpersistent message delivery mode. Nonpersistent mode does not provide guaranteed delivery but ensures delivery no more than once. In general, the nonpersistent mode is not acceptable for enterprise integration. While there may be times when the recipient does not require guaranteed delivery, this may change over time, or the message may be used for an alternative purpose without recognition that the message is being originated as nonpersistent. The minimal savings in processing are not worth the risk that messages will not be delivered to a critical application some time in the future.

JMS provides the ability to specify *time-to-live* for a message. This is another option that suggests that guaranteed delivery is not important. The value is when messages are directed to an application that is not active for an extended period of time, potentially resulting in an unacceptable backlog of waiting messages. In some cases, a message may become obsolete with age, and a subsequent message will make the recipient current. However, the application designer should be very cautious about making this assumption. In general, the application designer should look for other ways to control the buildup of unprocessed messages. Where the volume of messages is low, the messaging product should provide monitoring tools to detect delays, and corrective action may be initiated manually. Where the volume is high and a large backlog could accumulate quickly, the application designer should look for other control mechanisms such as periodic feedback from the receiving application.

Point-to-Point Messages

The terminology *point-to-point* can be misleading because it suggests that an application communicates directly with another application, as in the scenario discussed earlier, without a message broker. To the contrary, *point-to-point* in JMS simply means that the sender of the message directs the message to a specific recipient.

JMS allows, but does not require, that a product supporting JMS use a destination to designate a destination list. In this case, the implementation message broker product would receive the message, and copies of the message would be directed to each destination on the list. This is a desirable feature but generally not essential.

In point-to-point messaging, a destination is identified as a *queue*. A message is sent to a queue or received from a queue. A connection within an application may be used to receive messages from multiple queues. JMS does not define how queues are created; they are expected to be created administratively using the facilities of the implementation product. The application is expected to obtain a reference to a queue through requesting the reference by name from the Java Naming and Directory Service Interface (JNDI). JNDI is a standard Java interface to a name service, that is, an interface to the BSD name service.

In the enterprise integration architecture, point-to-point messaging should be used for controlling the mainstream flow of information between systems. In typical Enterprise Application Integration (EAI) solutions, business messages are communicated in this mode between COTS and legacy applications. This is equivalent to the exchange of files and file transfers for Electronic Data Interchange (EDI) with batch systems.

As business system domains and enterprise applications are integrated with workflow management, the point-to-point style of communication should be used to invoke remote processes. Workflow process requests should be sent as request-response point-to-point messages. A request-response message automatically passes a return address with the request, so each request specifies where the result is to be sent.

Publish-and-Subscribe Messages

In publish-and-subscribe messaging, messages are not directed to specific recipients, but are directed to *topics*. Interested recipients subscribe to a topic and can receive all messages directed to the topic or only those that meet specified selection criteria. Each subscriber is an independent recipient of messages, so messages consumed by one subscriber are also delivered to other subscribers. Messages that do not meet the selection criteria of a subscriber are not delivered or are held for that subscriber.

When a new subscriber requests messages for a topic, messages will be delivered from that time forward. If the subscriber has not specified a *durable* subscription, then when the subscriber becomes inactive, the messages that arrive while the subscriber is inactive are not held for delivery. If the subscriber is designated as durable, then when the subscriber is inactive, messages will be held for guaranteed delivery. Any essential business function that is driven by events should be designated as a durable subscriber. On the other hand, ad hoc monitoring applications may best be implemented as nondurable subscribers, assuming that they can remain active during the period of interest. The temporary creation of durable subscribers creates the risk that the subscriber will become permanently inactive, and the list of waiting messages will continue to grow indefinitely.

The messages communicated in the publish-and-subscribe style of messaging may be characterized as events. An originator of such a message does not know if there is an interested recipient and is not relying on a particular recipient acting on the message. This does not mean that the messages are not important, but rather that they provide signals for applications that should act when certain circumstances occur.

The topics to which messages are directed are types of events. It is expected but not required by JMS that topics could be defined in a hierarchy; this depends on the implementation of the particular product. With a topic hierarchy, general topics would include general categories of events with associated subcategories. A subscriber could then select an appropriate topic to receive a broad or specific category of events. Without the topic hierarchy, a subscriber may be required either to capture events from multiple detailed topics or to use selection criteria to restrict the messages received from a broad topic. The receipt of messages that are not of interest just adds to system overhead.

JMS does not define how subscriptions are implemented. There is an assumption that filtering messages will occur as near the source as possible. In other words, when there are no subscriptions for a particular message type, then messages of that type should be discarded when they are submitted for sending. On the other hand, when a subscriber for a message type appears, then this interest must be communicated across the network to cause messages of that type to be captured and routed to that subscriber. This may cause some delay in the initiation of message capture depending on the time it takes to propagate the interest to potential sources.

Message Format Abstraction

When different products implement JMS, they may use different message formats; a message format is not specified by JMS, so a variety of existing products can implement JMS. However, JMS does define a message format abstraction, which defines how an application views a message as well as associated data that must be communicated to the recipient. That abstraction is depicted in Figure 6.2.

We will not go into detail on the elements of the message format because that information is available from the JMS specification. However, we will discuss some of the elements as they relate to the enterprise architecture.

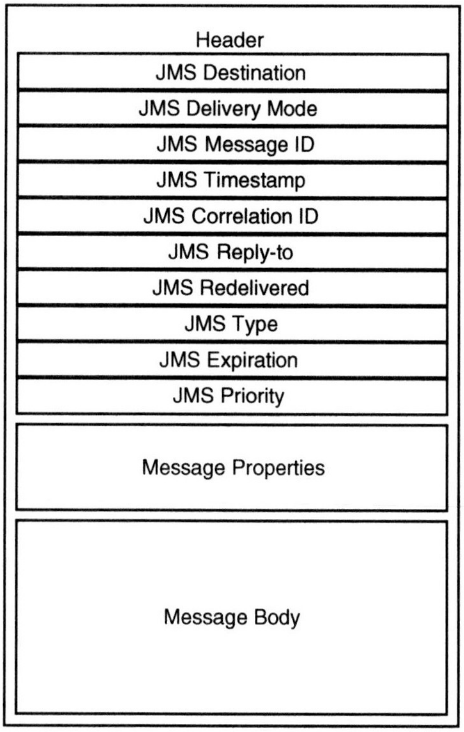

Header
JMS Destination
JMS Delivery Mode
JMS Message ID
JMS Timestamp
JMS Correlation ID
JMS Reply-to
JMS Redelivered
JMS Type
JMS Expiration
JMS Priority
Message Properties
Message Body

Figure 6.2 JMS message format abstraction.

Message Header

The message header contains essential information for delivering and controlling the message. We will briefly describe the header fields because they provide some additional insight into expectations of JMS.

Destination.   The destination may designate a queue or a topic depending on the style of messaging. The form of the destination value depends on the implementation product.

Delivery mode.   The delivery mode specifies if the message is persistent or nonpersistent.

Message ID.   The message ID is a string that is a unique identifier for the message. The scope of uniqueness depends on the implementation product.

Timestamp.   The timestamp field contains the time the message was submitted to be sent.

Correlation ID.   The correlation ID field is set by the application. It typically contains an identifier used to associate a response message with its request message.

Reply-to.   The reply-to field is used to communicate the originator of a message when a reply is expected. Depending on the application and the message type, it may be used for other information if a reply is not expected.

Redelivered.   The redelivered flag indicates that the message may have been delivered to the recipient before but was never acknowledged. This does not apply if the receiving session is transacted.

Type.   The type field is used to reference a repository definition of message type. This depends on the implementation product.

Expiration.   This field contains the Greenwich Mean Time (GMT) at which the message is intended to expire. It is computed from a value specified in the send method and GMT at the time of the send. If the time specified is zero, then the message does not expire. This could be useful for preventing queue overflow, but JMS does not define a mechanism for notification of expiration.

Priority.   The priority field contains a value from 0 as the lowest to 9 as the highest priority. Priorities of 0 to 4 are considered gradations of normal. Priorities need not be strictly enforced.

Message Properties

Message properties are optional, additional header fields. Properties are a list of name-value pairs for additional data about the message.

There are a number of JMS-defined properties that may be used by the JMS implementation; these have a JMSX prefix. The implementation product may have its own properties designated by a prefix of JMS_<vendor-name>. In general, applications should not rely on these vendor-dependent properties.

Applications may define additional properties. Properties are the basis for the specification of message selection, and thus property names must follow the rules for names in message selection specifications. In general, applications should include descriptive properties in event messages (that is, publish-and-subscribe) so that it is possible for subscribers to express interest in particular messages at a fairly fine level of granularity. This can reduce the level of network traffic in messages that are not really of interest.

Message Body

The message body contains the actual message. The content will depend on the application, but the goal should be to use Extensible Markup Language (XML) as the formatting syntax. This provides messages that are reasonably self-documenting and can be displayed easily. It also provides flexibility because items can be added to the XML message without disturbing the capability of existing applications to access items in which they have interest. Finally, where necessary, the use of XML as a consistent format will facilitate transformation.

JMS does not define the message body except that it specifies five general forms:

Stream message. A stream of Java primitive values.

Map message. A set of name-value pairs where names are strings and values are Java primitive types.

Text message. A string that may contain XML.

Object message. A serialized Java object that may be a collection object containing other objects.

Bytes message. A stream of uninterpreted bytes.

It is expected that most of the messages used for enterprise integration, including EAI, will be text messages containing XML.

API Object Model

The JMS API is expressed by a number of objects that provide the messaging service interface. The object model is defined in detail by the JMS specification and will not be repeated here. However, Figure 6.3 is included to illustrate the interactions between some of the key objects in the JMS model. The diagram depicts the sending and receiving of messages in a point-to-point style of com-

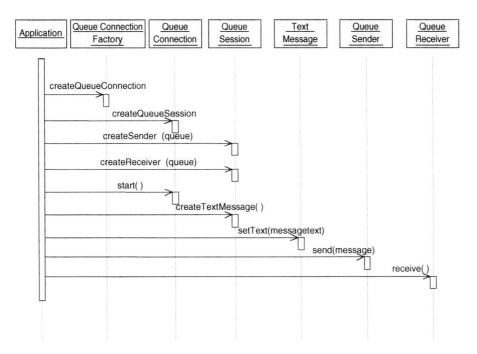

Figure 6.3   JMS object interactions for point-to-point messaging.

munication. The messages depicted by the arrows in the interaction diagram are all synchronous messages executed in Java.

The application obtains a reference to a queue connection factory (from JNDI) and sends a *createQueueConnection* message to obtain a queue connection. It then requests a queue session from the queue connection with the *createQueueSession* message. It could request additional sessions if it intends to operate multiple threads. It obtains a queue reference (from JNDI) for a queue to which messages are to be sent and creates a queue sender with the *createSender* message to the queue session. It obtains a queue reference for a queue from which it accepts messages (from JNDI) and creates a queue receiver with a *createReceiver* message to the queue session. It then sends a *start* message to the queue connection, enabling the sending and receiving of messages.

To send a message, it creates a text message by sending a *createTextMessage* message to the queue session. It then sends a *setText* message to the text message object to define the body. It also could set property values. It then sends a *send* message to the queue sender with the message as an argument. At this point it would be appropriate for the application to commit so that the application database is updated and the message is committed to the queue database and therefore available to be transmitted.

To receive a message, the application sends a *receive* message to the queue receiver. This message blocks until a message is received. After a message has been received and processed, it would be appropriate for the application to commit, thus updating the application database and causing the message to be removed from the queue.

Design Considerations

The JMS specification defines a vendor-independent messaging service. We have discussed it as a generic capability. The following design considerations provide additional insights on issues that arise in practical applications:

- Product interoperability
- Transformation service
- File transfers
- B2B messaging
- Security
- Scalability
- Application execution
- Exception handling

These are each discussed in the subsections that follow.

Product Interoperability

There are currently no standards for interoperability between message broker products. The solution is to create a bridge between the products where messages are received in a message queue from each product and forwarded to the output queue for the other product. Some of this can be accomplished within the functionality defined by JMS.

This works for point-to-point messages. The bridge functions in each message broker domain as a proxy for the other message broker domain. The proxy queues in one domain must function as destinations for all messages destined for destinations in the other domain. This creates an additional maintenance burden to create new proxy queues whenever a destination queue may receive messages through the bridge.

JMS does not support an effective bridge for publish-and-subscribe messages. A subscription should be propagated through the network to turn on a publication at the source. This assumes that the messaging product does not distribute messages for which there is no interest. Unfortunately, JMS provides no way to propagate a subscription across a bridge because subscriptions are not defined as being communicated to publishers. Consequently, the bridge as a potential publisher is not aware of new subscriptions and cannot forward them.

A fully functional bridge will be a solution that depends on nonstandard interfaces to the products involved. The design of the solution and the product interfaces also will affect the level of maintenance support required to accommodate changes in network configuration as well as addition and removal of destination queues.

Transformation Service

Transformation services have been developed to support the incompatibility of messages to be exchanged between systems for EAI. These products are either integrated into or used to extend messaging facilities. They enable the sender and receiver to communicate even though they may be using different message body formats. Of course, the content of the message body provided by the sender must have sufficient content with equivalent semantics that the format expected by the receiver can be created.

There are three different strategies for transformation:

- Transform each message from its originator format to its destination format.

- Transform the message at the source and destination so that messages are communicated in a standard format (decentralized transformation).

- Transform a nonstandard message when it is received by the message broker and, if necessary, transform it again if the destination requires a nonstandard format (centralized transformation).

The first strategy minimizes the number of transformations, but many transformations may need to be implemented. The other two always transform to and from a standard format. The second strategy associates the transformation with the nonconformant source or destination. This helps align responsibility with cost and control—there is an incentive to eliminate the need for the transformation. The third strategy centralizes cost and control. The centralization facilitates configuration and change management so that when the standard is changed, transformations for all affected sources and destinations can be implemented to support the transition.

The decentralized transformation strategy is recommended. If messages are communicated in XML format, then new elements can be added to the standard without requiring transformations for receivers. Sources can be updated independently to produce the new elements. When all sources are updated, then destinations that require the new elements can be implemented. The transition does not need to be synchronized globally.

The mechanism of transformation depends on the particular product. Generally, the transformation is defined in terms of rules. All messaging should be in XML format. If transformation is from XML to XML, then XML Stylesheet Language for Transformation (XSLT) can be used. XSLT also can be used to transform XML to other formats. Messages that are not originated in XML format will require other forms of transformation. It may be appropriate to first create an XML equivalent and then user XSLT to perform the transformation to the common format.

A more difficult transformation involves the merging of messages from different sources. This requires one message to be held pending the arrival of the message to be merged. Such a transformation is at high risk that matching messages will not arrive or will not be recognized as matching, resulting in both operational difficulties with growing queues and application integrity problems due to loss of input. The merge function is a specialized application that receives messages from the sources to be merged and produces merged output messages. Once the matching messages are identified, this transformation can be performed using XSLT.

Messaging product vendors typically have adapters for various technologies and enterprise application products. Not all vendors use XSLT or support the distributed transformation strategy. These should be strong selection requirements.

File Transfers

File transfers over the Internet are commonly performed using the File Transfer Protocol (FTP). FTP provides no guarantee that the file will be delivered once and only once, but using messaging to directly carry the content of large files could create serious performance problems for the messaging system. The answer is to use the two facilities together—use the messaging facility to manage the file transfer.

Figure 6.4 illustrates the exchange of messages between a file sender and a file receiver to control the transfer of a file. The file sender wants to send a file to the file receiver. This could be in response to a request for the file from the potential receiver. The sender sends a message defining the name and location of the file as well as other relevant characteristics of interest to the receiver. The receiver, when ready, executes the FTP to perform the file transfer. When the file transfer is complete, the receiver acknowledges receipt with a message. At this point, the sender no longer needs to preserve the file and can delete or move it, knowing that the receiver has it.

The receiver should take appropriate action to ensure that it cannot lose the file before responding with the transfer complete message. For example, the receiver could create a backup copy, or it could process the content of the file

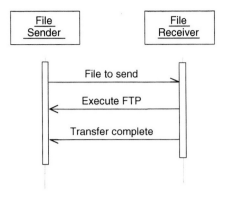

Figure 6.4 File transfer control protocol.

to update a database and respond with the transfer complete message when the database update commits.

If the file transfer should fail, the receiver should respond with a transfer failed message. The sender should respond to this message with a file-to-send message when any difficulty at its end has been resolved. In any event, the sender is informed that the file remains to be transferred, and the receiver knows that the sender is obligated to tell the receiver when to try again.

B2B Messaging

The infrastructure messaging service will communicate messages within the enterprise, but messages to business partners require an even more loosely coupled mode of message communication. Communication with business partners will be over the public Internet and must be assumed to be with incompatible message broker products. The industry direction is to communicate between enterprises using the HyperText Transport Protocol (HTTP) as the least-common-denominator protocol. HTTP can easily pass through firewalls, it is supported by all Web servers, and, like HTTPS, it supports secure communication based on digital certificates.

The enterprise business Extensible Markup Language (ebXML) effort, sponsored by the United Nations, defined a specification for reliable messaging using HTTP. The specification is based on each participant implementing a message service handler (MSH) for the HTTP communications. The ebXML message structure also incorporates digital signatures. This specification is key to flexible B2B communications. We can expect MSH products to be available by the time this book is published. Additional ebXML specifications provide for the specification of electronic documents and exchange protocols and the negotiation of complementary protocols between ad hoc business partners. Products implementing these additional ebXML specifications should be available in the near future. ebXML specifications are discussed in more detail in Chapter 9.

The enterprise infrastructure B2B messaging service incorporates an MSH for the B2B communication. It receives a message from the infrastructure messaging service that is destined for a business partner and wraps it as required by the ebXML protocol. Conversely, it receives messages from a business partner and forwards them through the infrastructure messaging service to the appropriate BSD queue.

Exchanges between business partners occur as conversations, that is, exchanges regarding a particular objective and subject matter. The conversation is guided by an agreed-on protocol. Each partner has a designated role in the conversation. The role identifies the appropriate destination BSD queue for incoming messages. A conversation identifier is associated with the BSD workflow process instance that manages the conversation. Each partner executes a workflow process with activities that receive a message, take appropriate action on the message, and send an appropriate response.

ebXML specifications anticipate the ability for an enterprise to electronically negotiate an exchange protocol with a new business partner, establish a connection, and conduct business. The technology is defined, the products will be available soon, and the specification of protocols and document specifications will be driven by the commitment of major corporations and industry consortia that recognize the business benefit of this capability. For current information on the status of such standards, see the Web site associated with this book (www.wiley.com/compbooks/cummins).

Security

The messaging infrastructure requires consideration of the following six security concerns:

- Authentication of a participating server
- Protecting the privacy and integrity of the message
- Authority of a sender to send to a specified queue
- Authority of a publisher to send to a topic
- Authority of a subscriber to receive from a topic
- Providing nonrepudiation of message content

JMS does not specify any interface for security, nor does it define security requirements for a compliant implementation product. In order to achieve effective security for messaging, the messaging product must address the first five of these concerns.

The implementation product must provide an interface to a participating server that ensures authentication of that server, and a secure connection must be established to ensure the privacy and integrity of the communication. Both the authentication and secure connection can be accomplished with Secure Sockets Layer (SSL) using digital certificates.

The authority issues can be more complex. The fundamental issue is the identification of an appropriate principal—the entity that is vested with the applicable authority. The user of the application that originated the message may be the principal, or the application itself could be the principal. Identifying the application as the principal reduces the number of principals to be authorized and provides greater flexibility, but this may not always satisfy security concerns.

Based on the principal identifier, the infrastructure messaging service must determine the authority of the principal to send a message to a particular destination, send a message for a particular topic (publish-and-subscribe), or subscribe to a particular topic. This can be based on access control lists for the message destinations and topics.

JMS does not define message properties for security information. Consequently, application properties must be defined to communicate the principal authentication information. At a minimum, the principal identifier should be passed as a message property for determination of authority. This assumes the integrity of the originating BSD because the communications between queue servers should be secure. However, this would allow any BSD to originate a message if it provides an authorized principal identifier. Consequently, it would be appropriate to require that the originating BSD also be authorized to send a message to the specified destination. This authentication can be based on the principal identifier of the output message queue server that is used for the SSL communication.

The last concern requires digital signatures. For the most part, nonrepudiation is not required for messages communicated within the enterprise. However, for communications involving money or the control of other valuable resources, digital signatures should be considered. For any transaction that would require a signature if conducted with paper, a digital signature should be considered for the communication of messages. In many cases, these should be the digital signatures of individuals.

These digital signatures should be transparent to the messaging service. They belong to the particular document. These documents should all be in XML format. Standards for XML signatures are discussed in Chapter 9.

Scalability

Scalability must be considered at two levels:

- The scalability of the JMS implementation product
- The scalability of the applications that use it

We will not examine the scalability of messaging products here; while it may be possible to make some assessment by examination of the product specifications, for the most part, the determination of product scalability must be through testing. Here we will examine factors to be considered in the design of applications and the features that messaging products must provide to support the scalability of applications. There are four primary concerns:

- Multithreading
- Load balancing
- Queue overload
- Unsubscribed topics

Multithreading

An application might accept a message from a queue or topic and complete all activity associated with the message before accepting the next message. In this case, the time to process N messages is N times the time to process one message. If the order of processing messages must be preserved, then the application should select a message, process it, and commit the transaction, causing the message queue and the application database to be updated before proceeding to process the next message.

Multithreading is an important way to improve performance over one message at a time. JMS defines a session as a single thread of control; it serializes the processing of multiple messages regardless of the number of receivers it may create. However, a connection can have multiple active sessions.

JMS does not define the semantics of concurrent receivers for a queue in the point-to-point style of communication. JMS allows multiple concurrent sessions, and as each session accepts a message from the queue, it will become unavailable for other sessions, and no message will be accepted twice. This would not, however, ensure the sequential processing of messages, particularly since a message could become available again if a session failed to complete the transaction.

JMS does define the effect of using two subscribers to the same topic in the publish-and-subscribe mode. Each subscriber will receive a copy of each message. Nevertheless, this can be used to achieve some level of multithreading. If subscribers specify mutually exclusive selection criteria, then each will receive a copy of messages from the set it has selected. This allows processing in multiple threads, but the benefit will depend on the arrival patterns of messages in each subset.

An optional JMS facility provides for the concurrent processing of messages by a subscriber—optional means that the implementation product may not support it. Under this facility, an application may associate several *server sessions* with a single JMS session, each server session executing in a different thread. Use of this facility would, of course, be a factor in the vendor independence of the application, and this facility should be used only if necessary to achieve a required level of performance.

Load Balancing

JMS does not define any facility for load balancing. Consequently, the implementation of load balancing falls to the application. If the work of serving a single queue is to be distributed across multiple servers, then the server receiving the messages must invoke processing on the other servers. If message processing is serialized by a single session, then off-loading to another server would provide little benefit and might degrade throughput. Improvement can only be achieved realistically if messages are processed concurrently, and the concurrent work is off-loaded to multiple servers.

Messages from a single queue might be accepted by connections on different servers, but this is not defined by JMS and would depend on the behavior of the JMS implementation product. Consequently, such an approach would be vendor dependent and would not be recommended.

Queue Overload

Queue overload can occur in several ways:

- A durable subscriber becomes inactive and does not return for an extended period of time (if ever).
- The application that processes messages from a queue is inactive for an extended period of time.
- An application goes into a loop or becomes deadlocked, and although still active, it stops accepting new messages.
- Messages are arriving at a rate that exceeds the capacity of the application to consume them.

The first situation is a likely consequence of casual use of durable subscriptions. Publish-and-subscribe communication frequently will be used for ad hoc applications and ad hoc monitoring of particular events. A durable subscription does not go away when the application is not active—it continues until explicitly terminated. Ad hoc subscribers are unpredictable because their use depends on current problems or analysis activities of people. If an application creates a durable subscription for a topic, then somebody must remember to terminate the subscription when it is no longer of interest, and furthermore, the subscriber cannot simply go away while messages accumulate, unless the rate of arrival and queue capacity are considered. Consequently, durable subscriptions should be reserved for regular production applications that will not leave their messages unattended.

The other three situations apply to the point-to-point style of communication, and generally speaking, it would be expected that the guaranteed delivery of messages is essential to their business function. These situations can occur unexpectedly. The first line of defense is for the JMS implementation product to provide a monitoring and alarm facility to detect a buildup of messages in a queue and warn the system administrator. Where message volumes are high or processes critical, designers should consider including a feedback mechanism whereby the receiver reports progress periodically so that the sender can determine if there is a potential queue overload.

Unsubscribed Topics

JMS does not define a way for implementations to inform applications when an event is of interest or when it is no longer of interest. Consequently, applications must produce events that may be of interest and let the implementation product determine when they are to be forwarded.

A good JMS implementation will filter events very close to the source so that there is minimal consumption of resources. However, there will still be a cost associated with each event issued. Application designers must consider carefully the need for events and the frequency of their occurrence. Wherever possible, the granularity of events, that is, the number of state changes they represent, should be reviewed, and events should be consolidated where practical. Particular attention should be paid to those events that occur with every business transaction.

Application Execution

JMS does not provide any mechanism to initiate execution of an application to process a message. An application must be active to receive a message from a queue or a topic. It is an unnecessary use of resources and an additional burden on the system administrator to have a number of applications executing just in case there might be a message for them.

To address this need, an execution service should be implemented. The execution service executes as a daemon within each BSD to monitor an execution queue. When it receives a message, it executes the appropriate application.

The particular execution environment will determine the manner in which the application is executed and the mode by which the message is relayed to it.

The Enterprise JavaBeans (EJB) specification defines such a facility, described as a message-driven bean. The message-driven bean is instantiated and executed when a relevant message arrives. This can then initiate an appropriate application process to handle the message. Message-driven beans are discussed further in Chapter 10.

Exception Handling

There are two levels of exceptions that a JMS application must consider:

- Exceptions arising in response to the invocation of a JMS function
- An exception communicated to a JMS *exception listener*

Exceptions returned from a function call must first be addressed in the context of the application. Unless they are exceptions that are anticipated and resolved programmatically, they should be reported to the infrastructure exception-handling service.

JMS provides for an exception listener to be registered with a connection. If the messaging service detects an exception on the connection that it cannot resolve, it will invoke the onException method on the exception listener. These exception notices are communicated asynchronously. Implications to the application, such as suspending execution pending resolution of the exception, should be resolved first. Then the exception should be reported to the infrastructure exception-handling service.

Summary

This chapter described the enterprise infrastructure to support asynchronous, store-and-forward messaging. It described the application of JMS as a vendor-neutral interface specification to available messaging products, and it has described supplementary services and protocols. This infrastructure capability is key to enterprise integration. It allows BSDs to operate and evolve relatively independently. At the same time it provides rapid delivery of transactions and events to those applications that are prepared to process them, thus enhancing enterprise responsiveness over batch mode operations. In addition, it provides a mechanism for communication that is reliable and flexible.

The key elements of these communications are the content and format of the messages. We touched briefly on this issue here and noted the goal to use XML as the message content syntax. We will examine this issue further in Chapter 9, where we explore electronic documents in detail.

As we move to workflow management to manage the integration and coordination of systems and components, there will be less direct communication of messages between applications. Instead, these linkages will be managed through the invocation of workflow processes. The nature and role of workflow management are explored in detail in the next chapter. The impact on the messaging infrastructure will reduce the need for transformation and increase messaging characterized by events and requests.

CHAPTER

7

Integrating Workflow Management

Workflow management is a key element of the enterprise integration architecture. It provides the automation of business processes to coordinate the activities of people and applications, potentially at all levels.

Workflow management products have been available for more than a decade. However, early products focused on the automation of paper flow within a local organization, often in conjunction with document archiving technologies. More recently, workflow management products have become more scalable and provide Web access. Work on standards has opened the door for the integration of different products, thus further enabling enterprise-level integration, particularly where multiple products are already in use.

Workflow management is not a solution that should be developed as an application. Instead, one or more workflow products should be purchased. Current products are the result of many years of experience with product and application development, and the custom development of workflow management would be equivalent to the custom development of a database management system.

In this chapter we will build on the introduction to workflow management from Chapter 3, beginning with the general workflow model and examining requirements and issues in the following areas:

- Process design
- Integration
- Scalability
- Product requirements
- Standards

General Workflow Model

This section will examine the nature of workflow management based on the workflow model discussed in Chapter 3. The workflow model diagram from Chapter 3 is repeated here as Figure 7.1 for easy access. The following paragraphs review and elaborate on the roles of the components.

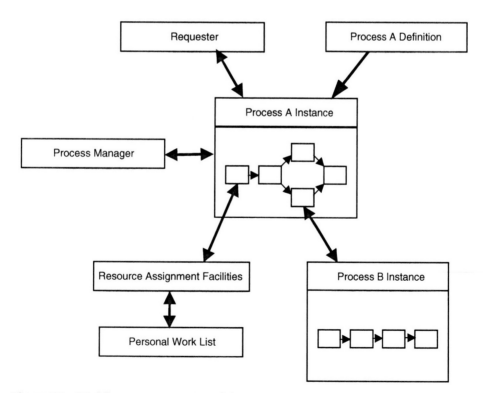

Figure 7.1   Workflow management model.

Workflow management begins with the definition of processes. This activity occurs offline using a process specification tool. Such tools typically provide a graphic depiction of the processes and provide interactive editing to ensure that the process structures are consistent with design constraints. The process definition will specify the activities of the process and their relationships and functionality.

The process definition is then installed for runtime execution. Different products will create the executable process definition in different forms. It may remain in much the same form as the build-time model, or it may be transformed to an implementation that executes more efficiently or takes less memory space. This version of the process defines how instances of the process will execute. It is the equivalent of a computer program that can be executed for different users to solve a number of similar problems.

The requester of a process provides values to variables that define the subject matter and parameters for the execution of the process. The requester will be notified when the process is completed.

When the process is executed, an *instance* of the process is created. The process definition typically is not replicated, but is incorporated by reference. The process instance holds information about the status of the particular execution, along with references to users and related subject matter.

The process executes its component activities according to the sequence and conditions specified in the process definition. Activities are executed in transactional contexts. When the status of an activity changes, the result is committed to persistent storage. Consequently, if the system fails, the process will resume after the last commit, typically at a point of completion of an activity.

Activities perform a variety of operations. An activity may include executable business logic directly or through the execution of application code. These activities are the equivalent of application transactional operations and may change the state of objects representing the subject matter, such as a purchase order or inventory status. An activity may invoke another process; the activity may then be suspended until completion of the subprocess. An activity may request a person be assigned to participate in the process, causing a request to be posted in one or more work lists. An activity may go into a wait state pending the occurrence of an event or, alternatively, the expiration of a specified amount of time.

Generally, a process may have multiple concurrent paths. This allows related activities to be active at the same time to reduce the duration of the overall process. At points along each path, activities may be suspended waiting for events to occur on other paths before proceeding. Similarly, an activity may be suspended pending an event from an external source.

When an activity requests the assignment of a person, it could specify a particular individual; this may be appropriate if a particular person participated in a related process. However, in most cases, the person should be specified in terms of qualifications or authority. The workflow manager will use an organization model to identify the potential participants. A request may go to a pool of people so that it appears in the work lists of all those who could accept the assignment. In this case, when a particular person accepts the task, it will be removed from the work lists of the others. The requesting activity will proceed when the person indicates that the requested task is completed. The activity also may initiate a timeout so that if the person does not complete the task in a specified time, then an alternative action may be taken, such as notifying the person's supervisor of the delay.

In the general case, a process may require other resources besides people, such as a room, a machine, materials, or a vehicle. The assignment of these resources typically is performed by invoking appropriate applications or processes or by requesting an appropriate action by a person to obtain them.

One of the common activities assigned to people is approval. For example, an employee initiates an expense reporting process by filling out an expense report. The process routes the report to the employee's supervisor for approval. The supervisor may approve the expense, but not have final authority to approve the amount involved. Consequently, the process will pass the report approved by the supervisor to his or her manager, and so on. Such routings are based on an organizational model defining reporting relationships and levels of authority. Typically, these models are incorporated into workflow management products. In the long term, general-purpose organizational models should be used for workflow management as well as for other purposes, such as security and accounting.

A person with appropriate authorization may obtain the status of a process. A participant in a process always should be able to get the status of processes in which he or she is participating. The requester of a process, such as the person who submitted the expense report, typically will have access to the status of the process. The owner of a process (that is, the process definition) should be able to examine the status of all instances of the process. In addition, workflow management products will provide tools for analyzing the performance of processes. Execution-time tools will show the status of current activity, and offline tools can be used to analyze process performance over time. These tools are key to process improvement.

Workflow products also will provide some level of intervention capability. If a process instance is suspended due to the absence of an employee, a supervisor may be allowed to change the person assigned. Other circumstances may necessitate redirecting the process flow to an alternative path. The nature and extent of process changes will depend on the capabilities of the particular product. Generally, changes made dynamically apply only to a particular process instance.

Process Design Considerations

Many factors must be considered in the design of processes to meet business function requirements. Examining all such factors would require a separate book. Here we will focus on more general design considerations associated with enterprise integration:

- Process closure
- Process scope
- Process state versus subject matter
- User roles
- Accountability and control
- Process back-out
- Long-running transactions
- Ancillary actions

Process Closure

A process should be viewed as a closed loop that accomplishes an objective of the organization. A request for a process implies certain expectations on the part of the requester. Completion of the process should yield the response to that request—the fulfillment of the organization's responsibility. This means that a process is not completed by passing responsibility for remaining work to another process. Instead, if work is to be delegated, the delegating process should make the request and wait for completion of the subprocess. The subprocess has responsibility for fulfilling the delegated work, but the requesting process has responsibility for responding to the initial request.

This is good business process design because responsibilities are clear. It is equivalent to the go-to-less programming model. Processes will become unmanageable if requests are passed off without a follow-up on the results. Each of the processes has a context. The result of each delegation should be considered in the context of the requester in order to achieve the most reliable and predictable result for the requester.

Process Scope

The scope of a process should be confined to a business system domain (BSD). We discussed the nature of a BSD in detail in Chapter 5. It is one or more applications that are tightly coupled, maintain a shared, consistent database, and are owned by a single organization. This means that the process is owned by the organization that owns the BSD, and the execution of the process occurs within the BSD. There are several implications here. First, the organization that owns the BSD likely will use a single workflow management product. Consequently, interoperability between different workflow products normally will be loosely coupled, that is, through asynchronous messaging. Operations performed by the workflow processes will be transactional within the host BSD. This means that the state of processes and the objects they operate on will be consistent at the end of a computational transaction and that they will be consistent when the system is recovered from a failure. Finally, the consistent state and accessibility of the process, its participants, and its subject matter provide support for role-based security (which we will discuss later).

Process State versus Subject Matter State

A process has a state that reflects its progress in the execution of activities along with other variables that define the context in which the process is being performed. A process also has subject matter, that is, information about the things the process is acting on. There is a subtle distinction here that should be reflected in the design of the process state and the subject matter object(s).

The process controls the sequence of activities. Its state reflects the activities currently active and variable values that are needed by the process to perform the requested function. The subject matter reflects the state of a business entity, something that has existence in the business, independent of the process. A purchasing process may be in an *issue request for proposals* activity. A purchase order and the associated product specifications are the subject matter; they contain the information necessary to perform the purchase.

As a general rule, the state of the subject matter should reflect changes that actually have occurred in the business. For example, if a purchase order is issued or the product has been received, then the purchase order record should be updated to reflect these actions. However, progress of the order through editing and pricing activities should be reflected by the process status, although the order may include a flag indicating that the order has been edited and a field containing the price after pricing has been performed. The reason for this distinction is to preserve process flexibility. For example, the price could reflect a retail computation, and a later activity might apply a discount for selected customers. Also, if an order is canceled, then the state of the order may be misleading because various actions may be required to perform the cancellation.

User Roles

A workflow process may involve a number of different users in different roles. These roles define the relationship of the user to the process and the work product, as depicted in Figure 7.2. As a result, roles relate directly to the manner in which each user participates in the process and the user's authority in the context of the process.

These roles are presented as a foundation for the definition of roles in specific workflow processes. Some processes will not realize all these roles; some processes may realize additional roles. Roles need not be defined in exactly the same way in every process. However, the use of consistent role types and names will make it easier to organize and understand the business processes.

Roles are important because they are a basis for activity assignments and access authority. For activity assignments, a role specification will have associated constraints on the persons qualified to take the role—this may include the fact that the candidate is not assigned a related role in the same process. For access authority, the role of a user will have a direct effect on what the user is allowed to do. Later in this chapter we will discuss security authorization further.

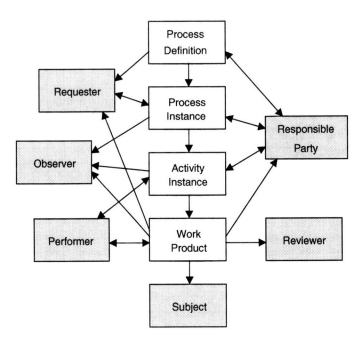

Figure 7.2   User roles.

Figure 7.2 depicts six different roles. We will examine the implications of each of these in the following subsections.

Requester

A *requester* is a person responsible for initiation of the process. The requester could have been assigned this role in one of three ways:

- The requester initiated the process directly.
- The requester initiated another process that requested this process.
- The requester was the responsible party for a process that requested this process.

In each case the person filling the requester role is determined when the process is initiated. There can only be one requester for each process instance, and that requester will seldom change. The requester provides the basis of authority for execution of the process.

The requester will be able to access information about processes he or she is authorized to initiate, and the requester provides the initial parameters of the process instance and may be given access to view the process parameters as the process progresses. The requester may be allowed to see the current state of the work product because the requester presumably has an interest in the outcome. The requester generally is not authorized to change the process, its state, or the work product.

Observer

An *observer* is simply an interested person. An observer can obtain information about the state of the process or the work product, but is not authorized to change anything. Observers are not actively engaged in the process but have an interest for other reasons, such as concern about the duration of the process or the quality of the result.

Depending on the nature of the process, there may be several different observer roles. An observer may be able to view only the state of the process. Another observer may be allowed to view the state of the process and the work product. Yet another observer may be able to view the process definition and history of the process instance.

The observer role and specializations of it will be determined by the relationship of the potential observer to other participants in the process or a process that invoked this process. Some of these may be determined at process initiation time, but most will be determined at the time the user attempts to access information about the process.

Performer

A *performer* is a person assigned direct responsibility for the result of one or more activities. There can be only one current performer for an activity so that there is only one person directly responsible for the result. A person becomes a performer when he or she selects the associated activity from a work list.

The performer is the only role authorized to change the work product. If others were authorized to change the work product, then the performer could not be held responsible for the result.

Subject

The *subject* is a person the process is about. For example, this could be a personnel process where the subject is an employee recommended for a raise, or it could be a customer whose car is being serviced. The subject may have very limited access to the state of the process.

Reviewer

A *reviewer* is somebody who will examine the work product and make an assessment. A reviewer could be a peer or a manager of the performer, or it could be someone concerned about the quality of the work product based on a relationship to the requester. A reviewer could be a person with authority to accept or reject the work product, thus affecting the resulting activities of the process. A reviewer may be selected or assigned when the process reaches a point where a review is required.

Responsible Party

A *responsible party* is responsible for the overall execution of the process. This person will monitor the process instances, receive alerts if there are errors or delays, and make changes in assignments if a current performer is unable to continue the process. The responsible party may be able to redirect the flow of a process instance to resolve a problem.

Accountability and Control

As with application programs, computers execute workflow processes. However, unlike most application programs, where humans are involved primarily in data entry, workflow processes may involve the participation of humans in many activities along the way. This requires closer attention to accountability and control, particularly where money or other resources may be at risk.

Actions reported by humans should be recorded for future reference, including the person, time, and date. In some cases, mechanisms may be required to ensure nonrepudiation, such as where the person is a customer or the employee of a business partner. Nonrepudiation mechanisms will be discussed further in Chapter 11.

Whenever a task or request is assigned to a human, the process should reflect the possibility that the human will not respond, will respond incorrectly, or will provide an acceptable response that does not properly reflect the action taken. Decisions made by humans must be within the scope of their authority. When authority is limited by a monetary value, and then when the person does not have adequate authority, the process must be designed to seek endorsement of a person with greater authority. Some actions always may require a concurring decision by two people, such as a programmer and a reviewer. Some actions may require that the person not have a personal interest in the result, such as approval of an expense report or a salary increase.

Process Backout

When application programs execute within a transactional context, a failed series of actions can be backed out automatically by the transaction control mechanism. The states of affected objects will be restored to their states prior to the beginning of the transaction.

Workflow processes involve many computational transactions. Typically, the results of each activity will be committed when the activity is completed, and additional commits may be performed at intermediate points for some activities. Consequently, when a process fails or is canceled, there is no automatic mechanism to undo the actions already performed. The backout for a process may be one or more alternative paths in the process, depending on its state when canceled, or there may be one or more separate processes designed to perform the necessary actions.

In some cases, a backout may be accomplished by saving the state of the subject matter objects before the process begins or by explicitly restoring them if the process fails or is canceled. However, this is seldom adequate because workflow processes affect circumstances outside the computer. It is not acceptable simply to forget that a product was shipped or a check was issued. There is also likely to be a need to examine the circumstances of the failure after the fact. Thus, a simple restoration of the subject matter state is seldom appropriate.

Long-Running Transactions

On the other hand, workflow processes can be used to break up long-running transactions into more manageable chunks. An application process may involve multiple interactions with a person or delegation of operations to other applications with unpredictable response times. If the full process is undertaken as a single computational transaction, referenced objects may be locked for an extended period of time, and if an error occurs, all work up to that point could be lost. If a workflow process is used to manage the activity, then units of work can be accomplished by individual activities and committed as they are completed. The workflow process ensures that the sequence of activities is performed and that there is no risk that completed activities will need to be redone in the event of a failure. Of course, it may be necessary to design backout processes to handle the occasional cancellation of a process.

Ancillary Actions

Sometimes circumstances in a process will require ancillary actions to be performed. For example, in fulfilling an order, the fulfillment process may determine that the inventory is now below a reorder threshold. The fulfillment process could invoke the reorder process, but this might delay the fulfillment process. There are two ways such actions may be initiated:

- With a nonblocking process request
- By issuing an event

If an activity performs a nonblocking process request, the requested process will be initiated, but the requesting activity will not wait for its completion. Support for this type of request will vary among workflow management products. The workflow management system will assure that the process is performed, but the requesting process does not depend on the completion or the result.

If an activity issues an event, the event may be communicated to any number of recipients through the notification service. The event may be of interest for ad hoc analysis or reporting, for raising an alarm, or for the initiation of other processes. In order to provide a product-independent mechanism for the communication of events, the workflow process should issue a message to a topic in the messaging, publish-and-subscribe service, discussed in Chapter 6. The messaging service will forward the event to all interested recipients, including recipients within the BSD and in other BSDs.

To complement the forwarding of events, there must be a mechanism for the initiation of processes based on events. An event handler is needed to receive each event and initiate the appropriate process. This mechanism is discussed further in the next section.

Integration Elements

Workflow management must function in the context of a BSD and interact with applications and other BSD facilities and services. This section will discuss the following elements of workflow integration:

- Process initiation
- Workflow context
- Application adapters
- Event detection
- Asynchronous process invocation
- Shared work products
- Security

Process Initiation

Processes are initiated in one of three ways:

- By a programmed request
- By a user
- By an event

A programmed requester has the same form as an invoking process, but it could be an application or other facility presenting the interface. A requester requests the instantiation of a process and passes parameters that form the context of the process instance execution—directly or indirectly defining the subject matter and parameters that will affect the execution of the process. The process will notify the requester when the requested process is completed. The requester also will be given a reference to the process instance so that it can direct messages to it during execution, such as status requests.

For a user to initiate a process, there must be a mechanism to initiate an instance of a selected process type and for the entry of parameters. The workflow management product may provide the mechanism for selection of a process and creation of an instance, but the entry of parameters will be unique to the particular process and will require specialized user-interface displays. The most flexible way to manage this input is with a process for this purpose. The user selects the input process rather than the primary business process, the input process leads the user through the necessary steps to enter the appropriate date, and the input process then invokes the primary function process. This also allows the primary function process to be invoked in other ways besides direct user input.

Event-initiated processes must be initiated as the result of the receipt of a message from a message broker publish-and-subscribe service. These are discussed in detail in Chapter 6. An event handler must receive the event message and function as a process requester. The event handler will initiate the process appropriate for the event and assign values to process context variables based on the content of the event message. For purposes of monitoring and control, it may be appropriate to attribute these requests to a person in the associated business organization. Often event-initiated processes are defined to address ad hoc problems, such as monitoring business activities or intervention in particular circumstances. In such cases, it is particularly appropriate for the request to be attributed to the responsible party.

Workflow Context

The context of a workflow process is the set of parameters associated with the execution of a process instance. These parameters will include references to persons in different roles, subject matter objects, and variables that will affect computations or how the process is performed.

The Object Management Group's (OMG) Workflow Management specification defines the process context as a sequence of name-value pairs. The initial names and their values are determined by the process definition and the particular request. Additional names and values may be added as the process executes to capture intermediate and final results. With a minor modification, the process context can be much more flexible and useful. Rather than specifying the parameters in name-value pairs, simply pass one parameter that specifies an Extensible Markup Language (XML) document. An XML document extends the concept of a name-value pair list in the following ways:

- It can provide more complex parameters in a well-defined structure.

- The structure can be accessed and managed with well-defined operations.

- The XML Document Type Definition (DTD) can define the content of the structure for editing.

- The same structure can be used to create associated user displays using XML Stylesheet Language for Transformation (XSLT).

For a process with subprocesses, attaching context documents for the subprocesses can extend the context document, thus capturing a deep history of the process execution. Different style sheets can be used to format displays with selected content for different purposes and different users.

Application Adapters

While workflow management products will provide ways for a process to execute an application, it is desirable to define a consistent interface to applications using adapters. The consistent interface will simplify programming and can facilitate the better recording of activities and communication with users.

It is suggested that the interface presented to the workflow process be equivalent to a workflow process interface. The application is then invoked in the same manner as a subprocess. If the workflow context is specified in XML, as described earlier, then the application parameters and results can be captured and accessed in an XML document defined for the application. The benefits derived from the XML context document described earlier then apply here as well.

Event Detection

Processes frequently wait for events. In some circumstances, an event may signal the completion of a necessary action such as execution of an application. In other cases, an event may signal an unexpected situation that should alter the execution of the process. Activities that normally fail to complete may wait for these unexpected events while other activities proceed with the normal work of the process. In either case, the waiting activity must be informed of the event.

Different workflow management products may provide different mechanisms for event detection. The simplest form is for the activity to check periodically for a change in a persistent data value. This could be a file or database entry uniquely identified for the event of interest to the activity, or it simply could be a check for the existence of a file produced by an invoked application.

The best general solution is to receive events from a message broker, but it may be more complex to implement when the more common approach, discussed earlier, may suffice. To receive events from the message broker, the waiting activity must subscribe to an event topic of interest and provide appropriate selection criteria to filter out irrelevant events directed to the same topic. Depending on the workflow product implementation, the event message may be received directly, or an event handler will be required to post the event in such a manner that the workflow product can detect it and activate the waiting activity. In some cases this may be the same form of detection as described earlier—periodic checking for a change in a persistent value.

Asynchronous Process Invocation

A process in one BSD may invoke a process in another BSD, just as it may invoke a process in the same BSD. However, the process in the remote BSD must be invoked asynchronously so that the BSDs remain loosely coupled. The key is to use XML so that the information exchanged can be passed through messaging, but it also can be passed through a firewall using the HyperText Transport Protocol (HTTP) to invoke a process in a business partner BSD.

The mechanism involves two new objects:

- A process request sender
- A process request receiver

The process request sender interfaces with the requesting activity of the primary process and the message queue for sending request messages and receiving responses. The process request receiver interacts with the message queue to receive process requests and interacts with the target process as a local process requester for the subprocess. Each of these will have a state associated with the particular process invocation in order to link the processes with the associated exchange of messages. The interface requirements for these objects are discussed at the end of this chapter.

Shared Work Products

When applications execute in a shared object environment, their transaction context provides the basis for resolving concurrent accesses. Objects are locked when in use and released when the transaction commits, thus forcing serialization of access.

Workflow processes involve a series of computational transactions. In order to achieve predictable results over these long-running transactions, the process must retain exclusive control over shared work products. This typically is achieved by a checkout, checkin mechanism, but it could be achieved using an independent concurrency control service or optimistic locking. The choice of mechanism may depend on the availability of a document management facility and the nature of the shared work products and their usage.

If a document management facility is used (such as a product data management facility), then a work product will be obtained for a process by requesting a checkout. When the process no longer needs to control the work product, the revised work product is checked in and becomes available to other processes or users.

The more general solution is to use a concurrency control service. All users of shared work products must agree to use the concurrency control service and to identify the shared work products in the same manner. A process that intends to use a shared work product will request a lock on the work product from the concurrency control service. If a work product with this identity is locked by another process, then the requesting process will be required to wait. When the process that holds the lock is completed, it will request the concurrency control service to release the lock, and the waiting process (or one of the waiting processes if there are more than one) will be given the lock it requested. Note that the completing process must explicitly release the lock. Also note that, as in other locking situations, it is possible for processes that lock multiple work products to become deadlocked with other processes, waiting for a lock that will never be released.

In optimistic locking, concurrent access to resources is not controlled. Instead, when an update is submitted, the resource is checked to see if the current state has been updated by a different process. If it has been updated, then the update request is rejected. This can be very efficient where there is little chance of two processes concurrently updating the same resource.

Security

In some ways, workflow management can simplify security authorization. Earlier we discussed six different types of roles: requester, observer, performer, subject, reviewer, and responsible party. Individuals will take on different roles in different processes and in different process instances.

The process logic is primarily responsible for determining the assignment of roles. Some role participants are determined by the source of the process request. Some role participants are determined by the process by which work is assigned. Still other role participants are determined by their relationships to the existing participants, the process, or the subject matter.

The assignment of persons to roles is part of the process context—essentially name-value pairs associating role names with person identifiers. When a user attempts to access information about a process or its work product(s), the person identifier can be used to associate one or more roles specific to the process instance. These can be added to the security context to affect security authorization controls, and they can be provided with response data returned to the Web server to affect the format and content of the Web display.

Process roles extend the general authority of individuals to access data and functionality as a result of their specific participation in a process. Although the determination of roles is embedded in the process specification, this is appropriate because role assignments are business decisions. At the same time, security logic is not embedded in the applications. A security service, such as Common Object Request Broker Architecture (CORBA) security, can use roles to restrict access to application data and functionality without any affect on application logic. In addition, where fine-grained security controls are not required, access to data and functionality can be controlled by the design of alternative Web pages selected based on user roles.

Note that in general, role assignments may change during the life of a process. Some performers may not be able to complete their assignments, and work will be reassigned to somebody else. Responsible parties may be replaced due to organizational changes. The role-based controls occasionally may need to reflect requirements to recognize previous role assignments for the same process instance.

Assessing Scalability

Most workflow management products were designed originally to meet the needs of managing departmental paperwork. As the scope of workflow management is expanded, the scale of activity may increase orders of magnitude. Enterprise-level workflow will become key to the operation of the business. It is important to assess the scalability of any product being considered.

The scale to be considered must go beyond the processes initially identified for workflow management. Even though the scope of application of a workflow product is limited to a BSD, once the technology is available and integrated, the number of defined processes and users will increase, with associated increases in the volume of activity. Consequently, the scalability assessment should anticipate considerable growth.

The following subsections will examine key factors to be considered in assessing scalability:

- Process definitions
- Active processes
- Number of users
- Threading model
- Execution distribution model
- Workload balancing

Process Definitions

Workflow management may be targeted for one primary business process. This may not seem like much. However, a well-designed process depends on many subprocesses, just as a well-designed computer program often will have many subordinate functions or subroutines. Special processes should be defined for the assignment of tasks, for handling exception situations, for accessing applications, and so on. A mainstream process could spawn the definition of a hundred supporting processes.

This may still not seem like a lot of process definitions, but it could have a performance impact if the workflow management product is designed assuming a small number.

Active Processes

A more significant scalability factor is the number of active processes. These should be considered at two levels:

- The number of processes that have been initiated and not completed (pending)
- The number of processes that are interacting with users or applications at a single point in time (active)

Consider, for example, an order-processing process. If an enterprise handles a million orders per year and it takes a week to complete handling the order, including shipping and invoicing, then almost 20,000 process instances will be pending at any point in time (1 million/52 weeks). If the number of orders is higher or the order cycle time is longer, then the number of pending processes will increase.

Generally, not all pending processes will be in computer memory if there is not any current activity with users or other applications. However, the number of pending processes could exceed the limits of tables held in memory. The more likely impact may be on user interfaces. When the number of processes is small, then they may be viewed in a scrollable list. When they get into the thousands, then the mode of access and display must change to be more selective.

The number of processes active at one time is more likely a performance issue. Each active process will require computer memory and compute time. The compute requirements for workflow management must be considered along with the computations performed with related applications.

Number of Users

Again, traditional workflow management installations involve small numbers of users—the members of a department. In enterprise installations, the number could be in the thousands, particularly if the workflow process has customers or suppliers as participants. Even if the participants are within the enterprise, some processes, such as for financial and personnel functions, could include all employees as potential participants.

As with the number of processes, the number of users could exceed table limits if information is held in computer memory. Similarly, the number of concurrently active users will have an impact on performance both in terms of computational requirements and in terms of network bandwidth. The design of Web pages can be a significant factor if access involves the downloading of large graphics or applets. Again, the workload of workflow management must be combined with the workload of associated applications that may generate additional Web pages.

The impact of a large number of users on security also must be considered. Security tables will be large, and security administration could be a nightmare if appropriate techniques are not defined for role-based authorization and possibly for the delegation of authority for security administration.

Threading Model

Large-scale systems require multithreading—the capability to process many independent requests concurrently—without requiring that one request be completed before the next can be handled. Some workflow management systems may have been developed for single-thread operating systems and may not be able to take advantage of multithreading. When there are many users and many processes, a multithreading implementation will be essential.

Execution Distribution Model

Workflow management products for large-scale applications should be designed for distributed processing. Even if they are, the manner in which the execution is distributed may have a significant impact on performance. The key performance factors will be database accesses and network messages. If the execution elements of a single process are finely distributed over multiple servers, then there may be excessive network activity. If process elements (such as process context, subject matter objects, or user information) are retrieved repeatedly from the database for every transaction, then there may be excessive database activity.

Load Balancing

Load-balancing facilities for the execution of workflow processes may affect the capability of the system to adapt to shifts in the level of activity in different types of processes or communities of users. Shifts may occur gradually over time, or they may be cyclic on a daily, weekly, monthly, or annual basis. The importance of load balancing may be a function of the nature of the business. However, more adaptive load balancing will reduce the risk of performance problems during peak periods.

Summary

In general, a scalability assessment requires both review of the product design—looking for risk factors—and testing with simulated workloads. Of course, a good starting point would be to assess performance in an existing installation of comparable scale, but currently, there are few large-scale installations of workflow products.

Product Requirements

There are a great many workflow management products in the marketplace. They have diverse capabilities and features. It is important that the product or products selected provide robust process definition capabilities, meet scalability requirements, accommodate integration with other system components, include appropriate management tools, and provide appropriate user interfaces and security controls.

While most workflow management systems in the past focused on document management, two new classes of workflow management have emerged more recently. One class has emerged from enterprise application integration (EAI), where tools have been developed to manage the flow of messages between applications. These products generally do not deal with human participation, but focus on message transformation and content-based routing. The other class has emerged from the development of Web portals. They focus on guiding a particular user through a series of steps to complete a desired action. These processes are limited in scope and generally involve only the initiating user.

The workflow management products needed for enterprise integration involve multiple users and typically provide more runtime control of the process.

The following subsections go into detail about workflow management features and capabilities to support the selection of a suitable product. Not all the features listed may be available in a single product. Thus, there will be trade-offs in the selection process. As products continue to evolve, this should become less of a problem. The capabilities and features are discussed under the following topics:

- Process definition elements
- Process definition tool
- Workflow execution
- Ad hoc changes
- Runtime user interface
- Compute environment
- Security
- Analysis tools

The capabilities and features discussed under each of these topics reflect both required and desired features. Many of the desired features are not currently available, but are included to suggest useful extensions for the future. The desired features are flagged with an asterisk (*).

We have included here features of process design tools, the runtime user interface, and analysis tools. These are not key concerns for enterprise integration and thus have not been discussed earlier. They are, however, important for the successful implementation of workflow management.

Process Definition Elements

The process definition elements define the language syntax for the definition of processes. The following list describes features and functions that are needed for the definition of processes:

Polling/status check activity.   An activity can be designated to poll or check a status indicator periodically on a specified time interval. This could be an ongoing check for a variable out of limits, or it could be, for example, a check on the activity of an application to determine if it has reached a desired status. Polling typically is used in the absence of triggering by events.

Timeout activity.   An activity can remain suspended for a specified period of time or until a specified event occurs (whichever occurs first). Typically, a timeout is used to recognize the failure of an action to occur, such as failure of a human to act on a work list or failure of a subprocess to be completed in an acceptable period of time.

Concurrent activities.   Activities in the same process can be defined to be active concurrently. This enables multiple concurrent paths, potentially involving different participants.

Activity start rules.   Rules can control when an activity starts. Rules may provide the mechanism by which multiple concurrent activities are initiated. Each activity determines if it should be started.

Conditional fan-out.   An activity conditionally can initiate multiple concurrent activities. This places control of the initiation of multiple activities in an activity being completed.

Conditional fan-in.   Initiation of an activity can be suspended until specified conditions are met regarding the results of other preceding activities. Multiple activities, representing multiple paths through a process, can be required to be completed. This is usually implicit at the completion of a process that has multiple concurrent paths.

Activity completion rules.   Rules can determine if an activity is completed. This can cause a path to be suspended until actions by an application or other activities meet the specified condition.

Preemptive completion of a process.   An activity can bring a process to either a normal or abnormal termination state even though some of its activities may still be incomplete. This can occur when two concurrent process paths are competing and the process is complete when one of the competing paths is completed. It also can occur when an activity detects a condition that calls for termination of the process. Depending on the condition, the termination may be considered normal or abnormal, and that status should be reflected in the result.

Resource selection criteria.   Most current workflow management products include facilities for representing resources, particularly people, within organizations. It must be possible for the process to indicate the type of resource required with selection criteria that reference attributes of the resource.

Process context specification.   The process has attributes to define parameters, including symbolic names and data types. The process context includes parameters provided when the process is initiated, variables used within the process, and parameters returned in the result.

Event-triggered process.*   A process is designated to be initiated by the occurrence of an external event. This would imply that the workflow execution has an integrated event handler. This facility can be implemented with a specialized requester component that receives an event message and requests the appropriate process.

Event-triggered activity.*   An activity specification will cause it to enter a wait state and to exit the wait state when a specified event occurs. This facility implies that the workflow execution includes an integrated event handler that will receive an event, determine if there is any activity waiting for that event, and, if so, cause the activity to exit the wait state and proceed.

Process Definition Tool

Workflow management products currently include a build-time tool for the creation of process definitions. In the future, these tools may become independent products. In addition to supporting the definition of processes with the elements just described, the tool should have the following characteristics:

Graphic interactive tool.   The processes are displayed graphically, and the process elements are added and connected with drag-and-drop interactive editing.

Visual distinction of task types.   The type of each process element must be visually identifiable in the graphic representation of the process.

Workflow Execution

The following list describes features that a workflow product may incorporate in the process execution:

Process definition versions. When existing processes are changed, active instances of the same process could be affected. Versioning distinguishes between old and new processes. This is particularly important when the processes are long-running because the new and old processes may both be active for some time in the future.

Process version effectivity control. Process definitions will be changed from time to time. In some cases, the effective date must be coordinated with changes to other processes or business circumstances. A new process definition should replace the existing process with the same identity only after the effectivity date.

Multiple active versions. When a process definition is replaced, there may be active instances. Changing the process definition for these process instances could produce undesirable results. It should be possible to continue the execution of active processes using the obsolete version (or versions) until each process instance is completed.

Event-triggered processes.* A process can be initiated as the result of the receipt of an event. This capability typically is not integrated into a workflow product due to the lack of consistent sources and formats of event messages.

Event-triggered activities.* An activity within an active process can be started or removed from a wait state as a separate path in the process as the result of the receipt of an event. This capability, based on the receipt of an external event message, is not typical of current products. Similar results should be possible when an event can be detected with an activity start rule.

Monitoring/polling activity. An activity should be able to examine the state of a resource, a variable, or a subprocess on a periodic basis to check for a change of state.

Interactive debugging support. The environment should support interactive examination of processes and activities as well as context variables to support debugging.

Stepped execution control. It should be possible for a developer to execute a process step by step to examine the flow and changes in variables for testing.

System environment library functions.   A library of functions must be provided for access to common system environment variables and functions, independent of the platform.

Propagation of preemptive completion.   A process should forward a notice of termination to active subprocesses when it is brought to either normal completion or abnormal termination so that the subprocesses will be terminated.

Ad Hoc Changes

Sometimes the normal sequence of events may not be appropriate for a particular process instance. The workflow management product should allow an authorized person to effect changes. A number of capabilities might be provided:

Skip or restart activities.   One or more activities can be skipped or restarted. Restarting an activity may be appropriate when an external action failed and must be repeated.

Reassignment/replacement of resources.   It must be possible to remove or replace resources, particularly people, for a particular process instance.

Alter the sequence of activities.   A different sequence of activities can be defined for a specific process instance beyond those activities that are currently active.

Runtime User Interface

The following list describes the desired characteristics of a runtime user interface:

Browser-based.   The user interface should be Web browser-based so that it can be accessed from diverse workstations and from remote locations.

Application user-interface integration.   The workflow user interface should be compatible with the user interfaces of associated applications for ease of use.

Display of process status.   There should be a display capable of depicting the current activities of nested subprocesses.

Graphic display of an active process.   There should be a graphic display of an active process depicting the status of the activities.

Process/activity context display.   It should be possible to display process and activity variables for an active process instance.

History/trace display.   A display should depict the sequence of activities executed within a process instance up to the current time. An extended display capability might depict activities remaining to be executed. However, this is unpredictable for tools that base activity initiation on rules instead of explicit activity dependencies.

Process definition.   It should be possible to display the process definition for an active process so that the user can see all activities that could be executed and their relationships as the process proceeds.

Work lists.   Personal work lists should indicate the nature and priority of pending tasks and the current status of processes and activities for which a person is assigned responsibility. The person should be able to access additional information about each item from the work-list display.

Runtime statistics.   The user should have access to current runtime statistics such as queue lengths (for example, work lists), the number of active processes, activity and process durations, and processes completed within a time period.

Compute Environment

The workflow management facility must function in a computing environment in a manner that is compatible with the environment and the other applications and services with which it interacts. The following list describes several aspects of this integration:

Transactional context.   The execution of workflow process steps and the associated applications and services invoked by workflow processes, as well as those that invoke workflow processes, must function in a transactional context so that concurrent actions are serializable (concurrent accesses are resolved) and actions completed (committed) are recoverable.

Messaging.   The workflow process steps must be able to interoperate with applications and other objects through an object request broker (synchronous messaging over a network).

Database.   The state of workflow processes and the associated context data must be made persistent in a database to ensure recoverability.

Multiple platform implementations.   Compatible versions of the workflow management system should be available for deployment on a variety of platforms. Specific platforms of interest should be identified for the enterprise.

Security

Using appropriate security facilities and services, the workflow management system must support access controls as described in the following list:

Integration. The workflow processes and the data on which they operate must be secure from unauthorized access or modification. It must be possible to appropriately integrate security controls with those of the BSD computing environment.

Process initiation. Processes must be initiated only by authorized individuals or by other authorized processes or services.

Process changes. Changes to process models as well as ad hoc changes to process instances must be restricted to authorized individuals.

Process status. Access to process status information must be restricted to authorized individuals based on the process context and assigned roles.

Process assignments. The control of assignments to workflow processes as well as access to information about assignments must be restricted to authorized individuals.

Work-list status. Access to a personal work list must be restricted to the individual assigned to the work list and authorized managers of the individual or the process.

Data access. Access to process context data must be restricted to authorized individuals based on the process context and assigned roles.

History access. Access to process history data must be restricted to authorized individuals based on the process and assigned roles.

Employee privacy. The workflow management system must support the need to protect employee privacy in compliance with local governmental regulations and company policy.

Analysis Tools

Workflow products provide various tools for analyzing process activity. The following are key capabilities:

Runtime statistics. It must be possible to report statistics on the status of the active system, such as queue lengths, the duration of activity executions, the number of active participants, process durations, and so on.

Variation exception reporting.* Exceptions should be reported for process variables that exceeded defined limits, such as the duration of activity, queue length, or percentage utilization.

Process flow analysis. Analysis tools should be available to analyze process history and report the use and duration of processes and activities, the use and workload of resources, particularly people, and the points at which bottlenecks have occurred.

Process integrity check. A tool should be provided for build-time analysis of a process model to identify logical inconsistencies such as loops or open-ended paths. Such tools can expedite the development of reliable business processes.

Simulation.* It should be possible to use process models to simulate process activity. Such models can be used to explore the impact of alternative processes, the allocation of work, or applications of technology. This requires components to simulate the submission of requests, interaction with external applications, and the assignment and participation of resources.

Standards

The BSD architecture and integration of workflow products should be based on industry standards so that products will be interoperable, they can be replaced by better products in the future, and process designers and users can rely on some degree of consistency in design principles and concepts. In this section we will discuss the following standards:

- Workflow management interoperability
- Resource assignment
- Organization structure
- Unified Modeling Language (UML) workflow process definition
- Loosely coupled process requests

Note that standards continue to evolve and that some of the standards described here are still under consideration. Please see the Web page associated with this book for current information.

Workflow Management Interoperability

The OMG has adopted a specification for interfaces to support interoperability between independently developed workflow products. Figure 7.3 shows the defined interfaces in a UML diagram. The key interfaces are WfProcess, WfActivity, WfAssignment, and WfResource.

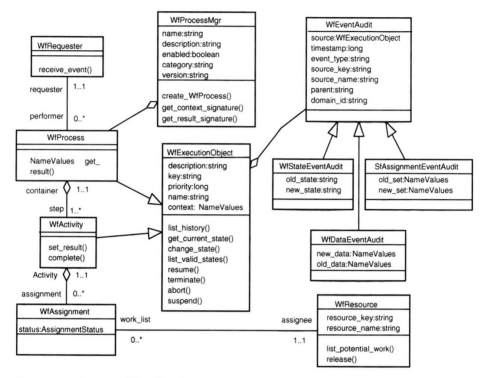

Figure 7.3   OMG workflow interfaces.

These interfaces allow a BSD to have multiple workflow management products that work together. They also facilitate the replacement of a workflow management product in the future. If a selected product does not conform to these specifications, it would be advisable to implement adapters for interfaces used in the integration in order to support interoperability, maintain vendor independence, and prepare for the future adoption of these interfaces.

Resource Assignment

The OMG is developing a specification for interfaces to workflow resource assignment facilities. This specification will provide a standard way to request the assignment of resources so that shared resources could be assigned to processes implemented in different workflow products. This is particularly important for the assignment of people, where each person should have one work list regardless of the source of assignments.

In lieu of the adoption of such a specification, the allocation of resources should be implemented as workflow processes. The interface is then simply a standard process interface with parameters defining the resource requirements. One workflow product can perform resource assignments, while others can perform the business processes. Implementating a resource assignment as a workflow process makes the assignment process visible and more flexible. This implementation can be replaced later by more a sophisticated resource allocation product if appropriate.

Organization Structure

The OMG has adopted a specification for an organization structure facility. Organizational information is important for the assignment of work and the routing of requests for approval. When incorporated in a workflow management product, these specifications will allow an organization structure facility to be purchased as an independent product and be used to support workflow management as well as other enterprise applications. Current products have organization information embedded in their process specifications. This should be separated to be a more consistent and robust representation that is available for other purposes as well.

UML Workflow Process Definition

The OMG is currently developing a UML profile (modeling subset) for the specification of workflow processes. This will enable the independent development of process definition tools and the portability of process definitions between different runtime workflow management products. When workflow processes are specified in UML, they will implicitly be expressible in XML Model Interchange (XMI) language. This will enable the exchange of process models between different tools and workflow execution products.

A standard modeling language for workflow process definition will not have an immediate effect on the application of workflow systems, but in the future it will improve flexibility and probably the quality of process modeling.

Loosely Coupled Process Requests

The Workflow Management Coalition (WfMC) has adopted a specification using XML and Simple Object Access Protocol (SOAP) as the form of messages to be exchanged for interoperability between workflow management products. This specification is based on the OMG/WfMC interoperability specification discussed earlier. The messages (and response messages) are asynchronous, and the XML form facilitates communication through firewalls. This was viewed as a way of extending the reach of workflow integration across the Internet.

However, this level of granularity of interactions is seldom, if ever, necessary between loosely coupled domains. A process request should be expressed as a single message with return of an acknowledgment. The acknowledgment should include a process instance identifier for future reference. A later message should return the process result. The Uniform Resource Locator (URL) of the request may determine the selection of the appropriate process, and a result URL may determine the routing of the result.

Much of the detail of the workflow interoperability specification provides access to the details of process activity. This level of detail should not be accessed between loosely coupled domains. Where remote users are to have access to status information about the process, the request acknowledgment also can include a status query URL. In the long term it would be appropriate to define a standard status request-response format so that status can be determined programmatically.

Interest has been expressed in the development of appropriate standards for a loosely coupled protocol, but there is currently no action underway. A simplified protocol is needed for interfacing to workflow systems using asynchronous messaging. This protocol would provide a consistent mechanism for both EAI and business to business (B2B) interoperability of workflow systems. See the Web page associated with this book for new developments.

Summary

Workflow management is a key element of enterprise integration. It makes business processes visible and flexible and expedites the exchange of information for a more timely response to customers and the resolution of problems. Integrating computer systems is not enough. The integrated enterprise must harmonize the activities of computers and the activities of people. Particularly in global enterprises, workflow is critical to supporting the collaborative efforts of people and providing easy access to applications and information.

Workflow management is also key to rapid process improvement. Analytical tools will assist in the identification of problems and the development of process improvements. The automation of workflow and the integral role it can play in the execution of business processes will facilitate the rapid introduction of process improvements and enforce compliance in order to rapidly transform the operation of the business.

CHAPTER

8

Providing Web-Based User Access

The Web is rapidly becoming the universal medium for user access to business systems. This is true for employees as well as customers and business partners. Web-based access allows users to interact with systems from anywhere as long as they have a computer running a standard Web browser.

Web-based user access brings four important elements:

- Users can have a variety of computing platforms.
- Users need not be members of a defined community.
- Users can access systems from anywhere.
- User access costs are low.

For these reasons, we should expect all systems in the future to provide Web-based user access. Alternatives are less adaptable, restrict user mobility, and are more expensive.

In this chapter we will examine the client and server facilities that bring the user and the application together through Web-based user access. We will examine these complementary roles and their interactions under the following topics:

- Web access environment
- Client facilities

- Web server facilities
- Session management
- Specialized client devices

We will begin by putting Web access into the enterprise context. Next we will discuss the basic client component, the Web browser, and various mechanisms for providing extended client-side functionality. We will then examine the complementary facility, the Web server, which links the user to specific functionality and provides the transformations between user interface and application functionality. These are coordinated beyond a single request-response through session management discussed next. Finally, we will briefly consider the implications of alternative client devices such as personal digital assistants and cell phones.

Web Access Environment

Traditionally, access to business systems has been confined to a small, well-defined group of users in one organization and in one office facility. The new generation of systems has an expanded community of users. Many members of the expanded community are employees from diverse activities of an enterprise who need information or who need to coordinate their activities. For some applications, the community of users extends to business partners and customers. A single business function can no longer dictate the device or software used to access the system, nor can the physical location of the user be predefined. Instead, a user comes equipped with a Web browser as the primary mechanism of access to any authorized system.

Within the enterprise, employees will have access to enterprise systems through internetworking of local-area networks (LANs). Outside the enterprise, customers, business partners, and employees away from the office will access enterprise systems over the public Internet and through enterprise portals. From the application standpoint, the same protocols will be used whether the user is inside or outside the enterprise. The accessibility of systems will be determined only by security constraints.

Most enterprises are in a state of transition to the Internet era. Legacy systems were not designed for Internet access. Some of these legacy systems will continue to exist for many years to come. At the same time, competitive pressures will demand that many legacy systems either be Web-enabled or be replaced by systems that provide Web access. The pace of business has quickened. Email and cell phones have increased the timeliness of communications between humans, but demands for streamlined business processes cannot be met by people acting as intermediaries between systems or by batch file transfers. The availability of Web technology allows people to access many different systems directly, and inputs are not expected to be held for a day until accepted by a batch process. The demand for streamlined response makes Web-based access to business systems a competitive necessity.

Web servers now can provide highly functional user interfaces through browser-based thin clients. The functionality of the Web-based interface has become key to streamlining interactions between humans and systems and thus the streamlining of business systems.

In Chapter 3 we described the enterprise architecture from a number of perspectives. The network model, presented again in Figure 8.1, illustrates the roles of the Web server. A Web server appears in the internal systems domain and in the public Web applications domain. In both these roles, the function of the Web server is essentially the same: to provide Web-based user access and to exchange Web page content and user input with associated business applications. The only difference in these two Web server roles is the level of

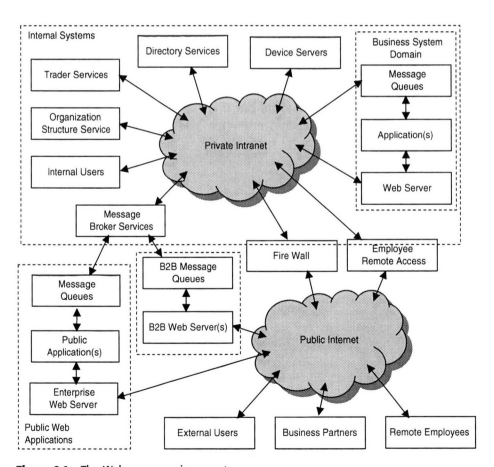

Figure 8.1 The Web server environment.

exposure to the outside world: One provides access from the private intranet, and the other provides access from the public Internet. The business-to-business (B2B) Web server is another Web server role. In this case, the Web server does not communicate with a Web browser but rather with another Web server for communication between systems. This role was discussed as part of the messaging service in Chapter 6. Here we will focus on Web servers that communicate with user clients.

The diagram depicts the network environment of the Web server. Now let's examine the role of the Web server in a typical Web application, as depicted in Figure 8.2.

In most cases, users will send a request to the Web server using a Web browser. The request will be communicated through HyperText Transfer Protocol (HTTP) communication. Depending on the nature of the request, the Web server will determine the identity of the user and may establish a secure mode of communication with the client browser.

The Web server will access the requested resource on the Web server. The resource may provide the response directly, or it may access a database or an application.

There are systems where a client is tightly coupled with an associated business application using synchronous message communication. This makes the client another node in a tightly coupled distributed computing environment. The goal is improved performance, but this extends the functionality of the application into less secure environments, and mechanisms for message exchange and security are more complex. This tight-coupling approach sel-

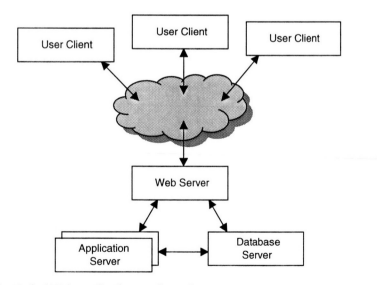

Figure 8.2 Typical Web application configuration.

dom will provide advantage with the increased functionality of current HyperText Markup Language (HTML). In addition, the ability to extend browser functionality with plug-in applications enables the development of highly functional and interactive applications for the client while preserving a loose coupling with the Web server through HTTP.

We will concern ourselves here with clients linked to applications through HTTP. This provides a clear separation of client and server functionality and a clear boundary for separation of security concerns.

Client Facilities

The participation and support provided to users and the performance, security, and functionality of enterprise applications depend on an appropriate balance of functionality and communications between the client system (that is, the user's computer), Web servers, and application servers. In general, the primary factor is the level of functionality and performance required on the client. The goal is to minimize the complexity of the client, avoiding application-specific software and security exposures while meeting the user-interface business requirements. There are a number of factors to be considered:

Provide adequate interactive performance.   If the user is engaged in the composition of a complex work product, this may require local computational support to provide an appropriate level of performance.

Ensure the integrity of system updates.   Client systems likely will be at greater risk of exposure and tampering because they are typically in less secure environments. This is particularly true of portable computers. The design should minimize dependence of the integrity of enterprise systems on client applications.

Minimize the risk of exposure of confidential data.   In order to minimize the risk of exposure of confidential data, it may be appropriate to minimize the amount of data downloaded to client systems. By minimizing client functionality, the data downloaded can be limited to that to be viewed by the user. The data also may be kept in a transient form rather than being stored in client files that could create a risk of later exposure.

Minimize network activity.   While the typical office environment may provide high-speed Internet communications, the system design should not assume that users will always be in the office environment. Remote communications often will be slow and unreliable. In addition, even with high-speed communications, the number of exchanges performed increases the load on servers significantly.

Enable disconnected user activity.   If a user is mobile or communication facilities are unreliable, it is desirable that the user be able to continue to conduct business without always being connected. This may call for periodic download of relevant information and upload of user inputs so that the user normally can operate in stand-alone mode.

These factors and the limits of browser capabilities must be considered for each business function and application—there are no simple formulas. While early Web browsers provided little functionality, current browser technology provides a variety of capabilities.

In the subsections that follow we will examine implementations of different levels of client functionality:

- Static pages
- Forms
- Active content
- Browser plug-ins
- Stand-alone applications

The purpose of this discussion is to provide an understanding of the nature and scope of client-side functionality, not to provide a tutorial on Web page development. The design of Web pages should begin with the simplest form (that is, static content) and progress to more sophisticated forms as required by the application. We will focus here on facilities that are supported by the leading Web browsers and Web servers. There are many other sources of information and Web authoring tools for Web page development.

The design of the client Web pages will determine the requirements of the server to generate the Web page and accept input. Web server components that can generate pages or accept inputs from them will be discussed later.

Static Pages

The simplest form of user interface is a textual or graphic display. A user specifies a particular Uniform Resource Locator (URL) to the Web browser, the browser requests the document from the Web server, and the browser formats the display as specified within the HTML document returned.

For example, a retail customer might want to access specifications on a product using a specified URL:

```
http ://www.ExampleRetailer.com/products/specs/
lawnmower/turbo2.htm
```

Based on this URL, the browser will submit a request to the www .ExampleRetailer.com server:

```
GET /products/specs/lawnmower/turbo2.htm HTTP/1.0
User-agent: Mosaic for X Windows/2.4
Host: www.ExampleRetailer.com
Accept: text/plain
Accept: text/html
Accept: image/*
```

The get request identifies the document requested, the browser, and the data types that are acceptable in the response. The HTTP daemon on the server will receive this request, parse it, and determine the type of response required and the availability of the document. Assuming that the document is available, the server will then send an initial response such as the following:

```
HTTP/1.0 200 document follows
Server: NCSA/1.4
Date: Fri, 25 Nov 2000 14:00:00 GMT
Content-type: text/html
Content-length: 5735
Last-modified: Tue, 17 Apr 1999 11:25:33 GMT
```

The status code of 200 in the first line of the response indicates a normal response. The server will then send the content of the `turbo2.htm` file.

There are few Web pages that are simply text-only documents. More often, a Web page is composed of a number of components including both text and graphics. The composite Web page consists of a primary document retrieved from the specified URL but with embedded references to other URLs for related components such as images and sound clips. In addition, some Web servers will recognize server-side include commands that will cause data from another Web server resource to be embedded in the HTML document at the server.

Some of the embedded URLs are links to other Web pages for the user to select; others are inline images or other components to be incorporated into the display. When the browser encounters an inline component, it issues another request to the server to retrieve the component. Consequently, one initial request may result in a number of requests, all occurring within the same network connection, in order to complete the requested display.

In many cases, an enterprise will define a common format for its Web pages that includes certain common selections and graphics. These elements may be incorporated in many enterprise Web pages using inline references. This not only achieves consistency in the Web pages, but the browser also will recognize the repeated components and retrieve them from its cache rather than repeatedly requesting the same elements from the remote server. This can improve performance significantly.

HTML defines a fixed set of element types for the specification of Web pages. For static Web pages, these include elements that define the document structure, such as head, body, and paragraphs, elements to define layout and appearance, such as headings, fonts, frames, lists, and tables, and links to other Web pages.

Cascading Style Sheets (CSS), an extension to HTML, provides a separation of formatting information from content. The basic concept of a markup language is to define the content of elements of a document so that it can be displayed appropriately in different formats. Thus, HTML defines headings, paragraphs, frames, tables, and so on so that a browser can format these elements to fit in a window. At the same time, various formatting features, such as relative positioning, fonts, and colors, are needed as formatting instructions. A number of formatting instructions have been included in the language to be embedded in the specification of individual elements. CSS formatting specifications also can be included *inline* in elements, but a style sheet can be *embedded* between the header and body to apply to the entire body of the document. Alternatively, a *linked* style sheet can be specified in the header of the document, incorporating a style sheet that may be shared by many documents.

CSS allows inline, embedded, and linked style sheets to be used together. The linked style sheet provides a shared foundation. The embedded style sheet will extend the style specifications and override the linked style sheet when there is a conflict. The inline style specifications will further specialize the styles for specific elements.

Much of the information accessed on the Internet is in the form of static Web pages. Static Web pages most likely will provide the framework for access to enterprise information, and static Web pages can be used to model Web services for consideration of page design, navigation, and content organization. However, static Web pages are not limited to fixed content. Many static Web pages will be generated dynamically on the server to reflect current information. We will examine the generation of Web pages later when we discuss Web server functionality.

Forms

HTML not only provides for display of information, but it also provides for the display of forms to accept user input. User input may be used to retrieve selected data from a database, to perform certain computations, or to create or update enterprise records. The browser does not know how the data will be used; it only provides the mechanism by which data elements can be entered and communicated to the server.

The request for a form looks the same as any other Web page request. The difference is in the document returned. Suppose, for example, that the Turbo2 lawnmower in our customer request for specifications earlier actually came in several models. The initial response might be a form from which the customer could select a particular model. The form could provide an input box for the model number, or it might provide a list of available models with a radio button selection for the model of interest.

HTML for a form with radio buttons for selection of a desired model is shown in the following code:

```
<H1>Request model number for product of interest.</H1>
<FORM
action=http://www.ExampleRetailer.com/cgibin/products/specs
method=post>
<P>
<INPUT TYPE="radio" NAME="model" VALUE=LM250>
Push mulcher
< INPUT TYPE="radio" NAME="model" VALUE=LM251>
Push rear bagger
< INPUT TYPE="radio" NAME="model" VALUE=LM252>
Rear wheel drive
<INPUT TYPE="submit">
</P>
</FORM>
```

The user enters information into the form, in this case by selecting a radio button, and clicks on the submit button. The browser will then submit the results based on the method specification. A *get* method, the alternative to *post* shown previously, will attach the name values as an extension to the URL. While this method is common, it is officially deprecated and should be phased out. The post method causes the values to be attached to a post request as an HTML body.

Note that the input from a form is an independent request to the server. When an HTTP request is satisfied, such as when the form is displayed, the network connection is terminated. The input from the form establishes a new connection with the same or possibly a different server. The content of the request, including the variables, would be interpreted appropriately if entered directly without first obtaining the form. This has implications to the design of interactive applications where an application requires a series of related user actions or requests.

Form input cannot be processed by a static Web server resource. The URL for submission of the form data must invoke logic to process the input data. This processing logic will be invoked as a Common Gateway Interface (CGI) script. We will discuss the processing of input later in the section on Web server facilities.

Active Content

Up to this point our discussion has focused on HTML pages with static content—actions are taken by the browser based on the document format specifications and element attributes. In this section we will examine two ways that the Web page can include executable code: JavaScript and applets. These are not the only ways available, but they are supported by the popular browsers, are used commonly, and are safe; that is, the user is protected from code that might corrupt the client platform.

The benefit of active content is that more application logic can be performed on the client, potentially reducing network activity and providing more effective interaction with the user.

JavaScript

JavaScript is a language for embedding executable code directly in an HTML document. It is not a dialect of Java but is a language interpreted by the browser. Code at the document level is used for initialization operations and to define functions invoked from elsewhere in the document. Within individual elements, event attributes specify the functions to be invoked when events occur for the associated elements. Functions can invoke subroutines to support more structured code.

The following code illustrates JavaScript embedded in an HTML document. Note that the script appears between <SCRIPT> and </SCRIPT> in the document header. The language attribute identifies this as JavaScript. Within the script element, the code is wrapped in an HTML comment wrapper. This makes the script invisible to browsers that do not understand JavaScript. The function of this example is to ask for the user's name and incorporate it in the heading when the page is loaded. Then, when the user selects one of the models, the JavaScript causes the model to be displayed as the selection. This example will be discussed in more detail later.

```
<HTML>
<HEAD>
<TITLE> Example JavaScript</TITLE>
<SCRIPT LANGUAGE="JavaScript">
<!-- comment wrapper
Name=prompt("Enter your name ","Name");
document.write
("<H1>Model selection for "+ Name + "</H1>");
function selected(model){
selection.value=model
}
// end of comment wrapper -->
</SCRIPT>
</HEAD>
<BODY>
<FORM action=
http://www.ExampleRetailer.com/cgibin/products/specs
method=post>
<P>
```

```
You have selected
<INPUT TYPE=text NAME="selection" value="">
Select one of the following models: <BR>
<INPUT TYPE="radio" NAME="model" VALUE=LM250
onClick="selected("LM250")"> Push mulcher
< INPUT TYPE="radio" NAME="model" VALUE=LM251
onClick="selected("LM251")"> Push rear bagger
< INPUT TYPE="radio" NAME="model" VALUE=LM252
onClick="selected("LM252")"> Rear wheel drive
<INPUT TYPE="submit">
</P>
</FORM>
```

There are a number of key capabilities enabled by JavaScript that allow much more functionality to be implemented on the client without access to the Web server. These capabilities are discussed briefly in the subsections that follow.

Dialog Boxes

JavaScript can be used to present a dialog box and accept input from the user. In the preceding example, the *prompt* function causes a dialog box to be presented to request the user's name. Dialog boxes are also very useful for alerting the user.

Data Entry Validation

JavaScript can be used to validate the values entered in a form. In the preceding example, only the radio button selections are available. However, if the user were asked to enter a model number in a single form field, the JavaScript function could be invoked to determine if the value were a valid model number and alert the user if the model number were incorrect.

Computations

JavaScript can perform a variety of mathematical computations such as basic arithmetic and trigonometric functions. JavaScript can be used, for example, to implement a browser-based calculator, applying computations to a result field based on button selections.

Actions on Events

Basic JavaScript actions are driven by events specified in individual elements. In the preceding example, each of the input radio buttons specifies that on the *onclick* event, the *selection* function should be invoked. Dynamic HTML (version 4.0) defines 18 intrinsic events that can be used to execute JavaScript code:

onload	onmousemove	onsubmit	onmousedown	onkeypress
onmoouseover	onkeyup	ondblclick	onblue	onchange
onkeydown	onclick	onfocus	onselect	
onunload	onmouseout	onreset	onmouseup	

As in the preceding example, the event action is specified in an associated element. In the example, the *onclick* event on the radio button element invokes the *selection* function with the associated model as a parameter. Events are available on all elements, but not all events are applicable to all elements; for example, the *onload* and *onunload* events only apply to the document body as a whole.

Dynamic Content Changes

JavaScript code can be used to dynamically change the document content. In the preceding example, the header is created dynamically to include the user's name, and the selected button value is entered in the selection field when the user selects a radio button. Much more extensive changes are possible, including changes to element attributes, such as font and color.

Access to Browser Characteristics

JavaScript code can access browser characteristics and use the information to tailor the page display. For example, the code can determine if the browser is Netscape Navigator or Internet Explorer.

Update of Browser Properties

JavaScript code can access browser attributes and modify them. For example, overriding the default colors will allow the browser color scheme to be changed.

Cookies

Cookies are records stored by the browser that contain data associated with a particular Web page or Web server interaction. Cookies will be discussed later as a device for managing user sessions. JavaScript code can access cookie data elements and assign values to them. This can enable further delegation of functionality from the server to the client.

Applets

Applets are Java programs that run in a Java virtual machine (JVM) under the control of a Web browser. From a browser perspective, an applet is equivalent to a graphic file. An applet file is downloaded in a similar manner, but instead of interpreting the file to render an image, the file is interpreted by the JVM.

The browser JVM is different from a JVM that executes normal Java application code. The browser JVM is designed to restrict the applet operations so that the applet cannot intentionally or otherwise damage the host environment. Consequently, applets cannot access client files or perform other input-output operations except operations on the browser display.

The applet is assigned a specific display frame area within the browser, the same as a graphic file. In this frame, the applet may manage the display to provide animation or interact with the user directly.

Applets provide a very powerful and portable programming facility for Web clients. Sophisticated logic can be incorporated in a Web page and executed on the client. The client is protected from destructive applets by the JVM. The Java code is platform- and browser-independent (it is supported by the popular browsers). At the same time, applets can be very large. The downloaded code must include supporting user-interface code because the applet must implement its own user interface within its frame.

Nevertheless, the work of HTML and applets can be integrated. JavaScript can invoke Java applet methods, and Java in applets can invoke JavaScript functions and access HTML object attributes. This allows applet code to extend the functionality of JavaScript.

Applets were very popular initially. However, since an applet must include a substantial Java environment to support its functionality, it may be very large to download. With the increased functionality of HTML and JavaScript, applets may have only limited use.

Browser Plug-Ins

Another approach to providing client functionality is through the execution of plug-ins. A *plug-in* is a program that is executed by a browser when an applicable data type is received. Plug-ins must be developed for each computing environment in which they will execute.

When the browser receives data of a type that it does not handle, it will look for a plug-in to handle the type and execute it. Plug-ins function in various modes. A plug-in can function like an independent application with its own window. Alternatively, a plug-in can display in a drawable area of the browser window. The browser can provide input data to the plug-in via a file or through other mechanisms. The plug-in can send HTTP requests or post messages and receive responses, it can perform File Transfer Protocol (FTP) requests to transfer files, and it can send mail. Because a plug-in executes as a client application, it can perform client operations that would be prohibited for an applet. The plug-in also can interact with applets or JavaScripts in the Web page that invoked it through Java application programming interfaces (APIs).

The selection of which plug-in to invoke is based on the name suffix of the data received by the browser. This is a Multipurpose Internet Mail Extensions (MIME) data type that should be registered with the Internet Engineering Task Force (IETF) to avoid conflicts.

A plug-in can be a very powerful approach to providing client functionality:

- Interactive performance should be very good because functions can be performed locally, and the application can be written in C or C++.

- The application functionality is not hampered by security constraints that limit access to client platform facilities.

- The plug-in also can implement sophisticated graphic techniques that HTML could not support or for which it would not provide acceptable performance.

- The user may execute the plug-in offline.

At the same time, there are significant drawbacks:

- The plug-in could perform risky operations or carry a virus that would corrupt the client platform.

- A different version of the plug-in must be developed for each possible user platform.

- An imposter plug-in could be installed on a client to corrupt the intended client functionality.

Stand-Alone Applications

Enterprise solutions should exploit the power and flexibility of personal computers and not always incorporate them as alternatives to dumb terminals. In appropriate circumstances, stand-alone applications should be implemented on the client:

- Network access may not be available always. It may be important to enable the user to move about freely and work in a variety of environments.

- The user simply may be capturing data or developing a work product that does not involve continuous access or interaction with shared information or services.

- The user may be doing analytical or creative work that can best be supported with a personal computer application operating independently.

- Some graphics or application inputs may be large and stable so that they need only be downloaded occasionally, allowing work to be done without network overhead.

- Reliance on a network may increase the risk of lost time and repeated work due to network failures.

However, these stand-alone applications should not duplicate browser functionality. This would be a major development and maintenance burden. A standard Web browser should continue to be the link to the enterprise as well as to other relevant Web sites for interactive activities.

These applications are *loosely coupled.* They receive input that does not require immediate action, and they produce output that can be processed when the recipient is ready. We have discussed the concept of loose coupling of enterprise applications and business system domains (BSDs) using asynchronous messaging. The same basic concepts apply here except that the participant is an application on a user workstation with a browser as the primary communication interface.

The most common form of loose coupling for workstation applications is through file transfers, typically FTP. While this is very straightforward, it is also unreliable, particularly if hundreds of salespeople are periodically submitting sales orders for processing.

E-mail is another alternative that provides greater reliability. Data can be formatted as e-mail messages or as attachments. This provides improved reliability, and the data messages will be held in the recipient's mailbox until they can be processed, both for the user and for the associated business application. However, users receive many e-mail messages, and these data messages could be overlooked. There is also potential for *spoofing*; an intruder could send a message pretending to be the business application or the user. Consequently, additional precautions would be needed to authenticate the sources of messages, and for some applications, messages may need to be signed and encrypted for validation and privacy.

Communication from workstations to applications should be through some form of asynchronous messaging. However, it would not be desirable to connect workstations directly to the message broker services discussed in Chapter 6. As we will see in Chapter 9, standards have been defined for message service handlers (MSHs) to communicate messages between business partners using HTTP. The MSH protocol can ensure once-and-only-once delivery of messages. This capability should be linked directly to the message broker services within the enterprise. This is an appropriate mode of communication for data being submitted by users for application processing. Delivery is assured, and messages are accepted by an application from a queue in the same manner as they are received from other loosely coupled systems. The MSH protocol comprehends the communication of signed and encrypted messages for security and accountability. However, this is less appropriate for data to be transferred to user workstations. Users need more control over the acceptance of work.

The preferred mode for transfer of data to workstations is through workflow management. Workflow management was discussed in detail in Chapter 7. A user will access a work list from the browser. Work to be done offline should be presented as an item in the work list. When the user selects the item, the associated data should be transferred to his or her workstation.

The simplest way to accomplish this transfer at this time is still FTP. In this transfer, the user is in control and will ensure that the file is received once and only once. The file transfer is just another browser action, and the FTP request can be just another link on the display.

Web Server Facilities

Web access is achieved through a complementary relationship between each client and the Web server. In general, the Web server responds to the HTTP requests. A request is received with a specified URL, possibly with parameters, and an HTML response is returned.

The primary task of the Web server is to invoke a resource specified in the request URL. The Web server will first determine if the user is authorized to access the specified resource; we will not examine authentication and authorization here because it is covered in depth in Chapter 11. If the user is authorized, then the data type designated by the resource-name suffix determines the specific action of the server.

In many cases the resource is simply retrieved and communicated back to the requester. These are called *static Web pages.* Not all requests are so simple. In many cases the content of the response is not predetermined. This simply might be a matter of taking input parameters, such as fields from a form, and computing a result to be displayed back to the user. Sometimes the response must incorporate information that changes over time, must be retrieved from a database, or must be computed by an application. Other requests may provide input to update a database or application. These active server pages are not simply retrieved but rather are executed. They can accept parameters, and they create HTML pages dynamically.

Generically, these active server pages are often called *CGI scripts.* Conceptually, they provide a gateway to database managers and applications. The specific interface protocol depends on the particular Web server implementation, but the basic mechanism is the same for a variety of Web servers. A number of languages are used to implement CGI scripts. The language must be supported by the Web server platform and must be able to comply with the Web server's CGI protocol to receive inputs and produce the HTML response.

Figure 8.3 depicts the three types of Web server components we will examine in the subsections that follow:

- Static HTML and objects
- Servlets
- Java server pages (JSPs)

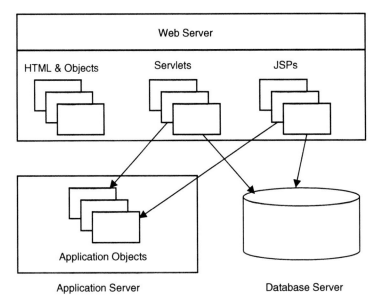

Figure 8.3 Web application components.

Servlets and JSPs provide computed page content. We focus on servlets and JSPs because they provide a good representation of the technology, because they are based on specifications developed with participation from a number of vendors, and because Web servers from a number of different vendors, as well as the Apache open-source Web server, support them. Specifications for Java servlets and JSPs were developed by the Java Community Process (JCP) under the leadership of Sun Microsystems. While the JCP is not an open standards forum, it does involve a number of different vendors, and the specifications have gained widespread acceptance.

Static Resources

A URL for a static resource identifies the resource and the directory in which it is located on the Web server. The resource type suffix determines the Web server treatment of the file. Static resources are files that are retrieved by the Web server and transmitted to the requesting client.

HTML

In general, the server retrieves an HTML file and sends it to the client without modification. The HTML file may contain hyperlink references and references to other objects to be included in the browser display. A hyperlink will become a new request if the user selects it. The browser acts on embedded object references to complete the display. Each embedded object reference becomes another server request by the browser.

Embedded Objects

Embedded objects include a variety of different data types, such as graphics, audio clips, and applets. The data type of an object is specified by the resource name suffix in the URL. The MIME data type determines how the data are processed by the browser. A graphic will be rendered in the display. An audio clip will be converted to speaker output. An applet will be interpreted by a JVM.

Plug-In Data

A browser does not process all data types. When the browser encounters a data type that it does not process, it will look for the data type in a plug-in application table. If the data type is associated with an application, the browser can invoke the application and pass it the file. The user may be given the opportunity to determine if the file is to be processed or saved.

Java Servlets

A Java servlet is a Java component that executes in a servlet container. The servlet container provides various interfaces and services to simplify the component implementation and make it portable to different server implementations.

Servlet Container

Each Java servlet is derived from the GenericServlet class, and most are derived from the more specialized HttpServlet class. These provide basic methods for processing various types of input requests. The servlet class is loaded into a servlet container that manages its execution. A container may create a number of instances of a servlet class and execute them concurrently. The container manages their initialization, execution, and termination.

The container also provides other objects to support the servlet. For example, ServletRequest and ServletResponse objects provide methods for the servlet to obtain input and produce output. An HttpSession object provides information about the session if the servlet is executing as part of a session.

When a servlet instance is created, the container initializes it by invoking its init method and passing a ServletConfig object. The ServletConfig object provides access to configuration parameters as well as a `ServletContext` object. The `ServletContext` object represents the application of which the servlet is a part and defines application parameters.

When a client request is received, the servlet container will invoke the service method on an instance of the servlet class, passing references to the associated `ServletRequest` and `ServletResponse` objects. The servlet obtains the input parameters, if any, from the `ServletRequest` object and sends its output to the `ServletResponse` object.

A servlet may be instantiated to handle a request and then be destroyed, but more often the servlet handles multiple requests, thus avoiding the need for repeated initializations. The servlet may restrict execution to one request at a time by implementing the `SingleThreadModel` interface. This does not prevent the container from creating multiple, concurrently executing instances of the servlet class. However, it is possible to restrict processing to a single instance of the servlet, resulting in true, single-threaded operation.

Content Creation

The content generated by a servlet simply may be a computation using inputs from the client. However, additional data usually are incorporated from other sources.

A servlet may create a response using other servlets. It can delegate to another servlet using the `RequestDispatcher` interface. The servlet can generate a portion of the response, invoke another servlet to produce the next segment of the response, and then produce the remainder of the response. The `RequestDispatcher` also can be used to forward a request without return so that the complete response is handled by a different servlet. Thus, a servlet can function as a dispatcher by redirecting requests based on input parameters. This capability facilitates the structuring of applications and the sharing of common elements among different Web services.

The servlet specification focuses on the behavior of a servlet as a Web component that receives requests and produces responses. A servlet may access files on the Web server to retrieve or store application data, but these would be rather limited applications. The specification does not define servlet interfaces to a database or supporting enterprise application. In order for a servlet to be portable, these interfaces also must be standard.

The expectation is that servlets will use Java Database Connectivity (JDBC) to interface to databases and the Remote Messaging Interface (RMI) to invoke methods on application objects on an application server. In order to locate remote services and application objects, servlets should use the Java Naming and Directory Interface (JNDI). Where it is necessary to send or receive asynchronous messages, Java Messaging Service (JMS) should be used. These are standard elements of the Java Platform 2 Enterprise Edition

(J2EE) environment that defines a broader architecture for Web-based enterprise applications. J2EE is discussed in greater detail in Chapter 10.

Benefits

Java servlets provide a number of important advantages over CGI scripts:

- Servlets and their containers are not loaded for each request, thus eliminating initialization overhead.
- Servlets are portable to different platforms that implement the Java servlet specification, allowing flexibility in the selection of platforms and migration to new platform technology.
- Servlet containers and the associated environment provide services that simplify programming and improve quality. For example, the container provides for session management, discussed later in this chapter.

At the same time, the Java servlet specification allows for considerable flexibility in implementation of the Java servlet container. Not all implementations will provide the same capabilities. For example, while the specification allows the same Java servlet to have instances executing on multiple hosts, not all implementations are required to support this. The goal of the specification is to enable different platforms to execute the same servlets, not to standardize the Web server functionality.

Java Server Pages (JSPs)

A JSP is a special form of servlet. The programming model is oriented to prescribing a page layout with computations to insert content at appropriate points in the page. This facilitates the separation of layout design from the creation of content.

The basic structure of the code for a JSP is a text document, typically HTML, with Java code interspersed. As each statement of the JSP is evaluated, the HTML encountered is placed directly in the output buffer, and the Java code is executed to compute content values, control the flow of execution, and produce additional output to the buffer.

The container manages the JSP code. The container functions much the same as a servlet container. It manages the JSP instance life cycle and buffers the input and output. In the following subsections paragraphs we will discuss:

- The JSP container
- The JSP content
- Associated objects
- Output composition

- Tag libraries
- JSP benefits

JSP Container

The JSP container provides an environment for execution of JSPs. At run time, a JSP implementation class with the interface `javax.servlet.Servlet` defines the JSP. The container loads a specified JSP implementation class (that implements a specific JSP) and creates an instance of it to process a request and produce a response. The container invokes the `jspservice` method to execute the JSP. The `jspservice` method is the translated version of the JSP code.

A new JSP instance may be created to handle each request, but more often an instance will be used to handle multiple requests. These may be handled concurrently, or they may be constrained to processing one request at a time.

The container eventually will destroy the instance, providing for completion of any active requests and allowing the JSP to perform any necessary completion processing. A JSP container is required to support HTTP but can support other protocols. The JSP model is well suited to processing and generating Extensible Markup Language (XML) documents.

JSP Content

There are four types of expression within a JSP specification:

- Template fragments
- Directives
- Actions
- Scripting elements

Semantically, the container processes these expressions sequentially to produce the output page. Each of these expressions contributes to the output in different ways. We will discuss each of them briefly.

Template Fragments

A JSP simply could be a static HTML Web page. As the page code is evaluated, that which is not explicitly a directive, an action, or a scripting language is assumed to be static content, and it is sent directly to the output buffer. This static content is the page template.

The template text may be interrupted by other expressions that produce other content that is placed in the buffer. In some cases, the active expressions may cause some static content to be skipped, depending on the request, or it may insert data retrieved from a database.

The template provides a basic framework for the JSP. Consequently, it may be created initially using a static page design tool. Inserting other JSP expressions extends the page document to include computed content.

Directives

A directive is a message to the container. It sets the mode of execution. For example, it may set page attributes such as buffer size or multithreading capability, and it may specify the URL of an associated tag library (discussed in the following sections).

Action Instances

Action instances are expressions in the document syntax that are recognized as invoking functionality. The syntax of an action is that of an XML element with start and end tags and a body. The element name is the name of the function to be performed, and attributes of the element become parameters of the function. Inserting a subordinate action within the body of another action element is known as *nesting*, just as subordinate elements can be nested within an XML element.

Action attribute values can be generated by scriptlets, fragments of scripting language code discussed in the following section, as long as the value is not required at translation time—scripting elements are only evaluated at run time.

Standard actions are defined for the JSP environment and are always available. Custom actions can be defined in a *tag library* (that is, an action definition library).

Scripting Elements

Scripting elements are fragments of executable code. Typically, the code is Java language, but the JSP specification allows for JSP containers to handle other scripting languages. There are three types of scripting elements:

- Declarations
- Expressions
- Scriptlets

Declarations are used to declare variables and methods. Both may be referenced anywhere in the rest of the page. Declarations have delimiters of the following form:

```
<%! . . . %>
```

An expression is a complete, executable statement in the scripting language. It may produce output to the buffer, it may perform computations, it may operate on objects, it may retrieve values or update a database, and so on. The expression is evaluated when it is encountered as the JSP code is processed.

A scriptlet is an expression fragment. Scriptlets may be inserted between fragments of the page template. The fragments of the page template will be inserted in the output buffer as they are encountered during evaluation of the scriptlets. Together, a sequence of scriptlets must produce a valid scripting language expression.

The scriptlet logic may affect what template fragments are encountered and therefore which are transferred to the output buffer. For example, scriptlets may make up segments of a conditional expression. Template fragments may be omitted from the output if they are embedded in the action segment of a condition that is not true.

The scripting language provides basic computational capabilities. Common computations can be defined in declarations, but they can only be shared within the scope of a single JSP. Actions, on the other hand, can be defined in a tag library and shared among many JSPs.

Objects

The JSP code can operate on objects as a mechanism of sharing information and performing computations. The container environment provides a number of implicit objects that define the container environment. For example, the `request` and `response` objects provide access to the request data and response variables, respectively, and a `session` object provides access to session information; sessions are discussed in greater detail later in this chapter.

A JSP also can create other objects. These objects are declared such that they are accessible within a certain scope:

Page. Accessible only within the page where created. Stored in the `pageContext` object.

Request. Accessible by pages processing the same request. Stored in the `request` object.

Session. Accessible by pages executing in the same session. Not legal if the page is not session-aware. Stored in the `session` object.

Application. Accessible from pages executing in the same application. Stored in the `application` object.

Objects are referenced through variables. The same objects may be accessed by both actions and scriptlets.

Output Composition

The JSP output is composed by the accumulation of output in the buffer. The output may be the result of execution of a single JSP, but it also may be a composite.

A JSP may include another JSP, invoking it at a specified point in the creation of the output. The output may then consist of content produced by the initial JSP, content produced by the included JSP, followed by the remaining content produced by the initial JSP.

A JSP also may forward a request to another JSP. It may forward the request before producing any output, or it could produce some output and then forward the request. However, if it produces output before forwarding the request, it must ensure that none of the output has been transmitted; HTTP will not allow the output to come from two different URLs.

These capabilities facilitate the structuring of Web applications so that elements of a Web page can be produced by shared JSPs.

Tag Libraries

Tag libraries were mentioned earlier. They provide for the sharing of actions (that is, functional elements) among multiple JSPs. The format of tag libraries and actions is defined to be independent of the scripting language. Consequently, the same components could be shared by JSPs implemented in different languages and environments.

Since a tag handler evaluates actions at run time, changes to a tag library may be installed without retranslating the JSPs that use it. This provides implementation flexibility.

The tag library also can be used to declare additional objects. The implicit objects will be instantiated when the library is invoked at the start of execution of a JSP.

Benefits

JSPs provide three key benefits in addition to those provided by servlets:

- The form of the JSP as a template with embedded computations and actions defined in a tag library provides a useful separation of layout from content computation that facilitates page development and flexibility.

- The tag library and ability to include or forward requests to other JSPs provide a sharing of component capability that contributes to consistency and productivity in the development of Web pages.

- The JSP specification defines a transformation of JSP code to and from an XML format. This facilitates the transport of JSPs to different tools and environments, enabling changes in technology without redevelopment of the JSPs.

Session Management

The HTTP is a stateless protocol. This means that each request stands on its own when a Web server receives it. The server does not retain information from the preceding request of the same user.

This eliminates problems with a user terminating a conversation in the middle and leaving the server waiting for the next input. However, it also complicates both the coordination of user actions and security of information to be carried from one request to the next. Such continuity between requests is described as a *session,* that is, the series of requests that accomplish some more complete objective or task.

Three alternative mechanisms are used to implement Web sessions:

- URL variables
- Cookies
- Secure Socket Layer (SSL) protocol

The Java Web server environment discussed earlier supports all three of these approaches. We will discuss each of these briefly.

URL Variables

HTTP provides for communication of variable values with a request. Variables were designed originally to communicate the values of form fields. However, they also can be used for other purposes.

For session management, a variable can be used to identify a session. When a page is communicated to the client, a session key can be embedded within it. When the next request is transmitted, it can carry the session key as a variable. When the server receives the request, it can then associate the request with the existing session using the session key value. The difficulty with this is that it is not secure. The session key is exposed to intruders.

Cookies

A cookie is a packet of information that is communicated between a client and server. The client retains the cookie until the next time it sends a request to the same URL. The cookie, like the URL variable, can be used to communicate session information. The cookie has the advantage that the information is not lost when the client visits another Web page. However, like the URL variable, the cookie is not secure.

Secure Socket Layer (SSL) Protocol

The SSL protocol is designed to manage a secure session. Early in the protocol handshake, a session is established, and a session key is defined for encryption of communications for the duration of the session. The session is broken as soon as the client directs a request to a different server.

SSL provides a secure session, but the protocol introduces considerable overhead, so it generally is not used unless a secure session is required.

Specialized Client Devices

Hand-held devices, such as cell phones and personal digital assistants (PDAs), are becoming popular for remote user access to systems. These devices place restrictions on the types of displays and inputs they will support. While a PDA may support a fairly sophisticated application, it will have significant display constraints. A cell phone, on the other hand, will have even tighter display constraints and limited functionality. The result is that Web pages must be tailored to the capabilities of the client device.

Currently, for static resources, it is necessary for the devices having different constraints to reference different URLs to obtain the same information in appropriate formats. This result is a duplication of effort for each different type of device that may be used. It creates hassle and confusion because the user cannot use the same URL on both his or her personal computer and cell phone.

Servlets, on the other hand, can be designed to generate different display layouts for different devices. This provides a single URL for access but still requires formatting for each device.

This technology is still in the early stages. It is likely that Web authoring tools and specialized Web server facilities will assist in minimizing the impact of these differences.

Summary

This chapter has described the Web-based facilities that will satisfy the user-interface needs of most applications. The basic architecture depends on a clear separation of roles between the client, the Web server, and the application:

Client. The primary role of the client is to render the display and capture input. If at all possible the client should rely only on a common browser. This preserves the greatest flexibility and platform independence. It also minimizes security risks because clients are often in insecure environments. Browser functionality can be extended with applets, plug-ins, and on rare occasions stand-alone applications. In any case, client communication with the Web server always should go through the browser.

Web server. The Web server is the primary control point for authentication and authorization. The Web server determines the format of the Web pages and guides interactions with the user. It communicates input to the application and incorporates content from the application into the Web page format. Where content is static, requires simple computations, or involves straightforward database retrieval and update, the Web server may perform these function directly, avoiding unnecessary complexity and network activity.

Application server. The application is responsible for accepting updates and providing content to be incorporated into the Web pages. Exchanges with the Web server should minimize network activity between the Web server and the application server. XML is a flexible format for this purpose and is discussed in detail in Chapter 9. Where user inputs involve a series of related actions, the application may participate in a session established by the Web server. The architecture of the application server is described in Chapter 10.

CHAPTER 9

Integrating with XML

The Extensible Markup Language (XML) is rapidly becoming the lingua franca of information systems. It is enabling communication between enterprise applications and between enterprises, and it is becoming the language of Web content. It also will become the preferred form for both business-to-business (B2B) and internal documents with legal effect.

XML is a syntax for textual expression of data structures. XML structures are fundamentally hierarchical in form and include tags that can be descriptive names of the data structures and primitive elements. The following is a simple example of an XML document:

```
<?xml version="1.0" encoding="utf-8" ?>
<Orders>
 <Order orderID="12345">
   <Customer customerID="8765"/>
   <OrderItems>
    <Item>
      <Product productNo="2234455"/>
      <Description>
       100-watt speaker, Mahogany case
      </Description>
```

```
        <Quantity> 2 </Quantity>
        <UnitPrice> 235.95 </UnitPrice>
      </Item>
      <Item>
        <Product productNo="23452345"/>
        <Description>
         CD Player, Mahogany case
        </Description>
        <Quantity> 1 </Quantity>
        <UnitPrice> 167.95 </UnitPrice>
      </Item>
    </OrderItems>
  </Order>
</Orders>
```

This document expresses a collection of orders containing one order. It is comprised of a number of elements, each with a tag name such as Order, Customer, OrderItems, and so on. Most tags are in pairs, defining the beginning and ending of each element, but some empty elements have only one tag such as Customer where the single tag is terminated with a slash (/). While an empty tag does not have an associated value, it nevertheless may have attributes. Some elements (Order, Customer, and Product) have attribute-value pairs associated with the initial tag such as the orderID="12345". Customer is an empty tag, but it does have an attribute value. Some elements, such as Description, have values expressed between their starting and ending tags, that is, between <Description> and </Description>. Element values also can consist of other elements, such as the elements between the beginning and ending tags of Order.

We will not be examining the details of XML syntax here because there are other books and formal specifications to address that need (see the References at the end of this book and on the associated Web page). We are concerned with the application of XML to enterprise systems, particularly its role in integration. We will examine the following topics:

- Benefits of XML

- XML extended technology

- XML impact on architecture

We will begin with a general discussion of the nature of XML and the reasons for its widespread and rapid acceptance. Next we will examine a number of technologies associated with XML that extend the basic capabilities. We will then describe how XML fits into the enterprise integration architecture.

Benefits of XML

XML is a relatively recent arrival on the information systems scene. The parent technology, Standard Generalized Markup Language (SGML), was developed many years ago and was the basis for HyperText Markup Language (HTML), the language of Web pages. XML became a World Wide Web Consortium (W3C) Recommendation (an accepted standard) in 1998. Since then, it has taken the world by storm.

A number of key characteristics of XML have moved it into the forefront:

- Nonproprietary
- Platform-independent
- HyperText Transport Protocol (HTTP)-compatible
- International
- Extensible
- Self-defining
- Common tools
- Transformation

Let's examine each of these briefly.

Nonproprietary

XML is a W3C specification. This means that any changes to the specification must go through a formal proposal and approval process that cannot be controlled by a single vendor. It also means that the specification can be applied without paying any license fees.

There are complementary specifications to XML that are proprietary. Limited consortia or individual vendors developed these complementary specifications to enable certain extended capabilities and applications. At the same time, there has been recognition of the need for industry standards, and these proprietary specifications are, in general, being replaced by W3C specifications.

Platform-Independent

XML is textual and does not contain any expressions that are specific to any platform. This means that an XML document is the same thing regardless of the platform that processes it.

When combined with Java, which can execute on most platforms, XML can be processed on different platforms with the same tools and applications written in Java. This is particularly important for integration of diverse applications and electronic commerce exchanges where the sender and receiver are often on different platforms.

HyperText Transport Protocol (HTTP)-Compatible

HTTP compatibility is a major benefit. XML can go anywhere HTML can go; XML has a more restricted syntax than HTML. This means that it can be communicated easily over the Web and passed through firewalls. It also can be communicated over secure links using HyperText Transfer Protocol Secure (HTTPs) with Secure Socket Layer (SSL). This is a key enabler for electronic commerce. Most enterprises already have a Web server and a firewall that enable Web access. XML leverages this existing connectivity.

International

XML is designed for international communications. It uses the Unicode character set with either UTF-8 or UTF-16 encoding. UTF-8 uses a variable number of bytes per character, but normal ASCII characters map to 1-byte UTF-8 characters. Consequently, UTF-8 is preferred in North America and Europe. UTF-16 uses 2-byte encoding with the potential for 16-bit pairs. The characters of most languages are encoded currently, and only 2-byte codes are used. UTF-16 is preferred in Asian countries because in some Asian languages the characters require multibyte encoding in UTF-8.

An XML document can include characters from any language. As we will see later, internationalization is also extended to other derivative specifications of the W3C.

Extensible

HTML has a defined set of tag names with specific meanings for the design of Web pages. As the technology evolved, new tags were added, often to support features of particular products. The adoption time for new tag standards is too long to keep up with advances in the technology.

XML is open-ended. New tag names can be defined as needed. In order to avoid the duplication of names, XML provides for the definition of *name spaces*. A document may indicate that a name is a member of a particular name space. That name space is identified by a Universal Resource Identifier (URI) in order to make it globally unique. As a result, XML document designers can use appropriate names and make them globally unique by qualifying the name with an appropriate name space identifier. An XML document can be composed of elements defined by several name spaces so that new documents can incorporate concepts defined in existing name spaces.

The free-form text structure of XML documents also adds to extensibility. If a document is extended with new tags, applications that have not been updated generally can ignore the new tags and continue to operate.

Self-Defining

The use of meaningful element names makes XML documents readable by humans without an associated specification or special tools. The use of name spaces and associated name prefixes enables the use of semantically appropriate names in the particular context. This is helpful in the design and debugging of documents but it does not provide the precise specification needed for computations.

The structure of an XML document is expressed as a Document Type Definition (DTD) or as an XML Schema. The DTD syntax was defined along with XML and eventually will be replaced by XML Schema. When a document specification is expressed as an XML Schema, the specification is itself an XML document. Thus, through the definition of new schema, the language is used to extend the elements and structure of documents. In addition, XML Schema specifications include robust data typing so that additional constraints and meanings may be attached to the values of elements. The document schema is incorporated by reference so that the same schema may be shared by many documents and used for validation to ensure that they are consistent.

Common Tools

XML is a subset of SGML. A number of tools are available that work with SGML, and these tools also work with XML. This gave XML a jump-start for initial acceptance. As consistent extensions and derivative technologies emerge, they can leverage SGML tools as well as tools developed specifically for XML. There are also a variety of open-source tools developed in Java, so they are available for multiple platforms.

Transformation

The structure of XML facilitates transformation. Transformations are specified using XML Stylesheet Language for Transformation (XSLT) and are commonly called *style sheets*. A style sheet in XSLT is an XML document. Style sheets are important for both presentation and integration. An XML document can be transformed to different HTML documents with presentation formats to support different display devices. An XML document also may be transformed to a different XML document format to meet the input requirements of an application.

Transformation is a critical capability to achieve compatibility for enterprise application integration and electronic commerce. Communications between enterprise applications and business partners often will involve incompatible record structures. Even if the specifications are the same, they likely will be incompatible at some point in the future due to software upgrades or the installation of new applications. Standard tools are available to implement transformations.

Summary

On first impression, XML appears to be much ado about nothing. The format is more expressive and flexible, but it is also verbose. However, basic benefits such as platform independence and HTTP compatibility started the trend, and as derivative specifications and tools have been added, the technology has gained value and momentum.

XML is now a key technology for Web access, B2B communications, and enterprise application integration (EAI). As we examine XML in greater depth, we will recognize additional value for enterprise integration.

XML Extended Technology

The XML language specification was adopted by the W3C in February 1998. This specification defined the basic XML syntax along with the DTD syntax to specify the structure of XML documents. As XML was applied, various extensions and complementary techniques were developed. Many of these were initially proprietary solutions, but many have been incorporated in specifications approved or under development by the W3C. As a result, XML is not simply the initial specification, but it is a family of specifications and tools that provides many extended capabilities. XML cannot be appreciated or exploited without an understanding of these extended capabilities.

We will not examine all the specifications and tools that have been developed, but instead we will focus on those specifications that are relevant to enterprise integration and are adopted or represent a strategic capability:

- Name spaces
- XML Schema
- XPath
- XLink
- XML Stylesheet Language (XSL)

- Document Object Model (DOM)
- Simple API for XML (SAX)
- XQuery
- XML Protocol (XP)
- Web Services Description Language (WSDL)
- XML Signature
- Universal Description, Discovery, and Integration (UDDI)
- Electronic business XML (ebXML)
- Resource Descriptor Framework (RDF)

This is not an exhaustive list of specifications or facilities, but it is intended to provide a general understanding of key XML technologies, particularly those that are supported by industry standards.

Name Spaces

Name spaces were added to XML in a January 1999 recommendation, shortly after XML was adopted. Name spaces provide the facility for the unique naming of elements.

A *name space* is a collection of names for a particular domain or purpose. Each name of the name space has specific meaning in that context. The same names may occur in other name spaces with different meanings. Uniqueness of name spaces is accomplished by using URIs. The global assignment of Internet domain names provides the foundation. Owners of a particular domain are then responsible for managing the name spaces within that domain.

Within an XML document, the name space URI is associated with a name space prefix that is shorthand for the name space UTI; for example:

```
<Order xmlns:zns="http://www.xyz.org/example-ns">
```

Here, the name space identifier (the URI) is associated with the prefix zns for the Order element. Consequently, names of elements within the Order element may be qualified using the zns name space prefix; for example:

```
<zns:OrderItem />
```

The URI need not refer to a real Web resource for XML purposes; it is used only as a unique identifier to differentiate homonyms. Nevertheless, it is useful for the URI to identify a Web page that describes the name space and provides a DTD or XML Schema for associated structures.

XML Schema

XML Schema is a specification for the expression of XML document specifications; these are documents that describe XML documents. XML Schema is a relatively new specification—it reached W3C Recommendation status May 2, 2001. We will examine DTD capabilities first and then the extended capabilities of XML Schema.

The initial specification for XML documents included specifications for DTDs. A DTD defines the structure of an XML document. With a DTD, a parser can determine not only that a document is syntactically correct (described as *well formed*), but also that it conforms to requirements for a specific document type (described as *valid*).

A DTD can define the following:

- Required and prohibited elements

- The elements contained within an element, defining the hierarchical structure of the document

- Required and optional attributes of elements and allowed attribute values

- Identifiers of elements within the document (ID attribute)

- References in one part of a document to an element in another part of the document (incorporation by reference)

- Shared segments of DTD specification incorporated from within or external to the DTD (entities)

A DTD can be included with an XML document, but the more important mode is for it to be incorporated from a common source. This provides the basis for sharing documents with a common definition. DTDs are used to define XML *vocabularies*. A vocabulary is a shared specification for documents in a particular area of interest.

Unfortunately, among other things, the DTD specification did not conform to XML syntax; that is, DTDs are not well-formed XML documents. In addition, support for data typing is minimal.

As a result, the XML Schema specification was developed. Since XML Schema is still new, it has not been widely accepted. However, it does have wide support and will provide several important improvements:

- It conforms to the XML syntax, so the same tools can be used to manipulate the specifications.

- It defines an extensive list of built-in data types.

- It provides improved control over element content.

- Complex data types can be defined as reusable entity structures and incorporated by name.

- Complex data types can be specialized with additional elements.

- Relationships between documents can be defined with keys as in conventional relational models.

XML Schema provides a much more robust representation and validation capability. This is important for any application of XML where documents are shared by different organizations, in particular in electronic commerce.

XPath

The XPath specification defines a mechanism for accessing elements within an XML document. XPath reached W3C Recommendation status in November 1999. It is a critical element of technologies and is discussed later, particularly regarding XML transformation and query facilities.

An XPath expression defines navigation from a *context* node to related nodes in a document. A node is typically an element but may be an attribute, a name space specification, a text string, and so on. Navigation may be in any direction, for example, to child elements, to a parent, or to siblings. If *axis* (direction) is not specified, then navigation defaults to child elements.

Navigation may be qualified by predicates—conditions applied to the nodes. Thus, navigation may be to the second `OrderItem` child or to the `OrderItem` that exceeds a particular price. XPath also defines functions that may be applied to compute results from the nodes accessed.

An XPath expression may return a `nodeset` or an elementary value such as a Boolean value, a floating-point number, or a string of characters. The following is a simple example of an XPath expression applicable to the example structure at the beginning of this chapter:

```
/child::Order/child::OrderItem
```

The initial slash (/) designates the root node of the document as the starting context. The expression would return the set of `OrderItem` nodes.

Since the default axis is child, the following abbreviated form will yield the same result:

```
/Order/OrderItem
```

Considerably more functionality is defined for XPath, but the preceding discussion should provide a basic understanding of its capabilities and role.

XLink

XLink defines a mechanism for linking XML documents or for linking an XML document to external resources. It attained the status of W3C Proposed

Recommendation in December 2000. The functionality is similar to the hyperlink specification in an HTML document but more robust. An XLink is specified with XLink attributes on a linking element within the XML document. These attributes define the participation of the element in the link.

A *simple* XLink attribute identifies the URI of a referenced resource, and additional attributes can define a human-readable title for the link, the intent of the external resource, and how it may be displayed. An *extended* XLink provides additional navigation capabilities. An extended link defines participating resources and arcs (relationships) between them. The links may be specified in the same or different documents so that one document may define links for other documents. Rather than relying on the document containing links to be loaded first, participating documents can refer to a shared *linkbase* document that will be incorporated whenever any of the participating documents are loaded. The linkbase arcs are incorporated as if they were part of the initially loaded document. The linkbase document defines how a number of documents are related, enabling relationships to be changed without opening or modifying the participating documents.

XML Stylesheet Language (XSL)

XSL includes two components: XSL Stylesheet Language for Transformation (XSLT) and XSL Formatting Objects (XSL-FO). We will focus on XSLT, which has a major role in XML as a medium of exchange of business data. XML-FO provides powerful capabilities for formatting Web displays and printed documents, including support for documents in languages that require right-to-left and top-to-bottom presentations.

XSLT defines XML documents that specify transformations of XML. One of the most common uses of XSLT is to transform an XML document into an HTML document for display on a conventional browser. The XML document could be data about an order or a part not designed for display. An XSLT specification can incorporate layout and presentation elements and restructure the information to provide an appropriate display.

While the creation of HTML pages from XML documents is a valuable contribution, the transformation of documents for exchange between applications and enterprises is of major importance. XML by itself provides a degree of decoupling systems by providing labeled, variable-length elements in Unicode text. XSLT transformation enables systems that expect different element names, value formats, and document structures to communicate with each other. Even if there are agreed-on standards, there will be times when the standards change, and it may be necessary to perform transformations on a temporary basis.

An XSLT document (a transformation specification) is composed of XSL template elements and functions as a declarative specification. An XSLT template acts like a predicate to select applicable source document elements. Attributes of each template determine when it is applied to the source document. XSLT uses XLink to navigate a source document. Generally, when a template matches the current context, it will be applied to perform its transformation. Multiple templates may match, and they will all be applied; the sequence of execution can be controlled by the designation of a priority.

Within a template, the elements are evaluated sequentially, depth first. In other words, each element is evaluated by evaluating each of its children and its children's children in sequence. The textual value yielded by each template element is contributed to the output. A template element may have mixed content, including text and elements. The text is output as encountered, as is the value of each element.

XLink is used to access elements so that the structure of the output document need not have any relationship to the input document. When an XLink reference returns a list of nodes, the value of only the first is output unless it is in the context of an `xsl:for-each` element that iterates over the collection (where `xsl` refers to the XSLT name space).

XSLT also includes conditional flow control expressions that provide a basic *if* statement and a *when* case statement. Templates also can be invoked by name from within another template using an `xsl:call-template` element. This provides a subroutine-like capability.

XSLT includes variables that are defined by an `xsl:variable` element and assigned a value returned from an XLink expression. Variable values may be used in conditional expressions and as transformation output.

These facilities provide a powerful transformation capability in a declarative mode, expressed as an XML document. This capability is fundamental to the power and success of XML.

Document Object Model (DOM)

The DOM defines methods for accessing an XML document as an object structure. These method specifications will be implemented according to the syntax of specific languages, so DOM is not an explicit application programming interface (API). The assumption of DOM is that the entire XML document will be loaded into computer memory as an object structure to be accessed and updated selectively. The API provides access to the document content without the need to deal with XML syntax.

The DOM structure involves a number of node object classes: `Element`, `Attr` (attribute), `Text`, `CDATASection` (character data), `Comment`, and so on. Objects of these classes have methods to support the retrieval and assignment of element and attribute values, the traversal of the structure, and the addition and deletion of nodes and document fragments.

DOM is particularly useful to support the processing of documents by applications. It provides the programmer with an easy-to-use interface that does not require an understanding of the XML syntax.

DOM also can be used to create XML documents. The programmer explicitly creates the structure by instantiating and inserting appropriate nodes. It is then relatively straightforward to generate a well-formed XML document from the object structure.

DOM level 2 supports events. Methods enable listeners to be registered or removed from specific nodes. Generation of events will be filtered against the node-type specification of the listener's request. A listener can be registered to receive events from any of the subnodes of the specified node. Events may be triggered by user-interface actions such as cursor movements or mouse clicks or by changes to the DOM object structure (mutation events). DOM level 2 also provides facilities to make it easier to trace and search the object structure.

Simple API for XML (SAX)

SAX is an alternative facility to DOM for programmatically accessing document content. Rather than loading the entire document into computer memory, SAX is a parser that invokes application functions as it encounters elements in the document. This means that the application can perform operations as the document is read, and it need not be capable of holding the entire document all at once.

SAX is not a W3C specification. There are a number of public-domain SAX implementations. The specifications and software were developed by an informal group of XML developers.

SAX has performance advantages, but it also imposes significant constraints on the application. The application must implement multiple handlers to be called by SAX. These handlers receive control with appropriate parameters as the SAX parser traverses the document. The order in which information is received is thus defined by the specific document. SAX does not provide any facility for changing the document.

XQuery

The XML Query language is intended to provide a standard way to query against XML documents. The language is still under development and may, in the end, have more than one syntax: a human-readable form and an XML-compliant form. Attention has focused on XQuery, which is a human-readable form.

XQuery is similar in form to Structured Query Language (SQL). It includes a path expression similar to the XPath abbreviated form, along with conditional expressions and computational functions. It can test for the existence of a condition or for consistent compliance with a condition (universality). It may be applied within a single document or across multiple documents. Although the path expression is similar to XPath, it is not consistent; a working draft document has been published to resolve this with future versions of XQuery and XPath.

In addition to the obvious capability of finding and extracting relevant data from documents, there are two other important benefits that make XQuery interesting. First, an XQuery request could be addressed to a virtual document rather than an XML document. The concept is that data may be stored in a database, but access to the database could simulate access to the equivalent XML document. This level of abstraction would provide a universal form of query expression that would not depend on the physical database schema. It provides not only portability of queries, but also increased flexibility in the design and evolution of database schema. Second, the declarative form of XQuery will facilitate optimization. The actual execution of the query can be optimized for the actual database schema and storage technology. This will become increasingly important when large volumes of XML documents are stored and queried.

Although XQuery is currently defined for retrieval only, it is expected that a future version will introduce an update capability.

XML Protocol

XML Protocol is a specification still under development, but it is a superset and refinement of the Simple Object Access Protocol (SOAP) proposed by Microsoft. A W3C Recommendation is targeted for late 2001. Consequently, we will focus on SOAP as an early version of XML Protocol.

SOAP is a remote procedure call protocol using HTTP. It opens the door to access of Common Object Request Broker Architecture (CORBA), Enterprise JavaBeans (EJB), and Component Object Model (COM+) objects over the Internet. The protocol provides a common XML form to send a message with parameters and receive a response using HTTP. This takes advantage of existing Web server and firewall technology that most enterprises already have in place.

SOAP is not restricted to using HTTP. SOAP messages are XML documents and can be transported using other protocols as well. SOAP messages also can be used for asynchronous messaging, where a message is sent and the sender does not wait for a response. Nevertheless, the focus of SOAP is for synchronous messaging, typically directed to CORBA, EJB, or COM+ object interfaces. Without standard middleware, application developers must explicitly program SOAP messages.

A SOAP message consists of three primary elements: an envelope that contains an optional header and a body. The following is an example of a SOAP message:

```
<SOAP-ENV:Envelope
 xmlns:SOAP-ENV= "http://schemas.xmlsoap.org/soap/envelope/"
 SOAP-ENV:encodingStyle=
  "http://schemas.xmlsoap.org/soap/encoding/">
 <SOAP-ENV:Body>
   <GetTotal>
    <OrderNumber>54321</OrderNumber>
   </GetTotal>
 </SOAP-ENV:Body>
</SOAP-ENV:Envelope>
```

The envelope contains name space and encoding specifications. The name space is for the SOAP message elements. The encoding specification provides a data type system corresponding to common programming language data types.

The `SOAP-ENV:Body` contains the message information. The message is directed to a `GetTotal` method with an `OrderNumber` parameter. A similar format is defined for the response:

```
<SOAP-ENV:Envelope
 xmlns:SOAP-ENV= "http://schemas.xmlsoap.org/soap/envelope/"
 SOAP-ENV:encodingStyle=
   "http://schemas.xmlsoap.org/soap/encoding/">
 <SOAP-ENV:Body>
   <GetTotalResponse>
    <Total>1234.56</Total>
   </GetTotalResponse>
 </SOAP-ENV:Body>
</SOAP-ENV:Envelope>
```

The response is similar to the original message except that, by convention, `Response` is appended to the method name.

The SOAP message header (omitted in the preceding example) provides for additional message-processing controls such as authentication and transaction management. A message with a header typically is directed to an intermediate network node for processing. The intermediate node processes the header and removes it from the message before passing the message on.

Web Services Description Language (WSDL)

WSDL is an XML specification for describing network services. It is a corollary to the interface definition languages of CORBA, EJB, and COM+. WSDL provides support to SOAP by defining the interfaces to which SOAP messages may be directed. Although WSDL has predecessors, it is still in the early stages of definition.

WSDL uses terminology associated with the Internet rather than the terminology of object interfaces. WSDL defines a *port type*, which corresponds to an object interface type. Messages are exchanged between ports. A *port binding* defines a particular port Internet address. The *port type* defines a set of *operations*, each of which may have an *input message*, an *output message*, or both. An operation may invoke an object method. Each message may have multiple *parts*. Each part has a *name* and a *type*. Parts may define message parameters for an object method.

While WSDL may be used to express object interfaces, it is more general. A port could be a destination for asynchronous messages. It also could be an interface for an asynchronous exchange of messages between enterprises to complete a particular business transaction.

The WSDL concept of port corresponds to the port concept in the Unified Modeling Language (UML) Profile for the Enterprise Distributed Object Computing (EDOC) specification under development by the Object Management Group (OMG). This specification supports the modeling of components with ports where the ports may exchange synchronous messages, asynchronous messages through a messaging service, or B2B messages over the Internet. The UML Profile for EDOC is discussed further in Chapter 10.

XML Signature

The XML Signature specification defines an XML structure for signing digital content. The signed content may be XML or any other digital objects. For XML, the signed content may be an entire document or a document fragment, that is, an element and its subelements.

A signature uses public-private key technology with digest functions. With this technology, the object to be signed is first processed to produce a hash value, and then the hash value is encrypted with the private key to produce a signature value. The signature can only be decrypted with the associated public key, which guarantees that the correct hash value could only come from the owner of the private key. This decrypted value is then compared with a hash value computed from the signed object using the same algorithm. Assuming that the public key is appropriately authenticated for the purported signer of the document, this provides both authentication and nonrepudiation of the signed information.

An abbreviated example of a basic digital signature is given here:

```
<Signature ID="OrderSubmitter"
 xmlns="http://www.w3.org/2000/xmldsig#">
```

```
<SignedInfo>
  <CanonicalizationMethod
   Algorithm=.../>
  <SignatureMethod
   Algorithm=.../>
  <Reference
   URI=...>
   <Transforms>
   <Transform Algorithm=.../>
   </Transforms>
   <DigestMethod
     Algorithm=/...>
   <DigestValue> ... </DigestValue>
  </Reference>
</SignedInfo>
<SignatureValue> ... </SignatureValue>
<KeyInfo>
  <KeyValue>...</KeyValue>
</KeyInfo>
</Signature>
```

The `Signature` element is the root element of a signature and has an optional ID attribute to distinguish it from other signatures in the same XML document. The preceding signature example contains three primary elements: `SignedInfo`, `SignatureValue`, and `KeyInfo`. First, we will look at the `SignatureValue` and `KeyInfo` elements. `SignatureValue` is the value computed by the encryption algorithm using the signer's private key. In an actual signature, the ellipses would be replaced by the encrypted digest value, computed as described in the `SignedInfo`, and encrypted based on the `KeyInfo`. `KeyInfo` provides information about the key used to decrypt the signature. In an actual signature, a digital certificate or a reference to one would replace the ellipses. `KeyInfo` is optional because it may be determined by the context of the signature (for example, the source of the digital certificate may be defined by an agreement or standard).

`SignedInfo` defines the content that is signed. It contains a `CanonicalizationMethod` element, a `SignatureMethod` element, and potentially multiple `Reference` elements. Each reference element identifies an object that is signed.

The `CanonicalizationMethod` is used to transform the object to be signed into a standard form. Any change to the signed object could invalidate the signature; thus, a minor change in format, such as spacing or indentation, could invalidate the signature even though the content of the object is not changed. The canonicalization method will put the object in a standard form so that such incidental changes will be removed. A specialized canonicalization transform might remove comments and formatting characters from an XML document so that the signature only applies to the substantive content of the object. This would be particularly useful where a communication such as e-mail may introduce extraneous end-of-line characters.

The `SignatureMethod` element defines algorithms used for hashing and encryption-decryption. In general, the signed information will be processed by a digest function to produce a hash value that is then encrypted to produce the signature value.

There may be multiple `Reference` elements. Each `Reference` element identifies an object being signed with a URI attribute. The signed object may be a fragment within the same XML document or an external object. The signed object is not changed by signing. The reference element includes identification of a digest function and a digest value. It may include transformations to be applied prior to signing. In an actual signature, the ellipses of the `DigestValue` would be replaced by a value computed from the referenced document or document fragment using the specified digest function.

The encryption for the signature value incorporates elements of the `SignedInfo` such as the canonicalization method to ensure that these elements as well as the reference digest value(s) cannot be changed.

There are numerous variations in the detail of a digital signature to accommodate different encoding techniques, different signed objects, and other refinements. What is important is that the signature provides authentication and nonrepudiation for one or more objects, providing assurance that validity is not affected by irrelevant format changes and accommodating a variety of encryption techniques.

Universal Description, Discovery, and Integration (UDDI)

UDDI is a multivendor initiative to develop a ubiquitous service for locating and establishing relationships with e-commerce services over the Internet. It incorporates XML along with other industry standards to provide this service in a consistent, platform-independent manner. The service accepts registrations from businesses, describing their services, and responds to queries to locate desired services. A UDDI Business Registry service currently exists, which is implemented on multiple servers by IBM, Ariba, and Microsoft.

The architecture of UDDI is equivalent to the Internet Domain Name Server (DNS) using globally distributed, synchronized directories. When a business registers with a particular directory, this registration is provided to the other directories. Access to the directories, both for registrations and for queries, uses SOAP messaging.

Each participating business provides information about its business, including the name, a description in multiple languages, contact information, associated business identifiers such as the business Dun and Bradstreet data universal numbering system (DUNS) code, and business domains: the industry, geographic locations, and products and services. The business also will provide specifications for e-commerce, including business process descriptions, service descriptions, and service addresses. The UDDI registry will assign unique business and service identifiers.

In order to provide shared protocols for conducting business, the UDDI service also provides a service-type registry. A service-type specification includes a name space URI that provides a description of the service, the identifier of the publisher of the service, and a unique service-type identifier. Industry-specific schema will provide shared vocabularies and document specifications for exchanges of information.

The result is a global, electronic yellow pages including information about the businesses and specifications on how it will conduct business electronically.

Electronic Business XML (ebXML)

ebXML is an e-commerce framework developed as a joint initiative of the United Nations Center for Trade Facilitation and Electronic Business (UN/CEFACT) and the Organization for the Advancement of Structured Information Standards (OASIS). The specification was adopted in May 2001. The goal is to facilitate development of a global electronic marketplace based on the Internet and XML.

Electronic Data Interchange (EDI) has been the basis for exchange of data between business partners for many years. Large numbers of transactions are communicated in batch files. Standards have been developed for the format of records for a variety of purposes. However, the batching of transactions delays business action, and the creation of new communications links requires negotiation and implementation of business and technical agreements and may take weeks or months to establish.

The Internet presents the opportunity to exchange data as events occur and with much greater flexibility. There is no longer a need to establish individual point-to-point communication links. Web technology has established basic protocols for secure ad hoc communications. Connections can be established anywhere at any time, and data can be exchanged. Retail sales over the Internet have become common practice. However, in retail sales, the seller defines the sale process and data exchange for a human customer. The customer has the ability to quickly evaluate the terms and adapt to the seller's process and data requirements. Effective exchanges of business data between commercial enterprises requires communication between computers that do not adapt so easily.

The ebXML initiative has defined a standard framework for electronically establishing ad hoc data exchange agreements between trading partners. The framework establishes XML standards for an enterprise to express its business capabilities, processes, interfaces, and message formats in a registry for open access. The registry entry is a Collaboration Protocol Profile (CPP). Whereas some enterprises will develop their own processes and record formats, over time, most are expected to incorporate standard protocols. As a result, a purchaser of products or services should be able to identify a potential supplier, find protocols in the registry that are complementary to his or her own, establish a working agreement—a Collaboration Protocol Agreement (CPA)—and conduct business transactions. These profiles and agreements are expressed in XML, and they define interfaces and messages to be exchanged in XML.

ebXML was an ambitious undertaking completed in a limited amount of time. The specification undoubtedly will be refined as products are developed. However, it provides a solid foundation for open electronic commerce. At the same time that the ebXML specification was under development, the UML Profile for EDOC specification also was under development, involving some of the same participants. Consequently, the EDOC specification provides elements for modeling ebXML collaborations and incorporating them in application components. This should facilitate the development of tools to support ebXML implementation and thus the acceptance of ebXML as the primary framework for global electronic commerce.

We will examine ebXML in additional detail under the following topics:

- Collaboration model
- XML documents
- Reliable messaging

Collaboration Model

ebXML specifies a comprehensive model for the conduct of electronic commerce. This model provides the framework for participation, the expression of capabilities and agreements, and the specification of exchanges.

Each participating enterprise must prepare a CPP. This profile defines the enterprise from an electronic commerce perspective. It may define multiple businesses of the enterprise; each such business is represented as a party in an electronic exchange. Each party may have different roles and different processes it follows. The party specifications also will include information on how to connect to the party and exchange data. Generally, the CPP will describe capabilities to participate in a variety of business relationships and alternative protocols. The CPP document is registered in the ebXML registry.

When one enterprise wishes to establish an electronic commerce relationship with another, it finds the trading partner's CPP in the registry and negotiates a CPA. The CPA incorporates relevant aspects of each partner's CPP to define the manner in which they will conduct business.

The CPA identifies participating *parties* within each of the trading partner enterprises. The CPA also identifies the *process specification* that defines the exchanges between the parties and the roles each of the parties will play in the process. A process specification defines the process each trading partner will follow from an external business collaboration perspective. It represents an abstraction of the various processes each partner may employ internally to support the collaboration.

The parties will engage in *conversations,* as defined by the business process, in which they will perform one or more *transactions.* A transaction is a unit of exchange consisting of a request, and potentially a response, directed from one party to the other. A conversation may involve multiple transactions to reach a conclusion. A party's *business service interface* defines the transactions that can be accepted by that party.

Transactions are performed by the communication of messages using a messaging service. Messages convey business documents expressed in XML. ebXML defines a reliable messaging service based on SOAP. The messaging service is discussed later in this chapter.

XML Documents

ebXML involves several XML documents. The relationships between the documents are illustrated in Figure 9.1.

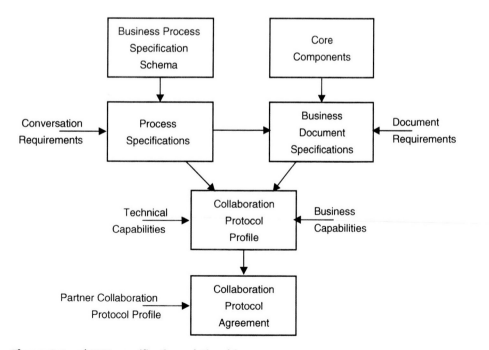

Figure 9.1   ebXML specification relationships.

The ebXML specification defines the business process specification schema. This determines the basic form of process specifications. Process specifications are developed to define conversations to meet particular business needs. Although they may be defined by individual enterprises, it is expected that, over time, coalitions or standards groups will define standard processes at least for industry groups.

Business document specifications define business documents that will be exchanged by business processes. The definition of documents is driven by the requirements of processes that use them. Business documents specifications will incorporate core components from the ebXML registry to minimize the diversity of document specifications.

The process specifications and business document specifications are incorporated by reference into the CPP of a particular enterprise. A CPP may define the enterprise as a number of potential party types engaging in a number of roles in business processes. An abbreviated skeleton of a CPP is given here:

```
<CollaborationProtocolProfile
 xmlns="http://www.ebxml.org/namespaces/tradePartner"
 xmlns:ds="http://www.w3.org/2000/09/xmldsig#"
 xmlns:xlink="http://www.w3.org/1999/xlink"
 version="1.1">
 <PartyInfo>
   <PartyId type="...">...</PartyId>
   <PartyRef xlink:type="...", xlink:href="..."/>
   <CollaborationRole id="..." >
    <ProcessSpecification name="..." version="1.0">
      ...
    </ProcessSpecification>
    <Role name="buyer" xlink:href="..."/>
    <CertificateRef certId = "..."/>
    <ServiceBinding name="..." channelId="..."
      packageId="...">
      xlink:type="simple"
      xlink:href="..."/>
    </ServiceBinding>
    <ServiceBinding channelId="..." packageId="...">
      <Override action="..." channelId="..."
      packageId="..."
      xlink:type="simple"
      xlink:href="..."/>
    </ServiceBinding>
   </CollaborationRole>
   <Certificate> ...</Certificate>
   <DeliveryChannel> ...</DeliveryChannel>
   <Transport>...</Transport>
<DocExchange>...</DocExchange>
 </PartyInfo>
 <Packaging id="ID">...</Packaging>
```

```
<ds:Signature>...</ds:Signature>
<Comment>text</Comment>
</CollaborationProtocolProfile>
```

We will not discuss the CPP structure in detail but will note some highlights. It begins with one or more `PartyInfo` elements. `PartyInfo` elements contain most of the relevant information. A party is the specific participant in a collaboration. Within the `PartyInfo`, one or more `CollaborationRoles` are defined. A role corresponds to a role in a process specification. A party could have multiple roles in a process. The `PartyInfo` also includes elements for specification of one or more digital certificates for security, one or more delivery channels for the receipt of messages, one or more transport protocols, and one or more message exchange protocols.

Each collaboration role defines the associated process specification by reference to a process specification document. It also specifies a specific digital certificate (by reference) and bindings to default and alternate delivery channels.

In addition to the `PartyInfo`, the CPP contains `Packaging` and `Signature` elements. The `Packaging` element defines how a message is to be composed of different parts, in particular where a message may include attachments. The `Signature` element is optional but may contain an XML digital signature to validate the CPP document.

The CPA brings together elements of the CPPs of two collaborating enterprises. Each CPP defines capabilities of the enterprise that likely will exceed the capabilities required for a single CPA. The CPP may define multiple parties, multiple roles within parties, alternative delivery channels and transport protocols, alternative digital certificates, and so on. The enterprises negotiate a CPA they can both support. This can be done electronically by finding a matching combination of CPP elements.

Reliable Messaging

ebXML also defines a messaging service, based on SOAP, for the exchange of messages between parties. In general, it is important that messages are reliably delivered once and only once, although the messaging service can support an optional best-effort level of service.

The message service is expected to be implemented by message service handlers (MSHs), one for each party to the collaboration. The MSHs send and receive messages for applications (they manage the ports). For reliable messaging, that is, once-and-only-once delivery, the MSH is expected to accept a message for sending and save it in persistent storage and, similarly, receive a message for processing and save it in persistent storage. For messages it sends, each MSH assigns a sequence number that is unique within the conversation to ensure that messages are not missed or duplicated.

Messages have a nested structure. An outer Multipurpose Internet Mail Extensions (MIME) envelope contains MIME parts so that a message can have attachments. The first MIME part contains a SOAP envelope. The SOAP envelope has a SOAP envelope header and SOAP envelope body that contain elements of the ebXML message. The SOAP protocol is extended to address-specific ebXML messaging requirements.

The ebXML Messaging Service specification defines the exchange protocol to deliver messages and resolve communication failures. It also supports a status request message, requesting the status of an earlier message.

The message structure supports digital signatures as defined by the W3C/IETF XML Signature specification. The entire message may be signed, and separate parts may be signed individually. The specification also defines default approaches to the authentication of the sender and receiver and encryption for confidentiality.

Resource Descriptor Framework (RDF)

The RDF specification defines XML for the description of Web resources. On first impression, this may seem to be a duplication of the UDDI or ebXML service registries or WSDL interface specifications, but RDF is not about services or a registry. RDF is about data to describe data—that is, meta data. The goal is to be able to classify and access information more effectively on the Web.

The basic element of RDF meta data is the triad *resource, property,* and *statement*. A *resource* is a Web resource—a unit of information available on the Web. A *property* is a named characteristic of a resource such as the *author* of a book or *date* of publication. A *statement* is a value of the property for the particular resource. A statement may be a string, such as an author's name, or it may be another resource. For example, an author statement could be a Web page for information about the author that might, in turn, have properties such as name, e-mail address, and affiliation. Thus, RDF descriptions can form a network of linkages, a semantic web of relationships between Web resources.

RDF does not define specific properties. The definition of properties is left to individual communities of interest. A community will define a set of properties as a name space. It is generally expected that the name space URI will be a Web page that defines the associated vocabulary. Some properties inherently have a set of possible values or require a particular form of expression to support classification and search. These characteristics also would be defined in the community vocabulary. Thus, any community of interest can define a meta data vocabulary for describing the Web resources of interest.

The Dublin Core set of 15 properties was defined in a workshop in Dublin, Ohio, in 1995:

- Title
- Creator
- Subject and keywords
- Description
- Publisher
- Contributor
- Date
- Resource type
- Format
- Resource identifier
- Source
- Language
- Relation
- Coverage
- Rights management

These property names have been used as HTML *META* element names to provide meta data for Web search engines. They provide a starting point for the development of RDF vocabularies for specific communities. Here is an example RDF meta data statement:

```
<rdf:RDF
 xmlns:rdf="http://www.w3.org/1999/o2/22-rdf-syntax-ns#"
 xmlns:dc="http://purl.org/meta data/dublin_core#">
 <rdf:Description about:"http://example.org/MyPage"
   <dc:Creator>Fred Cummins</dc:Creator>
 </rdf:Description>
</rdf:RDF>
```

The about attribute of the Description identifies the subject resource with a URL. The name space dc is associated with the URI for the Dublin Core, a well-known set of basic metaproperties of which Creator is one. Thus, the three elements are resource "http://example.org/MyPage", property Creator, and value Fred Cummins.

Summary

We have examined a number of XML technologies and standards. This has not been a comprehensive survey but has focused on key technologies based on accepted or emerging industry standards. Most of the specifications discussed are complementary—most are adopted by the W3C. Exceptions are Schema for Object-Oriented XML (SOX), which provides an important alternative to DOM, and UDDI, which provides a search facility to identify potential trading partners, a capability that is not addressed in ebXML. While some of these specifications are relatively new or in final stages of adoption, as a result of the momentum of the XML movement, viable specifications are implemented in products quite rapidly. In many cases products are developed before the specifications are final. In any case, we can expect that the basic functionality described here will be implemented, although details will continue to be refined. Additional capabilities and applications are still in the early stages of development, and others have gained a presence in the marketplace but may be only transient versions in this rapidly evolving field.

This discussion of XML technologies has illustrated the potential breadth of application of XML and the rich functionality available to support applications. XML has clearly emerged as a key technology for the Internet, but many of the same capabilities should be leveraged within the enterprise as well. In the next section we will examine the role XML should play in enterprise integration.

XML's Impact on Architecture

XML will have a widespread effect on enterprise architecture. As a nonproprietary, transformable, and Web-compatible representation of data, it is a key medium of exchange. As an extensible, free-form, self-documenting structure, it accommodates change. With name space specifications, it can resolve potential ambiguities. As a structure for signed documents, it can replace paper and microfilm. With Web access and meta data, it can facilitate access to information.

Some of these areas of application are depicted in Figure 9.2. XML provides a transformable representation of Web page content for processing and transformation by Web servers. It is a preferred form of data exchange between enterprise applications. It facilitates message transformation for communication of events and messages between enterprise applications. It is a meaningful form for archiving of business documents, particularly signed business

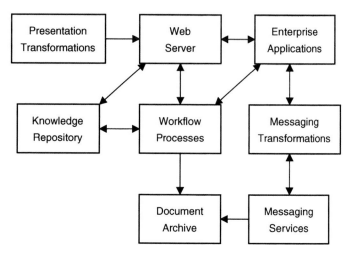

Figure 9.2 Architectural role of XML.

documents. Consequently, it is the preferred representation for business documents as they are developed and exchanged in workflow management. Finally, it provides a flexible form that supports classification and the search for knowledge management. We will now examine the key underlying XML applications represented in the preceding examples:

- Data interchange
- User interface
- Business records
- Knowledge management

Data Interchange

A fundamental role of XML is the interchange of data between systems. Independently developed systems can send and receive XML documents, and XSLT can be used to transform the documents for compatibility. The systems involved may produce incompatible but transformable documents for the foreseeable future, or the need for transformation may be transient, such as where systems are upgraded at different times.

In general, it is appropriate to exchange documents in a standard format as opposed to a format dictated by the sending or receiving application. The standard format is more likely to be stable, and the transformation associated with each application can be changed whenever the associated application changes. Consequently, it may be necessary to transform a document to the standard format when it is sent and transform it again when it is delivered, as required by the recipient. Over time, we would expect that enterprise application vendors will move to standard record specifications so that the number of transformations can be reduced. XML Schema should be used to define and validate the interchange format so that any inconsistencies can be identified quickly and objectively.

Within the enterprise, XML documents should be exchanged through a message broker for efficient, reliable delivery. External to the enterprise, and occasionally within the enterprise, documents will be exchanged over the Internet. This exchange typically will employ HTTPS for secure communications. The Reliable Messaging protocol of ebXML will ensure once-and-only-once delivery of messages.

Through ebXML and UDDI, XML provides the mechanisms for establishing electronic commerce relationships. UDDI provides facilities for finding businesses that offer desired products or services. For large corporations this facility may be employed between divisions or subsidiaries. ebXML provides the mechanisms for automatically establishing a shared process and document specifications for the conduct of electronic commerce. There is overlap between UDDI and ebXML, but preference should be given to ebXML as the industry standard.

A key aspect of these data exchanges is the development of standard processes and documents. Within the enterprise, processes usually are implicit in the applications. Documents are communicated when they become available or are requested. ebXML has provided the metamodeling facilities for the representation of shared processes in electronic commerce. It is expected that these will be developed and registered by various enterprises and consortia as needed and that the marketplace will provide incentives for convergence. In many cases, large corporations that want to streamline relationships with suppliers will drive this movement. These processes also may reflect application processes to some extent, but more important, they will reflect the need for reliable exchange of goods and services involving risk mitigation, legal issues, and negotiation protocols.

Many documents have been defined already, particularly for exchanges between enterprise applications—this has been driven by commercial-off-the-shelf (COTS) vendors. The Open Application Group (OAG) has been active in this area for several years. At the same time, many documents remain to be defined.

ebXML provides for the inclusion of document specifications by reference. The expectation is that documents will be defined to meet the needs of particular industries. In this way, specifications can be developed by a variety of interest groups without the need for a comprehensive coordination and reconciliation effort that probably would fail.

It will be important for the enterprise to be aware of and participate in various standards efforts for the development of process and document specifications. The goal should be to identify relevant existing standards, to leverage current systems and capabilities in the development of new standards, and to minimize potential adverse consequences of new or modified standards.

User Interface

XML has a major role in the implementation of user interfaces. Whether the user interface is with a thick client or a Web server and browser, XML should be used to exchange data with the underlying application. XML provides platform independence, ease of communication through firewalls, and standard transformation facilities. In addition, an XML document provides a format for communication of all the data necessary to populate a display as opposed to protocols that would retrieve individual field values.

Perhaps the most important benefit of XML for user interfaces comes from the transformation capability of XSLT. This is a key for flexible security authorization and alternate display formats, which are discussed in the following subsections.

Security Authorization

Security authorization logic often is embedded in applications. Applications are required to determine which fields a user is allowed to see or update based on a defined user role. In some cases, authority is conditioned on the specific information being accessed; for example, an employee, in general, can only see his or her own personnel record. When the characteristics of the role or the application change or new roles are defined, the application must be changed along with the user interface that provides the accompanying access. This constraint changes to adapt to business needs and to some extent increases the complexity of the application. The requirements and effects of role definitions and constraints often are difficult for the system owner to comprehend.

Most authorization constraints can be implemented in XML transformations on the data exchanged between the Web server and the application. The XML content produced by the application can contain all the data required for various users. The transformation can filter this content depending on the user's role. This can extend to authorization based on the user's relationship to the content if appropriate data are provided (there will be trade-offs to consider for including content-based authorization). Similarly, data entered can be filtered by an XML transformation on the input, preventing unauthorized updates. The transformation is separated from the application and directly defines the relationship of user roles to displays and inputs, so it is semantically closer to the system owner's perception and requirements of the system, and the application is not cluttered with authorization rules. Specification of each transformation is based on the user's role and, in some cases, the content.

Of course, the transformations must occur in a secure environment; for example, they cannot be performed on a computer under the control of an end user.

Alternative Display Formats

XML is essential for implementation of alternative display formats. The need for alternative displays occurs for three primary reasons. First, for productivity, it may be desirable to provide different display formats for different users depending on the job function as well as the security authorization role. The format of displays may have a significant impact on productivity for heavy users. Second, for internationalization, displays may be presented in different languages as well as different formats including the formatting alternatives supported by XML-FO (such as right-to-left text). Third, for alternative devices, a number of constraints must be applied. Much attention has been given to the use of wireless devices such as cell phones and Personal Digital Assistants (PDAs) for Web browsers. The constraints are both in the display real estate and in ease of input. Also, output to printers calls for special formatting considerations such as those provided by XML-FO.

Productivity, internationalization, and device constraints are three orthogonal requirements for user-interface design. This could result in a combinatorial explosion of transformations. However, productivity considerations usually are of concern to a relatively small community of users. Similarly, only certain displays and business functions can be effective with cell phones and PDAs. Consequently, these factors should be limited to only those displays where there is a clear need. In some cases, internationalization will only be relevant to certain user-interface facilities, particularly if the enterprise is centralized in a single country. However, for large, international corporations, the need for internationalization may be extensive.

Business Documents

Before computers came along, business records were paper documents. They could be read centuries after they were written because they were self-described and expressed in natural language. They had legal effect with signatures and seals to verify their authenticity. However, they were difficult to organize and retrieve, they took a lot of space to store, and they could be destroyed by fire or flood. Many documents are still stored in paper form. Those that occur in high volumes usually are copied to microfilm to reduce the storage space and facilitate retrieval. These microfilm copies are still difficult to search, and they require manual data entry or edits if they are to be processed by computer.

XML provides an alternative to paper documents. It can be self-describing with appropriate tags and associated schema. This would greatly reduce storage space and make documents retrievable by computer without human intervention. XML signatures can give XML documents legal effect, and the copies are just as legal as the originals, so risk of loss can be reduced by transmission to a redundant, remote storage facility. In addition, an XML signature can incorporate related referenced documents to ensure that referenced documents are unchanged from those intended as part of the original signed document.

Business documents are certainly important for electronic commerce. The opportunity presented by ebXML is to quickly establish business relationships and conduct business potentially without human intervention. The risks are high without documents with legal effect. ebXML incorporates XML signatures to produce legally binding business documents.

These documents must be archived to preserve their legal effect. Archiving must not change the content or format of a document, or the signature will no longer be valid. Although a transformation from XML to a relational database structure may be reversible, it may not be reversible to exactly the same format years into the future. Consequently, one of the following must occur:

- The documents must be stored as XML with their signatures.

- There must be an immutable pair of transformation algorithms to store and retrieve the documents without any net change to content or form.

- A canonicalization algorithm must be able to structure the document in a standard form regardless of variations introduced by transformations.

At the same time, because documents are associated with the schema that define them, new document formats with new schema can be accepted by the same facility, and XSLT transformations can be defined if the old documents are to be processed in a new document format. In any event, a proper archiving facility will allow large numbers of documents to be stored with minimal space requirement while preserving legal effect and providing effective retrieval capabilities.

Up to this point we have discussed XML business documents in the context of electronic commerce. However, the same basic concepts apply within the enterprise. Traditionally, paper documents controlled the authorization of activities, the transfer of resources, and the expenditure of funds. This provided accountability and control of corporate assets. As we have streamlined business processes, we have relied on computers to keep accurate records, but these records generally do not have legal effect, and the integrity of computer systems can be violated. Accountability and control would be more reliable and durable with electronic signatures. XML is the appropriate technology for the expression of these internal business documents and the attachment of signatures.

Workflow management is the focal point for creation of such documents. A business process implemented in workflow management captures data that define the results of the process. For appropriate accountability and control, the process also should capture data about the history of actions taken by individuals. Control points in the process should be contingent on attachment of signatures by appropriately authorized and authenticated individuals. These signatures not only authorize further action, but also authenticate the document and capture the basis of the action by the person signing. A signature may incorporate other objects such as a budget or an engineering design so that there can be no doubt about the basis of the signature.

Workflow documents are cumulative. As different activities are performed, new information is added or new versions are created for old information. Old signatures do not apply to the new material, but new signatures do. Some signatures may apply only to certain segments of or attachments to the document depending on the interest and authority of the person signing. The final document will incorporate various segments, some of which have multiple versions with a collection of signatures applicable to different segments and versions.

Since current workflow management products do not incorporate support for signatures, in the short term this must be addressed by other applications. Many workflow processes may never use signatures because they represent minimal risk and because of the added complexity of designing the documents and the processes that will manage them. In the long term we can expect that workflow products will provide support for capturing and signing business process data in XML. These documents will become the internal documents for accountability and control, and they will complement and extend the documents created for electronic commerce. Electronic commerce processes as defined by ebXML also will be implemented with workflow processes within the systems of each participating enterprise.

A distinction must be made between business documents supporting workflow processes and the artifacts that the processes operate on. The artifacts, in many cases, should not be XML documents. The distinction is where the artifacts have associated functionality accessed through object interfaces. For example, an engineering design or a manufacturing production simulation will not be usable as an XML document. Either artifact could be transformed to XML by some algorithm, but the XML documents would not be meaningful or usable without transformation back to the appropriate model.

Similarly, information about a customer or a part is stored more appropriately in a form that is convenient for application processing. At the same time, it may be appropriate to copy elements from the customer or part object into the process document to capture the relevant state of the customer or part at that point in the process. For example, the shipping address of the customer is relevant at the time of shipment because that is the address the carrier will act on regardless of what the customer's address of record is changed to later. At the same time, documents about customers and parts might be exchanged between applications using XML documents.

Even though process artifacts may not be expressed in XML, they may be signed. The XML signature in a process document can identify the artifacts as separate references and compute separate digest values for each. They are all incorporated in the signature, but they can be validated independently by their separate digest values.

Knowledge Management

Knowledge management involves the capture, classification, storage, retrieval, and application of knowledge. XML applies to the form in which knowledge is stored and the classification of knowledge with associated meta data, that is, metaknowledge—data about knowledge.

Knowledge will come in a variety of forms. Much enterprise knowledge will be in the form of textual assertions written by humans to describe a potential problem, an insight, a preference, or a constraint. Some knowledge will be in an encoded form to be applied by a computer. Encoded knowledge may be a rule-based system, a neural network, or a set of business rules (constraints). In all cases, we view units of knowledge as Web resources on the enterprise intranet.

When knowledge is a text document, it should be stored as or referenced by an XML document. When it is encoded knowledge, it should be represented by an XML document with a URL link to the actual unit of knowledge. In all cases, knowledge documents (XML) can have links to other Web resources that provide supporting material.

The knowledge documents also must contain an RDF element that contains metaknowledge that characterizes the knowledge. RDF defines meta data as a collection of resource-property-value triplets. For each category of knowledge, a set of properties must be defined. Primary properties will identify the business function context and the category of subject matter the knowledge addresses. Thus, the engineering department may have an XML document type for the design process for an engine cooling system. Additional properties might further qualify the context and subject matter, perhaps focusing on the water pump design and the rotor composition. Enterprise properties must be defined for security authorization requirements. These, in combination with a user's enterprise-level roles, and possibly local roles, will determine if the user is authorized to access a particular knowledge document.

The development of appropriate knowledge properties is a substantial undertaking, and the property set will evolve over time. However, as an XML document, it can be extended without adverse impact on existing metaknowledge. Similarly, the knowledge documents may continue to evolve. Some knowledge that is initially simple text may be refined to add structure and maybe encoding.

As XML documents, the metaknowledge and knowledge documents can be exchanged easily over the intranet, as can queries for a search of metaknowledge.

It is appropriate that the enterprise metaknowledge be stored in an enterprise directory so that it is available across the enterprise. This might be accomplished with a Web directory that can link users to appropriate subdirectories. At the same time, it is appropriate that the actual knowledge documents be held near where they are created and applied. This could improve performance, but in particular it keeps responsibility for the continued maintenance of the knowledge with the organization that depends on it. Knowledge management and other associated architectural issues are addressed in greater detail in Chapter 12.

Summary

XML must be incorporated in the enterprise architecture. Application of XML to data interchange and user interfaces are well established, and the scope of application will expand, as discussed earlier. Application to business records, particularly incorporating XML signatures, is just beginning to gain acceptance. Application to knowledge management provides a clear opportunity, but this has not yet been demonstrated. The enterprise architecture must exploit established capabilities by:

- Adopting XML as the form of business documents, including exchange of documents between internal systems

- Adopting ebXML as the basis for electronic commerce

- Implementing security technology (public-private key encryption) that supports electronic signatures

In addition, the enterprise must participate in industry standards efforts to shape and anticipate future developments and exploit the technology as it evolves.

Using Component Technology

The time and cost to modify business applications or develop new ones are major barriers to enterprise flexibility. Traditional applications tend to be large and monolithic, making it difficult to adapt them to new requirements, particularly when there are significant changes to business processes. Many enterprises have purchased commercial-off-the-shelf (COTS) applications to upgrade their systems while minimizing the time, cost, and risk of new application development. These solutions are effective for business functions that implement common industry practices and provide no competitive advantage. At the same time, these applications provide limited flexibility—often they impose new ways of doing business, and the enterprise may lose abilities that had provided competitive advantages.

The idea of purchasing existing software solutions is fundamentally sound, but for many applications, the purchasable units are too large and inflexible. The goal is to be able to purchase components that provide generally accepted functionality and combine them with custom components and flexible business processes to optimize the business function performance for the needs of the particular enterprise. When there are better purchasable components, it should be possible to replace the old ones without major impact to the rest of the system.

Even if components cannot be purchased to meet the needs of the enterprise, the development of systems with a component architecture improves flexibility and can reduce overall systems development and maintenance costs. Components force a well-organized system structure. Within a single system, common functionality most likely will be consolidated and encapsulated so that changes will be easier to define and require less pervasive modifications. If some components can be used in multiple applications, then even greater economy and flexibility can be achieved.

This chapter will examine the design of components and the applications built from components. We will establish requirements for using component technology and assess the state of the current technology—specifically Enterprise JavaBeans (EJB)—for meeting these requirements.

Component Strategy

Assembling complex applications from selected existing components is appealing for the following reasons:

- The cost of selecting components should be considerably less than the cost of developing new ones.
- If the components have market value, they probably will be better designed and tested than the first attempt at a custom equivalent.
- The cost of maintenance will be shared with other users of the same components.
- Components that continue to be marketed and maintained will keep the user abreast of new technology, so the user can exploit current technology with minimal impact.
- Competitive components should have compatible interfaces, so as better components are developed, they can be installed in place of the old components, keeping the user current with the latest solutions.
- The overall design of the system will be more flexible and adaptable to changing business needs.

With all these benefits, why are we not building all applications from components? There are a number of reasons. The development of component-based applications represents a strategic change from traditional approaches.

We will begin this section by examining where we are, and then we will look at the following topics:

- Barriers to application component development
- The changing landscape
- The expanded scale of reuse

Background on Component Technology

The concept of components in software design has been around since the early days of programming. Subroutines and functions were the earliest manifestation. Programmers recognized that they were programming the same logic repeatedly, and it saved a lot of time to program the common logic once, in a general way, and invoke it whenever it applied. This technology is still in use today.

Unfortunately, as the common functions became larger and more complex, it became more difficult to design them so that they would provide the appropriate solution in a variety of circumstances.

At the same time, software was evolving for operating systems, the management of different peripheral devices, and modules for the management of communications and data storage. System architectures evolved to accommodate the interchange of hardware components and the complementary software components. The personal computer market accelerated this evolution so that consumers could configure their computers with a variety of hardware components and associated software and also install selected applications. The market opportunities drove the development of standards that enabled this flexibility of configuration.

In application development, object-oriented programming improved the potential for the development of reusable components. Objects support encapsulation and polymorphism, which are important concepts for interchangeable components. *Encapsulation* describes an implementation where the user interacts with an interface without knowing the details of the implementation of the program logic or the data structures. *Polymorphism* characterizes the ability to interchange components of different types without affecting the logic in which they are used. These same concepts are manifested in interchangeable software components for configurating personal computers.

While object technology was touted as the solution to the development of application components, the marketplace in application components never emerged, and reuse of application objects still tends to be limited to closely managed teams of developers.

At the same time, a number of software components have emerged as products to support application development and enable the development of more sophisticated applications. The development of user-interface components and supporting services is a prime example. Without these components and associated tools, most applications would still be using character displays, and the Web would be mostly textual Web pages. Graphic user interfaces are products of object technology.

Object technology and systems software technology converged in the development of distributed computing architectures. Distributed systems are composed of application objects and services that can be executed on different computers. Each distributed unit encapsulates the logic and data it needs to perform its functionality. These distributed components are objects. At the same time, they are different from the original object-oriented programming objects because they execute independently, they are accessed over a network, and they may be implemented in different languages executing on different platforms. Standards developed by the Object Management Group (OMG) have established vendor-independent facilities for supporting communications between distributed objects and basic services to enable distributed object applications.

Barriers to Application Component Development

We now have the technology for integrating distributed application components and services. However, we still do not see a marketplace in application components emerging.

The critical factor is scale of reuse. The market for a component must be sufficiently large to enable the developer to make a reasonable profit. The expected revenue from sale of the component must more than offset:

- The cost of development
- The loss of investment in components that do not sell
- The cost of marketing and support
- The cost of ongoing maintenance and enhancement

The cost of development of a reusable component is substantially higher than that of a single-use component. It must be designed to function appropriately in a variety of situations, it must be more reliable, and it must have supporting documentation to enable customers to incorporate it easily.

The risk of loss of investment is high. The component may not appeal to customers, it may encounter competition, the technology or the business may change, rendering the component obsolete, or the market may not be as large as anticipated. In addition, the component will not sell without additional investment in marketing, and customers will not accept it if they do not perceive a commitment to support, ongoing maintenance, and enhancement of the product.

At the same time, the cost to the customer must be relatively low. There must be substantial savings over custom development. The savings must offset the customer's risk that incorporating the product will not be as easy as it appears, the product may not perform exactly as the customer expects, and the customer's business needs may change while the product does not.

In addition, customers must know what they are getting—assurance that the components will implement the functions they want and will work with other components to produce a functional system. There are not yet sufficiently concise and complete specifications to ensure the composability of components.

These same issues apply within a large corporation, where components might be developed for use in a number of applications. Candidate components usually are not of sufficient quality; there is seldom a willingness to invest in the necessary refinement, documentation, marketing, and support; and there is seldom an expectation of ongoing maintenance and support because that would require an internal product maintenance staff. In addition, the scale of reuse within the corporation is usually small, particularly compared with the world market. Consequently, the expectation of savings from reuse within the corporation is seldom sufficient to offset the costs and risks.

The Changing Landscape

In the last decade, many enterprises started adopting COTS applications for core business functions. These are very large software components. They are not tightly integrated with other applications or components, and they are of sufficient scale that they justify the installation of stand-alone computing environments, thus minimizing the need for compatibility with existing computing environments. The scale of these components was such that there was a major expectation of savings and a major opportunity for profit.

While these applications did not always meet expectations, they created an appetite for purchased solutions, and they created a market for products to support enterprise application integration (EAI). The development of EAI facilities, tools, and services reduced the cost and risk of integration with legacy applications.

The vendors of the enterprise applications recognized that there was a larger market for more focused solutions and more flexible applications. As a result, many have partitioned their products into a number of separable business functions and have incorporated workflow management facilities to tie together the separate business functions and support the implementation of different customer business processes. The scale of these applications is still quite large, so they still justify independent computing platforms and offer substantial savings over custom development.

While enterprise applications and technology have been evolving, standards for distributed object computing also have been evolving and maturing. The OMG has provided Common Object Request Broker Architecture (CORBA) standards for middleware and services that support distributed computing in a heterogeneous environment. Systems can be composed of components running on different platforms and using services implemented by different vendors. Several years ago, OMG initiated work on the CORBA Component Model (CCM) specification. This specification took several years to develop and defines standards to incorporate components written in different languages, including Java and C++.

During the same time period, Sun Microsystems developed the Enterprise JavaBeans (EJB) specification for distributed components and the Java Platform 2 Enterprise Edition (J2EE) specification for a Web-based application architecture. EJB and J2EE incorporate key CORBA middleware specifications. Some of the same companies contributed to both the CCM and EJB specifications, and a CCM container for Java is expected to be able to support an EJB component. The EJB specification, however, has gained wider acceptance and is part of the more complete J2EE environment. While the EJB and J2EE specifications are not entirely nonproprietary, they do represent the joint efforts of a number of different vendors, and the specifications are being implemented in a number of products. They incorporate the CORBA Internet Inter-ORB Protocol (IIOP), which allows EBJ components to interoperate with CORBA components and services written in other languages. It also incorporates CORBA Security and, optionally, the CORBA Object Transaction Service (OTS), enabling interoperability for transaction and security facilities.

Before CCM and EJB, Microsoft developed the Common Object Model (COM) component environment for desktop applications. This technology was very successful for the development of personal computer applications for the Windows operating system. A marketplace emerged in Dynamic Linked Library (DLL) and Visual Basic components for Windows applications. This architecture evolved through resource sharing on a local-area network (LAN) and eventually to a distributed objects technology now called Component Object Model (COM+).

While COM+ and its predecessors have had a significant impact on the marketplace by association with the Windows operating system, COM+ is a single-vendor technology controlled by Microsoft and supported only by the Windows operating system.

These three component technologies, CCM, EJB, and COM+, are all evolving in a similar direction and together represent the efforts of leading commercial software vendors. EJB stands out for its widespread acceptance and multiplatform implementations.

Recently, the OMG has adopted a Model-Driven Architecture (MDA) strategy for the development of standards. Future specifications will be expressed in the Unified Modeling Language (UML) with mappings of UML elements to implementation elements of specific technologies such as CCM, EJB, and COM+. This will greatly expand the applicability of specifications of application components and will enable the interoperability of components, even distributed components that are implemented in different technologies.

The Expanded Scale of Reuse

These standards are important both because they indicate a widespread trend and because they increase the potential scale of reuse of application components. CORBA products are available for most computing platforms. The Java language has gained wide acceptance as an application development language because the same application code can execute on many different platforms. The EJB specification has defined containers for the execution of Java components (so-called beans) where the container manages services and provides application support so that the component developer can concentrate on the application with minimal concern about distributed computing issues. Associated Java-based standards define interfaces for related services such as Java Database Connectivity (JDBC) and Java Messaging Service (JMS).

As these component standards have evolved, Web technology also has evolved to a separation of Web servers from application servers. This separation allows the user interface to be modified and tailored to different requirements with little or no impact on the underlying application. This also removes user interface requirements as a barrier to application component reuse.

The final factor in the scale of reuse is workflow management. Traditional applications have incorporated elements of associated business processes. As the business changes, the applications get in the way of adapting the business processes. Often the impact of change on the application is difficult to anticipate, and the necessary application changes may take considerable time and money. Workflow management provides the means to keep business processes visible and flexible. While application components provide low-level functionality, the workflow processes orchestrate their participation and the participation of humans in the overall business function. Not only does this provide business flexibility, but it also encourages the design of application components that incorporate discrete, generalized solutions that have minimal dependence on current business procedures. Thus, the application components will be better suited to reuse.

Summary

The strategy promoted in this book is to exploit industry standards, Web technology, and workflow management technology to develop and incorporate reusable application components. In the early stages, there will not be a significant market in application components, but the standards and technology will provide vendor independence and application flexibility. As the technology and marketplace mature, reusable components will emerge. To the extent that industry standards are developed for application component interfaces, the market potential will be improved, and the industry will grow. The enterprise that has implemented the distributed components architecture will be positioned to exploit this marketplace as it unfolds.

At this point, EJB with J2EE is the leading distributed component technology. Through working with multiple vendors and leveraging the power of the Java language, Sun Microsystems has produced a specification that is supported and implemented by a number of vendors on a number of platforms. For these reasons, we will focus on EJB with J2EE as the exemplar of distributed components technology in this chapter.

Component Specifications

A component must be sufficiently specified that one implementation can be replaced by another implementation and the related components will still function properly. In this section we will examine the various aspects of a component specification. The design of a component-based system must address all these aspects. Some of these will be determined by the selected component technology (CCM or EJB), some should be addressed by a system architecture, and those remaining must be addressed by the individual component specifications. We will discuss the following requirements for component specifications:

Basic properties. Components have several basic characteristics that affect the manner in which they participate in a system.

Interfaces. The composition of components requires compatibility of their interfaces.

Levels of granularity. The scale of a component affects the manner in which it interacts with other components.

Composition. Specifications are required to define how components are composed from more elementary components.

Shared infrastructure. Components must have a shared infrastructure incorporating communications facilities and shared services.

Development tools. Development tools are essential for consistent design, configuration, and deployment of components.

Basic Properties

Components have some basic properties that affect their suitability for different purposes:

- Network-visible
- Sharable

- Persistent
- Managed

We will discuss options presented by each of these properties and their characteristics.

Network-Visible

Access to a component may be limited to other components that are colocated in the same address space. Object-oriented programming languages provide this level of visibility. Other components may be visible on the network so that they can receive messages from components and services on other computers. Network-visible components sometimes may be accessed locally through their programming language interface, but this should be discouraged because it will bypass functionality incorporated in the network interface.

A network-visible component has an identifier within the scope of the network. Messages are directed to the component using this identifier. Consequently, network-visible components are passed by reference.

Components that are not network-visible, that is, local components, cannot be passed by reference over the network, but they can be passed by value; that is, their state can be copied. It is possible for a local component to be passed by value over the network and passed by reference locally.

Sharable

Sharable components can be engaged in multiple threads of control. Thus, they may be involved in concurrent transactions, and an appropriate mechanism must be provided to serialize the transactions to prevent conflicts. Components that are not sharable must be restricted to a single thread of control. Furthermore, a component that is not sharable may only exist for a single transaction, or it may exist for a sequence of related transactions. A thread that consists of a sequence of transactions for a single user is called a *session*.

Components that are not sharable can be network-visible, but care must be taken to restrict access to the single session so that there are no concurrency conflicts. Generally, these components carry a state that is relevant to the particular session, and they cease to exist when the session ends.

The same application functionality may be implemented with either sharable or nonsharable components. For example, either type may represent an order. If the component is sharable, it will maintain the state of the order for operations performed by multiple, potentially concurrent transactions. The state of the order will be saved at the end of each transaction for recoverability. If the component is not sharable, when a session begins, the state of the order will be retrieved from a database with a lock. The session will perform various operations on the order, possibly in the context of a sequence of transactions. At the end of each transaction, the state of the order is stored in the database for recoverability, but the order remains locked until the end of the session. At the end of the session, the database is updated, the lock is released, and the component is removed from memory.

Either approach is viable. The benefits of the shared component are that the state remains in computer memory to be available for the next transaction or session and fewer database retrievals are required. This is particularly important for component instances that are used heavily. The benefit of the non-shared component is that the implementation is simpler. The instance is always obtained from the database, and concurrency control is provided by the database.

Persistent

Persistence is the quality that the state of a component is expected to be preserved when the machine fails or is turned off. Not all components are persistent; they may exist only to facilitate operations within the scope of a transaction and then cease to exist. Persistence generally is achieved by storing the state in a database. Modifying the state in a transactional context and updating the database when the transaction commits results in recoverability, so the state in the database is always consistent.

The data structures of components often are different from the data structures of the associated database. This is particularly true if a relational database is used. Consequently, it is necessary for the database structure to be transformed to the component structure when the state is retrieved from the database, and when the database is updated, a reverse transformation is performed. Tools for implementation of the component should accept a transformation specification and provide the appropriate logic for database retrieval and updates.

Similarly, when component instances are retrieved using a query expression, the query should be expressed in terms of the component data structure, but it must be transformed to reflect the database structure in order to perform the database query.

The persistence mechanism requires an additional capability if the component is sharable. When a reference to an instance is requested, if the instance is already active (in memory), then the reference to the active instance must be returned. The same is true for instances identified by a query. If any are already active, then the active instances must be included in the query result.

Managed

Managed means that all instances of the component type are known and can be retrieved based on their identifier or through a query. Typically, all instances are managed on a single server. However, in a more robust implementation that supports load balancing and the integration of multiple implementations, instances of a type may be scattered over multiple servers and be reassigned dynamically to optimize performance. It must be possible to consistently locate instances through their identifier and through queries, if applicable.

A managed component also should support functions that apply to all instances of the type (the *extent* of the type). Queries on the extent of the type are one category of such functions. For example, a query might examine all orders to return those for a particular part. Other application-specific functions may apply to all instances as well. In particular, a robust implementation may support constraints or event-condition-action rules to be applied to all instances of a type.

Interface Specifications

Interfaces define the points of interaction between components. If the interfaces are not well defined and compatible, the components will not work together. A component may have multiple interfaces, that is, points at which it interacts with different components or for different purposes.

In this section we will consider the various requirements of interface specifications:

- Communication modes
- Data format
- Interaction protocol
- Relationships
- Type-based operations

Communication Modes

The basic form of an interface is determined by the mode of communication it supports. There are two essential communication modes for distributed components:

- Synchronous messaging
- Store-and-forward messaging

Synchronous messaging interfaces define the signatures of methods that are invoked while the sender waits for a response. Messages may have a transactional context and provide security authorization information.

Store-and-forward messages are delivered to a message queue. The sender and recipient, independently, determine the transaction and security contexts in which a message is processed. The recipient may receive messages as a specific addressee specified by the sender, or the recipient may be required to subscribe to a category of events it needs to perform its function.

Data Format

The data exchanged between components must be in consistent formats. In synchronous messaging, data are typed. Data types specify the structure of message parameters that are passed by value and the interface types of parameters that are passed by reference.

The data exchanged through store-and-forward messaging may be characterized as documents. A recipient will accept document types that meet accepted format specifications. The industry direction is for these to be Extensible Markup Language (XML) documents.

Interaction Protocols

A *protocol* describes the acceptable sequence in an exchange of messages. The sequence is defined in terms of the apparent state of a message recipient. Some interfaces have no protocol restrictions; that is, the interface will accept any message at any time. A simple protocol specification may be expressed in terms of preconditions; that is, a message is only acceptable when the recipient is in a certain state. A more complex protocol must be defined if there are restrictive state transitions.

State-transition constraints are particularly important in business-to-business (B2B) interactions, where the sequence of exchanges is less predictable. In general, a component will be expected to be in a particular state at the beginning of a process. The response to a message typically will indicate the state of the component for receipt of the next message.

Note that a protocol is defined in terms of *apparent* state, the state that is visible to the collaborating component. The internal state of a component may be much more complex and involve exchanges with other components.

Relationships

Component instances have relationships with other component instances. These relationships typically represent the relationships between concepts in the application domain, such as customers and orders, or in a workflow process between the process subject matter and participants. These relationships are part of the persistent state of a component.

Relationships are usually complementary—A expresses a relationship with B, and B expresses a complementary relationship with A. Relationships may be one-to-one, one-to-many, or many-to-many. When a relationship is updated and the related object has a complementary reference, it also must be updated.

Access to relationships, for traversals as well as updates, must be defined as part of the interface specification of a component. The methods employed could be defined for each relationship, but it is preferable to have a consistent protocol. The consistent protocol simplifies design and programming, and it also enables interfaces and supporting code to be generated from more abstract specifications.

Type-Based Operations

Certain operations are not associated with particular instances of a component, but rather with the component type generally. These include a request to create a new instance, find a particular instance, or perform a query on the set of all instances. Such operations typically are associated with a *home* or *type manager* interface.

Levels of Granularity

The level of granularity of a component describes the scope of its functionality and its relationships with other components. There are three fundamental levels of granularity to be considered:

- **Primitive component.**   One that is implemented directly rather than being composed of other components.
- **Local composition.**   A composition of colocated components.
- **Distributed composition.**   A composition that incorporates components on different computers.

We will discuss the nature of each of these briefly in the following subsections.

A Primitive Component

A primitive component is implemented directly in a programming language; it is not assembled from smaller components. Its functionality is implemented within a single address space, usually in a single programming language.

Primitive components execute the actual functionality of a component-based system. Compositions integrate primitive components to perform more complex functions. While a composition may include logic for interconnecting the components of the composition, it does not directly implement the actual application functionality.

Primitive components generally are single-threaded. They may participate in multiple transactions and multiple sessions, but these executions will be serialized. Some stateless components can participate concurrently in multiple threads; they essentially provide execution logic without a stored state.

Components at any level of granularity may be implemented directly in a programming language without any internal component structure. A component with complex functionality that could have been implemented through the composition of finer-grained components might be characterized as a *monolithic* component. A monolithic component could be an adaptation of a legacy system. There will be monolithic components that are highly optimized solutions to common problems. From the standpoint of their external characteristics, monolithic components should be indistinguishable from composed components that implement the same functionality. This interface equivalence allows for future redesign of the component for implementation of a component architecture.

A Local Composition

A composition within an address space, a local composition, may incorporate both primitive components and compositions of components that all execute within the same address space. Figure 10.1 depicts local compositions within an address space. Composition A consists of four primitive components. Composition B consists of two primitive components and a local composition. Composition C consists of two primitive components and two local compositions.

The components within the local composition usually will communicate through local (programming language) interfaces. These local interfaces usually will provide more efficient communication than remote-access interfaces,

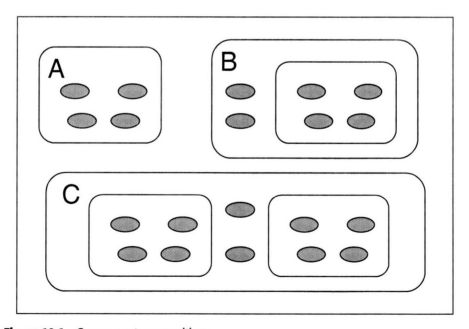

Figure 10.1   Component compositions.

and they may provide access to functionality that is not exposed to network access. Thus, in a local composition, components within A, B, or C in the diagram may be designed to be colocated, and the connections between them will not be required to anticipate the implications of remote accesses between them unless their interfaces are also accessed remotely.

A Distributed Composition

On the other hand, a composition may incorporate components that execute on multiple servers. Such a composition might provide a complex application function or an entire application. While such a composition could be designed to incorporate some components that must be colocated and others that can be distributed, the composition is much less complex if all the components of a distributed composition are designed to be distributed. In this way, the composition is concerned only with remote interfaces. In other words, it is preferable for compositions to be designed to be either local or distributed but not both.

When deployed, a distributed composition could be configured such that some or all of its components are physically colocated. This becomes a system management and performance decision as opposed to a component-specification decision. The composition is logically distributed, but its components may be physically colocated. The physical implementations of these components may constrain the degree to which they may be colocated. For example, if they are written in different languages, they may be executed on the same computer but in different address spaces so that they are logically distributed.

In Figure 10.1, compositions A, B, and C could be components of a distributed composition that are colocated on the same server. These components would interoperate as though they were remote, but the performance would be improved by the elimination of communications over the network. The elimination of network communication between them will improve performance, and in some cases the supporting environment (such as the component container) will provide further optimization based on colocation.

Composition

The structure of a component-based system is defined by composition from components. A composition connects components together to solve a more complex problem. Compositions may then become components for yet more substantial solutions.

Abstraction

Each component, and thus each composition of components, should provide an abstraction of its functionality that conceals the complexity of its implementation and the components from which is composed. This abstraction should place minimal constraints on the implementation while providing maximum flexibility in the ways the component can be used; in other words, the interface(s) should anticipate that the component(s) might be used in a variety of circumstances.

Abstraction provides system flexibility by minimizing the coupling between components and thus limiting propagation of the effects of change. It should be possible to change the implementation of a component, thus altering the performance or the nature of the solution, without affecting compatibility with related components.

Mechanisms of Composition

There are two fundamental mechanisms by which components can be incorporated in a composition: encapsulation and reference. Most component-based systems can be expected to use both these mechanisms, but some designs may make more use of one than the other.

Encapsulation involves a composition that contains its components and isolates them from outside access. The components are accessed only indirectly, through the composition interfaces, and the presence of the components may be hidden from users of the composition.

This form may be used, for example, where sharing of data is provided by a database, and the active components are transient instantiations. The data are retrieved from the database, and the component is instantiated for the particular transaction or session. When the session completes, the database is updated, and the component instance is removed. Different sessions may employ different compositions of components. When a session invokes a particular composition, the component is instantiated just for that session and then removed. Data that are shared by different sessions are incorporated in an appropriate composition for each session.

Figure 10.2 illustrates incorporation by encapsulation. The three process components—ordering process, order fulfillment, and order delivery—each operate on an order and its line items. When an ordering session is active, it instantiates the order and line items within the same composition. When it completes, the database is updated, and the composition is released. When the order fulfillment process starts, it creates its own instances of order and line items, and so on. Each of these processes takes exclusive control of the order and its line items when performing operations on the order. Typically, each process would consist of a series of transactions, and instances of the component would be active only during each transaction, so the order and order items would be under their exclusive control only for the duration of a transaction, not for the full duration of the process.

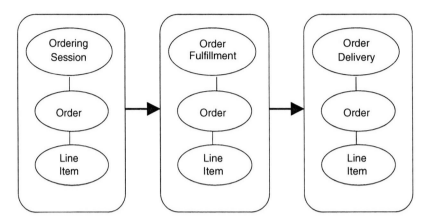

Figure 10.2   Incorporation by encapsulation.

Composition by *reference* involves connections between components that are independently visible and usable outside the composition. Figure 10.3 illustrates an example. An order may be created or updated by a customer ordering session. The customer session operates on the order by reference, sending appropriate messages to its independent order component. When the customer session completes, the database is updated, but the order component is not released. Then the same order component will be incorporated by reference in the order fulfillment process. Concurrency control is the responsibility of the order component because it is shared. In both composition by encapsulation and by reference, the order component is incorporated in both the ordering session and the order fulfillment processes. However, in composition by encapsulation, the state of the component must be retrieved from the database for each new session.

In general, incorporation by encapsulation is used for relatively fine-grained components, where there is no need to share instances of an encapsulated component independently. For example, in Figure 10.3, the order and its line items are encapsulated in the order component. Incorporation by reference generally occurs on larger-grained components, where an instance of the incorporated component is used in multiple contexts. For example, the order component will be the subject of actions in a number of contexts as it goes through the ordering, fulfillment, delivery, and payment processes and may be the subject of status checks and order changes as it goes through these processes.

In general, incorporation by encapsulation may provide greater opportunity for optimization through close coupling of the encapsulated components. Incorporation by reference preserves the independence of the components and provides greater flexibility in system configuration.

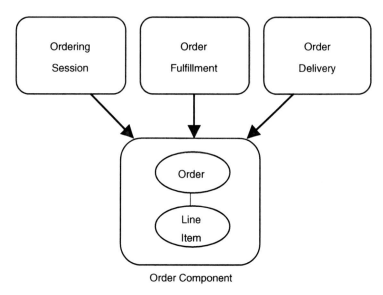

Figure 10.3 Incorporation by reference.

Process Components

Conventional information systems have evolved from the automation of specific activities to the automation of major business functions. In this evolution, aspects of the business processes have become embedded in the systems, often making the business processes less visible and more difficult to change.

Workflow management systems now provide facilities for visible and flexible implementations of business processes. The elements of business processes that have been embedded in information systems should be implemented in workflow processes. This is a change from the conventional object-oriented programming approach to implement process logic in methods on entity objects such as order and customer.

From a component architecture standpoint, this means that process components should be distinguished from entity components. The process components implement the business processes in ways that facilitate monitoring, analysis, and change of the business processes. The processes operate on the entities either directly or through engaging people in the process. The entity components represent the elements of the business and their relationships. Methods on the entity components should perform operations that are either computations or implementations of consistency constraints, but should not preempt business decisions or the sequence in which business activities occur.

This separation is reflected in the examples in Figures 10.2 and 10.3. The process components operate on the order and line item components. However, these examples do not show the relationships between process components.

Processes generally are linked in one of two ways: by event or by invocation. A process may directly or indirectly produce an event that causes another process to be initiated or altered. For example, the ordering session in Figure 10.3 might produce an event when the order is accepted. This could trigger an initiation of the order fulfillment process. The event could be produced explicitly by an activity operation, or it could be produced implicitly from the change of state of the order.

A process may be active and have an activity that is a subscriber for an event. An occurrence of the event may provide notice to proceed, or it may affect a condition that causes the flow of control to change. For example, an order fulfillment process might be waiting for inventory to be replenished and an event from the receipt of new material could enable it to proceed.

A process may invoke another process, where the invoked process occurs in a variety of circumstances and is defined once, or the invoked process is one that is performed by a different system or organization. For example, an order fulfillment process might invoke a back-order process when there is insufficient inventory to fill an order.

Where processes invoke other processes, the invoked process may be incorporated by reference or by encapsulation. Where processes are initiated or altered by events, it is appropriate to implement the processes as independent components, accessed by reference. They are active at different times, they probably represent different areas of responsibility, and changes to one process are not likely to affect the other.

Processes that are invoked in many different circumstances should be invoked by reference. It should be possible to alter any of the circumstances or invoke the process under new circumstances without affecting the calling process or other circumstances. For example, a purchasing process may be invoked in a wide variety of circumstances throughout the enterprise. In some cases it might be invoked directly by an individual; in other cases it might be invoked by a business process, such as an inventory-replenishment process or a back-order process.

On the other hand, processes designed to resolve exceptions might be defined separately from a mainstream process, but be encapsulated in the same component. For example, in the order fulfillment process, an item removed from inventory might be found to be defective. An exception process might be invoked to dispose of the defective item and replace it with another item from inventory. This exception process is closely aligned to the mainstream process and may be encapsulated so that only the mainstream process is visible on the network.

Shared Infrastructure

Distributed components require a shared infrastructure that provides supporting services. There are four key shared services:

- Transaction service
- Name service
- Messaging services
- Security service

These services provide common data and mechanisms that are essential for the interoperation of distributed components. We will discuss each of these briefly.

Transaction Service

A transaction service provides an identifier for each transaction, associates operations with a transaction, and provides the mechanism for commit or rollback when the activities of a transaction are completed. In a distributed database environment, it is important that a two-phase commit process is provided so that all the resources involved in a transaction are either committed or rolled back. In a distributed component environment, an additional *synchronize* phase is required to accomplish appropriate database updates from the component state. These issues were discussed in detail in Chapter 5.

Name Service

A name service is essential to provide for the translation from a logical identifier to a reference of a specific element in a distributed environment. It provides references to shared resources and to component-type managers or homes so that instances of the components can be created or located. A name service provices a hierarchical directory structure to group names into name spaces.

Messaging

Two modes of messaging must be considered: synchronous and asynchronous. These are implemented with different facilities.

Synchronous messaging supports the invocation of methods on a remote object as an inline request-response. A message directed to a local proxy is relayed and presented to the appropriate interface on a remote server, and the response is returned. The facility that provides this service often is described as an *object request broker* (ORB). Synchronous messages generally are executed in the context of a single transaction. The ORB facilities are highly integrated with the component implementations so that the complexities of managing the messages and responses are concealed from application developers.

Asynchronous messaging provides store-and-forward communications, discussed in detail in Chapter 6. These may be messages directed to specific destinations or events delivered to subscribers. The service often is described as a *message broker* service. A message broker accepts messages from output queues and forwards them to appropriate input queues. An asynchronous message is entered in an output queue in the context of one transaction and will be removed from a destination input queue in the context of a different transaction. The message broker provides guaranteed delivery, once and only once, through transactional control of queue updates. The application programmer uses the service through interfaces to the input and output queues.

Synchronous messaging will be confined to a single application or geographically local business function, a business system domain (BSD). Asynchronous messaging may be used locally, and it is the preferred mechanism for communication between independent applications and business functions, as in enterprise application integration (EAI).

Security Service

From a component perspective, a security service provides the linkage between authentication (determining a user's identity) accomplished at the user interface and authorization (determining authority). The security service may restrict access to interfaces and methods, and it may provide access to the principal (such as the user) identifier and authorized roles for access control implemented in the application. The security context must be carried with messages in a manner similar to the transaction context. Security issues are discussed in detail in Chapter 11.

Development Tools

Development tools are essential for building a component-based system. Modeling tools are needed to develop a robust design, implementation tools are needed to improve programming productivity and manage the composition and integration of components, and deployment tools are needed to compose independently developed components and configure and integrate components in a particular information systems environment.

Modeling Tools

Modeling tools should provide a robust representation of the system being developed and at the same time present different viewpoints that abstract the design for particular purposes. The Unified Modeling Language (UML) Profile for

Enterprise Distributed Object Computing (EDOC) specification has been developed in the OMG. This specification defines extensions to UML to address the design of components, component composition, the specification of protocols between components and between enterprises, the specification of process components, support for viewpoints, and the ability to specify and apply patterns. Additional specifications will define detailed models for business processes and mappings of the specifications to specific technologies such as CCM and EJB.

A robust modeling environment will facilitate the definition and refinement of components; it will enable the design to be validated from different viewpoints for consistency, completeness, and robustness; and it will help application developers focus on solving business problems rather than resolving technical complexities.

Implementation Tools

In addition to conventional development tools, tools are required to translate the design model discussed earlier and generate code for the implementation of the design in a particular technology. These tools must complement the services and facilities of the target environment.

Current modeling tools do not provide robust models, and code generation typically is limited to providing class skeletons. The UML Profile for EDOC specification will create a market for more robust tools.

Deployment Tools

Deployment tools adapt a component to a particular environment. A component that is designed for reuse should be deployable to a variety of environments, some of which were not known at the time the component was developed. This requires that certain details be defined for each deployment. The following are key aspects of deployment specifications:

- Assignment of components to servers
- Links to the identifiers of shared services
- Mapping of the persistent state of components to a database schema
- Transformation or qualification of component names for compatibility with the target environment
- Mapping of security roles of the environment to role references within the component
- Specification of asynchronous messaging destinations and event subscriptions
- Assignment or modification of interface access permissions

Tools are needed not only to improve the productivity of this activity, but also to ensure that the specifications are consistent and complete.

Component Technology

The preceding section has described the aspects of component design for a distributed components system. In this section we will examine EJB technology for the implementation of distributed components.

The focus of EJB technology is on primitive components. It defines a *container* environment in which components called *beans* can be deployed, allowing the same components to execute on a variety of computing platforms. The container specification provides a consistent integration of services necessary to support bean execution, but it does not ensure interoperability between beans deployed on different platforms, that is, different container products, computers, and operating systems. The specification provides some support for component composition, but it does not provide a component specification environment, and there are ambiguities that may interfere with component integration and interoperability.

In the following subsections we will examine EJB technology in greater detail, including the following:

- Component types
- Component features
- Containers
- Composition
- Specification ambiguities
- Interoperability issues
- Legacy integration

The EJB specification, along with the J2EE environment specification, provides much of a distributed computing architecture. At the same time, significant aspects are left to the implementers of this specification and the application developers that use their products. The subsection on specification ambiguities identifies areas where implementers of the specification may have significant differences that will affect the design and implementation of applications. The section on interoperability issues identifies issues that may affect the capability of components to interoperate, particularly if implemented on different platforms.

Component Types

The EJB specification defines five types of components:

- Entity beans
- Stateful session beans
- Stateless session beans
- Message-driven beans
- Value objects

Table 10.1 highlights the differences between these component types. We will discuss each of these component types briefly in the subsections that follow. Key features of EJB components, including the properties in Table 10.1, will be discussed in the next subsection.

Entity Beans

Entity beans are the most robust form of component. They will be used to model shared services and the primary entities of an application environment if those entities are implemented as sharable distributed objects.

Only entity beans are managed, can have relationships, and are supported by container-based persistence. This means that entity beans can be retrieved based on an identifier or by a query expression. The integrity of relationships is maintained, and the state can be stored automatically or rolled back at the end of a transaction.

Table 10.1 Differentiating Properties of EJB Components

	ENTITY BEAN	STATEFUL SESSION BEAN	STATELESS SESSION BEAN	MESSAGE-DRIVEN BEAN	VALUE OBJECT
Network-visible	Optional	Optional	Optional	No	No
Sharable	Yes	No	No	No	No
Managed extent	Yes	No	No	No	No
Persistence	Yes	Optional	No	No	Dependent*
Passed by value	No	No	No	No	Yes
Relationships	Local	No	No	No	No
Queries	Yes	No	No	No	No

*A value object will be incorporated in the persistent state of an entity or session bean.

Stateful Session Beans

A session bean only exists for the duration of one session. A *session* is defined as a series of operations performed by a single user. A stateful session bean has a state that is associated with the particular user session.

The session bean can retrieve data from a database, operate on the data, and then update the database. The session bean does not control concurrent access, and user operations are required to be sequential, not concurrent.

The session bean can operate in a transactional context and should if it is updating a database. In such a case, the database manager will manage concurrent access to the data.

A stateful session bean also might be used as a proxy for an entity bean. In this technique, the state of the entity bean may be copied to a similar session bean on a client system. The session bean then supports local interactive operations to improve performance. The entity bean is then updated at the end of the session.

Stateless Session Beans

Like a stateful session bean, a stateless session bean can only be used in one session. Unlike the stateful session bean, it does not have a state that is unique to the session, so when its associated session ends, it may be reused for a subsequent session.

A stateless session bean might be used to represent a database connection. The connection can only be used by one session at a time, but can be used by different sessions serially.

Message-Driven Beans

Message-driven beans are very lightweight. They exist to process incoming asynchronous messages; the receipt of a message activates a message bean. In effect, a message receipt is similar to a session; the message bean is dedicated to processing a single message. Like stateless session beans, message-driven beans have no persistent state associated with the message and thus can be reused for subsequent messages. The type of a message determines the type of message bean to be activated.

Value Objects

Value objects are not classified as components within the EJB specifications, but from an abstract modeling standpoint, they are components because they encapsulate data and functionality. Value objects are local-only components.

Value objects may be passed by reference locally (within an address space), but they are never passed by reference over the network—they are passed by value. Alone, a value object is not persistent, but it can be persistent vicariously if it is encapsulated in an entity bean or a persistent state of a stateful session bean. Nor does it control concurrent accesses. Concurrency control is implicit because it is either encapsulated in a component that provides concurrency control or a copy of its state is provided for use in a single session.

Value objects are used to represent concepts that are transient or are incorporated in other identifiable, persistent objects. Order line items and postal addresses likely will be implemented as value objects because they provide details of identifiable objects but do not need to be identifiable or persistent independently.

Component Features

In this subsection we will examine the features of EJB components in greater detail. This will provide greater insight into the architecture defined by EJB specifications. We will examine each of the following features:

- Network access
- Sharing
- Managed extent
- Relationships
- Persistence
- Queries
- Passing of state
- Transactions
- Security
- Composition
- Passivation
- Portability

Network Access

For an EJB component to be network-accessible, it must have a remote access interface and a reference identifier to which remote messages are directed. Entity beans and session beans (both stateful and stateless) can have remote interfaces or local interfaces or both. These interfaces actually direct messages to the bean container, the computing environment in which the beans are installed. This gives the container the opportunity to incorporate system services, such as transaction management, prior to invoking the target method on the bean instance.

Beans may be invoked through their remote interface even if the call is local. This allows beans to be remote or colocated transparently. A local interface reduces the overhead, but requires that the sender and receiver be colocated. It may also bypass container functionality such as concurrency control. Message-driven beans and value objects are not remotely accessible.

Sharing

Sharing refers to the capability of a component to participate in multiple concurrent transactions. This is accomplished through the use of a transaction identifier to serialize access from different transactions, that is, to execute as if only one transaction were executing at a time.

The container provides concurrency control for entity beans. When the bean is invoked for a transaction, it is locked until the transaction completes. Session beans can participate in transactions, but it is an error for the session bean to be invoked for a different transaction. The session bean is limited to one transaction at a time for a single user.

Message-driven beans and value objects cannot be shared. A message-driven bean executes for only one incoming message at a time. It may be reused after processing for a message is completed. A value object will exist either in the context of a bean or in the context of a session (user or input message process). Within either context, access will be restricted to one transaction at a time.

Managed Extent

Entity beans have a managed extent. All instances of the bean type are known. They have unique identifiers, and they are subject to retrieval by a query over the extent.

The other EJB components do not have managed extents. All component types have a home, or equivalent object, that represents the type for life-cycle operations. Only the entity bean home supports the retrieval of instances by identifier or by query, and only the entity bean home will support application methods compliant to all instances in the extent of the type.

Relationships

The EJB specification supports container-managed relationships. However, relationships are only between colocated entity beans, and relationships can only be accessed through local interfaces on entity beans. While this is a very important capability, the restrictions to colocated entity beans and access through local interfaces constitute serious limitations.

Relationships may be one-to-one, one-to-many, or many-to-many. The many relationships are implemented using local collections. Consequently, a *get* for a relationship will return either a local reference to a related entity bean or a collection of local entity beans of the type specified for the relationship.

The EJB specification provides for a cascade delete capability. In the deployment descriptor (the specification for bean deployment), cascading delete can be specified for a dependent entity bean. If an entity bean is deleted, then all related entity beans with cascade delete specified will be deleted as well. Cascade delete is only available when the primary entity is in a one-to-one or one-to-many relationship with the entities specified for cascade delete.

The EJB specification defines relationships sufficiently for use by application programmers, but it does not provide details of the implementation. Since relationships can only be local, they will only involve entity beans that are executing within the same container, so container provider vendors are free to employ significantly different designs.

Persistence

Persistence is the preservation of the state of a bean if the system is shut down or fails. A robust form of persistence is provided for entity beans through *container-managed persistence*. In container-managed persistence, the container retrieves the state of the object from the database when the instance is activated and updates the database whenever an associated transaction commits. Container-managed persistence provides a mechanism for mapping the structure of the entity bean data to the database schema. This mapping is applied for the interpretation of query expressions. Container-managed persistence also preserves the state of relationships between beans within the same container.

Entity beans and stateful session beans may have *bean-managed persistence.* Under this arrangement, retrievals of the state from the database and updates of the state in the database are the responsibility of the bean developer.

When an entity bean with bean-managed persistence becomes active, it is associated with a particular entity bean identifier. The container will invoke *load* and *store* methods on the entity bean, directing it to load its state from the database or store its state in the database. This provides synchronization of the database and entity bean state at appropriate points in a transaction. The entity bean (in other words, the developer) is responsible for loading and storing the proper state associated with its identifier.

Similarly, a stateful session bean may retrieve its state from a database and store its state in the database. The protocol is different from the entity bean protocol because the stateful session bean does not have an identifier for the relevant state. The container invokes methods on the stateful session bean after a new transaction has begun, before the transaction commits, and after the transaction has committed. This allows the session bean to load and store its state properly. The *after-completion* method call notifies the session bean if the transaction completed the commit (the database is updated) or the transaction was rolled back, making the state of the session bean no longer current. Note that for bean-managed persistence, the container does not provide support for relationships.

Queries

The EJB specification supports queries on entity beans that use container-managed persistence. Queries are very important in business systems for identifying instances that meet certain criteria or for gathering characteristics of a population.

A query is expressed in terms of the bean attributes and relationships and is translated to the database schema for execution. Query expressions are invoked by methods on the entity bean, but the query expression is specified in a deployment descriptor (an XML specification separate from the Java code). Consequently, queries cannot be created programmatically at run time, but query expressions do incorporate runtime parameters.

There are two types of queries: *find* and *select*. A *find* query retrieves a subset of all instances of a type. It returns an instance or a collection of the associated entity bean type that meets the query expression criteria. A find query is remotely accessible. A *select* query extends the scope of selection to related entity beans. It returns an instance or collection of attribute values or related bean instances. A select query is invoked on a local method and is not remotely accessible. The select query is more powerful because it traverses relationships to apply selection criteria and produce results, but the scope is constrained to colocated, related types.

Passing by Value

Bean attributes can reference local *value objects* that contain complex state structures. Local value objects are objects implemented in the local programming language that also can be instantiated in other environments on the network in the same or other languages. These objects do not have network interfaces, and therefore references to them cannot be passed to remote components.

Since value objects are not directly network accessible, there are two options for applying updates over the network:

- Invoke methods on the encapsulating bean to retrieve attribute values or apply changes to the value object.
- Retrieve a copy of the value object state, access relevant attributes locally, and then, if the copy has been changed, send a copy back to the encapsulating entity to update its state.

The first option results in high network traffic, but ensures the application of constraints, whereas the second allows much of the activity to be localized at the risk of inconsistent or conflicting updates.

The entity bean container serializes concurrent transactions that may access a value object within an encapsulating entity. A copy of the value object should be used only within the context of a single transaction so that it can be kept consistent with the primary copy managed by the entity bean.

In some cases, these objects can be implemented as entity beans. While they do not have unique identifiers, a unique identity can be inferred from the context of the containing bean. For example, order line items may be numbered sequentially, but require the order identifier to be uniquely identified outside the context of the order bean. The system designer must balance the system complexity and network activity associated with making these objects entity beans against the overhead and potential confusion of managing multiple copies when a value object is used.

While value objects will be passed by value over the network, they likely will be passed by reference locally. This can be a source of confusion and programming errors.

Transactions

In general, EJB components are expected to execute in a transactional context. The transaction service is expected to provide a transaction identifier and perform commit or rollback operations when the transaction completes. A two-phase commit is specified to support distributed databases. Transactions are *flat*; there are no nested transactions.

The EJB specification is compatible with the OMG Object Transaction Service (OTS), but OTS is not required. Interfaces to the transaction service are defined by the Java Transaction API (JTA) specification. This provides no assurance of interoperability between different EJB container vendors.

The EJB specification requires the capability to specify a bean as *nonreentrant*. This means that the container must raise an exception if a bean is invoked by a message in a transaction while it is still processing a message in the same transaction. This protects application logic that has not been designed for reentry.

The EJB specification does not require the capability to handle callbacks or requests from two or more different network sources within the same transaction context. In other words, a container may not be able to handle a message properly when it is received from a remote component that is processing a message from the current target component (callback). In addition, after a component has received and processed a message, it may not be able to process properly a later message received from a different source but in the same transaction context. In both these cases, the proper result would be for the second message to be processed as a continuation of the same transaction thread.

Security

The EJB specification requires security services compatible with the OMG Common Secure Interoperability version 2 (CSIv2) security specification. This provides for the principal authentication information to be passed with the message context. This allows access to be controlled at the interface or method level, and it allows the application to access authorization information for instance-specific authorization.

The specification requires role-based authorization, and the deployment descriptor provides for mapping the roles used in a particular component to the roles used in a target environment. In general, the security facilities and the mechanisms for mapping components to the execution environment are quite robust.

Composition

We discussed three basic levels of granularity in a preceding subsection:

- Primitive components
- Local compositions
- Distributed compositions

We will discuss the composition of an EJB system in terms of these levels of granularity.

Primitive Components

Primitive components are the five types that were discussed earlier: entity beans, stateful session beans, stateless session beans, message-driven beans, and value objects. The first four components are managed by an EJB container. The last, the value object, is a programming language object.

In addition to the component code, these components must be specified for purposes of composition. These composition specifications consist of interface definitions and deployment descriptors.

Although not explicit in the EJB specification, remote interfaces will be expressed in CORBA Interface Definition Language (IDL) to support IIOP for synchronous messaging between objects. For the Java programming language, these IDL interface specifications will be generated from the Java interface specifications, so they may be invisible to the developer. Four of the five component types will have interfaces specified in IDL. The message-driven components do not receive synchronous messages over the network and have no IDL interface. The value objects do not receive network messages, but their data structure is defined in IDL to be passed by value.

The deployment descriptors are XML documents that describe the remaining external characteristics of the components for composition. Value objects are sufficiently defined by IDL and their Java class definition that they do not need descriptor information. The deployment descriptor accompanies the component code in an EJB Java Archive (JAR) file.

A deployment descriptor can be a substantial document. As applicable to the bean type, the descriptor includes the bean name, its transactional characteristics, the security roles it uses, its data schema, query expressions to support query methods, and interfaces provided and interfaces used. For message-driven beans, the descriptor includes the message type the bean accepts and its acknowledgment mode.

Local Compositions

The bean descriptors define beans that must be colocated through the declaration of the local interfaces used. Local compositions can incorporate independently developed beans. The same container will manage all these components. Additional components may be incorporated in the same container through specifications in the deployment descriptor.

Distributed Compositions

Local compositions are collected into an EJB JAR file to define a distributed composition or a complete application. These compositions may include Java servlets and Java server pages (JSPs) to provide the accompanying Web interfaces. The deployment descriptors do not define how components interact. The composition is merely a grouping of objects expected to work together to provide desired functionality.

Passivation

Both the entity bean and the stateful session bean may remain active after a transaction commits. The entity bean is available for other operations by other users or processes, whereas the session bean remains available for the same user to continue a series of operations. Either an entity bean or a stateful session bean may be *passivated* between transactions. This means that the bean instance in memory is released to reduce the number of active objects on the server. However, passivation is not accomplished in the same way for both entity and stateful session beans.

Passivation of an entity bean eliminates the presence of the bean in memory, but the database is already current as a result of the last transaction commit. The entity bean receives a passivate message to perform any necessary housekeeping. When the entity bean is later activated, it follows the same process as described earlier for instantiation.

When a stateful session bean is passivated, it may have both a state that is stored in a database and a state associated with the session that is not normally persistent, that is, a transient state. Furthermore, the session bean does not have the unique identifier of an entity bean—it is a transient artifact that exists for the user session. Consequently, when the session bean receives a passivate message, it prepares for its state to be serialized and stored by the container in secondary storage. When the session bean is later referenced, its state is restored from secondary storage, and it may then also restore an associated persistent state from a database.

Portability

A primary goal of the EJB specification is the portability of components. The Java language and the availability of Java Virtual Machine (JVM) implementations on many platforms guarantee basic portability. However, much more is required for component portability. The EJB container is intended to provide additional facilities to achieve a consistent environment. It should be noted that a complete container product, in fact, not only is a runtime environment, but also includes the tools used to configure components, generate code, and install the components in a distributed environment.

The portability goal has been achieved to a significant degree. Beans can be developed that will execute in containers from different vendors and on different platforms. However, different vendors may extend the specification in different ways so that beans that take advantage of their features will not execute properly in containers from other vendors. In some cases, the extensions are important to the application, but to preserve portability, the bean developer must be careful to rely only on the EJB specification and not on the de facto capabilities provided by a particular vendor's container.

Specification Ambiguities

The EJB specification is the result of the combined efforts of a number of vendors. While the specification is more robust and flexible as a result, it also retains some ambiguities that allow for differences in implementations of different vendors. In this section we will briefly describe ambiguities under the following topics:

- Distributed instances of a type
- Callback
- Inclusive types
- Multithreading
- Relationships
- Handle durability

- Lazy activation

- Commit options

The concern here is that in some cases the ambiguity represents an important gap or shortcoming in the specification. Vendors will resolve these ambiguities in their implementations. While relying on a particular vendor's solution may result in beans that are not portable, the vendor solution in some cases also may have an important impact on an application.

Distributed Instances of a Type

The EJB specification is oriented toward the execution of all instances of a type on a single server, that is, in a single container. However, the specification suggests that some container implementers might choose to distribute instances of a type over multiple servers to provide better scalability and load balancing. This suggests that there would be multiple homes and an issue about which homes are responsible for which instances.

If instances of a type are executed on multiple servers, there is a more complex requirement for locating a particular instance. For entity beans, the home interface is designed to provide access to an entity bean based on its identifier. If an entity bean with a particular identifier is already active, requests must be directed to the active instance rather than causing a new instance to be created, possibly on a different server.

The specification suggests that when two requests are received for the same instance within the same transaction but the requests come from different source servers, in some implementations a duplicate instance could be created inadvertently (see the transaction diamond scenario discussion in the EJB specification).

Distribution across multiple servers also raises questions about relationships. Since relationships are only between colocated components, it would appear that relationships would be further restricted to those instances that happen to be executing in the same server, in other words in the same container.

Callback

The specification indicates that a callback may not be handled properly. A *callback* occurs when a bean (A) sends a message to another bean (B) that then sends a message back to the first bean (A) before returning from the initial message (sent from A to B). The desired result would be for the message to be accepted as within the scope of the same transaction. The EJB specification leaves the actual result up to the container implementer, so some implementations may allow a callback, but the application would then not be portable to containers that do not support it. Although applications can be designed to avoid this situation, this does restrict the design. In addition, when an application is assembled from components developed independently, there may be paths that inadvertently result in a callback. Thus, there may be a hidden defect or constraint on portability in a complex composition.

Inclusive Types

The object paradigm provides flexibility by allowing subtypes to be substituted for a type without affecting the logic that uses the type. Thus, Customer or Account types might be specialized to different subtypes to extend or alter the Customer and Account types for particular purposes. At the same time, these specializations can still participate as Customers and Accounts.

The same concept should apply to components of a particular type when performing queries. A customer with a particular identifier might be implemented as a specialization of Customer, yet it should be accessed through the Customer home. When it is instantiated, it should be instantiated as the specialized type. Similarly, relationships should accept specializations of the related types, and queries appropriately should traverse these relationships.

The EJB specification does not recognize the polymorphism of specialized types. The implication is that to query Customer, including its specializations, additional queries would need to be executed for each subtype, and relationships will link only the expressly defined types.

Multithreading

Multithreading allows concurrent processing within a server. A single-threaded server will handle only one request at a time, suspending subsequent requests until the first is completed. This creates a bottleneck, particularly if entity beans of a particular type must all be executed on the same server (the same container). The EJB specification does not require a multithreading environment.

Relationships

Relationships are confined to colocated components. This keeps the management and implementation within a single container and thus a single vendor's implementation. Consequently, except for the use of collections, each vendor is free to implement relationships in its own way.

Relationships in applications do not apply simply to small clusters of entities, but typically link all the entities in an application either directly or indirectly. Consequently, application developers are left to develop their own techniques for handling relationships between entity beans that may not be colocated. These relationships will not be consistent with local relationships because there are different issues to be addressed and access will be through remote rather than local interfaces. In addition, they will not be supported by container-managed persistence or queries.

The net result is that remote relationships are not likely to be portable, and related entity beans that are independently developed are not likely to be compatible.

Handle Durability

The EJB specification asserts that there is no standard for the structure or durability of an EJB handle. A *handle* is the identifier of a remote bean that is used to identify the bean in IIOP. The handle can be stored and later retrieved to access the bean it identifies. If handles had standard structure and durability, they might have been useful to implement remote relationships.

Lazy Activation

When an entity bean is activated, related entity beans also could be activated by recursively traversing relationships. This would improve performance over separate retrievals, but it may cause many beans to be activated that will never be used. Alternatively, the related entities might not be activated until they are actually the target of messages—lazy activation. Similarly, beans that are the result of a query should not be activated until they are actually the targets of messages. In some cases there could be thousands of instances returned by a query, and lazy activation would defer their activation until they are actually required for processing.

EJB does not specify or define design options for lazy activation. Since a query returns references to selected entity beans, either the entity beans must be activated to create the query response, or object references must be fabricated that would cause a bean to be activated if it is sent a message. This capability will depend on the container and associated ORB implementations.

Commit Options

The EJB specification defines three alternative commit strategies a container implementer may provide for entity beans:

- The state of an entity is held in memory between transactions so that the entity instance remains active and ready to receive subsequent requests. The database is updated as each transaction commits. The container ensures that the instance retains exclusive control over the state of the entity in the database.

- The state of an entity is held in memory between transactions, but the container does not maintain exclusive control of the state in the database. Consequently, the state of the instance must be refreshed for each new transaction.

- The instance is released between transactions, and the entity is instantiated from the state in the database for each new transaction.

These alternative strategies can have a significant impact on system performance. The first option optimizes performance by reducing the number of database reads. At the same time, if the database is shared, it will lock out other accesses for an undetermined duration. The second option preserves the object reference for network accesses, reducing the instantiation overhead of the third alternative and avoiding long-term locking of the state in the database. The third option eliminates the need for the container to implement passivation or the logic to determine when system loading calls for passivation—the instances are always passivated at the end of a transaction. Of course, it also avoids long-term locking of the database state.

The commit option may have a significant impact on application performance. If an entity is used in one transaction and is seldom used immediately in another transaction, then keeping it active has little value. However, a user frequently will interact with the same entity a number of times within a session, and certain entities, particularly shared services, may be accessed by many users, and the database accesses of the second and third options could have a significant impact on performance.

Component Interoperability Issues

As noted earlier, the focus of the EJB specification is the portability of components. This portability is achieved by using the Java language and by providing a platform-independent environment for the beans, the EJB container. However, portability does not establish interoperability. Interoperability requires that independently developed beans, potentially running on different platforms, will work together properly to achieve a more robust function. There are several key requirements of interoperability that are not addressed in the EJB specification, including the following:

- Transaction service
- Handles
- Message broker service
- Relationships
- Distributed instances of a type

We will discuss each of these briefly.

Transaction Service

The EJB specification requires that implementations support the JTA. This supports portability for beans, but it does not achieve interoperability between containers from different vendors or other CORBA-based components accessible with IIOP.

The EJB specification does require compliance with IIOP for synchronous message communication between servers. This provides the interoperability of synchronous messaging and a mechanism for conveying a transaction context, but it does not ensure the interoperability of transactions.

JTA provides an application interface that is compatible with OTS, but the EJB specification does not require that container vendors comply with the OTS specification for the exchange of transactional context data. Vendors that do comply with the OTS specification will be interoperable with each other.

Message Broker Service

The EJB specification requires the asynchronous messaging service to be compatible with JMS. JMS defines the functionality of a message broker service from an application perspective. Generally, a message broker service will involve message queues on each application platform and a server that functions as a communication hub. Message broker products are designed to work with a variety of platforms, and the JMS specification should be sufficient to ensure interoperability at this level.

In a large enterprise, there will be more than one message broker service, and it will be necessary to connect the message broker services to deliver messages across the enterprise. For point-to-point messaging, this can be achieved with a bridge that receives messages from one message broker and forwards them to another message broker.

However, JMS does not provide for the interoperability of the publish-and-subscribe service. For an efficient implementation, events will not be distributed across the network if there are no subscriptions; when a subscription is presented, such a service will enable the communication of the requested event from potential sources. This requires a mechanism for communication of the activation request that is not defined in the JMS specification. This might be remedied by a bridge between products if an activation request were visible to the bridge application, but JMS does not provide for the delivery of subscriptions to turn on publications. Therefore, there is no way for a JMS-compliant bridge to propagate a subscription in order to turn on dormant publication sources.

Handles

The EJB specification explicitly leaves the structure and durability of handles undefined. An application will use a handle to store a reference to an EJB instance for future use. Since the structure of the handle is not defined, the environment that creates the handle must decode it when it is to be used to access the target object. Consequently, handles cannot be shared across different platforms. The fact that handle durability is not defined means that handles cannot be relied on consistently for future reference, and application developers will need to devise their own mechanism for creating persistent references to EJB instances.

Relationships

The EJB specification provides requirements for relationships managed by a single container, but relationships in real systems are much more extensive. If a relationship extends from a bean in one container to a remote bean in a different vendor's container, there are additional issues to be resolved:

- A remote interface is required to enable the addition or deletion of a relationship of one instance to be propagated to the other participating instance.

- If the persistent state of the participating beans is stored in a relational database, a relationship may be stored as a single foreign key reference, and many-to-many relationships will be stored in a separate table. This requires the coordination of updates to persistent storage.

In addition, relationships represent a fundamental element of system design. The interfaces for access to relationships should be consistent to enable them to be generated from application models and to provide a consistent interface for application programmers.

Legacy Integration

Legacy integration with components is not much different than without components. There are three basic modes:

- Shared database
- Legacy wrapper
- Enterprise application integration

Shared Database

A component-based application may share a database with a legacy system. The components retrieve and update their state in the shared database. For updates, database locks will be required to prevent conflicts. For read-only operations (where no updates are involved), locks may not be necessary.

The components may be application components (EJBs) or Web server components (servlets or JSPs). If the new component-based application involves the participation of a number of entities, then it is appropriate that the state from the shared database be implemented in EJB. The commit options discussed previously must be considered for the potential impact on legacy system performance. Either entity or session beans may be used depending on the architecture chosen for the component-based application. If access to the legacy database is for display only, then it may be accessed directly from Web server components.

If the new application involves two databases—the legacy database and the component-based database—it is essential that the transaction service and the databases support a two-phase commit. This will ensure the consistency of results across both systems.

Caution is required if the legacy database is used for read-only as part of update activity in the new application. It is possible for multiple reads from the legacy database to yield an inconsistent view of the legacy database, thus producing inconsistent results in the new application.

Legacy Wrapper

A legacy wrapper can be developed to interface directly with the legacy application logic, thus incorporating the legacy system logic into the new component-based application. This can be very challenging even if commercial products are used to implement the interface. The application developer needs a much deeper understanding of how the legacy application is implemented because its functionality will be part of the final system.

It may not be practical to implement the legacy wrapper as EJB components because legacy systems typically are not written in Java. Consequently, it may be necessary to implement the wrapper as CORBA objects written in the native language of the legacy system. Since EJB components communicate using IIOP, they also can interoperate with CORBA objects.

The legacy wrapper may involve multiple interfaces. The design goal should be to make the legacy system appear to be a large-scale component from the perspective of the rest of the system. In this way, eventually it might be replaced by another large-scale component composed of smaller components. In order to achieve this objective, the designer must represent the functionality of the legacy application as a composition of components, as depicted in Figure 10.4. In order to provide greater compatibility, it may be appropriate to implement the CORBA objects as CORBA components. However, although the specifications suggest this level of compatibility, this must be demonstrated with actual CORBA component container products.

Often an interface to a legacy system is implemented through a simulation of the human interface. Products are available for interfacing with legacy user-interface facilities, but compatibility with the J2EE environment would need to be determined for the particular product.

There may be no way to implement a two-phase commit. Consequently, there is a risk that the component-based system could fail after updating the legacy system, and the two systems would be left inconsistent. The application developer will need to consider the consequences of this inconsistency and define ways to detect it and resolve it either automatically using compensating transactions or through human action.

One way of recognizing this situation is for the component-based system to commit the transaction with a *pending* indicator to be updated after the legacy update is completed. In this way, if the new system fails, the pending indicator will provide information about transactions that must be reconciled. On the other hand, if the legacy system fails before completing an update, the new system will require logic to back out of the committed pending state.

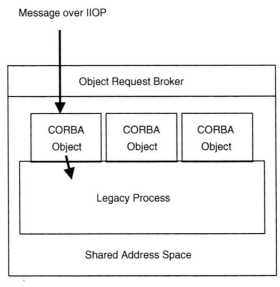

Figure 10.4 EJB legacy wrapper.

Enterprise Application Integration (EAI)

The most widely accepted and flexible mode of integration is using store-and-forward messaging and EAI tools. Products are available to facilitate the development of interfaces with legacy systems. The interaction between the legacy system and the new system will not be synchronous, but will be accomplished through the exchange of asynchronous messages. While the two systems may be out of synch momentarily while messages are exchanged or held in queues, the guaranteed delivery of messages provides a high degree of assurance that they will be updated consistently.

Nevertheless, the developer must ensure that the sequence of messages received by the legacy system properly represents the sequence of commits in the new system. When the new system is processing multiple concurrent transactions, it is possible for the effect of an update to be posted before another transaction commits data that do not reflect the update. This may require that transactions share a common element that forces the sequential processing of certain interdependent transactions.

Component Modeling Technology

A specification for modeling component-based systems is being developed in the OMG. This UML Profile for EDOC will be finalized shortly after this book is released. The specification supports modeling that is independent of specific technical implementations. Example mappings to specific technologies will be included, but formal mappings will be adopted by the OMG in subsequent specifications. The EDOC specification provides a number of important capabilities:

Recursive composition.   The composition model provides a consistent representation of components and compositions so that a composition can consist of primitive components and compositions. A composition can be as small as two primitive components (or even one component adapted to a particular use) and as large as a complete enterprise (although this scope is probably impractical as a single model).

Pluggable components.   The specification of component interfaces and semantics will be sufficient to determine if one component can replace another. This includes the interfaces provided and interfaces used, protocols of exchanges between components, the communication of messages and events, and data structures exchanged.

Degrees of coupling.   The ports (more generic than *interfaces*) provide for the specification of synchronous messaging, store-and-forward messaging, and Internet messaging [such as HyperText Transport Protocol (HTTP)]. They also provide for the specification of the message exchange protocols.

Event-based coupling.   Specifications may include the definition of event conditions and event notice content to support publish-and-subscribe coupling.

Process framework.   Components may be processes, from embedded computational processes to workflow processes engaging people. This specification provides a framework for a later OMG specification that will define the details of workflow process logic.

Ad hoc monitoring.   Ports can be specified to accept ad hoc requests for the notification of events from an individual instance or from all instances of a type. This enables the integration of a component with a system that was not designed to support the component.

Patterns.   A mechanism is defined for the specification of patterns and the unfolding of a pattern for a particular circumstance. This will improve the consistency and productivity of design activities.

The UML Profile for EDOC specification is important for three reasons:

■ It provides a robust specification of components at all levels of scale.

■ It provides the basis for tools to generate much of the code for applications, dramatically reducing programming effort and improving quality.

■ It provides component specifications that are sufficiently robust to enable a marketplace in replaceable components.

In addition, the UML Profile for EDOC is a key element of the OMG MDA strategy. It enables the specification of robust, technology-independent application models. Technology mappings will make these models applicable to multiple implementation technologies. Tools are currently being developed to generate code from the UML models. In the future, it will be possible to port an application to a new technology by regenerating the code from the specifications.

Summary

A number of architectural and design issues must be considered in the development of a component-based system and in the development of components for reuse in multiple systems. The EJB specification resolves many of these issues, particularly the development of portable components. However, a number of issues remain to be resolved by the container product developer and the application developer. Consequently, the stage is not fully set for the composition of large, multiplatform, multivendor systems.

The ambiguities in the EJB specification may affect the portability, interoperability, and performance of components. The developer must consider these in the selection of a container product and in the design of the components and the application.

At the current stage of development, container products should not be mixed within the scope of a business system domain (BSD). The use of different vendor products for different BSDs should not be a problem except to the extent that sharing components between domains will require care to ensure that they do not rely on any vendor-specific design choices or extensions. There will still be an issue with the use of multiple-vendor products to provide the message broker services between BSDs.

The UML Profile for EDOC specification under development in the OMG will greatly enhance the ability to design components and compose systems. The specification will be sufficient to define plug compatibility, and it will enable the development of code-generation tools to reduce the cost and improve the quality of components.

However, the development of sharable components is not just a technical problem—it is a business problem. First, standard specifications are required for common business entities and functions. Without these, components will still be incompatible. Second, the design of marketable components requires additional investment in design and implementation. Finally, customers will not accept components if they cannot rely on long-term support from the component supplier. These issues apply both in the open marketplace and within a large corporation.

While the technology and the marketplace are still evolving, we are on the threshold of the development of large-scale systems with component architecture. Investment in EJB technology is an important step to position the enterprise to exploit component technology as it continues to unfold.

Ensuring Enterprise System Security

A decade ago, system security was relatively straightforward. It involved a logon with a user ID and password, restricted access to physical facilities, and selective user access to application functions and database fields. User terminals were in restricted environments and accessed specific applications. Most enterprise computers were behind locked doors, and communications were over dedicated lines.

The explosive growth of personal computing, the Internet, and distributed computing have increased security risks dramatically and thus the need for close attention to security vulnerability and defenses. The Internet, in combination with internal enterprise networks, now provides potential communication paths to nearly all computers in the world. A computer virus can spread around the globe in a matter of hours. Crucial business data are communicated between computers over common carrier facilities and through public Internet service providers (ISPs). Customers and business partners are conducting business over the Internet, and the number and sources of security threats have increased orders of magnitude.

Security can no longer be something added on. It must be an integral part of the enterprise architecture, and it requires continued attention as the technology changes and new applications are developed. Threats come from inside as well as outside the enterprise: A 1999 survey by the Computer Security Institute reported intrusions by employees in 55 percent of the organizations surveyed.

This chapter will examine the security needs of the integrated enterprise:

- Security requirements
- Security techniques
- Security strategy

The intent here is to develop an understanding of the elements of security and provide a strategy for the design of enterprise systems and the selection, application, and configuration of security facilities.

Security Requirements

In this section we will examine the following security requirements as a basis for understanding the relevance of security techniques:

- Secure physical environment
- System integrity
- Recoverability
- Authentication
- Authorization
- Communication
- Nonrepudiation
- Monitoring
- Administration

Secure Physical Environment

The first step in achieving system security is to control physical access to the computer systems. Traditionally, computer systems have been housed in limited-access facilities. With the growth in personal computers and local servers, much enterprise computing occurs in less controlled environments. The business systems and data are no more secure than the physical environment of the computer.

The interconnection of distributed computers requires communication over facilities in uncontrolled environments. These facilities can be wiretapped, providing outside access to the data being exchanged. Access to the communications also may create opportunities for electronic access to the computers involved. Communications necessarily will continue to be over physically insecure facilities, so this must be considered in system designs and network protocols.

With the increased use of notebook computers on the Web, enterprise client computers may be connected from anywhere in the world. In addition, notebook computers often are stolen, carrying enterprise information and applications that may represent additional security risks. The design of client systems must consider the risks inherent in the client computer environments.

Whenever enterprise systems rely on client computers to maintain information or restrict access, there is a greatly increased security risk. When application logic is executed on client computers, there is a risk that this logic will be corrupted and that the integrity of the associated enterprise system will be compromised.

In general, system designers must be sensitive to any risk of physical access to computers or communications links and take appropriate steps to either restrict access or implement other security precautions.

System Integrity

System integrity depends on the proper functioning of the operating software, consisting of the operating system, middleware, access methods, and so on, and the applications that execute in the environment. Proper functioning must be considered at two levels: Does the software do only what it is intended to do? and Does it allow opportunities for someone to do something unacceptable?

Both operating software and applications carry the risk that they contain illicit logic intended to perform functions that violate the trust of the system owner. The only way that most, if not all, system owners can mitigate this risk is by obtaining software from trusted sources. The developers of software must have appropriate processes for reviewing code, testing components and systems, securing their work products, and protecting products from corruption during distribution to customers. Software downloaded from questionable sources on the Internet creates a high risk to system integrity. Viruses are the most insidious form of corrupt software. Individual users must understand that an e-mail attachment may contain executable software even if it is not identified as an executable. For example, a document may contain macros that will be incorporated in the logic of a word processor with virtually unlimited capabilities to access other data and applications on the personal computer.

Both operating software and applications also carry the risk that they will allow a user or intruder to do something unauthorized. This covers a broad range of possibilities. The most obvious is allowing user access to data or functionality that should not be authorized. The most obscure may be an input that causes program logic to be overlaid with an intruder's code or the ability to use data obtained in different requests to infer confidential information.

The first line of defense against such intrusions is again to obtain the software from trusted sources that design, review and test the software to detect and correct such loopholes. Restricting the population of persons who have access to the systems also can mitigate the risk of intrusion. The reason security is a greater concern on the Internet is that millions (or maybe billions) of people have Internet access, and significant numbers of them may be intent on breaching the security of enterprise systems.

If the number of persons with access to a system can be restricted, there is less risk that some will attempt to use the system in illegitimate ways. If the population is also restricted to a defined group of people who can be held individually accountable, there is further mitigation of risk.

Consequently, limiting access to an enterprise intranet reduces the risk to systems accessible from the intranet. Limiting access to a local-area network (LAN) further limits the risk to associated systems.

Recoverability

System malfunctions and failures will occur. A system is not secure if it cannot be recovered. Recoverability generally is achieved by maintaining a record of system activity and establishing successive checkpoints or committed states from which the state of the system can be restored. The frequency of checkpoints and committed states will determine the amount of work that may be lost if the system fails.

Unexpected termination may occur as a result of a hardware or software error or power outage. It also may occur as a result of sabotage. If a malfunction is detected immediately and there is a recent checkpoint or committed state prior to the malfunction, then operations may be resumed with minimal disruption of business activities.

Occasionally, a hardware or software malfunction will go undetected, allowing many transactions to be completed before the malfunction is discovered. Such a malfunction simply could be a computer error, it could be created intentionally through acts of an insider, or it could be introduced through some form of intrusion such as a virus. Due to the potential for such failures, an organization should be able to recover from a point in time prior to the malfunction, which could be weeks or months in the past, depending on the subtlety of the malfunction. In such cases, the problem is seldom simply one of restoring the system, but the external effects of the malfunction must be corrected as well. Checks may have been written incorrectly or goods delivered without payment. The enterprise must maintain independent audit trails of system actions that might need to be reviewed for corrective action.

Authentication

The enterprise likely will provide some information, and possibly some computer functionality, to anyone who visits the enterprise Web site. In these cases, it is unnecessary to obtain a reliable identifier for the user, although it may be desirable from a marketing perspective to attach an identifier for future use.

Nevertheless, for most enterprise system data and functionality, the user must be known as a basis for determining what the user is allowed to do and, in some cases, as a basis for holding the user accountable. There are two general populations of users to be considered: those who are known ahead of time and those who were unknown previously. In general, employees, some supplier personnel, and some distributor personnel will be known, and current or previous customers may be known.

The known population can be assigned identification information, such as a user identifier and password, so that they can be authenticated when they access a system. The enterprise may have no interest in most Internet users, but the enterprise will be particularly interested in those previously unknown users who may become customers.

Currently, the primary mechanism for the identification of new customers is through credit card numbers. Credit card companies have enhanced this self-identification by providing some degree of liability protection against the fraudulent use of credit card numbers on the Internet. There is also some degree of protection from fraud if the credit card owner is the only one who can receive the benefit of the credit card transaction. For example, the product is shipped only to the address of the credit card owner.

Once the enterprise has established a relationship with a customer, the customer becomes a known user and can be issued a unique identifier and password for future transactions with the enterprise.

Regardless of the form of user identifier, presentation of the identifier and password to the system must not allow an intruder to obtain the user's password. There are various techniques for preventing exposure of the password, but some systems still accept passwords as Uniform Resource Locator (URL) parameters or other textual input. This risk is increased substantially when a user uses the same password for many systems.

Authentication is not necessarily complete when the Web server accepts the user. The server may be in a less secure environment, or the user's request may be relayed to other systems. In such cases, there is a need for end-to-end authentication. The final recipient of the input must be able to authenticate the originator of the input. In some cases, a user identifier may be sufficient, but if the intermediate facilities are less secure, then the final recipient may require a more secure form of identification.

For many users, a simple logon and password mechanism is no longer sufficient. Users access many different systems. For each system, they must have a different identifier and password. This is a source of some frustration for customers, but for employees, who may need to access many different systems to perform their jobs, this can be a source of lost productivity.

Within the enterprise, the intranet has dramatically improved the potential scope of access by employees to information they need to do their jobs better. With a traditional logon approach, they must enter an identifier and password every time they access a different system, even though they are certainly known to the enterprise as employees. They should be able to identify themselves once, at least during a period of continuous activity, and access systems throughout the enterprise according to their level of authority. The enterprise should not need multiple identities and passwords.

Customers have a similar problem dealing with different enterprises. This is a more difficult problem because a single identifier for multiple enterprises must come from a source that all the enterprises trust. The credit card number comes from a trusted source, but it is not trustworthy because of the accessibility of credit card numbers. The use of a personal identification number (PIN) in addition to the credit card number has improved the security of debit transactions, but the PIN typically is only four digits and could be compromised as well.

The authentication of users is not the only concern. Users and business partners must be assured that business communications are occurring with the proper server. Consequently, authentication protocols should contemplate the authentication of both the client and the server to each other, whether the client is a user or another computer.

Authorization

Once a user is identified, the system must determine if the action to be taken is authorized for that user. Certain authority may be granted to any user to provide access to public information or to initiate a business relationship. When the user wants to establish a business relationship, the user identity will provide the basis for determining the scope of the user's authority and the acceptability of the business relationship.

A user may have general authority based on his or her relationship to the enterprise. This authority also may be a function of the user's relationship to the data to be accessed. For example, if a customer submits an order, then the customer may be given authority to access information about the order. At the same time, the customer should be denied authority to access information about another customer's order. Similarly, an employee may be authorized to view information from his or her personnel record, but should be denied access to another employee's personnel record unless he or she is the manager of the other employee.

Within the enterprise, users will be granted authority to access information and perform operations relevant to their job functions. Access to information may be fairly broad so that they are able to make decisions from an enterprise perspective and so that they have information of interest to them as employees. For the actions performed in their job function, their access may be limited to particular subject matter and to records associated with their particular business unit. When they access certain records, some fields may remain hidden, and they may not be authorized to change certain other fields. Consequently, it must be possible to define authority at different levels of granularity that depend both on the job function of the user and on the relationship of the user to the data being accessed.

The user's relationship to the data may be determined directly from the data as for the employee record, or it may be a function of the user's participation in an associated process. For example, an employee cannot be allowed to approve his or her own expense report. The person approving an expense report must not be allowed to change it without the approval of the person who submitted the report. This separation of responsibility is determined by roles defined by the business process.

Finally, user authority may depend on the state of the associated business transaction. For example, a customer order cannot be changed after it is shipped, and an expense report cannot be changed after it is approved. While there may be business procedures to accomplish the same result with appropriate controls, the user will not be allowed to change the record directly after a critical state has been reached. In other business transactions, different users may have different authority as the transaction progresses through various stages.

Communication

A system may receive a request to perform an action or accept input. The sender may need assurance that the intended recipient received the request. The receiver may need assurance that the request was originated by an authenticated and authorized source and that the content has not been altered. Furthermore, if the content is confidential, there should be assurance that an unauthorized third party cannot understand an intercepted copy.

Even if a user has been authenticated, a message might be intercepted and changed, or an imposter might continue to interact with the system after the authenticated user has discontinued activity. The protocol for the communication of information must provide assurance that the sender and receiver are who they purport to be, that the message has not been altered in transit, and, if necessary, that the message content is kept confidential.

Nonrepudiation

Nonrepudiation refers to the ability to capture information from an identified source and refute attempts of the source to deny responsibility. For example, in order to conduct business electronically, it must be possible to establish agreements electronically. In traditional business, agreements are established with paper documents signed by the parties. A document provides evidence of the substance of the agreement, and the signatures provide evidence that the parties concurred on the particular document. To achieve the equivalent result electronically, it must be possible for each participant to provide an electronic signature for the document that could only be created by them for the particular document.

Internal to the enterprise, there are numerous transactions that traditionally have been conducted with paper documents and written signatures. As we have converted many of these transactions to be computer-based, the signatures have been dropped on the assumption that each user will be authenticated properly and that the contributions of each user will be identified reliably and controlled by the computer system. This may be sufficient when illicit transactions will be recognized after the fact, the person(s) can be held accountable, and the adverse effects can be reversed. However, some illicit transactions are not identified or reversed so easily. Where resources are transferred out of the enterprise, and sometimes when resources are illicitly transferred within the enterprise (complementary credit and debit of accounts), the unauthorized action may not be detected until a reversal requires legal action. When there is the potential for legal action, there is a requirement for legally enforceable documents.

Monitoring

System activity should be monitored to identify security threats or intrusions. Monitoring should include consideration of the following circumstances:

- Unusually high network traffic, particularly traffic that is not consistent with legitimate activity. High network traffic may indicate a denial-of-service attack, where an intruder directs a flood of activity to a Web server, making it unavailable for legitimate business.

- Frequent attempts to access Web services by unauthenticated users. Frequent requests that fail authentication suggest that an intruder is attempting to discover a legitimate identifier and password in order to gain access to the system.

- User accesses to highly restricted system functions and resources, particularly unusual activity. Accesses to highly restricted facilities should be reviewed both by the users themselves and by managers to ensure that the accesses are legitimate. Unusual activity could indicate either that an authorized user is no longer trustworthy or that the user's identity and password have been compromised.

■ Authenticated users repeatedly denied access. When a user repeatedly attempts to access facilities without authorization, this suggests the potential for improper conduct by the user, but it also may be a fraudulent use of the user identifier and password by somebody who is not aware of the limits of authority of the legitimate user.

The goal of monitoring is to detect and eliminate any security threat or breach of security as soon as possible and potentially to take legal action to deter the intruder.

Administration

Security administration involves a number of responsibilities:

■ Users must be reliably identified as who they say they are.

■ Users must be assigned unique identifiers and proof of their identity (a password).

■ The identifiers of users and their access authority must be defined to systems.

■ Identifiers that are no longer valid or acceptable must be recognized.

■ New identifiers and/or proof of identity must be issued when users forget or expose their proof of identity.

Administrative authority must be restricted to trusted individuals, the scope of authority of each should be limited, their actions should be undeniable (nonrepudiation), and depending on the level of risk, their specific actions should be reviewed and possibly approved by another person. Automated administrative processes can provide further assurance of the integrity of the administrative activity.

Administrating security may be performed internal to the enterprise, but it may be appropriate to delegate this responsibility to an outside organization. An independent organization may provide greater protection from corruption, and it should provide some level of indemnification if users are not identified properly before being given proof of identity or if a breach of security in the issuing organization causes damages to the enterprise.

Security Techniques

Comprehensive coverage of the topic of system security would require a book in itself. The discussion here is limited in several ways. First, we will not address aspects of physical security and system integrity but will assume that systems are housed in appropriately secure environments, changes to software and applications are controlled properly, and appropriate precautions are taken to address recovery from malfunctions and catastrophic events. Second, we will not address business process issues related to the identity of users and the definition of their authority. Finally, we will not examine all possible security protocols and techniques, but will focus on a set of techniques that provide a system of security in the integrated enterprise.

We will examine the applicable security techniques under the following topics:

- Password authentication
- Cryptography
- Digital certificates
- Digital signatures
- Secure communications
- User roles
- Authorization
- Firewalls

Password Authentication

The basic mechanism of authentication is achieved with an identifier in combination with a password. The identifier asserts a particular identity, and the password is used to confirm or deny the identity. This is evident in the typical system login process, and it is inherent in all other authentication mechanisms. To be authenticated, the user must have something unique that only that person knows or possesses.

Only the identified user and the system for which the password provides authentication should know the password. It must be chosen from a large domain of possible passwords and contain an unpredictable combination of characters so that it will be difficult for somebody else to guess its value. The user must keep it secret from other potential users.

Variations on simple login/password authentication include biologic characteristics and card keys. For example, a user may be identified from a retinal image, a fingerprint, or a voice pattern. These characteristics uniquely identify the individual, but they require a specialized, reliable input device that will only accept input directly from the individual; otherwise, the identity could be faked. A card key provides identification, but does not ensure that the cardholder is the person identified. A card key could contain a digital certificate (discussed later) with a password to activate the digital certificate. A card key is easier to carry around than a personal computer, and it would allow a user to use different computers. However, it still requires an independent password. A card key may require a special input device, or it could be a personal computer (PC) card as specified by the Personal Computer Memory Card International Association (PCMCIA). A PCMCIA card can provide better security by performing the cryptographic operations internally rather than making the owner's private key available to the host personal computer.

Of course, in the traditional password access model, the system being accessed by the user must have the password value (or the unique biologic identifier) in order to compare it with the value submitted by the user. This increases the risk that somebody other than the identified user will gain access to the password value. The risk is further increased if the password is transmitted to the host computer over public communication facilities.

A relatively simple improvement is provided by the HyperText Transfer Protocol (HTTP) version 1.1. The user sends an identity to the host system, and the host returns a response with a challenge phrase or *nonce*. The nonce may be a string of meaningless characters or a string of information about the current transaction. The user browser then returns a computed value (a *hash value*) derived from the nonce using the user's identity and the user's password. The host then performs the same computation and compares the result with the value submitted by the user. If they are the same, then they must have used the same password, and the user is authenticated.

Such schemes still require that the host have a copy of the user's password. It is desirable for users to be able to access many systems without the need to remember different passwords or get explicit authorization for every system they may need to access. However, if the same password is used for multiple systems, the risk of exposure is increased—the password is no safer than the most vulnerable system.

Another mechanism that is used quite widely is an automatic sign-on. A security server authenticates the user. The user provides all identifiers and passwords he or she uses to access other systems. After that, whenever the user attempts to access another system, the security server intervenes and performs the logon automatically using the user's identifier and password from its security directory. This accomplishes a single sign-on, but it also creates a system bottleneck. In addition, it does not eliminate all the administrative overhead associated with managing user identifiers and passwords on all the systems involved.

A more sophisticated mechanism, sometimes called *public key technology*, involves the use of two complementary keys: a public key and a private key. This mechanism supports a single sign-on capability and has other far-reaching implications for security that will be discussed in greater detail in the next subsection.

Cryptography

Cryptography is the use of various mechanisms to encode (or encrypt) information so that the information content is hidden and then decode (or decrypt) it, revealing the original information to the recipient. There have been many forms of cryptography. The forms used today to encrypt data exchanged with computers use computational algorithms where the encoding is based on a key provided by the user. Consequently, the encoding algorithms are standard, but the encoding is different for each user because the key is different.

There are two basic models of encryption for computer information: symmetric and asymmetric. We will discuss them in the following subsections.

Symmetric Single Key Encryption

With symmetric encryption, the same key used to encrypt the information is used to decrypt it. Consequently, both the sender and the receiver must know the value of the key. If an intruder can determine the value of the key, then the intruder can intercept messages and also decrypt them. If a key is small in length, then the number of possible values is also small, and an intruder may be able simply to try all possible combinations to discover the key. If the key is a word or character string that is meaningful to the user, then the intruder may be able to guess it. The longer the key length and the less predictable the character string, the more difficulty the intruder will have discovering its value. At the same time, the longer the key, the more computational resources will be required to perform the encryption and decryption, and the more difficult it will be for the user to remember it.

A number of symmetric encryption algorithms have been developed over the years. Data Encryption Standard (DES) is one that has been around since the 1970s. It uses a 56-bit key. This key length was adequate originally, but with increases in computing power and sophisticated encryption-cracking techniques, it is no longer adequate protection from a determined intruder. Variations on DES have been used to increase the effective key length.

RC2, RC4, and RC5 are proprietary algorithms of RSA Data Security, Inc. These support the use of keys up to 2,048 bits in length. Due to past U.S. export restrictions, limited versions of RC2 and RC4 have been used with 40-bit key lengths for Web browsers and Web servers. With the easing of restrictions, this will change, but it may take some time before most users have browsers that support stronger encryption algorithms.

Asymmetric Public Key Encryption

Asymmetric encryption involves the use of two complementary keys. One key is kept secret, and the other key is made public. Either of the keys can be used to encrypt a message, and the other is required to decrypt it.

Figure 11.1 illustrates the two modes of communication. If a message is encrypted with the private key, then anybody can decrypt it if they know the sender's public key. This does not protect the message content from being revealed, but it provides assurance to the recipient that the message originated from the holder of the private key. Conversely, if a message originator uses the recipient's public key to encrypt a message, then only the recipient, who knows the private key, can decrypt the message.

There are two public key encryption algorithms in general use: RSA and ElGamal. Both typically use key lengths from 512 to 1,024 bits. A patent on the RSA algorithm was held by RSA Security, Inc., and the ElGamal algorithm was

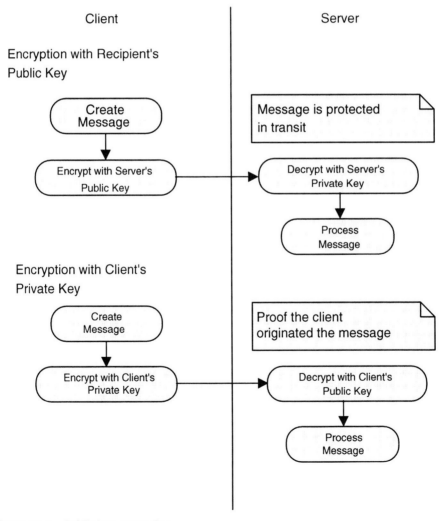

Figure 11.1 Public key encryption.

not patented. The RSA algorithm patent expired recently, so it may see increased use in the future.

Using a public key algorithm, a user can be authenticated by any system that knows the user's public key. The user contacts the system and receives a challenge phrase, a string that is different for each request. The user encrypts the challenge phrase with his or her private key and returns the ciphertext result. If the system decrypts the ciphertext successfully with the user's public key, then the user is authenticated. Generally, the user will include additional information in the return message so that the message content is unpredictable and decryption by an intruder would be more difficult. For example, the user might include a key to be used for the symmetric encryption of subsequent exchanges because symmetric encryption is more efficient.

Some security experts recommend that users be issued two key pairs. One key pair is used for authentication, and only the user knows the private key. The other key pair is used for the encryption of stored data. This provides protection for data stored on a laptop computer. Both the user and the enterprise know the private key of the stored data key pair. In this way, if the user forgets or loses the private key, the enterprise can still retrieve and decipher the stored data.

Message Digest Function

Another way to protect the integrity of message content is to use a message digest function. A message digest function transforms a message into a fixed-length hash value. Unlike encryption, the message cannot be derived from the hash value, but as a practical matter it is impossible to change the message and produce the same hash value. Consequently, if the sender creates a hash value and the receiver uses the same message digest function and obtains the same hash value, then the message has not been changed. In order for the receiver to be assured of the validity of the sender's hash value, it is encrypted.

Typically, the hash value is encrypted with the sender's private key and decrypted with the sender's public key. Encryption of the hash value requires much less computation than encryption of the entire message with a private key, and the encrypted hash value can be used to prove the content of the sender's message because only the sender could create an encrypted hash value that would be decrypted properly with his or her public key.

Digital Certificates

A *digital certificate* is an electronic document signed with the private key of a certifying authority (CA) as proof of identity of its owner, the person to whom it is issued. The certificate owner may be a person or a computer—servers have digital certificates to provide proof of their identities.

A digital certificate contains information about the recipient-owner of the certificate and its public key. Decrypting the certificate with the well-known public key of the CA validates it, and thus the identity of the owner and the value of the owner's public key are authenticated; that is, in order to decrypt with the CA's public key, the certificate must have been encrypted with the CA's private key. The format of certificates is defined by the International Organization for Standardization (ISO) X.509v3 standard.

While the digital certificate will establish the identity of the owner, it cannot establish that the owner presented the digital certificate. This is accomplished with the owner's private key. If the purported owner of the certificate is sent a random value, the rightful owner will know the private key for the certificate and can return the random value encrypted with the private key. If the encrypted value decrypts to the original random value with the public key from the certificate, then the sender is authenticated as the owner of the certificate.

Certificates are the backbone of the Public Key Infrastructure (PKI). The PKI is the combination of software products, certification authority, protocols, services, and agreements that use digital certificates to support secure exchanges of information between parties. Of course, the certificate is only as good as the integrity of the CA.

The level of trust provided by certificates depends on the method of identification of the certificate owner by the CA, the security of the CA's private key, the liability accepted by the CA for fraudulent certificates, and the strength of the encryption provided, that is, the length of the keys.

Certificates can be used in a number of ways. For example, in order to send a secure message, a client requests a certificate from the intended message recipient. The recipient returns a certificate by a well-known CA that has a well-known public key. The client decrypts the certificate with the CA's public key to obtain the intended recipient's public key and other identifying information. The sender can then use the recipient's public key to encrypt the message to be sent. Only the intended recipient can decrypt the message.

If the owner's private key is compromised, then the certificate is no longer valid. Certificate revocation lists are used to identify invalid certificates. Due to the potential size of such lists and the level of activity against them, revocation lists often are ignored in practice, but this will not be the case for sensitive applications in the future. Typically, certificates expire in a year, so the number of certificates on revocation lists is limited to the number that are revoked in a year.

Certificate integrity also depends on the ability of the owner to protect his or her private key. Since the private key is a rather long and meaningless string of characters, it would be very difficult to remember. Instead, the key typically is encrypted with a simpler user-selected key, and the encrypted form is stored on the user's computer. Unfortunately, if the user's computer is lost or corrupted, the user will lose the use of his or her certificate. If the user-selected key is short or obvious, a thief might be able to use the certificate to impersonate the owner. At the same time, the user should be aware of the theft of his or her computer and notify the enterprise to revoke the certificate.

Digital certificates provide a more powerful and flexible facility for authentication as well as related functionality. However, login/password authentication will be around at least as long as some current legacy systems. Facilities that provide automatic sign-ons to multiple systems using passwords typically accept digital certificates as one form of user authentication. Consequently, it is appropriate to implement some form of automatic sign-on facility to support single sign-ons with certificates and accommodate the fact that some systems will continue to use passwords.

Personal certificates can be issued by the enterprise for employees. This is recommended for large enterprises to provide employee authentication to multiple systems. The certificate is encrypted with the enterprise CA private key and identifies the employee and the employee's public key. The enterprise public key is known to all enterprise servers and is used to validate the employee identifier and public key. Similarly, each enterprise server holds a certificate issued by the enterprise, and an employee browser can use the enterprise public key to authenticate the server and obtain its public key.

The issuance of certificates by the enterprise provides several advantages. First, the enterprise controls assurance of the employee identity when the certificate is issued. Second, the revocation and reissue of certificates may be coordinated more closely with the hiring and firing of employees. Third, the enterprise does not need to place its trust in an outside certificate authority (CA) to ensure the proper issuance of certificates and the protection of the CA private key. On the other hand, an outside CA provides the separation of control of certificates from enterprise management, which could be considered better protection of stockholder interests. The outside CA also may be able to achieve economies of scale by serving multiple enterprises, and the CA should provide some form of indemnification and risk mitigation for losses resulting from improper issue of certificates (the identity of the person is not validated properly) or exposure of the CA private key.

Digital Signatures

The purpose of a digital signature is to attach a person's acknowledgment, approval, or endorsement to a document, equivalent to placing a signature on a paper document. The difference between paper and electronics is that an electronic document can be changed easily. A digitally signed document cannot be changed without making the signature invalid. A digitally signed document has the added benefit that a copy is as valid as the original.

Figure 11.2 illustrates a document signing process. It uses a message digest function in combination with public key technology to provide authentication of the message content. A digest function is used to create a hash value from the message content. The signer of the document encrypts the hash value using his or her private key. The encrypted hash value is then communicated with the original document.

In order to authenticate the message, a recipient uses the same digest function to create a hash value from the message. The recipient also decrypts the sender's signature using the sender's public key. If the two hash values are identical, then the message is authentic.

Any number of persons may sign a document in the same manner. For example, this might apply to an internal purchase request. The purchase request document would be signed by the originator and sent to his or her manager for approval. Depending on the dollar value of the purchase request, it might be necessary to obtain signatures from several managers up the chain of command. Each would be assured of the legitimacy of the request, and the last signature would provide the authority for the purchasing department to issue the purchase order. The document with attached signatures then can be stored as a record of the transaction and provide accountability for the action.

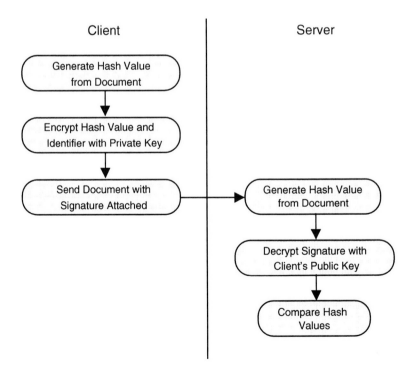

Figure 11.2 Authenticating a signed document.

Note that the document must remain exactly the same throughout the process, or a different hash value will be generated by the digest function. This means that the document format cannot be changed, and values cannot be converted, such as units of measure. However, it is possible that the message could be structured so that a later signer of the document could add an attachment. In this case, that signer would produce a hash value for both the original document and the attachment. Subsequent signers might add attachments in the same manner.

In enterprise application integration (EAI), messages communicated between applications may pass through a transformation function. This achieves a compatibility of exchanges between applications without modification of the applications to send or receive new formats. EAI transformation would invalidate the signature of a signed document. One way to preserve the signature is to retain the original message and signature and pass it along with the transformed message. The concatenated message, consisting of the original message and the transformed message, can be signed by the transformation service. The recipient can then authenticate the endorsement of the original message using the originator's signature and authenticate the transformation using the transformation service signature. The recipient will rely on the integrity of the transformation service in accepting the transformed message as the information to be acted on.

The United States recently adopted legislation giving digital signatures the same legal effect as signatures on paper documents. This enables the creation of enforceable electronic contracts. In combination with digital certificates, this will reduce the risks and drive expansion of the scope of electronic commerce.

The W3C adopted the XML Digital Signature specification in April 2001. This provides a standard format for creating and expressing a digital signature as an XML fragment. The Electronic Business XML (ebXML) initiative sponsored by the United Nations Center for Trade Facilitation and Electronic Business (CEFACT) has incorporated the XML Digital Signature specification in the format of signed messages for the exchange of documents in electronic commerce. Signatures may be created for all or parts of the documents, as well as attached documents or referenced documents. These specifications were discussed in greater detail in Chapter 9. These standards efforts likely will accelerate the use of digital signatures.

Secure Communications

A number of protocols have been developed for the secure exchange of data over the Internet. Unfortunately, some of these have been slow to gain acceptance, probably due to U.S. government restrictions on the export of strong encryption algorithms. In this section we will examine the following protocols that have gained significant attention:

- Internet Protocol security (IPsec)
- Secure HyperText Transport Protocol (S-HTTP)
- Secure Sockets Layer (SSL)
- Pretty Good Privacy (PGP)

IPsec Version 6

The Internet Engineering Task Force (IETF) has been developing a new version of the Internet Protocol, IP version 6 (IPv6), that will provide optional encryption at a low level in the Internet communications stack. This will enable two computers to authenticate each other and exchange encrypted communications. The protocol will not require the modification of application software and is completely transparent to applications.

However, since it is a machine-to-machine protocol, it cannot provide facilities at the application level, such as the authentication of persons and documents as provided by certificates and digital signatures. It also is expected to use 56-bit DES encryption, which is no longer considered strong encryption.

Secure HTTP (S-HTTP)

CommerceNet and a consortium of business users developed S-HTTP for use in electronic commerce. While it provides support for digital signatures, it has not been adopted widely as yet.

S-HTTP performs much the same sequence of exchanges as SSL. The server, and optionally the client, provides certificates for authentication. The client provides a session key encrypted with the server's public key. However, S-HTTP is specific to HTTP and thus to Web access. The server certificate and encryption options are included in the S-HTTP header information. A user interaction may switch between secure and unsecure exchanges. A secure exchange will be invoked with a URL starting with shttp://.

Because S-HTTP is specific to HTTP, the cryptograpic operations are more visible to the end user. The user can sign documents and authenticate and store signed documents. These are valuable capabilities, but because very few browsers and Web servers have implemented S-HTTP, it is not a practical solution, particularly where transactions are to be conducted with previously unknown users on the public Internet.

Secure Sockets Layer (SSL)

SSL operates at an application level, for example, between a browser and server, using certificates and session keys. SSL has been accepted widely among browser and Web server vendors.

In SSL, the server, and optionally the client, is authenticated using a certificate. For HTTP communications, SSL is invoked on a Web server with a URL that starts with https://. Figure 11.3 illustrates the exchange for authentication to establish a session key. The client sends a greeting to which the server responds with the server's certificate. The server may request the client's certificate, but this is optional; if the client fails to send a certificate, the server may terminate the exchange. If the client provides a certificate, then the server can obtain the client's public key. The client can obtain the server's public key by using the CA's public key to decrypt the server's certificate.

The client uses the server's public key, from the certificate, to encrypt a session key and sends it to the server. The server cannot use the session key if the server is an imposter because it must use its private key to decrypt the session key. If the client provided a certificate, the client also sends a verification message encrypted with its private key; this message will be meaningful only to the server if the client's public key can decrypt it (proving that it was encrypted with the client's private key).

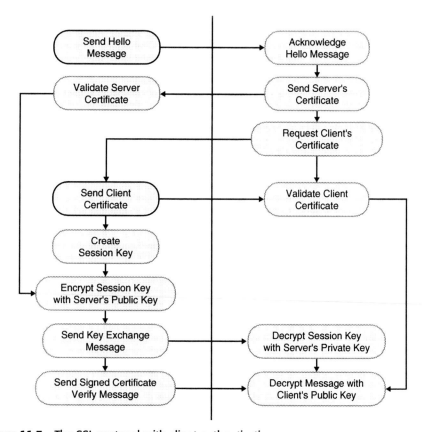

Figure 11.3 The SSL protocol with client authentication.

SSL is not tied to any specific application, and thus it can be applied to other applications besides HTTP, such as the File Transfer Protocol (FTP), the Network News Transport Protocol (NNTP), and the Simple Message Transport Protocol (SMTP), that is, e-mail. However, since the security logic is hidden at the information-exchange level, SSL does not provide digital signatures and the storing of digitally signed documents.

SSL is incorporated in the ebXML specification for the reliable messaging of XML documents for electronic commerce. The ebXML specification uses the same certificates for digital signatures on commercial documents expressed in XML. These signed documents may be communicated over the reliable messaging service, encrypted by SSL.

Pretty Good Privacy (PGP)

PGP is an open source program developed about 10 years ago for e-mail privacy. It employs asymmetric encryption with public-private key pairs and digital certificates, but the digital certificates are not compliant with the X.509v3 standard.

The intent of PGP is to provide the general population with a way to protect their e-mail messages. Messages may be signed for authentication and nonrepudiation, and they can be encrypted to protect privacy. Signing employs a message hashing function, and encryption employs symmetric encryption with a session key.

Rather than require that a CA issue certificates, the strategy with PGP is for individuals to create their own certificates. Individual users then accept and validate certificates from others based on the source and endorsement by other known users. Certificates may be shared with others through certificate servers. These servers may provide no direct assurance of the validity of the certificates; the signatures of others who have endorsed them validate the certificates. In a simple scenario, an e-mail originator who wishes to protect a message requests a certificate from the intended recipient. The originator then encrypts the message using the recipient's public key to encrypt the session key.

PGP has been accepted widely for e-mail protection. It is now competing with Secure Multipurpose Internet Mail Extensions (S/MIME), which was originated by RSA Data Security, Inc., as an ISO X.509v3-compliant protocol. It is likely that a new standard will incorporate features of both. In the meantime, PGP provides a widely available facility for e-mail protection.

User Roles

An enterprise may have thousands of employees and thousands of system elements with requirements for access restriction. In addition, the enterprise may have customers that will become identified only when they attempt to access enterprise systems. It is impossible to define specific authority on an individual basis. Instead, authority must be defined in terms of roles, with a set of authority rules associated with each role. Then a user can be associated with one or more roles, and authority can be defined appropriately. Not only does this simplify the level of detail required for granting authority, but it also allows the grantor to think in terms of the job or activities of the user instead of specific data elements or operations he or she might need to access.

We will now examine three general classes of roles to be defined and their implications for controlling access to systems:

- Organizational
- Contextual
- Subject matter

Organizational

The most general type of role is determined by the person's relationship to the organization. This includes customer, supplier, and employee. Thus, when a known user signs on, he or she will immediately have a basic role, such as customer, supplier, or employee.

Relationships to the organization also define more specific roles associated with particular job functions in the organization. A person may be an employee and the manager of a particular department. As the department manager, he or she may have the general authority of a manager at a particular level, defining dollar levels of authority for transactions such as purchase orders and expense reports. This level of authority may be applied across the enterprise.

Figure 11.4 illustrates hypothetical relationships between generic roles, which characterize a level of authority, and position roles, which define a position in a particular organization. Note that the arrows represent an inheritance of authority; for example, a manager has the authority of a supervisor and more. The horizontal lines suggest an association, such as where the engineering department head is a manager. The generic roles may be associated with a level of authority, such as dollar values, whereas the position roles may be associated with authority over a business domain, such as particular business processes, types of subject matter, groups of employees, and financial accounts. Employees can be assigned generic roles that are applicable across the enterprise, whereas position roles will be applicable only to particular business domains.

Generic
Roles

Position
Roles

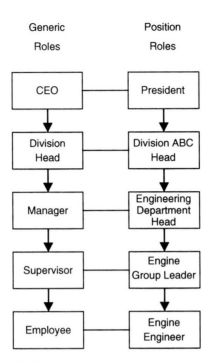

Figure 11.4   Organizational roles.

Contextual

A role may be based on the context of a particular activity the user is performing. For example, a user may have the role of requester with respect to a particular expense report. The requester can create and enter data in a new expense report, view the status of the expense report as it is routed for approval, and recall and change it prior to final approval.

A contextual role is assigned dynamically and likely will be assigned for a limited period of time based on the life of a process or work product. It is associated with a particular activity and reflects the user's responsibility and authority with respect to that activity and the associated information.

For some activities, such as expense reporting, a user may only be required to be an employee (a general role). Others may have approval roles. Not all users can take on such roles. In some cases, a user only will be allowed to take on a particular role if he or she is already assigned to another role in a related activity. In other cases, a role will be assigned based on organizational relationships, such as where an approver may be required to be a submitter's manager. Or a role may be assigned only if certain relationships do not exist in order to ensure separation of responsibility. Consequently, the assignment of roles often will depend on existing roles, associated activities, and organizational relationships.

Subject Matter Content

Allowable authority also may depend on the subject matter content. This corresponds to the object state level of control discussed earlier. For example, a manager cannot approve an expense against another manager's account and can only approve an expense for a subordinate. This may be similar to roles based on process participation, but these restrictions would apply when no process is active and when a person is to be assigned to a role within a process.

The subject matter also may define a relationship with the user that will determine the user's authority. For example, an employee may request access to a personnel record. If the record is the employee's own, then he or she may be allowed to read it all, but if it is for another employee, he or she may only be allowed to see the person's name, work phone number, and department. On the other hand, a manager may be allowed to see the complete records for employees who work for the manager.

These are typically application-logic authorization controls. However, this logic need not be embedded in the application, but may be determined by the user-interface logic on the Web server. The data supporting the decision must be available from the application. For the manager example, the manager's relationship to the account and the employee, if any, must be known. For the employee record example, the employee identity should be available from the record to be displayed, but if it is not the same employee requesting the information, then the user's supervisory/managerial relationship to the employee in the record must be known.

Summary

Roles provide a very powerful and flexible way to define authority. Where roles are static, such as those associated with a job function or organizational position, they can be used for determining general authority for most systems across the enterprise. Roles based on organization also will provide basic authority for access within the associated business system domain (BSD), that is, access to departmental systems. In particular, the authority to access information and initiate processes typically will be based on organizational roles.

Some roles are determined dynamically by the context of the user's activity of his or her operations. These roles correspond to the dynamic assignment of responsibility in business processes.

Further restrictions on access may be determined by the subject matter. These constraints may be based on a combination of role and subject matter, such as where a manager can access the records of his or her employees.

Roles are key to aligning authorization to the needs of individuals to function effectively in the enterprise.

Authorization

Authorization involves mechanisms to determine if a request should be accepted and processed based on its source. Up to this point we have examined ways to authenticate the identity of a user to ensure that messages exchanged with a user are not altered, to keep the message content confidential (encrypted), to hold the originator accountable for the message content, and to associate users with roles. The next step involves the application of business policies and rules to determine if the user has sufficient authority for the request to be given effect.

We will start by discussing the differences in the level of granularity at which controls are applied, and then we will examine the specification of controls based on user roles.

Access Control Granularity

Access control can occur at several levels of granularity associated with different system elements. As the granularity of control increases, so does the system overhead associated with access control. Possible levels of access control are described as follows:

Web server.   A Web server is the front door to a security domain. A user may be stopped at the front door and only allowed to proceed if he or she is authorized to access something in the domain. This is where initial authentication generally will occur. Based on this authentication, the basic authority of the user will be established.

Web resources.   The Web server can control access to specific Web resources based on user authority. Information-only resources may be unrestricted, whereas specific, functional resources may be restricted to certain users. This provides a high-level restriction on what aspects of the application can be accessed. The available pages may achieve implicit restrictions by limiting the available commands.

Alternative Web pages.   Web server components determine what users see and what they can enter by the design of the Web pages. Consequently, different users may be given different Web pages reflecting their authority. In some cases, the same Web server component may create alternative pages based on the user's authority. For some users, a selected Web page may provide comprehensive data and the ability to update. For other users, a selected Web page may limit the content and the fields that can be updated.

Object types.   In a distributed objects environment, a user may be restricted to accessing particular types of objects. The security system would be required to control access at the object interface level—all objects of a particular type. With this access control, every message directed to a particular interface type will be checked to see if the user is authorized to access that type of object.

Object methods.   Access also might be restricted to particular methods on an interface. Again, all messages to a target object of a particular interface type will be intercepted. The security intercept will determine if access to the method being invoked is controlled and if the user is authorized to invoke the method. This level of security has slightly more overhead than the object-type level because the access control lists will be longer.

Object state.   In many cases, the authority of a user will depend on the particular object instance being accessed, not on just the interface type or method. This authority may be a function of the status of the object (the stage of production of a purchased product), the subject matter (the type of product being purchased or the dollar amount of the expense), or the relationship of the user to the particular instance (the salesperson for the particular sales order). Unless these controls can be implemented at the user-interface level, they must be applied by the application logic. The application must access the user's identity and credentials from the security system and apply the appropriate rules.

Common Object Request Broker Architecture (CORBA) security, defined by the Object Management Group (OMG), supports authorization for object types, object methods, and object states. CORBA security provides the mechanism by which principal credentials are passed with the messages communicated over the network. Consequently, when a message arrives at a server, the Object Request Broker (ORB) provides the opportunity for the security system to check interface and method access authority before the message is forwarded to the object. This provides authorization without application awareness. The security credentials are also available for access by the application to exercise control, particularly where authorization depends on the state of the specific object instance or its relationship to the user.

The application designer must strike a balance between security granularity and performance. Control at the method level can provide assurance that certain functions and data elements cannot be accessed inadvertently through some indirect request path. However, intervention at the method level requires the interception of every message by the security logic.

Authority Specifications

Roles provide characterizations of people's functions and responsibilities as a basis for determining their authority. Roles must be mapped to the system elements that are required for them to perform those roles. The following are several mechanisms to accomplish this mapping:

Access control lists.   When certain actions are requested, the security mechanism will check an access control list (ACL) for authorization. The ACL contains the roles that are authorized to take the associated actions. Thus, authorization is simply a matter of determining if a user's role matches a role that authorizes the action. ACLs may be used at most levels of granularity, but they are not particularly useful for state-based authority.

Access decision functions.   An access decision function (ADF) is an alternative to an ACL. Instead of checking for a role in an ACL, an ADF is invoked to apply appropriate rules. The ADF authorization rules may involve access to the state of the target object. The ADF returns a result indicating if access should be allowed or denied. This keeps the security logic outside the application code, but it may still be sensitive to changes in the application, particularly changes in possible states and definitions of variables.

Application logic.   An application may access the user's credentials to determine if an action should be authorized. The application then may alter the content of the response or deny access based on the user's role, identifier, or relationship to the particular object being accessed and its current state. The application also may alter the credentials, such as adding a role, thus affecting subsequent access decisions. Here the authorization rules are embedded in application code.

Web page content.   The preceding specifications focus on the authority of a user to access specific functionality or data for an application. Controlling Web page content provides an alternative mechanism for restricting access. A request to the application may return a set of potential Web content values for display. The mapping from the response content to the Web page format can control the selection of content based on the user authority. This approach allows the system owner to see what various users will be able to access rather than attempting to interpret the detailed controls in terms of various users and circumstances. Similarly, acceptance of a user request can be controlled by the Web script based on the user's role.

ACLs and ADFs provide controls outside the application and can be applied at various levels of granularity. This minimizes the impact on application complexity and keeps the security controls independently visible. The control of access at the Web page level embeds security controls in the Web page logic, but the specification of content for Web pages is much easier for a system owner to understand and validate. It keeps the security logic out of the primary application and expressed at a business level.

Firewalls

A *firewall* is a computer or software component that restricts communication from a network environment to a computer or restricted network environment. The restrictions are intended to prevent communications that might violate security or corrupt the protected resources.

There are three primary firewall mechanisms: IP filtering, network address translation, and proxy services. These may be implemented individually or in combinations in different firewall products.

IP filtering.　IP filtering operates on the IP packet header information. Typically, it will control the passage of IP packets based on the sending and receiving of IP addresses and ports. The IP filter is unaware of the content of the packet, that is, the data being passed to an application. IP filters can bar access to specific services such as the FTP or the System Network Management Protocol (SNMP) by filtering out packets directed to the associated ports. Filtering can control both inbound and outbound packets.

Network address translation (NAT).　NAT converts the IP address of packets received by the firewall to addresses of target servers and ports behind the firewall and, conversely, converts the sender address for outgoing packets. NAT was developed originally to deal with the limited availability of global IP addresses. It has become very useful for firewall protection by hiding the IP addresses of internal facilities from the public Internet. Note that NAT is not effective with applications and protocols [such as CORBA/Internet Inter-ORB Protocol (IIOP)] where IP addresses are embedded in the application data.

Proxy services.　Proxy services operate at the application data level. Messages are received by the firewall server and may be transformed and/or redirected to the appropriate application servers. Conversely, outgoing messages will be transformed, and any references to the protected server will be replaced. The proxy services break the network layer connection and provide control over the application data content. Proxy services are used for IIOP firewalls so that IP addresses embedded in the message content can be converted appropriately.

In addition to these basic firewall mechanisms, firewalls also may incorporate additional functionality:

Source authentication.   The source of a message may be required to first establish its identity for messages to be allowed through the firewall.

Activity monitoring.   The firewall can monitor intrusion attempts and excessive activity of various types to warn of security threats.

Encrypted tunneling.   Firewalls can provide an encrypted connection between two private networks using the public Internet. This is commonly called a *virtual private network* (VPN). The two private networks functionally can appear to be one integrated network.

Part of the value of a firewall is that it has a single-minded purpose so that it is less likely to have loopholes where an intruder might get through or corrupt its function. Firewalls that are implemented as software on an application server are more likely to be vulnerable to attack.

Security Strategy

The integrated enterprise requires a security strategy: a consistent approach that addresses the variety of situations encountered in the enterprise. This section will describe such a strategy, addressing:

- Authentication
- Authorization
- Domain separation
- Business documents
- Security domains

Authentication

The enterprise should establish a PKI. Authentication should be based on digital certificates for known users. A CA must be established to issue certificates for known users. Contracting for CA services should be considered for the separation of responsibility and potential long-term economies. Processes must be put in place for ensuring the identity of digital certificate recipients (new employees) and for identifying certificates to be revoked (employee terminations). Servers must be updated to use digital certificates for authentication and authorization.

Automatic logon facilities should be implemented for the transition and for legacy systems to eliminate the need for users to log onto each system. The automatic logon facility should accept the user's digital certificate for authentication.

Authorization

Authorization should be based on roles. The enterprise must establish a base set of roles that apply across the enterprise. These include roles that define broad levels of authority and roles that apply in common patterns such as workflow product approval. These roles should be stored in the organization directory for access across the enterprise.

The application of roles as well as the definition of application-specific roles occur within particular application and service domains. Application-specific roles that are associated with organizational position responsibilities should be stored in the organization directory. Additional roles required for various process and application contexts must be defined and managed for the particular domain. It would be desirable, however, to have an enterprise-wide role definition directory to prevent duplication and encourage consistency.

Mechanisms for the specification of authority will be domain- and application-specific. Unless required by security concerns, the control of access at the level of the Web page, that is, the user interface, is preferred because this minimizes the performance impact and enables the system owner to express restrictions in terms of the user interface instead of internal application elements.

Domain Separation

As the use of Internet technology and personal computers emerged, enterprises created private *intranets* and separated them from the outside world with firewalls. This protects the enterprise systems from outside intruders. However, as the private intranet has grown, many more people can gain access behind the firewall. Often offices with fairly open access are part of the intranet. Conference rooms are often wired for intranet access. In addition, employees are carrying laptop computers to remote sites and then connecting to the intranet through public telephone lines and ISPs. The firewall may still have value, but a significant number of security violations are coming from within enterprises. Protection from intruders already on the private intranet merits just as much attention as protection from the public Internet.

Enterprise systems should not be viewed as a single environment to be protected from outside intruders. The information systems landscape should be partitioned into a number of domains along organizational and functional boundaries. Different domains merit different degrees and types of protection. Some environments are inherently less secure, and the design of systems should reflect the risks to computers, software, and data in such environments.

In addition, enterprise systems should be designed and integrated in a manner that contains the impact of security violations when they occur. Just as a ship is partitioned with bulkheads to contain flooding, enterprise systems should be bounded so that an intrusion is confined to a limited area. These security domains should be aligned to business functions so that responsibility for the domain is clearly defined, and a limited set of people are in charge of the functions performed by the domain. Security must preserve separation of responsibility with bounded domains of accountability and control.

Figure 11.5 illustrates the relationships between typical enterprise security domains. The enterprise exists within the domain of the public Internet. Typically, the enterprise has an intranet, separated from the Internet, that connects people and systems within the enterprise. Note that these internal domains include infrastructure services (e-mail and message broker) and office environments.

These domains may have two points at which they interface to a broader domain: a Web server and a messaging server. Each Web server should have a firewall to minimize the risk of intrusion. The office and plant domains typically are composites of smaller domains, so firewall protection may be implemented at the LAN access point or on individual servers. In addition, personal computers should have firewall software both for protection within the intranet and for protection when they are used on the public Internet. While the intranet is safer than the public Internet, it nevertheless presents the potential for a devastating intrusion if all enterprise resources are open to attack.

Message queues represent another avenue for access to domains. These represent a lesser risk because the message exchange functionality is quite specific, and messages generally are coming from within the enterprise over

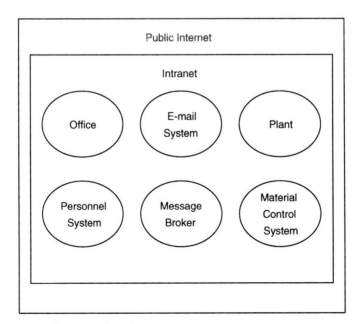

Figure 11.5 Typical security domains.

secure links. Nevertheless, sources of messages should be restricted to sending specific types. Messages from an external business-to-business (B2B) message server must be strictly constrained as to message type and internal recipient.

Business Documents

The enterprise must move to the use of XML documents for signed business transactions. The key enabler for electronic business documents is digital certificates for all participants. Digital certificates form the basis for digital signatures.

The implementation of products supporting the ebXML standard will position the enterprise for B2B electronic commerce using documents with electronic signatures. Specifications for processes and documents based on the ebXML framework should be developed in conjunction with business partners to enable electronic transactions.

Employees should develop a practice of using electronic signatures for e-mail–based business transactions internally. The capability to support digital signatures should be a key requirement for the selection of workflow management products so that internal documents can be created, signed, and approved in workflow processes.

The enterprise should consider providing digital certificates to established customers so that they can conduct secure transactions. This is a longer-term undertaking and must be evaluated in the context of the particular enterprise.

Security Service Elements

Security for the integrated enterprise involves a number of service elements at three different levels: as part of the enterprise infrastructure, as part of each BSD, and incorporated in each application.

Infrastructure Elements

The infrastructure provides facilities and services that are shared across the enterprise. The enterprise CA will assign digital certificates to employees and potential business partner employees and customers. The CA may be a contract service, but there must be business processes within the enterprise for the proper identification of persons receiving digital certificates and for the revocation of certificates when employees leave or the certificates are compromised. An enterprise-revoked certificates directory must be maintained and accessible for authentication.

There also must be authorization facilities for specific infrastructure services such as infrastructure directories, the messaging service, system management services, and so on.

For the transition from logon/password-mode authentication to digital certificate authentication, the infrastructure may include an automatic logon facility. This will accept a digital certificate and automatically log onto systems that require a logon/password so that the user does not need to keep track of multiple passwords and sign onto each system accessed.

The infrastructure messaging service must support the secure control of message delivery. Publishers of messages do not control where their messages will be delivered. The messaging service must be able to authenticate and determine the authority of subscribers. Similarly, recipients of messages, either point-to-point or published messages, must be protected from receiving messages from unauthorized sources. The messaging service should provide an authorization of message senders that are sending messages of particular types or direct messages to particular destination queues. In addition, it may be important for the messaging service to guarantee the identification of message sources so that recipients can determine if they are acceptable. Alternatively, assurance of the source and validity of the message could be accomplished with signatures.

BSD Elements

Wherever possible, authentication for access to BSD facilities will use digital certificates. Legacy and COTS systems that require logon/password access should be accessed through an automatic logon facility. BSDs with public Web server access may use logon/password access for previously unknown users.

Each BSD will have some form of support for authorization. Generally, this will involve a security directory with ACLs associated with user roles. Roles will be obtained from the organization directory or may be assigned dynamically by the application(s).

BSD message queues should be accessible only from a messaging service server. These communications should be secure, and each server should authenticate the other.

Application Elements

Applications will vary greatly in their approach to implementing security. In all cases possible, the user identifier should be based on authentication with digital certificates. Authorization should be based on roles. Where possible, access should be controlled at the Web access level and not within the application or in middleware. Defining access in terms of authorized interfaces is much easier for business managers to specify and understand, and this usually will minimize security overhead.

Security Domains

We will now examine the security measures appropriate for six different categories of security domains:

- The public Internet
- The private intranet
- Workplace domains
- BSDs
- Demilitarized zones
- Shared services domains

The Public Internet

The public Internet is the electronic world in which we live. It provides customers, business partners, and remote employees with the ability to connect to the enterprise from anywhere at any time. It also provides the employees and systems of the enterprise with access to information and services outside the enterprise. The public Internet is where a significant aspect of the enterprise business is conducted.

At the same time, we share the Internet with millions of people and systems, some of which may pose a threat to the enterprise. We have no knowledge or control over the paths our messages may travel through the Internet. And we can assume, in general, that communication channels are not physically protected from intrusion.

When we conduct business over the Internet, we need insurance that we know who we are talking to (authentication), that our communications are protected (integrity and privacy), that we can create legally binding agreements (signatures), and that our systems are protected from attack (firewalls).

Unlike the other domains, the public Internet involves potential users we do not know—particularly potential customers and business partners. If they are just seeking information, then it may be desirable to capture information about who they are, but authentication is not a particular concern. If, on the other hand, they want to engage in a business transaction, then authentication becomes an issue.

The authentication of unknown users relegates identification by reference to some other known authority, for example, a credit card company or a CA. Today, the most common form of identification for business transactions is a credit card number. This is not a particularly reliable form of authentication, and it limits the practical scope of business. In the long term, we can expect certificates and the PKI to provide reliable authentication. Consequently, in the short term, our systems serving the public Internet should be designed for both.

In the current environment, it is difficult to develop a legally binding agreement with a previously unknown party. A credit card number provides a weak form of endorsement. An electronic signature requires public key cryptography supported by a certificate. S-HTTP provides a mechanism for attaching signatures to documents, but it has not gained widespread acceptance. This technology has been slow to develop, in part due to U.S. export restrictions on cryptographic algorithms. With the adoption of U.S. legislation making electronic signatures legally binding, we can expect industry standards to emerge in the near future.

The conduct of business transactions over the Internet requires protection of the communications with encryption. SSL provides the necessary encryption and is generally available on popular browsers and Web servers. Although use of a client certificate is optional in SSL, any server-to-server transaction should require a client certificate.

The Private Intranet

The primary difference between the private intranet domain and the public Internet is that within the intranet, all users and servers should be known. In addition, the browser and server software can be controlled to implement standards that may have not gained widespread acceptance.

The risk of attack on client and server computers is reduced on the private intranet, but it should not be ignored. Particularly in a large enterprise, the intranet is not really very private. It's more like a safe neighborhood.

While password sign-on has been the traditional form of authentication for known users, in the integrated enterprise an employee may need to remember many identifiers and passwords to gain access to different systems. In addition to the burden on the employee, this multitude of passwords also creates an administrative burden to create and replace forgotten passwords. Risks are also created by the need to store and protect passwords in many different systems.

The recommended approach is for the enterprise to issue digital certificates for employees. The certificate can be used as the basis for authentication throughout the enterprise, for SSL-encrypted communications, and for digital signatures. Digital signatures will enable the widespread elimination of paper documents. In addition, applications do not need password files that could be exposed, and there is no need for the administration of user identifiers and passwords on every application. While each user must remember the code to unlock his or her private key, that code only works on the device where the private key is stored.

In some cases, users will not always have their personal computers in their possession when they need to be authenticated. One approach is to store the digital certificate and encrypted private key on a smart card. The card can be carried by the user and plugged into other systems that require authentication or other certificate-based operations. The user can enter the code for access to the private key as required. The ad hoc client device need never see the private key, and the private key encryption code only works with the smart card, which remains in the user's possession. Such approaches are still evolving in the marketplace.

Workplace Domains

The typical workplace has multiple computers connected to a LAN with a shared file server and printers. In an integrated enterprise, the LAN will be connected to the intranet. The LAN is an extension of the intranet. In a large enterprise, the intranet has many users and can be accessed by determined intruders who connect in a conference room or unoccupied office. The intranet is more secure than the Internet, but represents a significant risk of intrusion. Consequently, access to LANs should require authentication.

It is desirable for visiting employees to access the intranet through the LAN and be able to use the local printers. At the same time, the local file server contains files that belong to the local business unit and should not be accessible to a visiting employee.

The visiting employee, on the other hand, should be able to access his home-base file server through the intranet from the remote LAN. The employee digital certificate should identify the employee wherever he or she goes within the enterprise.

Within the workplace LAN, it may be acceptable to communicate with the local file server without encryption; this will depend on the security of the workplace environment. However, when an employee communicates with the server from a remote LAN, the communications should be encrypted using SSL. The server must differentiate between local and remote IP addresses.

Up to this point we have not specifically addressed user authorization. The primary concern has been authentication. In the workplace environment, different users may have different authority for access to file server resources. This should be addressed through normal file server security based on the user identity from the digital certificates.

With enterprise firewalls and restricted access to workplace LANs, the workstations used by employees can be quite secure. While employees can reach out to other intranet resources and public Internet resources, others inside and outside the enterprise should not be able to reach in to attack the workstations. On the other hand, experience with the Code Red virus has demonstrated that workstations and servers inside the enterprise can become carriers of a virus that attacks the vulnerabilities of other workstations and servers on the intranet.

In addition, many employees now use their portable computers on the public Internet from outside the enterprise intranet. Some will access the Internet through an ISP that potentially restricts the communication in a way similar to the enterprise firewall. This is typical of dial-up Internet access. The employee computer can only function as a client, not as a server.

Newer services, however, provide a less encumbered and potentially more dangerous link to the public Internet. A user can set up a personal Web site on his or her personal computer. Hackers can direct messages to these user computers the same as other servers on the Internet. Hacker programs are constantly probing the Internet for unprotected servers. Consequently, users who use these open connections to the public Internet must implement firewall software on their personal computers.

Business System Domains (BSDs)

The BSD was defined in Chapter 5. A BSD is one or more computers supporting one or more synchronously coupled applications that are managed by a single organizational unit, usually at a single site. The scopes of the business organization, computations, and the physical computing facility are aligned. Where a BSD extends over multiple sites, the channels of communication should be highly secure and high performance because communication interruptions and delays would have a direct impact on the operation of synchronously linked components.

A BSD should exist in an appropriately secure facility. Specific people should have access to the physical facility for operation and maintenance, certain people should control changes to the hardware and software, and certain people should know the access keys of digital certificates of BSD servers.

A BSD is expected to have two modes of communication with the outside world: a Web server for communication with humans and a connection to a message broker for communication with other systems.

The Web server is the primary point of user access to the BSD and the primary point of security risk. A BSD server may be on the public Internet or on the private intranet. A BSD that is performing a core business function should only be connected to the private intranet to reduce exposure to outside attacks. A BSD that is supporting public services or access by customers and business partners will be connected to the public Internet. The publicly accessible BSD should have limited business functionality to limit the potential damage from a breach of security. Protected business functions are performed by internal BSDs, and BSDs exchange information through message

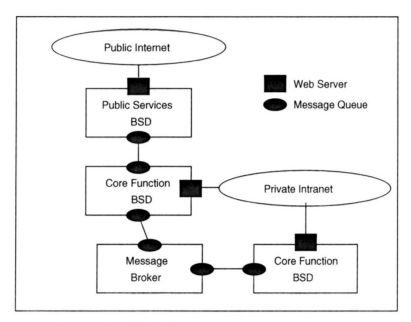

Figure 11.6 BSD network relationships.

broker services. Figure 11.6 illustrates the relationships between BSDs and message brokers.

Known users are authenticated to the BSD server using their digital certificates. On the public Internet, other authentication mechanisms such as credit card numbers may be required, as discussed earlier. Communications are encrypted using SSL. If appropriate, documents created, reviewed, or authorized by a user are signed with a digital signature based on the user's digital certificate.

Similarly, communications with the message broker are authenticated and encrypted using SSL and are based on the digital certificates of the communicating domains.

Within the BSD, we must be concerned with authorization. A BSD may manage a variety of data and provide a variety of operations and services. Different users will have different authority to access these data and services. Authorization is based on roles and is implemented at different levels of granularity depending on the application. Static roles, such as organizational responsibility, are defined in the organization model provided from the organization directory (discussed in Chapter 5). Dynamic roles, based on user activities, are defined and associated with particular users within the BSD.

Demilitarized Zones

Web servers provide the primary access to enterprise applications. They are the primary point of exposure of these systems. Not only do they provide the intended functionality, but because they have complex capabilities, there is also a risk that an intruder will find some way to bypass authentication and authorization controls and perform unauthorized functions or alter the functionality of the Web server.

In order to reduce this risk, Web servers are placed behind firewalls that have limited functionality and only allow certain types of requests to pass through. In the event that the Web server may become corrupted, links from the Web server to other servers also may pass through firewalls. Consequently, the Web server is isolated between a firewall connection to the outside world and a firewall connection to the internal application servers. This is commonly called a *demilitarized zone*. In some cases, communications with the internal applications are only allowed to originate with the internal applications so that a corrupted Web server would not be able to initiate activity with the internal systems.

The use of a firewall implies a fairly direct connection and interaction between the Web server and the application. In order for the firewall to be effective, the exchanges must be quite well defined so that the firewall can bar any other communications. The firewall also should restrict communications to specific enterprise application IP addresses and ports.

Asynchronous queued message communications may be used between the Web server and the application. This provides reliable and relatively timely transfers of information. An intermediary should accept messages; filter them for type, content, and destination; and forward them to an authorized application or Web server queue. This mechanism avoids making the application or the Web server synchronously dependent on each other. When a client completes a transaction, the message is committed to the queue; then the message simply remains in the queue until the recipient accepts it and commits the input transaction.

If timeliness of information is not a priority, then batch file transfers may be appropriate. The application used to read the file can check for invalid input. If the files are transferred by FTP over the intranet, then additional controls should be applied to ensure that files are transferred between the proper sources and destinations.

Shared Services Domains

Shared services domains are computing services that are part of the information infrastructure. They are special types of BSDs that support the integration

and management of the enterprise systems. They include the following
services:

- System management services
- Security services
- Organization directory
- Message broker services
- E-mail services

Like BSDs, each of these may have a Web server for user access and message queues for the exchange of messages with other systems. In addition,
each has unique security issues to be considered as a result of their cross-
domain functionality.

System management services.   System management services can have
significant control over the operation of systems and facilities through
the reconfiguration and control of operating parameters. Close attention
must be given to control of SNMP messages.

Security services.   The core of the security services is the management of
digital certificates, including proper identification of applicants for certificates and the recording of revoked certificates in an appropriate directory. Security services must establish business processes for the
administration of certificates; these processes should be automated so
that they are widely accessible and reliable. Security services also
include the specification and maintenance of authorization for infrastructure services. This must have supporting business processes to
ensure the orderly control of changes.

Organization directory.   The organization directory must be maintained
to reflect changes to the organization structure, personnel assignments,
and role assignments. The directory must address structure, assignments, and roles for the enterprise as a whole and role assignments for
security within BSDs, that is, local role assignments. Appropriate
processes and controls must be put in place to implement these changes
on a timely, reliable, and authorized basis.

Message broker service.   The message broker service provides great flexibility in the integration of systems and the communication of events.
This capability also must be controlled to ensure that messages and
events are not introduced fraudulently into the network because messages will be exchanged across BSDs. For some messages and applications, it may be necessary to restrict message sources. This may include
the need for secure connections between the message broker and the
sources and destinations.

E-mail services.   E-mail can come from anywhere and go anywhere. In some cases, e-mail may be used by applications to send notices to people. These messages could be forged. It may be appropriate to require a mechanism such as PGP to digitally sign such messages. Messages also may carry viruses. The e-mail service should filter messages for attachments containing viruses even though the personal computers also have virus detection software.

Summary

The security strategy developed here relies heavily on domain separation and digital certificates. Domain separation relies on firewalls and the separation of networks. Digital certificates integrate enterprise security in the following ways:

- Digital certificates provide uniform authentication for employees, systems, and possibly business partners.
- Communications are secured with SSL based on digital certificates.
- Digital certificates support digital signatures.
- Digital certificates support a single sign-on across the enterprise.

While supporting protocols are not yet widely accepted on the public Internet, digital certificates and public key technology can be implemented within the enterprise. Their adoption will greatly improve enterprise security, reduce the security hassle for employees, and enable the replacement of paper documents with signed digital documents, supporting further streamlining of business operations and the expanded scope of electronic business.

Supporting
Enterprise Intelligence

Up to this point, the primary focus of the enterprise architecture has been on support for mainstream business systems—the systems that run the business minute to minute and day after day. However, support of routine operations is not enough. The enterprise must be managed to develop products and services, improve processes, respond to opportunities, and prepare for the future. It must be managed intelligently.

In the past, planning and decision making tended to align with the chain of command of the organizational hierarchy. Managers would make decisions for the organization within their area of responsibility. Top-level management would make decisions that affected the enterprise as a whole and resolve issues between departments.

As business has become more complex and decisions require greater analysis and expertise, much of the responsibility for managing the enterprise has been delegated to specialists, or *knowledge workers*. These knowledge workers may focus on their primary area of responsibility, but they often draw on information and contributing experts from across the enterprise. Internet technology, accessibility of powerful computing resources, and the low cost of massive amounts of storage capacity have further expanded the opportunity for this delegation and cross-enterprise collaboration, planning, and decision making. Events in one part of the business can be communicated quickly to other parts of the organization for appropriate action. Employees making plans and decisions in one area can tap information and experts in other areas of the business to make more informed decisions and improve the plans or reduce risks, achieving enterprise-level optimization instead of only local optimization. Large volumes of historical data can be accumulated and analyzed to identify patterns and trends.

In a sense, top managers have expanded their capabilities and reach through delegation to experts. This delegation is only possible to the extent that pertinent information is available to those who need it and they can collaborate to achieve enterprise-level optimization. In this environment, many different people make management plans and decisions: engineers, salespersons, accountants, project managers, systems analysts, buyers, production supervisors, and quality improvement specialists. The enterprise is managed not by functional islands, but by a collective enterprise intelligence that is integrated across business functions. Top managers define the business, provide the vision, and create the incentives, but they do not have the expertise or the time to participate in every decision that affects the operation or future success of the enterprise. Where the risks are high, problems are not being resolved, leaders disagree, or there are no good choices, then the level of decision making must be escalated to engage top management.

Enterprise intelligence is the integration of people and systems, sharing information, collaborating on solutions and plans, and communicating decisions and events so that the enterprise responds intelligently in a manner reflecting enterprise-wide optimization. It is a strategic objective to enable the enterprise to achieve and maintain competitive advantage.

This chapter will look at both the business and architectural requirements of enterprise intelligence. The business requirements will describe the business needs for systems and people to work in harmony to achieve optimal operation of the enterprise. The architectural requirements will define the technical supports required to achieve this harmonization.

Business Requirements for Enterprise Intelligence

In this section we will examine the following business requirements of enterprise intelligence:

- Strategic objective
- Planning and decision making
- Data sources
- Organization

- Synthesis of intelligence
- Modeling and simulation
- Personalization
- Knowledge management
- Collaboration

Strategic Objective

The business intelligence strategic objective is for knowledge workers throughout the enterprise, potentially including the virtual enterprise (including business partners), to have access to needed information, share insights, and combine their skills to achieve optimal management of the enterprise. Knowledge will not be lost to the enterprise when individuals leave or retire. The enterprise will function as a harmonized community to optimize the enterprise operation and future direction. Knowledge workers include employees at all levels who are responsible for identifying problems and opportunities, developing plans and solutions, providing information, or making decisions that affect the operation or future of the enterprise. Knowledge workers should work in harmony to manage the enterprise.

Responsibilities and relationships must be defined so that persons with the right expertise are aware of and act on problems and opportunities. Levels of authority must be defined so that the appropriate persons allocate resources and accept responsibility for risks and the mitigation of risks.

Enterprise intelligence will be reflected in decision making and planning throughout the enterprise. Knowledge workers will act in the best interest of the enterprise. Decisions will be optimized from an enterprise perspective.

Knowledge workers must be notified of events or circumstances that are relevant to their area of responsibility and expertise, and they must be able to access relevant data through views appropriate to their area of interest in forms that support their analysis. They also must be able to expand certain views and particular elements to obtain additional detail, and they must be able to aggregate and compare equivalent data from different segments of the business.

In order to understand, analyze, aggregate, compare, and assess the credibility of data, knowledge workers must have information about the sources, integrity, semantics, and basis of measures of data retrieved. The data must be consistent or undergo appropriate transformations to support comparisons, aggregations, and modeling of hypothetical circumstances or events.

Knowledge workers must have the appropriate tools to retrieve needed data from sources throughout the enterprise and perform analyses. These tools will vary from simple reports, to data visualizations, to models and simulations, to collaborative environments.

Finally, knowledge workers must have access to enterprise knowledge, both from documents and humans, and be able to communicate and coordinate with other experts from different disciplines and activities. Collaboration is key to gaining insight from an enterprise perspective and developing more effective solutions.

Managers and knowledge workers must operate in a harmonized enterprise that provides consistent and meaningful data and knowledge, manages predictable and consistent business processes, supports collaboration, and responds to change quickly and consistently.

Planning and Decision-Making Horizons

It is important to understand the different planning and decision-making horizons of knowledge workers, as depicted in Figure 12.1. Some plans and decisions will have an immediate effect, whereas others may take considerable time to implement. The objectives, data needs, and methods differ. We have defined three horizons for purposes of considering appropriate mechanisms of support:

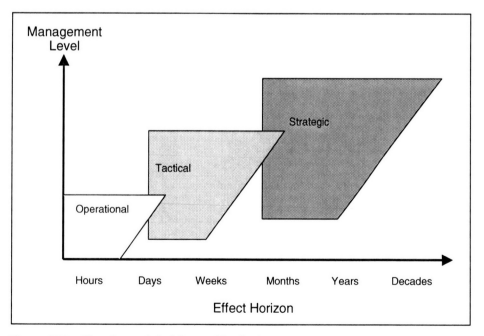

Figure 12.1   Planning and decision-making horizons.

- Operational
- Tactical
- Strategic

We will consider each of these in the following subsections.

Operational

Operational planning and decision making affect current activities, generally within the same day or week. These may be decisions affecting current production, such as job assignments, workload balancing, rework, facilities maintenance and repair, priorities, and expenditures.

Operational data will include orders, resources, defects, schedules, and units of production. Generally, management information will be an aggregation of counts and exceptions, but when aggregate data suggest that limits have been exceeded or when events of particular concern occur, then data on specific instances may be of interest.

Within each department, certain current data may be of particular interest. These data would indicate if appropriate progress is being made on the routine work of the department—for example, data on routine accounting transactions, engineering assignments completed on time or delayed, shipments and receipts of materials, number of defects or scrapped parts, daily sales, and so on.

These data are derived from routine business transactions that are essential to the primary mission of the enterprise. They are of interest because they may provoke decisions that will have an immediate impact on the conduct of business, such as the production of products or services, the consumption of resources, or the realization of sales.

Operational monitoring and analysis may reveal problems or opportunities that cannot be resolved immediately. These issues should be referred to tactical planning and decision-making processes for further analysis and, if appropriate, allocation of resources to address the issue. Examples might be a production machine that cannot be repaired, a product design flaw, or an inability to meet the demand for a particular product or service.

Tactical

Tactical planning and decision making involves actions intended to occur in the near future, typically in less than a year. Activities to install new equipment, analyze and improve business processes, select an alternate supplier, hire new people, or make changes to a computer application are typical tactical activities.

Some activities related to longer-term efforts also may be tactical. During a product development program or a systems development project, it may be necessary to alter the plan, reassign resources, or modify objectives to keep the effort on schedule. These actions affect work in the development domain within the near future but may require consideration of the implications years into the future.

Generally, tactical decisions are different from operational decisions because the consequences of the decisions are more far-reaching or significant or implementation requires more time and effort. It may be desirable to base the activities on current operating data, but it may be necessary to examine historical data or observe the situation over time to devise an appropriate solution.

Typically, it is not necessary for tactical activities to have access to up-to-the-minute operational data, and it may not be necessary to have continuing access to historical data. The problems addressed are either sufficiently understood with recent operational data or the necessary data can be collected within a short period of time. Most tactical decisions deal with the resolution of problems that affect current operations.

Tactical activities may uncover the need for a longer-term strategic solution, and they may provide a short-term remedy in lieu of a strategic solution.

Strategic

Strategic planning and decision making affect activities in the more distant future, typically 1 to 5 years. They are strategic because either they require effort over a prolonged period of time or they are in anticipation of longer-term changes in resources, technology, or marketplace. The drivers for strategic planning and decision making generally come from outside the enterprise in the form of technical advances, market shifts, environmental factors, politics, or competition.

Strategic planning and decision making for the enterprise generally will involve top management of the enterprise because they may have a significant long-lasting impact on the success of the enterprise. Strategic enterprise decisions may involve the issue of new stock, investments in new endeavors, acquisitions, and marketing strategies. Implementation may involve research and development and organization and culture changes. At the same time, there may be strategic planning and decision making at lower levels in the organization with a more limited scope impact. Strategic plans might involve the development of a new product line, implementation of new computer applications, changes to the skill set of a department, or substantial changes to facilities or business processes. These strategic plans should be aligned with the enterprise strategic plans.

Strategic activities seldom need data from current operations. The problems to be solved are raised by historical trends, external factors, or basic changes to product or process technology, not transient operational problems.

Strategic issues may not even be visible in current production data. They may be observed in data collected over a period of time and analyzed for trends or correlations. At the same time, it may be appropriate to monitor current data at some level to recognize if current operating experiences no longer support assumptions that are the basis of a strategic direction.

Data Sources

Knowledge workers in general will need data from many sources. Knowledge workers involved in operational decisions will be interested primarily in local data and data that are a consequence of local operations. Tactical knowledge workers will be interested in data with broader scope in terms of both the organization and time. Strategic knowledge workers will likely be interested in historical data and sources beyond the scope of the enterprise involving competitors, markets, customer satisfaction, new technology, and economic factors.

Data also may come from models. One pervasive model is a budget. Other models may reflect business process performance, product cost breakdowns, and product distribution models. Models may be a shared basis for action or a hypothetical projection of the future. Specialized models will often exist in particular problem domains, such as mechanical stress analysis models, production sequencing models, distribution models, performance simulations, and business process models.

Data that are available locally are usually easiest to obtain. The leadership of the particular organization likely will appreciate the need and ensure their accessibility. As the scope of interest broadens and the planning horizon becomes more distant, the ease with which the needed data are accessed and the consistency of the data likely will diminish. When data are obtained from outside the enterprise, they may be easier to obtain if the source is a vendor or is compensated for making the data available. Other data, such as customer and competitor data, may be more difficult to obtain—such data might be available from third parties in the business of providing industry data.

Enterprise intelligence depends on knowledge workers having access to the data they need. In some cases, the data are simply not available or the benefit is not worth the expense. In such cases, the knowledge worker will need to make assumptions or projections based on available data and experience. However, where data exist, enterprise intelligence calls for defining appropriate sources and making the data consistent and accessible to those who need them.

Organization

Organization structure information is a key element in achieving enterprise intelligence. In order to perform ubiquitous planning and decision making, participants throughout the enterprise must have well-defined roles, authority, and relationships. Roles establish the subject matter and thus the input data of an individual's planning and decision-making efforts. Roles suggest the information viewpoint of interest to the individual, and role assignments also should serve as the principal basis for security access authorization. Authority determines constraints on actions, such as spending limits or the types of processes that can be initiated. Relationships determine potential additional or alternate contributors and can be a basis for ensuring separation of responsibility in decisions affecting enterprise assets.

In addition to the organization structure, enterprise intelligence requires the ability to involve people with relevant skills and knowledge. This includes information regarding potential participants that goes beyond the capabilities implicit in their job assignments.

This information must be readily available throughout the enterprise. It is key to engaging the right people in the work of the enterprise, and it is key to harmonizing their efforts to optimize enterprise performance.

Synthesis

Access to data alone does not achieve enterprise intelligence. Data are primary inputs to the development and application of intelligence. More meaningful forms must be synthesized from raw data. Three different levels of synthesis accomplish the transformation of data into intelligence:

Data to information.   Data are assembled, aggregated, converted, organized, and presented so that they reveal relationships, trends, and exceptions. Reports typically provide information. For example, a computer-aided design (CAD) system manages data about points and lines, but these have little meaning until they are presented as features such as edges, holes, and protrusions. These features are abstractions of the detail that present concepts and relationships, that is, information, not obvious from the raw data.

Information to knowledge.   Information can be used to develop generalizations about behavior, events, and thresholds. Knowledge is an understanding of cause and effect. Knowledge may be inferred from observations and experiences over a long period of time. This knowledge of cause and effect may be expressed as rules to infer when effects of interest are or will occur. Knowledge may be obtained from experts and translated into rules for the development of expert, rule-based systems.

Knowledge to intelligence. Intelligence is the ability to produce purposeful behavior—to act in pursuit of objectives. Knowledge is transformed into intelligence or, more specifically, intelligent behavior when inferences are used to make plans and decisions based on objectives, priorities, values, and risks. Intelligent systems apply knowledge to data and information to interpret circumstances of interest and take appropriate action. Intelligent actions generally occur through the synthesis of knowledge from multiple sources to achieve objectives such as reduce cost and improve quality. Much of the intelligence of the enterprise occurs through people analyzing information, applying knowledge, and making decisions about appropriate actions to achieve objectives.

Figure 12.2 depicts the three levels of synthesis of intelligence. This is not a one-way process, but an iterative process. As information, knowledge, and intelligence are realized, they raise new questions and new investigations. This drives new analyses and inquiries. Inquiries require that the user focus on relevant data, information, and knowledge; develop abstractions and models to characterize the problem; examine the problem from different viewpoints with different visualizations; and realize new insights. These different levels of inquiry and synthesis suggest the kinds of tools needed to support enterprise intelligence.

Modeling and Simulation

A *model* is an abstract representation of a set of circumstances and relationships. A model simply may be an abstraction of the real world, or it may represent a potential set of elements and relationships for planning, design, analysis, or construction. A model typically incorporates constraints and the

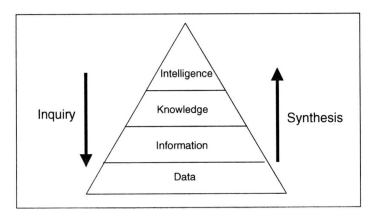

Figure 12.2 Synthesis hierarchy.

mechanisms to maintain consistency with the constraints. Based on constraints and relationships, a change to one element of a model may be propagated to maintain consistency. A model may be as simple as a spreadsheet that accepts data in certain cells and propagates the effects of the data entered to other cells. A model is an integration of information and knowledge. A model that has an objective function, for example, to optimize throughput, provides some degree of intelligence because it is balancing values.

Simulation uses models to analyze and predict consequences. Often intelligent decision making involves consideration of many interacting factors. The consequences of the interactions may be difficult to comprehend, and the net effects of the interactions may be difficult to predict without a model. Often simulations are dynamic systems where a series of inputs are provided over time according to a schedule or statistical arrival rate function. The model may propagate the effects through constraints, or the input transaction may travel through a series of operations, simulating the effects of queues and servers. Simulation occurs with a spreadsheet when the user experiments with different data values or changes formulas for computations to produce different results.

Simulations provide support for a what-if analysis. A user provides data to a model that reflects the circumstances of interest. The user may then enter hypothetical data or modify constraints and relationships to examine the possible consequences of an action.

Figure 12.3 depicts the role of modeling. Information, knowledge, and objectives are inputs to the modeling activity. The modeling activity may

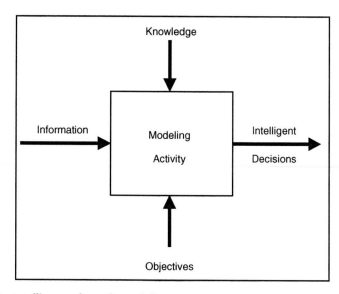

Figure 12.3   Intelligence through modeling.

involve exploration of alternative solutions, or it may evolve as the shared representation of a collaboration solution. The result is intelligent decisions.

Personalization

Personalization is the tailoring of services to meet the particular needs and interests of individuals. Personalization improves individual productivity and quality of work.

A modest level of personalization occurs where the interface to a system is based on a user's role—display content and format may be designed for each potential user role. Individualized personalization requires the capture of information about the individual and the tailoring of the presentation or interactions to address the individual's particular needs or preferences. In some cases, the individual explicitly performs the personalization.

Personalization has become important in dealing with customers in order to give them a positive experience in dealing with the enterprise and to make it easy for them to satisfy their individual needs in acquiring a product or service.

Personalization for enterprise intelligence can occur at many levels, including the following:

- Information in forms that are useful to the individual
- Mechanisms to keep the user informed of events
- Convenient access to relevant knowledge
- Models for the application of knowledge and intelligence
- Support for collaboration with others for enterprise-level intelligence

Personalization may be achieved explicitly or implicitly. When a user is assigned a specified role or saves a Uniform Resource Locator (URL) for future reference, these are explicit forms of personalization. When the system captures information about the user, such as buying habits and demographic data, and uses it to alter the content and form of information presented, this is implicit personalization. Both kinds are important, but caution must be used with implicit personalization because the user may experience a loss of control or be irritated with being presented with information he or she did not ask for.

The organization model should reflect role-level personalization of interfaces so that an individual may consistently obtain data in a form suitable to his or her role with certain abstractions and aggregations applied and possibly with certain report layouts or data visualizations. It is important to enable the individual to further personalize the presentation of information using workstation-based tools, where templates and parameters can be saved and applied locally. Personalization helps the individual do his or her job efficiently without doing a new investigation to obtain current data on the same subject matter.

Customer relationship management (CRM) is an extended form of personalization. Not only can the customer's interaction with the system be tailored to the individual's interests and needs, but the system also may actively initiate activity with the customer or provide ancillary services to maintain contact or promote products and services. The customer should see the enterprise exhibit intelligent behavior.

Knowledge Management

Knowledge is the generalization of facts, relationships, and behavior. It comprehends cause and effect. Experts have knowledge that can be used to explain or predict behavior or consequences.

Knowledge that is only available from experts has limited utility and may be lost to the enterprise when people leave. Managers always have been concerned about the preservation and use of enterprise knowledge. Knowledge management involves the retention of and access to knowledge that is of value to the enterprise.

We will first examine the forms of knowledge to be managed and then examine the knowledge management process.

Forms of Knowledge

We will consider three forms of knowledge:

Human knowledge.   Knowledge of experts and others who have experience in a particular domain.

Passive knowledge.   Knowledge that is recorded but must be retrieved and applied to be useful.

Active knowledge.   Knowledge that is linked to models or the real world and is invoked automatically to provide advice or invoke appropriate actions.

Human Knowledge

Individuals capture human knowledge through experience and analysis. Individuals retain the knowledge in their heads. The knowledge may or may not be consistent, complete, and well organized. The individual applies the knowledge by recognizing circumstances similar to his or her experience and using the knowledge to infer conclusions and predictions about the situation at hand. The human continues to refine the knowledge through additional experience and feedback regarding the accuracy of his or her conclusions and predictions.

Passive Knowledge

Passive knowledge is captured by recording generalizations and conclusions about facts, usually from human experiences and typically in the form of documents. Passive knowledge also may be generated by processing facts and creating generalizations such as the trends and correlations derived from the analysis of market data. This knowledge is applied when humans match a situation to relevant knowledge and use the knowledge to draw conclusions and make predictions. The knowledge is refined by human efforts to revise and extend the documents or by creating new documents and phasing out old ones.

Active Knowledge

Active knowledge is in a form that can be linked to operational systems or models in a way that enables it to be applied automatically. Typically, such knowledge is in the form of rules or constraints that are applied whenever relevant facts change. These may be triggers in a database, formulas in a spreadsheet, constraints in a CAD system, or rule-based expert systems.

Underlying such systems is a model. The model represents the problem domain—for example, records of production activity, a budget in a spreadsheet, a CAD part design, or a credit application. The rules and constraints are expressed in terms of the model, and the rules and constraints are linked to the relevant elements of the model so that they will be evaluated when the facts change.

Active knowledge generally is refined by human efforts to correct or improve performance. However, some systems, such as those based on neural networks, learn from experience and continue to learn as they receive feedback on the correctness of their conclusions or predictions. In this case, the capture, recording, and refinement of knowledge are automatic. The role of the human is to define the appropriate context, to provide the experience in an appropriate form, and to give feedback on the results.

Knowledge Management Process

The knowledge management process is concerned primarily with capturing, preserving, and using knowledge as an asset of the enterprise. Here our focus will be on capturing human knowledge to create accessible passive knowledge. Most of the enterprise knowledge at risk of being lost is human knowledge. Knowledge that can be formalized as active knowledge is a small fraction of the total knowledge, and it applies to relatively specific problems that justify a substantial investment in codification.

We introduced the model of Figure 12.4 in Chapter 1. It is a human process that can be augmented with technology. The same process is applicable to active knowledge that may be acquired and applied by computer, but we are

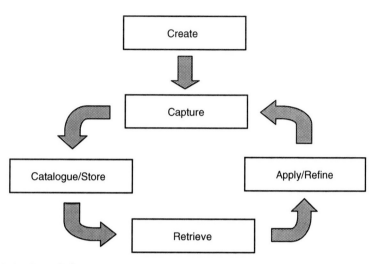

Figure 12.4 Knowledge management process.

more concerned here with human knowledge that is not encoded easily and may be lost to the enterprise if not managed effectively. We will examine the potential for technology support in each of the activities.

Create

Deriving insights from experience and analysis of problems or phenomena creates knowledge. The principal enablers for creation of knowledge are access to information and collaboration with other experts. If relevant information is not available in an appropriate form representing sufficiently broad experience, the creation of new knowledge will be encumbered. Similarly, new ideas and insights often require synergy between experts with different backgrounds or techniques.

Capture

Capture of this knowledge requires the following:

- Recognition that there is knowledge to be captured
- A mechanism to facilitate capture and classification in a useful form
- Incentives to get people to apply the extra effort and give up control of their knowledge

While knowledge may be generated during a productive endeavor, it may not be recognized or fully appreciated until the endeavor is completed. A key point for capture is where the person or group performing the productive activity seeks acceptance of their work product. At that point, they are in a position to explain the basis of their result and may be required to do so. This is knowledge that could be captured. At that same point in the endeavor, the person reviewing the result will apply knowledge to evaluate the result, and the basis for review issues or questions is additional knowledge of the reviewer that could be captured. The result of the iteration between producer and reviewer may be a refinement of the knowledge that is the basis of acceptance of the work product.

Catalogue/Store

Once knowledge is captured, it must be catalogued for future reference. This involves the capture of metaknowledge, that is, information about the knowledge. The metaknowledge will be the basis of future retrieval of relevant knowledge.

It must be easy for humans to create the metaknowledge. Metaknowledge for certain types of processes and work products should have similar meta attributes. The human submitter should be given a form that includes defaults for the particular product and process and meaningful choices for the other attributes.

Retrieve

The retrieve function is a search and access capability. The search is over the metaknowledge based on attributes that are similar to the problem situation at hand, where the knowledge is needed. Retrieval may also require a search of the content of documents for relevant words or phrases. While there might be a repository for metaknowledge, the actual stored knowledge may be very voluminous and will continue to change over time. Consequently, the storage of knowledge may be distributed if it is classified and accessed easily. The results of a meta knowledge search can identify where the knowledge is stored.

Apply/Refine

Knowledge is applied by mapping a new situation to the concepts considered in the knowledge. The application will provide insight on the current situation and may provide insight to generalize or refine the knowledge. For human and passive knowledge, this process is still a human process.

Collaboration

Collaboration is key to enterprise intelligence. Collaboration involves people working together to combine their knowledge, apply their values, and improve the quality of plans and decisions. Collaboration is essential to enterprise intelligence; otherwise, solutions will tend to be suboptimal, reflecting the experience, knowledge, and objectives of individuals who are focused on certain business functions or problem areas.

The following steps are typical of a collaboration:

- Identify a collaboration leader.
- Define the problem.
- Identify and engage participants.
- Establish collaboration medium.
- Perform collaboration.
- Produce results.

We will briefly discuss the nature of each of these steps.

Identify the Collaboration Leader

The first step is to identify the person who will lead the effort. This person has primary responsibility for defining the nature of the effort, engaging participants, obtaining resources, and moving the process forward. This assignment may be by virtue of the nature of the problem, the area of responsibility, or some process of recruiting according to expertise and availability.

Define the Problem

The first challenge for collaboration is to define the problem—what is the nature of the task, and what are the objectives for success? The nature of the task and objectives will determine the qualifications of people to get involved. The problem description also will provide participants with an understanding of the effort they are being asked to join.

Engage Participants

The next step is to get the right people involved. In a large enterprise, where individual circles of acquaintance are a fraction of the enterprise, this can be very challenging. It requires some form of personnel directory that will support a search for qualified people. The participants must not all bring the same perspective and capabilities but must be chosen for their diverse perspectives and expertise.

In addition to identifying candidates, engaging participants will involve determining their availability, providing funding, providing information on the situation and the problem, and scheduling participation. These will tend to be a function of the corporate culture and the available collaboration mechanisms.

Establish the Collaboration Medium

Collaboration requires a medium of exchange: a place or mechanisms by which the collaborators can interact, exchange ideas, and develop consensus. The medium of exchange could be a face-to-face meeting, a videoconference, a teleconference (audio), a managed process, an electronic bulletin board, or an e-mail exchanged through a distribution list.

The choice of medium will depend, to some extent, on the nature of the problem, the collaboration mode, and the availability of the participants. If participants cannot meet at a common place, then the collaboration cannot be face to face. If they can meet at a common time, then teleconferencing or video-conferencing may be options. If participants cannot meet at a common time, then collaboration must be through store-and-forward communications such as e-mail, a bulletin board, or a managed process.

Collaborate

Collaboration can be accomplished in a variety of ways. We will examine approaches to collaboration by considering three basic variables:

- Authority of participants
- Communication mode
- Modeling approach

Authority of Participants

Collaborators may participate with different levels of authority. The leader has primary responsibility for organizing and directing the collaboration.

The goal of the collaboration may range from simply obtaining input to producing a consensus result. If the goal is simply to obtain input, the leader will have strong authority for determining the relevance and importance of contributions and the substance of the result. This is weak collaboration and may have limited success, particularly if participants have experienced similar collaborations in which their inputs were ignored or not acknowledged. Participation will be ensured if the participants work for the leader, but then their participation may not be as objective or their perspectives as diverse.

Strong collaboration works toward a consensus. Participants have the opportunity to influence the result and will be more committed to it. In strong collaboration, inputs, proposals and discussions are the basis for creation of a consensus work product. This could be a specification expressed as text and diagrams in a document, it could be a CAD design where participants have participated in shaping the model, or it might be a project plan constructed interactively. In strong collaboration, the leader will keep the process orderly and on schedule with minimal authority over the content of the result.

Communication Mode

Communication modes may be synchronous, asynchronous, or managed. Most undertakings will involve a combination of these communication modes.

Synchronous. Synchronous communications can occur when collaborators participate at a common time. Each participant's contribution is observed by the others as it is made. Synchronous communications occur in a face-to-face meeting, a teleconference, a videoconference, or a chat room.

Asynchronous. Asynchronous communications are prepared by individual participants, independently, and communicated for other participants to consider at their convenience. This enables collaborators to participate when their individual schedules permit. It does not preclude some or all of them participating in the same time period, but typically the assumption is that they are working independently. Asynchronous communications occur with the exchange of documents, e-mail, and bulletin boards. Asynchronous communications reduce the pace of contribution, but often the contributions are considered more carefully because they must be prepared and must stand on their own when received by other participants.

Managed. Managed communications occur under some form of controlled exchange. The participants may each have defined roles in a formal process. Or contributions could be solicited and combined according to a schedule or protocol. Managed communications occur with a workflow process, a project plan, or on an event-response basis. Participants each contribute their part to the whole when it is time for their contribution and the inputs they need are available.

Modeling Approach

The purpose of collaboration is to produce a work product that reflects the experiences, perspectives, and expertise of multiple participants. The work product is a model that defines the solution. It could be a diagram, a document, a spreadsheet, a complex design, or a prototype. The model is where the pieces are integrated to validate and illustrate the combined contributions.

The modeling approach will affect the communication mode and the nature of the contributions. There are three modeling approaches: ad hoc, structured, and assembled.

Ad hoc. Ad hoc modeling starts with a blank slate. Participants may each produce a proposed solution or a partial solution for others to consider. As participants present partial solutions, aspects may be accepted as part of the result so that a solution emerges over time. This form of modeling is necessary when the problem is unique or the goal is to explore unconventional solutions. This approach will take time, and it also may be more subject to the strength of individual personalities, particularly in synchronous communications.

Structured.   A structured model begins with a framework based on experience with similar problems in the past. The structure might be a document outline, an architecture, a general design, or a development process. Collaborators may contribute to the fleshing out of the framework wherever they see an opportunity to contribute their expertise. This reduces the time but preserves interaction and consideration of tradeoffs.

Assembled.   An assembled model begins with well-defined components. This partitions the problem and allows participants to be assigned to specific components where they will concentrate their efforts. Collaboration is through reviews and reconciliation of interfaces, but each segment tends to be the product of a weak collaboration. This approach is most common where a similar solution already exists. The design of an automobile for a new model year is typical. Most of the parts are already defined, but they must be adjusted to meet styling and performance objectives.

Some collaborations will employ all three modeling approaches, progressing from ad hoc to assembled as the problem becomes better understood and useful structure becomes apparent.

Produce Results

The collaboration could conceivably continue endlessly. Conditions of closure must be defined early in the effort and applied. The conditions typically will be that certain objectives will be achieved in the model and/or a time limit will be reached. The collaboration will be most successful if the result represents a consensus.

Consensus is not always possible. Participants may not agree on or accept the enterprise-level optimal solution. Opinions simply may differ. In such cases, the leader or an outside arbitrator (such as a higher-level manager) may need to take control and define the result.

This may mean that the arbitrator takes control of the model, considers the various contributions, and configures a final solution that balances different concerns. The arbitrator then takes responsibility for the quality and effectiveness of the result.

In any case, the collaborators should see the final result, be acknowledged for their contributions, and receive feedback on the ultimate success of the solution. This feedback is important for improving both the collaboration activities and solutions in the future.

Summary

Collaboration takes many forms. The form will be a function of the problem, the urgency, the participants, the available models, the similarity of experience, and the supporting facilities and services. The enterprise integration architecture can affect the choice of participants, access to information about the problem, the nature and quality of the model, and the facilities that support modeling and collaboration.

Establishing Architectural Support for Enterprise Intelligence

Enterprise intelligence requires an environment in which people and systems work together to observe, analyze, interpret, predict, define objectives, plan, and make decisions to achieve maximum value for the enterprise and respond quickly to changing circumstances. The enterprise integration architecture does not produce information, knowledge, or intelligence. These come from applications and people. The architecture must support the applications and people with an environment that enables access, communication, collaboration, and harmony.

In this section we will examine how the architecture can support enterprise intelligence through the following:

- Engaging and supporting people
- Data access
- Presentation of information
- Knowledge management
- Supporting intelligent behavior

Engaging and Enabling People

People are an integral part of enterprise intelligence. Computers and telecommunications improve the speed, accuracy, and productivity, but in the final analysis, people run the business. People bring the following qualities to planning and decision making:

Experience. The ability to determine when a problem is unusual or a result is inconsistent.

Responsibility.   A personal stake in the quality of the result.

Judgment.   The ability to apply often competing qualitative values to decision making.

Vision.   An understanding of the overall situation and the desired future state.

Enterprise intelligence requires that issues engage the right people so that people with the right experience, responsibility, judgment, and vision participate in various planning and decision-making activities. For these people to be productive, they need support that accommodates their individual needs. Finally, they must be authorized to access enterprise data, information, and knowledge appropriate to their area of responsibility.

The architecture should address these requirements through the following:

- An organization directory
- An assignment mechanism
- Personalization
- Authorization

We will examine these in the following subsections.

Organization Directory

An organization directory is essential for engaging the right people and supporting their activities. The directory should provide information about where people are in the organization, their level of responsibility, the roles they are assigned, and their competencies. The core of this directory is an organization model. The Object Management Group (OMG) has adopted a specification for an organization structure facility to provide a shared source of information on an organization. The organization directory service described here is broader in scope.

The organization structure aspect of an organization directory will provide information about the individual's area of responsibility, and it will provide information about the chain of command for job assignments and decision making. An individual's level of responsibility implies the degree to which the enterprise relies on his or her capabilities and the degree of personal commitment the individual has to the enterprise. Roles provide more specific expressions of the responsibilities and authority of an individual. Roles also will provide the basis for the individual authority to access data, information, and knowledge.

Finally, the directory should include individual competencies. Competencies include various measures of the individual's capabilities, such as education, certifications, test scores, and performance ratings. The OMG is defining interface specifications for a competency facility to support searches for individuals or services that meet specified qualifications.

Many different users may need to access the organization directory information for a variety of purposes. At the same time, roles will determine authority to access data and applications, and some of the information about people may be personal and confidential. Consequently, the directory should be a shared service that provides information on people based on the purpose and authority of requests.

Assignment Mechanism

Problems and issues need to be assigned to people in an efficient and reliable manner. The organization directory provides a basis for assignments, and in some cases, the selection of candidates may be automated. However, in many cases, selection will require human involvement. In this case, the first assignment is to somebody who can make an assignment. It should be possible to automate the assigner assignment in most cases based on the source and general subject matter of the issue.

Assignments should be done with a workflow management system. There may be a number of candidates for an assignment, and the request can be posted in all their work lists. The candidates can then consider if they have the expertise and the time to respond. In the mean time, the request will not be lost, and if there is no timely response, an alarm can be raised for further action by the assigner or a person of higher authority.

Once the assignment has been accepted, the performer may determine that others should address portions of the solution. The performer may then issue subordinate requests for action to other people, posting the request in multiple work lists.

This process works as long as there are willing performers. Unless they are in the same department as the source of the problem, acceptance of the request is likely to be viewed as conflicting with their responsibilities to their local organization. At least in a large enterprise, the process must incorporate a mechanism for cost allocation. The assigner may specify the appropriate allocation.

Personalization

The architecture should provide an environment that can be tailored to the individual in order to enhance quality and productivity. Key elements are the following:

- Distribution lists
- Event subscriptions

- Bookmarks and hyperlinks
- Application configurations
- Solution templates
- Presentation templates

Knowledge workers not only respond to assigned problems, but they are expected to be on the lookout for circumstances that call for their attention based on their area of interest and responsibility. Consequently, distribution lists should direct issues and events to persons who may respond directly or may recognize relevant patterns or problems with a common solution.

It also should be possible for individuals to subscribe to particular events or define rules to fire on events in circumstances of interest. Events of interest will reflect current and potential problems and will change over time for individual knowledge workers. The knowledge worker may react to individual events or accumulate a history for analysis.

Knowledge workers also need to be able to access relevant stored knowledge quickly. Much of this knowledge will be in the form of textual and graphical documents. Once relevant knowledge has been located, it should be easy for the knowledge worker to capture the reference for the future. Browsers provide the fundamental bookmark capability to store URLs for future reference. In addition, the knowledge worker should create his or her own documents and Web pages giving structure to the problem domain and providing hyperlinks to material available on the Web.

It is also important that applications are configured for the roles of users and that knowledge workers are able to configure applications to suit their individual preferences, level of proficiency, and techniques. Role-based configuration is based on both authorization restrictions and the viewpoints needed for each role. These may be defaults that can be further tailored by individuals. Unfortunately, configuration parameters usually are specific to the applications, as are the mechanisms for making the selections persistent, so configurations can only be shared if common applications are used.

Knowledge workers often will solve problems more quickly by leveraging solutions to earlier, similar problems. In order to do this, it must be possible for the knowledge worker to save and selectively retrieve solutions. To make these examples more useful, they should be catalogued and possibly generalized into templates or rules, thus functioning as knowledge for future problems. It should be possible for individuals to capture, catalogue, and generalize their experiences without the burden of making them useful to a broader community. We will discuss support of knowledge management more later.

Finally, different knowledge workers find different visualizations useful depending on their role, their skills, their problem-solving techniques, and their personal preferences. Each knowledge worker should be able to tailor the form and content of data visualizations and capture the parameters for future reference. When similar problems arise, the knowledge worker can then apply familiar templates and compare visualizations with prior cases to identify similarities and differences.

In summary, the architectural requirements for personalization involve primarily mechanisms for receiving appropriate assignments and subscribing to events of interest, providing mechanisms for organizing information and knowledge, and providing for capture of examples, templates, and configurations for future reference. The basic capabilities of the first requirement are addressed with e-mail, messaging, and workflow management. The second requirement is supported by Web access along with storage and retrieval of metaknowledge. The third requirement is addressed by using common personal workstation applications to support personalization and the sharing of work products.

Authorization

Knowledge workers cannot function without access to relevant data. In addition, they need access to appropriate tools for analysis, collaboration, and composition of solutions.

Data Access

Internet technology has enabled communication with systems everywhere. Web access technology has provided the capability to display information from diverse sources on an ad hoc basis. What is missing is authorization for employees to access proprietary data without prior explicit authorization.

Employees should have access to any data necessary to their function based on assigned roles, not based on an identifier and password for each system they need to access. This requires a single sign-on capability that does not depend on explicit authorization for each system (for example, an automatic logon facility). The single sign-on provides authentication of the user. The identifier then must provide access based on authorization.

These roles must have enterprise-wide scope. Often roles are defined in terms of a particular application. As such, they may be known only to that application. Knowledge workers may have application roles, but they also need enterprise roles that are applicable and accessible throughout the enterprise. The organization directory service (discussed earlier) must make this information available throughout the enterprise.

Ad Hoc Authority

Roles provide a persistent definition of authority. However, collaboration will require ad hoc authority. Collaboration teams will require access to shared facilities, such as an e-mail distribution list, a shared repository for documents, and models; access to conference calls; and so on. These should be easy to establish so that collaboration groups can be established quickly and can be productive immediately.

A collaboration leader should be able to establish and maintain a collaboration group. Members of the group should then have access to all collaboration facilities in the context of the particular collaboration. Thus, the creation of a collaboration group should implicitly establish an e-mail distribution list, a shared repository, a conference-call capability, and so on. The leader should be responsible for adding and removing members if the group membership changes.

The sharing of information among collaboration team members also creates implicit authorization. Members with authority to access certain data will share that with the other members through meetings, e-mail, and the shared repository. The authorized member implicitly extends authority to every other member of the collaboration group.

The problem of implicit authorization is not new. It happens in face-to-face meetings all the time. However, in face-to-face meetings, the authorized contributors are aware of who is participating in the discussion. With electronic collaboration mechanisms, this is not always the case. In addition, in face-to-face meetings, it is possible to present material without giving out copies, thus maintaining control of broader distribution.

There are currently no rigorous solutions to this problem. At a minimum, members of the collaboration group should be kept aware of and have access to information regarding the level of authority of each of the other members. The leader has a particular responsibility when selecting and adding members to the group to ensure that each new member has the appropriate authority to access the information already shared by the group.

Data Access

Data are the raw material of enterprise intelligence. The architecture must support access to data from many sources. In addition to the data, users must have data about the data, that is, meta data. Meta data will provide insight on how to access data and whether particular data are appropriate for a particular purpose.

In the following subsections we will begin by considering sources of data. We will then consider the role of meta data and data standards.

Data Sources

Internal data reflect the operation of the business. They include facts about the business organization, personnel, facilities, products, resources, practices, customers, suppliers, and so on, and they include transactions such as orders, purchases, shipments, payments, personnel actions, and product programs. These data we will classify generally as *operating* data. Knowledge workers often will need data collected over time to examine trends and relationships.

In the following subsections we will first consider access to several sources of internal data, each with somewhat different architectural implications, and then consider access to external sources:

- Sentinel events
- Operational databases
- Reporting databases
- Data warehouses
- Reference data
- Process traces
- External sources

Sentinel Events

In the course of business operations, certain circumstances are of particular importance, calling for immediate consideration. These *sentinel events* should be communicated to the appropriate people and systems for further action.

From an architectural perspective, there are two categories of sentinel events: ongoing events and ad hoc events. Ongoing events are produced by design. Whenever an ongoing event occurs, an event notice will be generated. As a result, they are always available to be monitored. Ongoing events should be published to a message broker environment to be forwarded to all subscribers. Ad hoc events are produced to address a current need. This may be to monitor circumstances related to a particular problem or to take a distinct action that is not a normal part of routine operations. A trigger for an ad hoc event may be attached for all instances of an entity type, such as all orders, or it may be defined for specific instances, such as a publicly traded security. This would enable, for example, particular action to be taken on any order over a certain total sale or initiate a sale if the quote for a particular security reaches a certain value. Ad hoc event notices should be directed to specific recipients because they exist for a particular purpose. When the event is no longer of interest, the trigger should be removed.

Sentinel events may be directed to people or processes. It may be convenient to transform events directed to people into e-mail messages so that the people will receive the events whenever they read their e-mail. Events that require specific attention must be directed to processes. A process provides greater flexibility in directing the event, considering workloads, vacations, types of events, and priority. When a recipient does not act within a certain period of time, a process can detect the delay and reassign or escalate the problem.

Operational Databases

Current operating data include current facts and active transactions. These are the data that support the operation of the business and operational decision making. These data typically are stored in operational databases. They are updated to reflect the current state of the business, sometimes moment to moment. People managing the operations will have local responsibility and access to the associated systems. Typically, their needs for data will be addressed specifically by the systems so that they can obtain moment-to-moment information.

Generally, these data are not needed for collaborative decision making unless the collaboration is among members of the particular operating department or team. Even in such cases, the collaboration will take on a more tactical perspective. On the other hand, experts may see things in operating data that others do not, so the ability to obtain access may be important on a broader scale even though timeliness is not an issue. For example, a purchasing agent may be interested in the performance in product quality and timeliness for a vendor being considered for a new contract.

Reporting Databases

Tactical decision making requires relatively current operating data, but it also requires selective retrieval and reporting. These ad hoc activities may interfere with the performance of mainstream systems, and consequently, reporting or ad hoc query databases often are created to off-load this activity. Since these queries do not require up-to-the-minute data, the database can be updated periodically, with periodic extracts of relevant data from the operational databases.

Reporting databases, sometimes called operational data stores (ODSs), also provide a separation between operational systems and reporting activity for security and reliability purposes. Data may be limited to entities and attributes that are appropriate for outside observation, and high levels of activity or denial-of-service intrusions will not affect the mainstream business operation.

In addition, the transfer of data from operational databases to reporting databases provides the opportunity for transformation. Many operational databases will be in legacy systems that do not conform to shared data standards. Extracted data may be transformed prior to loading into the reporting database. Reporting databases do not, however, reflect the operation of the business over time—they reflect the operation at a recent point in time.

Data Warehouses

Data warehouses, on the other hand, are designed to provide historical data covering long periods of time. Operational data, particularly transactional data, are loaded into a data warehouse when the transaction is complete. This minimizes the level of update activity against the data warehouse and enables the data warehouse to be optimized for data retrieval.

Data warehouses have been applied predominantly to capture historical sales data. These data support analysis of market trends and customer behavior. The analyses do not require current operating data but rather require the ability to examine activity over extended periods of time. Data warehousing also has potential application in other areas of the business such as production (for example, relationship of defects to other factors), distribution (for example, timeliness of delivery and damaged goods), and warranty (for example, occurrence of repairs related to product, dealership, geography, and so on).

Reference Data

Many data about the business are relatively stable. These *facts* are not changed by routine operations, and they may be replicated in numerous databases throughout the enterprise to improve performance of operational systems.

These data nevertheless will be important to planning and decision making, and they do change from time to time. Consequently, knowledge workers will require access to reference databases, and changes to the reference data may need to be correlated with operating data, particularly historical operating data.

In some cases, because not all systems may be operating on the same reference data, it may be important to include the reference data with the operating data when extracting for reporting databases or data warehouses. In any event, it is important to maintain effectivity timestamps for all reference data so that the appropriate reference data values can be determined when examining historical data. Note that even with effectivity timestamps, there may be inconsistencies if clocks are not synchronized or distribution of updates is delayed.

Process Traces

Process improvement is an important aspect of managing the enterprise. Process improvement may be focused on quality improvement, cost reduction, or improved responsiveness.

Process traces provide an important tool for process improvement. These data generally are provided by workflow management systems along with tools for analysis of the traces. Traces can be used to trace back to the root cause of defects. They also can be used to analyze throughput, bottlenecks, and prolonged operations. Traces of user interactions or *click streams* also may be captured to provide insights on the effectiveness of Web page designs and the interactive processes followed by system users.

Traces most often will be performed when a particular process is under study. Usually the period of tracing will be of short duration sufficient to capture a variety of circumstances. The analyst may be interested in delays, events preceding an error or defect, problems with particular resources, and opportunities to eliminate steps or idle resources.

In the case of click-stream analysis, the analyst may identify problems with the user finding appropriate information or opportunities to draw the attention of the user to relevant information or, for customers, to draw attention to a purchasing opportunity.

These are usually tactical decisions, and the data capture is ad hoc. However, where major business processes are being traced, a variety of subprocesses may be invoked to achieve the end result. In this case, the traces could extend to processes across the enterprise. For example, a special order for a complex piece of equipment could produce an engineering order for special engineering and subordinate orders for specialized components. Orders for specialized components could produce production orders to produce those components and purchase orders to obtain lesser components and raw materials. Consequently, a deep understanding of the primary order process could involve understanding many of the subordinate processes.

Changes to the main process could affect the basic structure of operations and the way the product is engineered. This would likely be a strategic planning and decision-making activity. At the same time, the data to support this analysis may be relatively current, so long as variations on product orders and production processes are represented adequately. It also may be necessary to use current data because the needed data have not been captured in the past.

External Sources

The enterprise does not operate in a vacuum. Intelligent decisions often require data about the outside world, including the following:

- Economic data such as stock market figures, interest rates, energy prices, and the consumer price index
- Environmental data such as weather and natural disasters
- Regulatory data such as tariffs, taxes, transportation restrictions, and product standards
- Market data such as sales statistics and market share
- Competitor data such as new products, major sales statistics, and pricing

These and other data from external sources will be important for intelligent planning and decision making. In some cases, these are facts to be considered in analyses of other data. In other cases, they may convey facts that have a major impact on the business and require immediate attention in a tactical time frame.

In the past, much of this data was captured manually either informally or by persons with specific responsibilities to monitor outside events. With the World Wide Web, many of these data are available online. Client systems can be designed to monitor certain Web sites, capture data on a continuing basis, and monitor changes to trigger event notices. However, this approach is not recommended as the general solution. The design of Web pages will change, the client system may not identify the correct data elements for extraction, or the owner of the Web server may object to continuous requests that have an impact on the performance of other clients and either restrict or deny access.

For data that are needed on a continuing basis, the enterprise should subscribe to an appropriate service. The service should provide the data in a well-defined format, preferably Extensible Markup Language (XML), and a standard mode of communication should be established depending on the frequency of transmissions and volume of data to be communicated.

The following are several examples of modes of communication that can be employed for continuing updates:

E-mail notices. Data on relevant events can be communicated by e-mail. This can be useful, but performance may be affected by slow delivery and the need for users to filter out unwanted messages.

Client Web request with continuing response. Once the client system establishes a connection to the data source server, the server can continue to send updates as they occur. This could apply, for example, to providing the equivalent of a stock ticker tape update.

Supplier client submitting data. The supplier system could act as a Web client, connecting to the subscriber's server and entering data as form parameters or an XML document. The supplier-client system should only connect when it has new information to provide.

Periodic or ad hoc File Transfer Protocol (FTP) file transfers. Either the subscriber or the supplier could initiate a file transfer, although it is more efficient for the sender to originate the transmission when the file is available.

Message Service Handler (MSH) message exchange. Messages can be exchanged by a MSH over HTTP as defined in the ebXML specifications for reliable business-to-business (B2B) messaging. The messages can be delivered to applications through the messaging service either as point-to-point messages or events.

The last approach will be preferred in the long term, but the others may be necessary based on the capabilities of the data provider.

These modes focus on continuous monitoring and update from outside sources. As with internal sources, there are events of interest that should be communicated and other data that will only be of interest when relevant to particular problems. Where data are being received on a continuous basis, it will be desirable to provide a mechanism to pass on only events of interest. For data of only ad hoc interest, knowledge workers can be given Web access to appropriate external services.

Because the enterprise likely will pay for data services provided, it may be necessary to restrict access to knowledge workers who have a need to know. Access to these external sources may be controlled through a proxy server that authenticates the knowledge worker and determines if he or she has an appropriate role for access to the outside service. This would avoid the need to grant explicit authorization to access the service for each knowledge worker.

Data from outside sources also will be needed with semantics and formats that are compatible with data from inside sources. Transformation facilities will help provide format compatibility, and both transformation and interpretation of the data will be facilitated if they are obtained in an XML format.

Meta Data

Meta data is data that describes data. When data comes from many sources, it is important to have associated meta data to ensure that it is transformed, stored, and interpreted properly.

There are two basic roles for meta data:

- Provide technical specifications for the conceptual model, storage structures, transformation, and communication of data.

- Provide business information regarding the source, quality, and meaning of the data.

The OMG has adopted a Common Warehouse Metadata (CWM) specification so that meta data can be defined consistently and exchanged between systems and tools. The CWM includes a number of metamodel packages to describe different aspects of enterprise data such as the following:

- Specifications regarding the sources and accuracy of data elements
- Storage structures for object-oriented, relational, record, and multidimensional data stores
- XML structures for exchange of data
- Data transformations from source to target formats
- Transformations from storage structures to abstractions for Online Analytical Processing (OLAP) tools
- Specifications for data mining to discover knowledge in data
- Specifications for rendering data visualizations
- Definitions of business nomenclature, synonyms, and related terminology
- Specification of processes for data transformations and their initiation criteria
- Specifications for the recording of process executions to capture the lineage of sources and transformations of data

These meta data are consistent with the Unified Modeling Language (UML) metamodel specified by the OMG and may be exchanged using the XML Model Interchange (XMI) standard also specified by the OMG.

Meta data is expected to be stored in a shared repository. The OMG CWM specifications, as for other UML metamodels, are designed to be stored in a metaobject facility (MOF), a repository that conforms to the OMG MOF specification.

The CWM provides support for transformations of data from different sources to different storage structures and for use by different tools, so it enables the use of a mix of products that might otherwise be incompatible. The key is transformation—a transformation engine that operates from the CWM transformation specifications is essential. Compatibility of tools with lineage and accuracy specifications is important for providing business users with insights into the validity of their analyses.

Compatibility of specifications for visualization, OLAP, and data mining are less essential, but would provide flexibility in the choice of tools in the future.

The CWM is based on an extract-transform-load (ETL) model of business data analysis. Thus, the expectation is that standing processes will be created to extract data from all sources of interest, pass the data through appropriate transformations, and load a data warehouse to support a variety of queries and analyses. Because of the ETL focus, the CWM does not explicitly address certain other meta data also important to support enterprise intelligence, including the following:

- Data source mapping identifying the sources of data based on a common conceptual model

- Query transformation to convert a query based on the common conceptual model to a set of queries appropriate to the associated data sources

This meta data would support the ad hoc retrieval of data from heterogeneous sources. For example, data from diverse reporting databases might be brought together for cross-enterprise analysis of an operational problem, or data from diverse external sources might be retrieved on an ad hoc, as-needed basis. This would be a valuable complement to the CWM capabilities.

Data Consistency

Data consistency is crucial to enterprise intelligence. If data are not consistent, they cannot be aggregated or compared. There are several aspects of consistency to be considered:

- Reference data model
- Semantics

- Basis of measures
- Synchronization of sources
- Industry data standards

We will discuss each of these in the subsections that follow.

Reference Data Model

A reference data model defines a shared understanding of the way concepts that exist in the enterprise are classified, identified, described, and related. It provides the basis of a unified vocabulary. Consequently, when reference is made to a customer, it is understood who qualifies as a customer, how a particular customer is uniquely identified, the data that should be stored about a customer, and how customers are related to other concepts in the enterprise.

Although not all data in the enterprise may be consistent with the reference data model, it should be possible to define the correspondence of elements and often the necessary transformations.

The common reference model should be reflected in any data warehouse because these data will be important long into the future. This also would provide the basis for a unified expression of queries, as noted earlier, which could be translated to the equivalent queries to address diverse data models of different data sources.

Semantics

Inconsistency of data semantics is a potential problem whenever data are combined from different sources. The semantic inconsistency may come in a variety of forms, but generally it relates to some form of classification. These are concerns that go beyond the use of different terms to describe the same thing.

For example, customers from one source might include employee purchasers, and another source may not. Date of sale might be the date an order was placed from one source, and it might be the date of delivery from another source. One source might evaluate the cost of inventory on a first-in, first-out basis, whereas another evaluates it on a last-in, first-out basis (yielding a lower value when costs are rising). Often these differences may not be critical to the analysis, but sometimes the effects can be significant.

These differences cannot be resolved through transformation. Appropriate meta data can help the analyst recognize these differences so that the impact can be considered.

Basis of Measure

Attributes that are measures must have a consistent basis to be compatible. For example, if sales figures from one source are weekly and from another source are monthly, there is no way to accurately convert one basis to the other because the beginnings of weeks do not align with the beginnings of months. If the figures were for days and weeks, the basis would be different, but a transformation could add days to obtain accurate weekly figures.

Synchronization of Sources

Data warehouse data represent the business activity over time. Although current operating data represent the current state of the business, the current state is a result of actions that occurred over time. In either case, these data may be combined with data from other sources for analysis, and the results may be misleading if the data are not synchronized, that is, aligned with respect to time.

For example, if production figures are computed from a reporting database for current figures and a data warehouse for historical figures, there will be times where both databases have records of transactions relating to the same periods. Some of these may be the same transactions represented in both databases. Similarly, operational or historical data may require synchronization with reference data. If a product design has changed, the impact of the change cannot be evaluated unless the operational data can be separated into production before and production after the product change.

The need for synchronization may seem obvious, but it may not be obvious when the data capture and database structures are being designed.

Industry Data Standards

The enterprise may invest millions to define consistent data specifications, but this investment is at risk whenever a commercial-off-the-shelf (COTS) application is introduced. Furthermore, although enterprise data may be consistent, it may be inconsistent with data from external sources.

Whenever possible, the enterprise should work to align its reference model, and ultimately its applications, with industry standards. This will minimize the risk of inconsistency.

Industry standards are still evolving, so there is no universal reference model. However, there are standards in specific domains. Industries that must share data as part of their everyday business have standards for those exchanges that incorporate a shared data model. The Open Application Group (OAG) is a prime source of internal business data standards. They focus on exchanges of data between enterprise applications. The OMG has defined some data standards implicitly in the specification of interfaces to applications. These standards will likely be more explicit as the OMG moves to model-based specifications and the more robust specification of components under the Model Driven Architecture (MDA) strategy.

The enterprise reference model should be as closely aligned to these industry standards as possible. In order to minimize the risk of misalignment in the future, it is advisable that the enterprise participate in the development of future industry standards.

Presentation of Information

Information is derived from data by organizing and transforming the data to reveal inherent properties that may not be apparent in the raw data. For the most part, this involves transformations for human interpretation, such as the following:

Views.   Abstractions from complex models to focus on data of interest for solving particular problems or for individuals with particular expertise.

Aggregation.   The computation of totals for relevant categories and intersections such as sales by region and product line.

Filtering.   Identification of occurrences of particular interest or those that are outside certain boundaries or norms such as exceptionally high or low inventories or periods of high absenteeism.

Visualization.   Transformation to graphic displays showing relationships usually between two but sometimes three dimensions or changes in a dimension over time.

Statistical analyses.   Mathematical characterizations of the range of values of variables, relationships between variables, or changes in the variables over time.

Appropriate presentations of information generally are built into applications for routine operational decision making. This includes facilities for the analysis of workflow processes and Web click streams. With Web technology, these presentations could be made more widely available to knowledge workers throughout the enterprise.

Presentation of events for local purposes may be adequate for broader analysis. Often, a graph of the occurrence of events or changes in an associated variable can be of general interest. However, it may be preferable to filter events differently for different recipients, and it may be desirable to aggregate events from multiple sources. The information of interest is the fact that the event occurred with relevant variables. The circumstances under which it occurred likely will be the subject of further inquiry and should be satisfied by other data capture and analysis techniques.

Although applications generally will support local needs for information, they are not likely to support broader tactical and strategic analyses, often requiring different transformations and combining data from multiple sources, depending on the particular problem to be solved.

Consequently, the presentation for analysis should be performed locally to the user of the data, typically on the user's workstation. This means that the data should be retrieved or communicated (in the case of events or messages) in a common format and transformed locally to reveal information.

OLAP tools for analysis of data from a data warehouse are highly developed. These tools are capable of retrieving appropriate data from a database or data warehouse and performing various user-domain transformations to support analysis.

For many users, report generators, spreadsheets, and business graphics will provide the necessary functionality to support analysis. These are most appropriate for operational and tactical decision making.

As long as the operational and tactical decision making is based on local data, existing tools typically support adequate report generation and retrieval of data for spreadsheets and business graphics. Where data are to be combined from different sources, the solution is not as straightforward.

If data are needed to support certain kinds of analysis on a routine basis, then it may be appropriate to establish specialized reporting databases or enterprise ODSs that contain data from across the enterprise. Periodically, database update files can be collected from multiple sources and loaded into the database. Then existing tools can be used to extract and present the data to support analysis. This is the ETL approach characteristic of support for data warehouses.

In the long term, consistent interfaces should be implemented to source systems to support response to ad hoc queries. The query should be expressed in terms of the enterprise reference data model, and the response should be consistent with the enterprise reference model.

Knowledge Management

Forms of knowledge and a generic knowledge management process were discussed as business requirements earlier in this chapter. Here we will consider how the enterprise integration architecture can support knowledge management through the following activities:

- Create
- Capture
- Catalogue and store
- Retrieve
- Apply/refine

Create

Humans or machines create knowledge. Knowledge from humans may be in natural language form, necessitating that humans use it, or it may be encoded, such as where a developer codes a rule-based system. Knowledge created by machine also may be in human- or machine-interpretable form. Some knowledge created by machine is expressed as visualizations of data and concepts. Other knowledge generated by machine can be applied directly by machines, such as rules generated from data relationships or the weights associated with a neural network.

Creation of knowledge is supported by access to data, information, and other knowledge. These may come from computer storage or from other people. The architecture can support access to relevant stored data, information, and knowledge. It can also provide access to competency data and other references to human experts who should participate in collaborations to solve particular problems and develop new knowledge.

Capture

Knowledge that is encoded is captured easily because it is generally already in a form in which it can be stored. Generally, it is encoded to address a particular problem where the application of encoded knowledge will improve the quality or reliability of certain decisions.

Most knowledge is in the heads of humans. It takes particular effort to put such knowledge in a form that is meaningful and can be stored for future reference.

Knowledge usually is not a primary work product, but instead, it is the basis for the decisions made to accomplish the task or produce the work product. Consequently, it is usually not required that knowledge be expressed for an individual to complete a task. Capture of knowledge requires additional time and effort, and there are natural disincentives for doing work that is not required to achieve a defined assignment.

Capture of knowledge must be tied to the business processes where knowledge is developed or used. Knowledge is the basis for a decision. If we can identify where a decision is made and capture an explanation, then we have captured knowledge. A key point for identification of decisions is when a work product is approved. The knowledge worker should be able to explain any innovative approaches, and the reviewer should be able to identify any reasons for disapproval. There is at least some incentive to identify knowledge at such decision points. However, the participants still must take the time to express the explanation in general terms so that someone not knowledgeable about the particular work product will understand the knowledge.

If the business process is managed as a workflow process, there is additional opportunity to encourage the capture of knowledge. When the knowledge worker completes the task, he or she can be encouraged to enter explanations for any atypical aspects of the work product in order to answer the reviewer's questions before they are raised. In addition, the reviewer can be prompted to enter explanations for any reasons he or she finds the work product questionable or unacceptable. Before the work product can be accepted, the knowledge worker's explanations must be accepted or resolved, and the reviewers concerns must be resolved by further explanations.

These explanations should be captured by a knowledge management application that is Web-enabled so that knowledge can be entered from anywhere and accessed from anywhere. The knowledge should be expressed as a brief assertion followed by an explanation that elaborates on the assertion and the circumstances under which the knowledge was applied.

Catalogue and Store

Knowledge must be catalogued and stored for future reference. Cataloguing is based on meta data—data that describes data. In this case, we may call this *metaknowledge*—data about knowledge. Metaknowledge must be associated with each retrievable unit of knowledge—a document, a set of rules, a neural network, and so on—so that it can be located under relevant circumstances.

Part of the metaknowledge will relate the knowledge to the particular task from which it was derived. When existing knowledge is applied to a new work product, it becomes an explanation for the new work product. In addition, meta data can be associated with work products so that similar work products and associated knowledge can be retrieved. These relationships to work products provide explanations later on, when a decision may again come into question or changes are being considered due to concerns on related work.

The meta data for knowledge is expressed as a set of resource-property-value triples described by the resource descriptor framework (RDF) in Chapter 9. Each business function should have a set of knowledge properties defined for different types of activities and work products. The values of these properties must be entered when the knowledge is captured. These properties should include security restrictions to be used to determine who is authorized to see the knowledge. The stored knowledge is valuable intellectual property and should be restricted to those who have a valid need to use it.

The metaknowledge, as an RDF element, is stored in a knowledge repository to support searches. The actual knowledge may be stored in distributed Web-accessible servers, usually near where the knowledge was created or will be used. There is no need to centralize storage unless there is a concern about security. It is expected that most knowledge will be stored as XML documents including the associated metaknowledge. These will be stored as Web resources and may include URL links to associated Web resources.

Retrieve

Retrieval of knowledge should be supported at two levels: (1) retrieval based on metaknowledge and (2) retrieval based on textual content.

Retrieval based on metaknowledge will be used for well-classified problems such as product design decisions or the correction of production variance. This knowledge can be characterized with appropriate RDF properties. Meta-knowledge captured as RDF elements is consistent for categories of knowledge and could be stored in a relational database for retrieval with conventional queries. However, metaknowledge likely will evolve over time as the need for additional properties becomes apparent. Consequently, it is preferable to define the metaknowledge as an XML structures and retrieve it with XQuery. XQuery is discussed in Chapter 9. Database management products are becoming available for the storage of XML and retrieval with XQuery. This provides a more flexible storage facility to accommodate the evolution of metaknowledge, and the database management system will provide the optimization of query processing.

Not all problems will have clear associations with categories of knowledge or will relate well to the predefined RDF properties. These are the less routine problems and those that require out-of-the-box thinking. For these problems, a search based on textual content of knowledge is appropriate. Web search engines are designed for this task.

Retrieval based on textual content may produce volumes of irrelevant knowledge if the retrieval criteria are not sufficiently selective. Different search engines provide different selection criteria capabilities. The engine should support searches by phrases, Boolean expressions (*and*, *or*, and *not* operators), and proximity of terms. Some search engines will allow the proximity to be specified as the number of words separating the specified terms. The engine also should recognize alternate forms of the same word, such as plurals and alternative tenses.

Ideally, retrieval could be triggered by the characteristics of a current work product. An agent could associate characteristics of the work product under consideration with the meta data of stored knowledge. This is a problem for further research. This triggering of knowledge retrieval could provide an incentive to search for relevant knowledge earlier in the business activity rather than waiting until the work product is considered completed, only to discover that existing knowledge should have been applied.

Apply/Refine

Humans must apply knowledge captured in natural language form. When it is interpreted and applied to new situations, new insights or earlier oversights may be recognized. In such cases, a new knowledge document should be created. This may be treated as a supplementary document or a new version of the prior document. If it is considered a new version, it should include a reference to the old version, and the metaknowledge for the old version should be removed from the repository.

Encoded knowledge can be applied automatically if it is linked to appropriate data that describe the situation. The knowledge may be a simple list of rules that fire whenever their conditions become true, or it may be a knowledge-based system driven by an inference engine that manages the execution of the rules. Diagnostic systems use rules to analyze the interaction of a number of factors to arrive at a diagnosis that characterizes the cause of a problem and may suggest a solution.

Creation of encoded knowledge will require considerable effort and expertise. In addition, these knowledge-based systems are only effective for limited-scope problems. Consequently, such solutions will only be justified when there is a lack of human expertise or repeatability of results is critical.

Knowledge-based tools for monitoring current operational data may be characterized as agents. The agent system may be active on an ongoing basis, or it may only be activated when there is interest in recognizing certain circumstances. In either case, the agent likely will maintain an abstract model of the current situation and update it with events produced by the operational system(s). Rules are linked to the model in order to detect relevant situations and apply the knowledge. The abstract model enables the agent to be located remote to the systems it is monitoring, and it enables the agent to function without having a performance impact on the operational systems. Loose coupling is particularly important to both the operational system and the agent if the inferencing mechanism is complex, so that it is computationally intensive.

Knowledge also may be applied to models outside the mainstream operational environment. In this case, agents might be tightly coupled or integrated into the model-based applications such as production scheduling or engineering design.

Supporting Intelligent Behavior

Intelligence is the application of knowledge to arrive at a solution that addresses desired objectives. We distinguish intelligence from active knowledge in a manner similar to the distinction of intelligent action from a reflex in a human. The reflex is a direct response to a stimulus; both the stimulus and the response may be complex, such as where a human reacts to observing a vehicle about to hit him or her. Intelligent action requires consideration of multiple objectives or constraints and the consequences of alternative actions. In simple terms, it involves optimization.

Figure 12.5 depicts various knowledge supports for the knowledge worker. We have already discussed some of these in other contexts. Stored knowledge is the subject of knowledge management. Metaknowledge provides information about knowledge so that relevant knowledge can be retrieved. This may include metaknowledge about people to help find experts when stored knowledge is not enough. Enterprise experts also will be identifiable in the organiza-

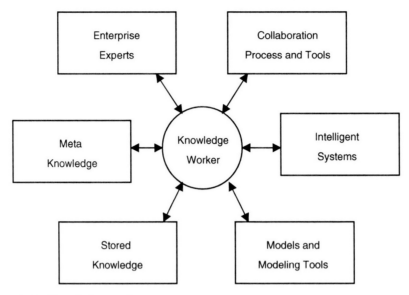

Figure 12.5   Knowledge-worker supports.

tion directory, which will provide information on the competencies of everyone in the organization. We will round out this topic with discussions on models, intelligent systems, and collaboration. The enterprise integration architecture provides the environment in which these techniques can be linked to the real world and shared by users.

Models

Fundamental to intelligent behavior is a model of the problem domain. Humans maintain a mental model of their environment in order to behave intelligently. They conceptualize a mental model of a problem situation in order to make intelligent decisions. Often more tangible models such as drawings, specifications, or computer models support these mental models.

Models are abstractions of the real world. As such, they focus attention on aspects of the real world that are relevant to a particular problem domain. Models that maintain consistency or propagate changes effectively incorporate knowledge about constraints in the real world. Thus, the model incorporates some knowledge, provides a basis for structuring and expressing knowledge, and facilitates refinement or development of new knowledge by supporting the consideration of alternative scenarios.

Models implemented as computer applications can be supported by the enterprise integration architecture. The architecture provides access to data representing past and present states of the enterprise. This data can be used to build complex models and to examine the variety of circumstances that occur in the actual operation of the business.

Intelligent Systems

The trial-and-error process of working with models is characteristic of intelligence, whether a human or an intelligent system performs it. Intelligent behavior is the result of a directed search, considering multiple factors to arrive at an optimal solution (or one that is reasonably optimal given the available information, time, and resources for searching). An intelligent planning system will explore a variety of alternative approaches to finding an optimal plan, considering various constraints and factors such as available resources, costs, duration, risk, and so on. A familiar example is a chess program exploring many possible moves and considering potential actions by the opponent before making each move.

Intelligent systems often are used to provide advice to humans. Knowledge of experts is encoded for a particular class of problem, and then many other knowledge workers can get advice from the intelligent system to take advantage of the expert's knowledge.

Intelligent systems exist in well-defined problem domains. These tend to be limited to particular operational decisions where the environment and relevant factors are relatively stable. Intelligent systems tend to be fragile. They work well within a certain range of anticipated circumstances, but they may be seriously flawed if circumstances exceed those normal bounds, and the system may not distinguish circumstances that are unusual.

The architecture can make intelligent systems more available through Web access, and it can support the application of intelligent systems to operational problems by providing access to data and events.

Collaboration

Problems where there is no encoded knowledge or those involving judgment require human intelligence. Often the intelligence of a single person is sufficient, but where the problem is high risk, complex, involves multiple objectives to be balanced, or requires diverse expertise, it should be resolved through collaboration—the participation of multiple humans.

We discussed various aspects of collaboration in the earlier section on business requirements. The architecture can enhance collaboration in the following areas:

- Identifying a leader
- Engaging the right participants

- Establishing a communication medium

- Sharing a model

- Accessing relevant information and knowledge

- Managing the process

We will discuss the architectural aspects of each of these.

Identifying a Leader

A workflow process should manage identification of a leader. When an event requiring action occurs or a problem is identified, a process should be initiated. The process may be able to select a leader automatically based on the type of event or characterization of the problem. If not, then it can assign the task of identifying a leader to an appropriate person. The workflow process can then continue to manage the collaboration activities.

Engaging the Right Participants

Engaging the right people involves identifying candidates and obtaining their commitment to participation. We discussed issues of identifying the right people earlier in this section. In order to engage them as collaboration participants, a process is required to determine who is actually available and willing, and to arrange for the appropriate allocation and funding of their time. This process can be performed via e-mail, but it could be performed more efficiently if those involved participate in a workflow process.

Establishing a Communication Medium

The primary criterion for selecting the medium of exchange is the availability of participants. If they can schedule concurrent time, the exchanges can be synchronous. If not, then communications will be asynchronous. In general, a collaboration that continues for a significant period of time, in excess of a few weeks, likely will employ both synchronous and asynchronous communications.

Scheduling meetings is a capability already supported by some e-mail systems. Some extend this capability to scheduling meeting facilities—a conference room (if they can physically get together), a chat room (on the Internet), a telephone conference call, or videoconferencing facilities.

If participants cannot meet concurrently, then communications must be in an asynchronous mode. Common forms of asynchronous communications are e-mail distribution lists and news groups. An e-mail distribution list should be created and maintained for the collaboration participants.

Regardless of the mode of communication, participants must be able to share information, including the solution model and supporting information, knowledge, and ideas. These require a shared repository. The shared repository should be established at the outset of the collaboration activity.

Access to the repository should be restricted to the collaboration participants. The leader may manage additions to the repository to provide consistent classification. Entries should include documents unique to the collaboration activity as well as hyperlinks to relevant documents stored elsewhere. Documents created for the collaboration activity but of value to other activities should be filed in a knowledge repository, registered in a meta-knowledge repository, and referenced by hyperlinks.

Sharing a Model

Participants must work toward a shared model of the problem and ultimately the solution. The mode of sharing will depend on the mode of communication. If communication is synchronous, then participants should actively share a common model. If they are in the same room, then a video projection of a workstation display enables them to view, comment on, and jointly evolve the model. This can be done to some extent with videoconferencing, but models communicated by video often have poor resolution. Internet-based facilities are available for sharing a common workstation display. Used in conjunction with telephone or Internet-based voice communications, this is similar to sharing the same model within a conference room.

Accessing Relevant Information and Knowledge

During the collaboration, participants will need to obtain additional data, information, or knowledge relevant to the problem. This may provide insight on the context of the problem, the variations that should be considered, or similar solutions that might be applied or adapted. We have already discussed architectural issues regarding access to data, information, and knowledge, so we will not repeat that here.

Managing the Process

Collaborations should be managed through a workflow processes. Particularly at the outset, a process is needed to assign a leader, establish an e-mail list, establish a shared repository, and engage participants. During the collaboration, the process may be unstructured, reflected in the workflow process as a collaboration activity pending completion. If work is divided among several performers, then each may be given a separate assignment, and his or her activities can be tracked concurrently. Once the collaboration is complete, the workflow process again can provide structure to closing the pursuit from publishing the result to releasing resources and catalogueing a final record of the material collected and the final product.

In addition to supporting an orderly approach, the use of a workflow process facilitates monitoring the status of the various activities in process and tracking the progress on various active collaborations.

Summary

This chapter described the business requirements for enterprise intelligence and then examined requirements for the enterprise integration architecture to support enterprise intelligence. Many of the requirements have been identified already for other purposes, independent of enterprise intelligence. There are, nevertheless, some key architectural features summarized in the following outline:

Organization directory.   Although the needs for an organization model and authorization directory were discussed earlier, the personnel directory incorporates and extends these with personnel competencies that facilitate the engagement of people from across the enterprise in collaboration to solve problems from an enterprise perspective.

Digital certificates and role-based access authorization.   Although role-based authorization has been discussed, the importance of this approach increased when we examined the need for knowledge workers to access data, information, and knowledge from across the enterprise. Without role-based access authorization, knowledge workers would be constantly encumbered by the need to obtain authority to access another system for needed input.

Access to external data sources.   Prior to this chapter we have not discussed the need for access to external data sources. This is essential for solving many problems with an enterprise perspective. It raises the need for various Internet-based methods to request and obtain data from autonomous heterogeneous sources.

Sentinel events.   Although the use of events to monitor operations has been discussed, the role of events in supporting enterprise intelligence provides a new perspective. Events can trigger processes and individual awareness of a problem that needs attention, speeding the result and ensuring that action is taken by appropriate knowledge workers.

Meta data repository.   The meta data repository is key to providing consistent data and defining the semantics and quality of that data so that knowledge workers can assess the reliability of their observations and conclusions. The CWM meta data standards developed by the OMG provide for this expression of data quality along with models for the management of data warehouses and the integration of analysis tools from different vendors.

Reference data model.   The need for consistency of data has been discussed from the standpoint of the integration of systems. This chapter has highlighted the importance of a common reference model for effective management of the enterprise.

Knowledge repository and search.   Retention and access to enterprise knowledge is a growing concern as the pace, complexity, and level of competition of business increases. The enterprise cannot afford to repeat mistakes. A Web-enabled, searchable metaknowledge repository provides a partial solution to this concern. More is needed.

Agents.   Agents have been introduced as a mechanism to monitor aspects of business activities, to recognize relevant circumstances, to sometimes take corrective action, and to support intelligent planning and decision making. Consistency of the architecture and access to consistent data and events is essential for the easy integration of agents. Otherwise, the development of agents is further complicated by the development of adapters and translators and the associated modification of production systems.

Shared models.   The use of models as a mechanism of analysis is common practice in all disciplines. Typically, it is an individual activity. Here we have highlighted the importance of sharing a model for collaboration and the need to facilitate that sharing among distributed collaborators.

Collaboration repository.   A collaborative effort involves the gathering and sharing of information and knowledge as well as the development of a solution model. The collaboration repository makes these artifacts available to all members of the group and can make them available for reference after the collaboration is completed for later adaptation of the solution or application to similar situations.

Enterprise workflow.   Workflow management has been described earlier as the automation of local processes that may incorporate other processes for enterprise integration. Collaborative processes involve people from across the enterprise. This highlights the importance of having standard interfaces to facilities for personnel work assignments and for facilities to manage individual work lists.

The enterprise integration architecture is a prerequisite to enterprise intelligence. Enterprise intelligence is the result of the harmonization of efforts of people and computer systems through better communication, coordination, and collaboration, and the ability to adapt quickly to address problems and opportunities with an enterprise perspective. It is not a solution, but an objective to be continuously pursued.

This chapter has described a vision of enterprise intelligence and how it can be enabled with the enterprise integration architecture. In the next and final chapter we will examine the challenges of implementing and exploiting the enterprise integration architecture.

CHAPTER

13

Implementing the Architecture

While much of this book is devoted to the technology of enterprise integration, enterprise integration is first and foremost a senior management responsibility. The fundamental challenge is for management to create a harmonious business environment supported by information systems. People develop systems, people select products, people manage business functions, systems complement the business activities of people, and people accomplish the ongoing process improvement. The people of the enterprise must be organized, motivated, and led to achieve enterprise integration. This requires effective management strategies.

Management strategies must address the four different domains depicted in Figure 13.1. Each of these domains represents different challenges. Each of these will be addressed in various ways throughout this chapter.

In Chapter 1 we examined the changes occurring in information technology and the potential impact on the enterprise. In Chapter 2 we outlined design objectives for enterprise integration. Subsequent chapters examined the elements, technologies, and integration of systems in an enterprise integration architecture (EIA). In this chapter we return to the management perspective to examine the changes necessary for transformation of enterprise systems to

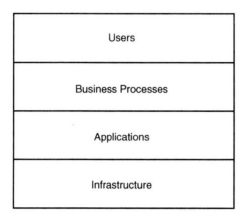

Figure 13.1   Enterprise integration management domains.

implement the integration architecture and exploit the technology through the following initiatives:

- Strategic planning
- Creating service-oriented business processes
- Changing user mindset
- Implementing the infrastructure
- Managing the infrastructure
- Setting application integration goals
- Managing application development
- Setting standards
- Managing change
- Consolidating information systems management
- Considering critical success factors

We will begin with strategic planning because transformation to the EIA is a long-term undertaking that must complement the strategic objectives of the business. From there we will consider a number of issues related to changing business processes, the organization, system architecture, and the management of systems. Finally, we will consider the critical success factors—key factors that will drive a successful transformation.

Strategic Planning

Transformation of the enterprise to exploit the EIA is not just a technical problem; it requires a business commitment and support from the entire organization. In order for the enterprise to derive the full benefit, it must change the way it does business.

As a consequence, strategic planning is essential. The transformation must complement the strategic business plan of the enterprise. We will consider the key elements of strategic planning that are directly related to systems transformation. These key elements are the following:

- Shared vision
- Business objectives
- Business processes
- Timetable for change

Shared Vision

The leadership of the enterprise must have a shared vision of the future of the enterprise. This is a fundamental element of strategic planning in general, but it is also essential to realize the value of systems transformation.

The shared vision should be a comprehensive description of the enterprise in the future with close attention to the impact of technology. It should include the nature of the business, target markets, relationships with business partners, products, personnel, growth projections, location of business operations, competitors, key technologies for both business systems and products, and critical success factors. Information technology not only must support this business vision, but it also must be recognized as a major driver for change, enabling new business models and creating new business opportunities. Information systems also will be a more integral part of business operations through the automation of business processes and supporting collaboration among knowledge workers.

The shared vision should comprehend the implications of Internet technology and enterprise integration. The key implications are the following:

- Virtual enterprise
- Event-driven operations
- Rapid change

- Continuous improvement
- Web presence
- Harmonized enterprise

We will discuss each of these briefly in the following subsections.

Virtual Enterprise

The Internet has eliminated barriers to communications both within the enterprise and with business partners and customers. As a result, in order to remain competitive, the enterprise must have communications capabilities to establish closer working relationships. Although the legal boundaries of the enterprise will still exist, the operational boundaries will expand to include participation with business partners and closer relationships with customers. These expanded operational boundaries are characterized as the *virtual enterprise*—the community of participants in the business endeavor.

While the virtual enterprise expands beyond the corporate enterprise, some functions of the enterprise may be moved out of the corporate enterprise—outsourcing. The EIA not only provides for integration of internal business functions, but it also enables the integration of business functions performed outside the corporate body. The corporate leadership must examine which business functions are critical to the competitive position of the enterprise and which could be performed more effectively by business partners that specialize in particular business functions. This is the commercial off-the-shelf (COTS) solution taken a step further.

The future shape of the virtual enterprise will have a significant impact on plans for business systems transformation. The nature of business functions and relationships will change, and some business functions may be no longer within the corporate enterprise.

Event-Driven Operations

Although many systems provide online access to users, many, if not most, mainstream systems in conventional enterprises communicate through batch communications. This introduces surges and delays in business activity. These surges and delays reduce the enterprise's ability to respond and prevent potential optimization of business operations.

Internet technology has opened the door to the communication of events as they happen. For example, rather than receiving and batching a number of customer orders, each order is processed as it is received. In some cases, an order might be shipped before the next one is received. This change in mode of operations has far-reaching consequences not only in the design of systems, but also in the way people do their jobs.

This mode of operation is not necessary for all systems. In some cases, optimization is achieved by sequencing a batch of requests for more efficient operations. Even when events are communicated immediately, it is not always appropriate to expect immediate action. If immediate action is always expected, then resources may be idle much of the time so that they are always ready to respond to an incoming event. In addition, the technology for immediate communication is not free, although it is much less expensive than in the past.

Corporate leaders must consider where the business should be event-driven and balance the costs of supporting technology and business transformation against the business benefits of rapid response.

Rapid Change

The pace of change in business has accelerated. Much of this has been driven by globalization and changes in social, political, and economic forces, but it also has been driven by advances in technology. An effective enterprise architecture will enable more rapid change in the business systems and the conduct of business. The demand for change is experienced by all enterprises. The ability to change will be a key competitive advantage.

The design of products and services, along with the business operations directly associated with the production or delivery of products and services, will be the primary focus of change. The corporate leadership must anticipate the nature of changes in order to be responsive and at the same time operate efficiently. A business designed to do practically anything may not do anything particularly well. At the same time, the EIA will facilitate change in the business systems. The plan for the transformation of systems should reflect priority for business functions that are most likely to be affected by change.

Continuous Improvement

Implementation of the EIA must not be viewed as a one-time transformation but rather as the beginning of continuous improvement. The architecture should position the enterprise to incorporate incremental changes in the business processes, the organization, the applications, and the supporting technology. The enterprise should be managed for continuous improvement not just in response to changing external forces, but also as a result of continuous reassessment and evaluation of new ideas to make the enterprise more effective at all levels.

Web Presence

The enterprise presence on the World Wide Web is of major importance. The Web has become the primary source of current information. The Web puts a face on the enterprise for customers, investors, partners, regulators, employees, news investigators, and the public in general. It is important that the Web presence of the enterprise properly addresses the interests of each of these user communities.

The ease with which users access information about the enterprise will suggest the ease with which they may expect to do business with the enterprise. The aesthetics, openness, and usefulness of the Web content may affect attitudes toward the enterprise that have consequences in the marketplace as well as in the political and regulatory arenas. The accessibility and presentation of products and services will have an impact on sales, perhaps more than conventional advertising. The Web paths leading to the enterprise will determine its visibility.

The corporate leadership must understand that the Web should be a major element of advertising, sales, public relations, education, and recruiting. The corporate home page and other primary pages must communicate a proper image of the corporation and provide rapid access to key information and services. A proper Web presence is not a technical challenge, but it is a leadership challenge with the support of talented people who know how to deliver the image defined by the leadership.

Harmonized Enterprise

Effective management, improvement, and adaptation of the enterprise require consistency of information and effective coordination of activities across the enterprise. It must be possible to combine or compare data from different segments of the business. The data must originate from well-defined and consistent processes, or the computations and comparisons will be flawed. Data and knowledge must be shared, knowledge workers must collaborate, and knowledge workers must have both the information and access to relevant enterprise knowledge to make decisions that reflect an enterprise-level perspective. The harmonized enterprise achieves the consistency of information and the sharing and coordination of efforts to achieve enterprise-level synergy, economies, and rapid response to problems and opportunities.

Business Objectives

Corporate leaders must examine the operation of the business for improvements that will yield competitive advantage. Typically, these improvements will fall into one or more of five fundamental objectives: new business, increased market share, cost reduction, quality improvement, and improved responsiveness. The opportunities and competitive pressures created by the Internet and related technology are key factors in the identification of objectives and the necessary transformations. The plan for systems transformation must be driven by business objectives. The leadership must determine the priority objectives and translate these into initiatives to transform the business.

At the same time, the benefit of this technology may not be realized by the transformation of systems one application at a time. Often the benefit will come from synergy between applications, changes to cross-functional processes, and economies of scale. As a result, the leadership must examine the return on investment of different timing of initiatives and combinations of initiatives, as well as the return on investment of initiatives considered individually.

The infrastructure is a critical element of the EIA. Once the appropriate infrastructure exists, the cost, risk, and duration of efforts to implement new systems will be reduced significantly. However, when the infrastructure is not yet established, the cost of implementing initial applications will seem excessive, and the benefits of enterprise integration may be minimal. The corporate leadership must accept the cost of infrastructure as a long-term investment and remove that cost as a consideration in the design of individual applications. At the same time, the timing of infrastructure investment and thus the return on investment may be affected by the order in which specific application changes are undertaken.

Business Processes

The infrastructure and Internet technology will enable the cross-functional automation of business processes. In the past, improvements to business systems were localized. A new application would improve the productivity or quality of a particular business activity within a particular business function. This is no longer the case. Technology has changed the distribution of workload, barriers to communications, and needs for special skills. There are no longer rooms of accounting clerks passing paper transactions; the roles of drafters and engineers have merged with computer-based design, and distribution patterns are changing with direct shipping and Web-based sales.

For the last decade, business process reengineering has been a key source of business improvements. Business process reengineering incorporates opportunities provided by the technology, but it focuses on the improvement of business processes.

In business process reengineering efforts, often computer applications still are viewed as mechanisms to improve the productivity or quality of particular business functions. However, the business processes no longer are separated from the applications; often they are embedded in the applications and the linkages between applications.

A critical aspect of systems transformation is to remove the business processes from the applications and implement them as workflow processes that are visible and manageable independent of the applications. Separation of business processes from applications will improve the ongoing ability to respond to change and will enable rapid, ongoing, and continuous process improvement.

Consequently, the transformation involves not only the transformation of applications, but also the emancipation and transformation of business processes. This will have an impact on the organization structure as well as the roles and responsibilities of people in the organizations. Business function managers will regain control of their business processes and must learn to manage them.

Timetable for Change

The corporate leadership must develop a realistic timetable for change. The changes needed are not simply the introduction of new technology, but they are also most likely fundamental changes to the way of doing business. The effort will involve not only the cost of developing new infrastructure and systems, but also the restructuring of the organization and changes to people's jobs—potentially at all levels.

This requires top-management commitment and participation in the planning and management of the transformation effort. The timetable must reflect the consideration of competitive pressures, return on investment, business operation during transitional phases, commitment to architectural specifications and standards, and the timely implementation of supporting infrastructure.

The initial timetable must extend over several years. As work progresses, the timetable will change, and new initiatives will emerge. The effort will be ongoing as the business, the technology, and the business environment continue to change. The goal must not be simply to implement a transformation but to become adept at continued transformation.

Creating Service-Oriented Business Processes

Many business processes are designed as a thread through the organization that eventually produces desired results. The decisions, the responsibility, and the control are fragmented. Nobody is responsible for the business process from end to end, except maybe the CEO of the enterprise.

Business processes, like software systems, should be implemented in a service-oriented structure. A business unit receives a request and is responsible for producing a result with appropriate side effects within that area of responsibility. The objective and responsibility of the process and associated organization are well defined and apply from the time the request is received until the result is returned.

This provides the same benefits as those ascribed to object-oriented programming. The interfaces between business units define what services are available, but generally do not limit how they are implemented. This approach provides flexibility in the implementation and the potential for substitution of an alternative implementation (or organization). The organization is accountable for meeting the objectives of its processes, and it can alter the processes to improve the result as long as it does not have an adverse impact on other business units with related processes.

The model also reinforces the consolidation of functionality to achieve economies of scale and uniformity of function. If the business function is to be changed, then the affected processes are well defined and encapsulated in the business function. Changes in the way of doing business are more likely to be localized instead of being scattered through multiple organizations because related operations and decisions will be made by the same organization for related processes.

The service-oriented organization can effectively parallel the automated business systems so that responsibility for the way of doing business rests with the same organization for both manual and automated operations. This aligns accountability and control better and enables the organization to be more responsive.

This model does not preclude delegation, that is, the invocation of a process in another organization, but the responsibility for completion of a process remains with the organization that owns the process. Responsibility for completion of the subprocess rests with its associated organization. Consequently, the ordering process is the responsibility of the sales organization and continues to be a sales responsibility until the product is delivered. The ordering process may invoke the fulfillment process for retrieving the product, packaging it, and shipping it. The fulfillment process may invoke the production process when inventory is low, and the production process is responsible for getting the product produced to replenish inventory and ensuring that materials are on hand when needed. Each of these has clear objectives and requires a responsible organization that either has the resources to fulfill the objective or delegates to another organization that provides the needed service.

Changing User Mindset

Enterprise integration requires changes in the roles of people and the way they think about and do their work. The computer becomes an integral part of the work of most people in the integrated enterprise because it is the vehicle by which information is retained and accessed and which activities are coordinated. The central role of the computer requires the mindset of people to change. There are four key changes:

- Computer literacy
- Process automation
- Process ownership
- Information sources

Computer Literacy

Computer literacy, of course, is an important requirement. People will not be able to function effectively in the integrated enterprise if they are not comfortable with fundamental computer operations. Managers must recognize that some people are very intimidated by computers and cannot type. These people must be given the basic skills and develop the confidence to incorporate the computer into their work.

Process Automation

People are comfortable receiving assignments from another human, reporting to a human, having progress reviewed by a human, and so on. With process automation, the worker will receive assignments from a computer and report results to a computer. Some systems will be very rigid in making assignments and structuring the work. This may offend some people, particularly those with the highest skills and most experience, because they know to get the job done without a cookbook, and they probably get it done faster and better. People must learn to work with the processes, and they must have the opportunity to tailor or improve the processes, within limits. Managers also must find new ways to assess performance and provide positive feedback to reinforce work that exceeds expectations. Managers also must learn how to design business processes to ensure that technology helps people be more effective and use their strengths rather than treating them as mere automatons, expected simply to do what they are told.

Process Ownership

Process ownership, including control over how the process works, will return in large measure to the associated business function organization. As the scope of computer applications has grown, much of the control over how work is done has shifted to system developers and the information technology organization. With the implementation of business processes in workflow, it will be possible for the business manager to see and control much more of the way things are done. With this control comes responsibility and creative work. When the way of doing business changes, the manager has primary responsibility for determining how the processes should change and who will make the changes.

Information Sources

In organizations dominated by paper and human processes, information often is exchanged directly between humans. Even when information is in computer systems, humans with access are often the sources of information for other humans. In the integrated enterprise, humans who have a business need for information will be expected to get it directly from the appropriate system, not go looking for a human who can get it. In the short term, there will be difficulties: People will not know where to find what they want, how to ask for it, or what it means when they get it. People will need information but not have the authority to access it. In the long term, however, access to information will be more timely, and the information will be more accurate.

The key is to define clear management commitment to information accessibility and make sure that the systems provide the appropriate user interfaces and access mechanisms to enable access. Information on a piece of paper or in someone's head is data unknown to the organization. Data in the system should be accessible to anyone who needs them, and the system should be the preferred source.

Implementing the Infrastructure

Shared infrastructure is a key goal of the EIA. The fundamental benefits of shared infrastructure are connectivity and economies of scale. To achieve these benefits, the infrastructure must incorporate certain standards and be shared by multiple applications and users.

In addition to providing consistent interfaces to infrastructure facilities, standards are important for achieving infrastructure abstraction. Abstraction enables users to work with a service or facility with a simplified mental model of how it works so that they need not understand the intricacies of the technology to use it effectively. For example, the controls of an automobile provide an abstraction of the underlying design of the engine, transmission, steering, and suspension systems.

Users and application developers should not be concerned with the complexities of the infrastructure, nor should they be concerned, in most cases, when the underlying technology of the infrastructure changes over time. For example, with the possible exception of performance implications, users should not care if the infrastructure communicates over twisted pairs, coaxial cable, fiber optics, or microwaves. The interface and message content should be the same, regardless of the transport technology. In addition to enabling the infrastructure to be upgraded or to exploit economic opportunities, this abstraction enables applications to evolve and infrastructure capacity to be adjusted without the need for coordination of design.

In general, it is not practical to implement a comprehensive infrastructure at one time. The investment would be substantial, and the benefit would be limited. The scope of infrastructure should expand over time. Because common facilities can be shared by multiple applications, the common facilities may be integrated into the infrastructure, to be managed independent of the applications.

In the following subsections we will consider these key components of the integration infrastructure:

- Network facilities
- Knowledge worker personal computers
- Consolidated server operations
- Authentication services
- Defenses against intruders
- Application services

Network Facilities

At this stage, network facilities generally are accepted as the foundation of the information infrastructure. Systems with dedicated terminals and associated single-application network facilities are disappearing quickly. In some business functions, dedicated terminals and direct connections still meet business requirements and provide economical solutions. However, the enterprise, in general, requires Internet technology to enable many systems and users to interact with many different systems and people both within and outside the enterprise.

Core network capabilities include electronic mail, file transfers (FTP), messaging with message-oriented middleware, and Web access (HTTP). These facilities enable fundamental information sharing involving many users and many computers. In general, this level of infrastructure is essential for an enterprise to survive in the current business environment.

Knowledge Worker Personal Computers

Infrastructure must extend to the deployment and support of common personal computing facilities for employees who work with information—that is, knowledge workers. All knowledge worker personal computers should use the same or at least compatible office automation software. This includes a word processor, a spreadsheet application, a presentation and graphics application, and electronic mail. These are fundamental for the exchange of business information.

Knowledge workers, and probably all employees, should have Web access through a standard Web browser. This is essential for access to relevant information on the public Internet as well as access to information and applications within the enterprise. Knowledge workers will require this as a critical element in performance of their jobs. Other employees will require this for access to personnel information, corporate policies, and other administrative functions.

Finally, shared support services should be established to keep personal computers up to date, ensure virus and intruder protection, help users resolve problems, obtain the benefit of quantity purchases of software licenses and hardware, and ensure connectivity to the Internet.

This infrastructure component is also accepted generally, although support services still may be provided locally and somewhat informally in some cases. In general, shared support and common personal computer applications yield substantial economies of scale, particularly when employee productivity and reliable, secure operation of the business are taken into consideration.

Consolidated Server Operations

Traditionally, centralized management of computer operations was generally an accepted strategy. Computers were expensive and complicated, requiring special protection and support and demanding high utilization to achieve economies of scale.

With the development of powerful microprocessors, personal computers, and application servers, many systems were moved out of the data-processing centers and onto departmental and personal computers. This was driven both by economics and by the need for flexibility. Users of the technology were able to implement new solutions without the overhead and bureaucracy of the data-processing organizations.

However, this transition fragmented the enterprise, introduced diseconomies of scale, and increased risks that previously had been managed by the data-processing organizations. The scope of departmental systems has grown, and the systems are becoming increasingly complex and indispensable to the business operation. Competitive pressures have increased the need for integration of systems and streamlining of operations. Internet access has increased the need for round-the-clock operation, high reliability, and security.

There is again a strong need for consolidated server operation. Use of hardware is no longer the primary driver, but security, reliability, and shared operations and support personnel are major drivers. Web applications are expected to be online around the clock. Failure of Web applications creates an immediate risk to the reputation of the enterprise. Web access also raises security risks. As the systems of the enterprise become increasingly integrated, they become critical to the moment-to-moment operation of the business. The enterprise can not afford to leave control of these critical operations to individual departments that do not have the expertise, the disciplines, or the resources to operate their systems with the necessary degree of security and reliability.

Consolidated server operations should include the following services:

System administration.   Operation of the servers, monitoring activity and resource loading, corrective action for overloads or failures, and system security administration.

System maintenance.   Monitoring of system performance, installation of new hardware and software as well as upgrades, and reconfiguration of systems to accommodate new applications and changing workloads.

Application support.   Coordination of application changes, monitoring of application performance, resolution of problems, application backup and recoverability assurance, and application security administration.

Help desk.   Response to routine user questions and problems and input and status reporting of service requests.

Change control.   Coordination and control of hardware, software, and application changes to ensure compatibility of software, proper validation and authorization, ability to retract changes and restore operations, and minimal disruption of business operations.

Preproduction testing.   Maintain a simulated production environment, conduct system software and application testing to ensure compatibility and acceptable levels of performance, and support user acceptance testing.

Disaster recovery.   Maintain a plan and the ability to recover in a timely and orderly fashion from a disaster that destroys major computing and communications facilities.

Each of these services requires special skills and disciplines that for most enterprises will be difficult to achieve and maintain for independent departmental systems.

Note that the full benefit of consolidation will not be realized as long as different applications use different hardware and supporting software. Migration of applications to common platforms and technologies will improve the ability to achieve economies of scale and to provide a high level of expertise in support of each application.

Authentication Services

Authentication is the mechanism by which the identity of a system user is determined. Authentication will yield a user identifier that is the basis for determining who has access to an application and what they can do. Traditionally, authentication was implemented for individual applications. This was acceptable as long as employees were limited to accessing specific applications and the community of users of an application was limited and well defined.

However, the Internet has changed this. Employees are expected to reach a wide variety of applications to access information from across the enterprise. With application-based security, the employee must be issued an identity and password for each application. This soon becomes a major headache for the user, and the administration of passwords becomes an obvious source of duplicated overhead and a potential security risk from disclosure of passwords.

Rather than an extension to applications, security should be considered an extension to network facilities. A user should be identified to the enterprise as a basis for determining that user's authority to access data and applications and for providing secure communications and accountability as the user conducts business.

Various techniques have been developed to provide a *single sign-on* capability, and various techniques may be used by an enterprise as it evolves to the EIA. A common technique is for the user to access the network through a security portal. The security portal authenticates the user and maintains information on all the user identifiers and passwords for access to applications. The portal intercepts authentication requests and automatically signs on for the user. This eliminates user hassle. However, it does not eliminate the barrier to access a user faces when there is a need to access a system not authorized previously, and it does not eliminate the administrative overhead of assigning and maintaining many identifiers and passwords.

Another technique is to assign each user a single identifier and password and propagate that identity and password to all applications the user might access. This reduces the redundant administration, but it increases the risk from exposure of passwords—if an intruder breaks into the password file for any system, then all systems are exposed.

The preferred solution is a public key infrastructure (PKI). This is security as an infrastructure service that uses public-private key pairs for authentication and encryption. This technology provides a digital certificate for user authentication on all systems. The common certificate minimizes administration, minimizes risk of exposure, and provides support for encryption and digital signatures. Digital certificates also provide the basis for authentication and encryption of communications between servers.

Support for PKI requires a *certificate authority* (CA) to issue certificates. The CA certifies the identity of users and the validity of their certificates. It also maintains a directory of certificates that are no longer secure; that is, the user's secret key has been exposed.

PKI is currently appropriate where the community of users is well defined, such as with employees and business partners. Even established customers can be issued digital certificates by the enterprise. However, at this time, and probably for some time into the future, we cannot assume that a member of the general public who accesses our Web site can be identified with a digital certificate. There is not yet a generally accepted CA that will ensure user identity and accept liability for fraudulent use of credentials. Until such an authority is established, ad hoc transactions over the Internet likely will be based on credit card numbers and be limited to small monetary value. Even when an authority is established, it will take a number of years before most people have digital certificates.

The infrastructure should be designed to support a common approach to security along with shared services to ensure consistency and achieve economies of scale. The infrastructure must support a strategy for transition to PKI. PKI and related security issues were discussed in greater detail in Chapter 11.

Defenses against Intruders

Security is a major concern in this era of the Internet and enterprise integration. It requires careful design, vigilance, and reliable defensive measures. Defense against intruders requires central control and services as part of the infrastructure.

Intruders do not always come as impersonators of legitimate users; intruders may find other ways to access system facilities without being accepted as a user. Although defenses against such attacks could be implemented for each application, centralized management of infrastructure facilities will yield economies of scale, support rapid response to attacks, and facilitate the implementation of consistent barriers to reduce risks. Three primary forms of attack must be addressed:

Unauthorized access. Unauthorized access occurs when an intruder finds a way to circumvent authentication and authorization controls. This typically occurs as a result of security faults in a Web server operating system. The primary defense is the use of firewalls. The strategy is to limit the nature of communications from the outside to reduce the risk that an intruder will find a security gap.

Corrupt software. The most common form of corrupt software is a virus. Infrastructure services can provide four primary defenses against viruses: detection of virus attachments in e-mail, distribution of warnings and updates to virus-detection software on personal computers, management of the deployment of software products to ensure that they come from computers of legitimate sources, and configuration of personal computer systems and software to minimize the risk.

Denial-of-service attacks.   Denial-of-service attacks typically take the form of onslaughts of requests that overload a Web service. The Web service either fails or response time is so poor that service is virtually denied to legitimate users. Defenses involve detection, filtering of requests, and identification of the source. These are capabilities that should be built into the network infrastructure.

Application Services

In order to enhance application reliability and economies of scale, shared application services should become part of the infrastructure over time. Prime examples of shared services include the following:

Backup/restore.   Application data should be backed up periodically and stored off-site. Occasionally, application data must be restored from a backup on request from a proper authority.

Software distribution.   If applications have distributed components, upgrades to the components must be distributed and coordinated to ensure integrity of the upgrades, timely installation, and compatibility with the infrastructure and related systems.

Message transformation.   Message transformation facilities achieve compatibility of data exchange between different applications without the need to modify the individual applications. These facilities are used primarily for the integration of commercial-off-the-shelf (COTS) applications, but they also can resolve transient incompatibilities of data exchanges being upgraded.

Organization directory.   Information on the organization structure is fundamental to the business. It is essential for the proper distribution of information and for directing requests to the appropriate individual for action or authorization. This will become increasingly important as business processes are implemented with workflow management systems. It should be a common point of reference for secure access authorization.

Managing the Infrastructure

Enterprise integration requires a solid foundation of shared facilities and services with flexible communications. This infrastructure should reduce the scope and effort of individual application development activities and at the same time accommodate diversity in the technology and design of applications.

It is useful to analogize to the national infrastructure. When a new home is built, it relies on the existing infrastructure of roads to access it; utilities that provide water, sewers, power, and communications; government services such as police, fire department, and trash removal; and so on. As a consequence, the effort required to build the home is reduced, and the occupant's comfort, security, and linkage to the rest of the community are greatly enhanced by the supporting infrastructure. The equivalent quality and scope of today's community infrastructure would never be built for a single home.

We are focusing on the computing and communications infrastructure that supports integrated business systems. This infrastructure must be managed for reliable operation, security, and linkage of the business systems. There are five primary management responsibilities:

- Investment
- Unification
- Ownership
- Evolution
- Change control

We will discuss each of these briefly in the following subsections.

Investment

Infrastructure requires investment. It cannot be justified or built one application at a time. It requires investment in the design, the hardware and software components, and the implementation. The value of the infrastructure is realized through economies of scale and flexibility over multiple applications.

Consider, for example, one aspect of the community infrastructure: the telephone system. A telephone system cannot be justified by the needs of one, two, or three subscribers. The justification is in being able to communicate with a large number of subscribers on an ad hoc basis at an economical individual cost. The impact of economies of scale has been demonstrated more recently by the emergence of the Internet. The Internet was interesting and useful, but its real value and impact came when it reached a critical mass of subscribers. In both cases, there was substantial investment ahead of the realization of value.

Unification

The infrastructure must be connected and functionally consistent in order to provide reliable, secure, and flexible support to business applications. The scope and implementation of infrastructure may vary according to the needs of the environment or the systems supported, and it may vary as new technology is introduced. However, there must be *one infrastructure*. This means that certain services are shared and that there is connectivity between services and applications.

It is appropriate to view the infrastructure as layered. The base layer exists in all environments. Generally speaking, it includes communication facilities, directory services, Web services, security services, and asynchronous messaging services, including e-mail. Above this base layer may be several variations of a layer specialized to different environments—for example, an office layer, a plant layer, a retailing layer, and so on. These variations likely will exist because of the different characteristics of the systems and the environments. They likely will include other specialized services such as local-area networks (LANs), shared file servers, workstations, and workflow management.

The nature and scope of the application-dependent layer also will vary with the age of legacy systems. Old systems, developed before the effort to unify the architecture, will make minimal use of the infrastructure. As new systems become legacy systems, some of the infrastructure also will become legacy. There must be a continuing assessment of the impact of these incompatible legacy layers. At some point, the cost of maintaining and supporting this layer may justify the replacement or major rework of an application. This should be considered a cost of infrastructure unless there are also substantial improvements to the functionality or efficiency of the associated business function.

Regardless of the specializations, the infrastructure must be viewed as a unified environment. While the telephone system across the nation varies considerably in the equipment used, the communication media (for example, wire, fiberoptics, microwave, or radio), and the ancillary services, it is a unified system—anybody can call and talk to anybody else even though they may use different kinds of telephones and employ multiple communication media and service providers on a single call.

Ownership

The infrastructure must have an organizational owner. This does not mean necessarily that one organization is responsible for all the investment or all the operational control. It does mean that there must be control over the architecture and protocols that enable the infrastructure and the systems it supports to operate and interoperate reliably, securely, and efficiently.

At a minimum, ownership means defining the scope of infrastructure and the associated standards. The implementation and operation of the infrastructure can be decentralized so long as standards for shared services, interfaces, and protocols are enforced. However, in general, the enterprise will be able to ensure the quality of the infrastructure better if the shared services and facilities are the responsibility of one organization.

Evolution

The infrastructure must not be cast in cement—it must evolve as new services are developed, new technology emerges, and economic factors change. The evolution must be managed. This is where modularity of design and industry standards are important. It will not be possible to upgrade the entire infrastructure at one time; upgrades must be rolled out. In general, upgrades must be backward-compatible so that old facilities will continue to function as new facilities are introduced.

Backward compatibility is important to the infrastructure, but it is crucial to the applications that rely on the infrastructure. It is not acceptable to require major changes to applications to accommodate an infrastructure upgrade, but it may be necessary to make some application changes to realize the benefit of the new infrastructure. This balance between infrastructure improvement and application impact must be managed carefully with an enterprise perspective and attention to quality of service. Infrastructure changes that have an impact on business operations or personal productivity without the proper organizational groundwork will result in significant human problems regardless of the projected value on paper.

Change Control

Change control may be the most critical aspect of infrastructure management. Changes occur as a result of evolution, but they occur more often in the configuration of services and facilities to accommodate new users, applications, and the workload. Changes must be evaluated carefully and deployed in an orderly manner.

Testing is the primary control point for functional changes, including changes in hardware and software versions as well as new products. These changes must be tested in an environment that is reasonably representative of the production environment. Changes that do not meet testing requirements must be rejected.

It may not be possible to test all changes to configurations in a nonproduction environment, but the impact of configuration changes should be evaluated carefully and, if possible, simulated to assess performance impact.

Installation of changes must be orderly so that they are performed properly, they can be linked to associated adverse consequences (for example, a problem occurred when a change was introduced), and they can be revoked if they create serious problems. Change is a major source of risk to the business and must be managed as such.

Setting Application Integration Goals

Enterprise integration is about systems functioning in harmony. The establishment of a common infrastructure will go a long way toward implementation of the EIA. However, enterprise integration requires appropriate participation by applications as well.

Obviously, all the applications in an enterprise cannot simply be converted to the new architecture—many legacy applications will continue to serve the enterprise for years to come. In addition, many enterprise needs may be met by COTS applications. These will come with their own architectures. As a result, the degree of integration will vary from one application to the next.

As with infrastructure, efforts to implement consistent architecture in applications must be balanced against the cost of modifying or redeveloping existing applications. The extent to which consistent architecture will be achieved should be evaluated for each application. The following subsections describe successively greater degrees of application compliance.

Loose Coupling

Loose coupling is the use of asynchronous messaging for the exchange of data between applications. This technology has been accepted widely for enterprise application inegration (EAI)—the integration of COTS and legacy applications. Loose coupling minimizes the propagation of effects of changes between systems, and it implies the capability of one system to accommodate delayed action by another.

Applications must be aligned with business system domains (BSDs). Applications that are tightly coupled are considered to be within the same BSD and recoverable to a consistent state. If applications cannot be recovered to a consistent state, then they are considered to be in different BSDs. Typically, legacy systems and COTS enterprise applications should be viewed as independent BSDs. BSDs are loosely coupled.

As new interfaces are required to integrate with legacy systems, they should be through asynchronous messaging. The requirement for new interfaces occurs most often when there is a need to integrate newly developed or COTS applications. EAI tools facilitate the rapid development of legacy system adapters.

In addition, application interfaces should be designed to make key events available. These events should be available on a subscription basis to address ad hoc needs for monitoring as well as integration of other applications.

Web Access

In general, applications should be accessible using a standard Web browser. This mode of user interaction provides the greatest degree of flexibility and accessibility of systems. Specialized client software should be avoided wherever possible.

New applications must provide Web access. COTS applications should no longer be acceptable without Web access. Over time, many legacy applications should be Web-enabled—particularly if there is a need for ad hoc users (for example, employees who may only have occasional need to access the system).

Certificate-Based Access

As soon as practical, applications should be transitioned to using digital certificates for authentication. This provides the mechanism for authentication of users across the enterprise without prior identification on each system.

Based on certificate authentication, the application should implement role-based authorization that recognizes enterprise-level roles for all users in addition to specialized roles for local users.

The priority given to this capability depends on the scope of the need for access to the application. Applications that are only of interest to an associated business group are low priority.

Workflow-Based Process Automation

Workflow management capabilities should be put in place without waiting to support a specific application. Current manual processes should be automated with workflow management, thus establishing the workflow environment, providing users some experience with workflow management, and establishing user work lists. Managers and workflow designers will need to develop skills in the design of workflow that empowers people and streamlines the business without dehumanizing or micromanaging individuals. Applications should be designed to separate workflow management from application functionality. Standard workflow management facilities should be used to implement these business processes so that they are visible, analyzable, and adaptable.

It may not be feasible to separate workflow management from legacy and COTS applications, but separation should be an important factor in the selection of COTS applications. Major COTS vendors are moving toward workflow-based management of business processes to provide greater flexibility in the adaptation of their products to the needs of particular enterprises. Workflow management should be used to achieve greater synergy and coordination between systems and people.

Over time, the integration of applications should shift from the message sending typical of EAI to the integration of workflow processes. It should be possible to examine the status of a process, including the status of any processes it may have initiated in other business functions and applications.

Observance of industry standards will enable a process to request another process that executes in a different workflow management product.

Other Shared Services

A number of other shared infrastructure services were described in Chapter 4: system management, archiving, business-to-business (B2B) messaging, and organization directory management. Applications should incorporate these services as the opportunity arises.

Using infrastructure system management services may not yield significant savings for COTS and legacy systems, but it will achieve more reliable operations over time. It may be practical for COTS and legacy applications to use the infrastructure archiving and B2B messaging services, particularly if they are Web-enabled and use asynchronous messaging for integration.

Information about the organization may be embedded too deeply in the logic of COTS and legacy systems for them to be converted to using the organization directory service. Nevertheless, as workflow management use increases and the organization transitions to digital certificates for authentication, the use of the common organization directory will become increasingly important.

Shared Technology

It is not essential to the EIA that applications employ common technology, but there are significant benefits in economy of scale, development productivity, and application adaptability if common technologies are employed.

Over time, the preferred technology will change, and new applications will exploit these advances. This evolution should be managed to prevent gratuitous proliferation of techniques. As new technologies are introduced, guidelines should be developed to identify inconsistencies with the architecture, adapt the architecture where appropriate, or define appropriate application exceptions. These assessments should recognize the full cost of deviation, including lost development and operations productivity and higher development and operations risks.

Migration Strategy

Adaptation of applications to the EIA is a long-term effort. As new applications are developed in compliance with the architecture, they will need to interface with existing, legacy applications. As the business changes, legacy systems may be adapted, and where possible, these modifications should be consistent with the EIA. Similarly, as COTS applications are selected, compatibility with the EIA should be a factor in product selection.

In this regard, there are two key events in the life of legacy applications: implementation of loose coupling and implementation of Web access. These events represent an opportunity to migrate the legacy application toward compliance with the EIA.

Implementation of loose coupling may occur as a result of the need to outsource a related application, the need to integrate a COTS application, the implementation of a new application, or the need to geographically distribute related applications. In some cases, this simply means changing the mode of communication with the legacy system.

However, in some cases, the design of the legacy application assumes interaction with a related application within the context of a single transaction. When this is encountered, there is a key decision to be made: Either the related applications will continue to be colocated and characterized as a single integrated business system or the dependency must be broken.

If the related application is being replaced or there is a strong desire to separate the applications for independent operation or management, then the dependencies must be examined in greater depth. It is likely that a linkage performed within the scope of a single transaction was a matter of convenience when the applications were developed; that is, it was easier for the calling application to invoke the other application directly than to post a request for later action. In this case, it may be possible to convert the mode of communication to use asynchronous messaging, enabling each application to complete its transaction independently. This is the preferred solution.

If the dependency remains unresolved, it is probably because the action occurring in the requesting application depends on data managed by the secondary application. If the data in the secondary application affect the result of the primary application, then removing the accesses from the scope of a single transaction could result in an inconsistency between the applications.

This dependency can still be resolved asynchronously, but it involves more complexity than the automatic retraction of a failed transaction. The asynchronous operation must determine, in the end, if a consistent result has been reached. If it has not, then compensating actions must be performed, possibly in both systems, and if a user initiated the action, he or she also may have to make appropriate adjustments or reenter a request.

As a final alternative, the data of the secondary application may be replicated in the environment of the primary application. This replicated data may be updated with asynchronous messages as changes occur. This enables the primary application to complete its action in a single transaction within its own environment. This has the advantage that the end user will experience good performance in completion of the transaction. However, there may still be situations where a true inconsistency can occur and must be detected and resolved through compensating actions.

Managing Application Development

Enterprise integration requires that applications meet integration requirements. We will not examine all aspects of application development here, but we will focus attention on five integration requirements that require particular management attention for enterprise integration:

- Infrastructure foundation
- Standards compliance
- Reuse discipline
- Design reviews
- Integration testing

Infrastructure Foundation

Applications must be developed to plug into the enterprise infrastructure. This will constrain application design and will be a source of opposition from some application developers. Application developers must not be allowed to avoid the infrastructure and develop or acquire their own alternative facilities and services. Either they must use the infrastructure as is or justify changing it.

In many cases, new applications will be the drivers for infrastructure change. New technology will offer new business value. However, the cost-benefit analysis must go beyond the individual application. It must consider the cost of associated changes required to the infrastructure and other applications as well as the potential long-term impact on enterprise integration.

Standards Compliance

New applications must comply with all infrastructure standards and applicable industry standards. Compliance with infrastructure standards is part of accepting the enterprise infrastructure as the application foundation. In addition, applications must incorporate other industry standards in order to achieve long-term flexibility, maintain vendor independence, and support enterprise integration at the business function level.

Data standards are the most fundamental. They enable the communication of information between systems and for management information. Interface standards are important for the integration of applications and services. At a minimum, it must be possible to loosely couple applications through standards for asynchronous messaging. In addition, it is important that standards for finer-grained components be incorporated where possible in order to provide flexibility and interchangeability of applications and finer-grained components in the future.

Reuse Discipline

Earlier we discussed reuse in a broad context for achieving economies of scale. Here we are concerned with achieving reuse in the development of applications. Reuse of software components is important for achieving consistency as well as improving the quality, cost, and flexibility of applications. The same types of reuse discussed earlier are applicable to application development: common systems, shared services, shared components, and specifications reuse. We will consider these four types of reuse from an application-development perspective.

The development of common systems brings the added challenge of reconciling differences between operating units. This begins with the development of common data specifications but goes much further. Those who will use the system may view the undertaking as a threat, and top management commitment and support are required to force people to work together toward common goals of consistency, efficiency, and quality improvement. A person with strong skills in negotiation and insight into the needs of the business that cut through provincial attitudes should lead the project. It may be very difficult to introduce common systems until the individual units see it as necessary to their own success.

Shared services support multiple applications over a network. These could be shared databases, or they could be applications that respond to requests. These will provide the greatest degree of consistency because they consolidate development as well as production support. However, shared services may be less flexible and responsive to needs for change, and they may introduce performance concerns.

Shared components come in two primary subtypes: executable modules and reusable source code. *Executable modules* are generally software products or library modules that provide specific computational functions. These modules are not expected to change and must be treated as black boxes because developers do not have access to the source code. They are not portable across platforms. *Reusable source code* provides the opportunity to examine the inner workings of the component, and it also opens the door to alteration. When alterations are made, the long-term benefit of being reusable code is eliminated; the only benefit is in the reduction of development time by starting with something that works. Components written in the Java language are highly portable both because of the Java virtual machine (JVM) and the supporting components that provide a consistent abstraction of different operating environments. There is already a marketplace in Java components, but these are still, for the most part, computational components as opposed to components that implement business functionality.

Specifications reuse involves the development of robust specifications. The OMG Model Driven Architecture (MDA) will enable tools to generate interoperable, executable code from Unified Modeling Language (UML) specifications. Specification reuse can provide portability of the application or component through the ability to generate code to different platforms. A particular benefit of specification reuse is the durability of the application in the face of changing implementation technologies and infrastructure. Even if the specifications are not shared by different organizations, the application may be able to exploit changing technology and adapt to changing business needs long after other implementations would be obsolete.

In the development process, as in the larger context, reuse requires management commitment and support. The development process must determine the applicability of each of the preceding types of reuse. This includes reuse of both existing components and components that should be developed for future reuse in other applications. However, identifying the candidates is not enough. There are four key elements to successful reuse:

- A willingness to reuse rather than reinvent
- Design for reuse
- A commitment to support
- A cost allocation mechanism

The first requires appropriate incentives. Developers and their managers will have a preference for the approach with least risk. An unknown black box represents a greater risk than a solution that can be designed and controlled for the particular project, unless it is obvious that the capabilities of the black box would be difficult to reproduce.

Design for reuse requires special skills and the anticipation of how a component may be used in the future. This requires extra effort by highly skilled people. It also requires an initial investment that is greater than that required to satisfy the needs of the first application. Consequently, design for reuse has a cost deterrent.

The commitment to support means that there will always be somebody to upgrade the component as needs arise and technology changes, and there will always be somebody with the expertise to assist in the proper use of the component and the resolution of problems when they arise. Consequently, this is a financial commitment that represents a risk to the component owner. It also requires commitment by the owner organization to give priority to the needs of those using the component and objectively consider the needs and impact on all applications when developing new versions.

The commitment to support will not survive if there is not an appropriate mechanism for allocation of costs, at least within a large enterprise. If the support organization is viewed as overhead, then it will always be at risk. If the cost is allocated and supported by the applications and organizations that use the component, then there is ongoing justification for the commitment of resources.

Note that successful software product vendors meet all these requirements. Software products are, by definition, reusable components.

Within and enterprise, small-scale reuse often succeeds where stable, relatively small application development organizations attempt to reuse their own work products. Reuse fails where the scope of reuse extends to organizations that do not accept both the benefit and the burden of reuse.

These are all management issues. Design for reuse is a technical activity, but it will not occur without management commitment. Reuse will not be successful, except on a very small scale, without a management commitment to addressing these issues.

Design Reviews

Design reviews are a key element in ensuring that an application will use the infrastructure properly, comply with applicable standards, and use appropriate sharable components and services. Design reviews must involve knowledgeable people from outside the development team; at least some of these should be from the infrastructure management organization. Criteria for the evaluation of the design should be documented so that developers understand what is expected. However, reviewers should consider other design factors as well.

Design reviews must occur at several stages in the development process:

- When a conceptual design is proposed
- When a general design is completed
- When system integration begins
- When the application is ready for user acceptance evaluation

If an early design review is avoided, substantial work may become committed to a flawed design. As a result, there will be opposition to correcting the flaws, and corrections will not be as effective as a good initial design. In addition, without the design review, the project may be undertaken without an adequate understanding of the cost and complexity, creating the risk that shortcuts will be taken later in the project.

Intermediate design reviews are necessary to keep the development on track and identify problems that may emerge as the details unfold. By the time system integration testing begins, the application should be reasonably complete, but detection of problems through reviews usually will be less costly than discovering them during testing or later.

The final review should occur before user acceptance. The user should not invest time in evaluating a flawed design, and the developers should not release a flawed design. At this stage, it will take considerable management commitment to correct flaws, particularly if correction will delay the implementation. However, a lack of commitment at this stage will tend to under-mine the commitment at earlier stages in future projects. In addition, the actual cost of avoiding corrections at this stage could be very high after the applica-tion is moved to production operation. The flawed application may affect the operation of other applications and the integrated operation of the business as well.

Integration Testing

The application must be tested thoroughly to ensure effective integration with the infrastructure and related applications. As with the final design review, the application should not go to user acceptance testing without first demonstrating that it will function properly and with an acceptable level of performance and impact on other systems when integrated. This requires a test environment that simulates the production environment. This environment should be maintained for testing of future releases of the same application.

Testing should be viewed as a distinct discipline. Resources, including peo-ple, hardware, and software, should be assigned to integration testing. These people should not be part of the application development team. Their role is to ensure that nothing is introduced into the production environment that will adversely affect other applications and infrastructure performance, fail to meet performance and reliability expectations, or fail to incorporate infra-structure services as appropriate. The testing team must have the authority, with management support, to stop deployment of a system that does not meet acceptance criteria. This power may be very painful if it is exercised, but recog-nition that the power is real will alter behavior earlier in the project when the problems typically begin.

Setting Standards

The enterprise integration architecture depends on the adoption and applica-tion of standards. This is an ongoing process.

Preferred standards should be those defined by an industry consortium that represents a diverse group of participants, not a single enterprise. Too often de facto standards are defined by vendor dominance in the marketplace. These proprietary standards give the advantage to that vendor in terms of both prod-uct compliance and the ability to change the standard. Although proprietary standards will continue to be a factor, industry standards should be applied wherever possible.

Now we will explore the key standards needed for enterprise integration. Later we will consider the approach to adoption and application. There are five key goals for standards:

- Internet participation
- Interoperability
- Productivity
- Adaptability
- Management information

We will examine each of these in the following subsections.

Internet Participation

Internet participation has become critical to the success of the enterprise. Internet participation requires compliance with standards. This is the domain of most rapid change. Standards for Web access are relatively stable, but standards for electronic commerce are in the formative stages. Early adoption of standards in this domain may be risky, but if electronic commerce is a critical element for the future success of the enterprise, then the enterprise should participate in the development of standards and balance the risk of adopting failed standards against the risk of lost business.

The primary organizations for the definition of Internet standards are the World Wide Web Consortium (W3C), the Internet Engineering Task Force (IETF), and the Enterprise Business XML (ebXML) initiative of the United Nations Center for Trade Facilitation and Electronic Business (UN/CEFACT).

Interoperability

Interoperability focuses on the capability of applications, components, and services to work together to meet enterprise requirements. Interoperability focuses on interfaces and protocols, not the implementations behind the interfaces. This preserves the opportunity for innovation and enhancement within applications, components, and services without affecting related facilities.

A number of interoperability standards exist for an infrastructure: networks, middleware, and infrastructure services. Some standards are emerging for applications. In the Object Management Group (OMG), interoperability specifications focus on synchronous interfaces—requests and responses completed within the scope of a single business system domain (BSD). In the Open Application Group (OAG), standards focus on the format and content of asynchronous messages exchanged between BSDs.

Productivity

Standards enhance productivity by improving the predictability of results, thus reducing rework and the diversity of skills required of persons engaged in using the technology.

The Java 2 Enterprise Edition (J2EE) architecture defines standards for an application environment. It defines a complementary set of interfaces and services along with a general configuration of an environment in which application components can be executed. Once developers have skills and experience with this environment, they can develop new applications much more quickly and reliably. J2EE and other Java-based specifications are products of the Java Community Process (JCP), which unfortunately is not an open forum.

Development productivity is further enhanced if applications can be constructed using components. A component-based application architecture will be more flexible in the long term. Components that are shared among multiple applications will improve development productivity and probably achieve higher quality. Components that are purchased should provide substantial savings and achieve higher quality if they are successful in the marketplace. As much as possible, the components should be compliant with industry standards. If they conform to industry standards, their interfaces are more likely to be compatible with other components, and ongoing improvements to purchased components will be driven by competition with similar products compliant with the same standards. OMG is developing more robust modeling techniques in the Unified Modeling Language (UML), which will enable the specification of interchangeable components that may be implemented in different technologies. This supports the OMG MDA strategy in which specifications for applications and components will be expressed in technology-independent models, enabling standards-compliant products to be implemented and ported to different technologies.

In system operations, using a consistent set of hardware and software products enhances productivity. The selection of consistent products often turns into the implicit definition of standards based on the selected products. Although the products should be consistent for effective operations, they should be selected based on compliance with industry standards to preserve the ability to replace them in the future. Adoption of standards should come first. In any case, application developers should not rely on the nonstandard features of selected products unless absolutely necessary.

Adaptability

There are four primary ways standards contribute to system adaptability:

- Abstraction
- Consistent business object model
- Workflow management
- Data exchange

We will discuss each of these briefly.

Abstraction

Abstraction involves the hiding of complexity. Standards facilitate the hiding of complexity by providing well-defined interfaces. A well-designed interface will allow for diversity of implementation while ensuring consistency in interface behavior. Encapsulation in object-oriented programming is a special case of abstraction where the interface is to a computational element that has both data and functionality and the specifics of the implementation are concealed behind an interface that defines allowable operations.

Abstraction is important for interfacing with application components, supporting services, operating systems, and business functions generally. When abstraction is achieved using standard interfaces, then the adaptability of the system will be improved because efforts to develop and approve the standard have contemplated a variety of implementations as well as a variety of usage contexts, and the interfaces reflect the potential for this diversity.

It is particularly important that a clear abstraction be defined for the infrastructure. The abstraction should provide the appropriate application services and support, but with the potential for a variety of infrastructure implementations. This enables changes and enhancements to the infrastructure to be implemented with minimal impact on applications, and it improves the potential for applications to be reused in different environments with minimal modification.

Consistent Business Entity Model

A number of concepts and associated data representing business entities are shared between different functional areas of the enterprise. In order for them to communicate and cooperate effectively, these concepts and data should be expressed in consistent ways. Consistent definitions and representations of business concepts are essential for the harmonized operation of the business.

For example, customer, order, employee, department, and other entities are incorporated in many functional areas and systems. These also have identifiers, quantities, units of measure, and other attributes that should be expressed in consistent forms.

Within the various systems, these business entities may be represented as objects—incorporating both data and associated functionality. If the entities are defined with a common business object model, then the implementations may be reusable for multiple applications.

The data, if not the objects, representing these entities will be shared across the enterprise through communications between mainstream systems. Sharing is required in daily operations, but it is also essential for effective management of the business—operationally, tactically, and strategically. It must be possible to compare results of different business units, different product lines', or different time periods using consistent data, or the comparisons are meaningless.

If data are not consistent, then transformations may be required, and in some cases, transformations may be difficult or impossible. For example, if production figures are captured on a weekly basis, it will be impossible to accurately convert these figures to monthly production figures.

Data standards should be consistent with industry standards first. In this way, compatibility problems will be less likely to occur in the future if COTS applications are installed or applications or services are outsourced. Industry standards have the added benefit that they reflect the perspectives of a number of enterprises and may resolve problems that individual enterprises or internal departments may not uncover until reconciliation is much more expensive.

This, of course, must be balanced against the value of proprietary solutions that provide competitive advantage. Such claims should be given careful scrutiny, because competitive advantage is seldom a result of unique representations of business entities and more often is achieved through specialized processes and leveraging special knowledge, skills, or relationships.

Workflow Management

Although business processes will, in some cases, reflect standard business practices (such as accounting practices), the primary goal here is to implement standards that enable the consistent management of business processes. Consistent, well-defined processes are essential to the harmonized enterprise—data about the processes are meaningless if the processes are not known and consistent.

Industry standards for workflow management systems are still under development, and those available have not been widely accepted. However, it is important to take advantage of standards-compliant products as they become available for the following reasons:

Interoperability. Business processes can be implemented using different workflow management products, and interoperability standards will enable integration of these processes across the enterprise.

User access. Users may need access to information about the status of processes in different parts of the business, and some users will participate in processes defined using different products. Each user should have a single work list by which he or she responds to assignments from any workflow product. Often a process in one department will invoke a process in another department. It should be possible for a user to trace these links to determine the current status and identify delays.

Process management. Standard process specifications will support tools to define processes for execution in different workflow management products. Process definition standards will enable transfer of processes to different execution environments and thus support the implementation of common processes in different business units.

Process analysis. Consistent process models and event recording will enable the use of common process analysis tools for identification of bottlenecks and opportunities for process improvement.

Data Exchange

Extensible Markup Language (XML) is rapidly becoming the dominant form of data exchanged between systems, both for EAI and B2B exchanges. The use of XML documents provides improved flexibility in addition to providing a format that can be exchanged easily over the Internet and through firewalls using the HyperText Transfer Protocol (HTTP). In addition, common software functions are available for the manipulation and transformation of XML documents.

Various standards organizations are defining XML-based specifications for particular document types. For example, the OAG focuses on specifications for EAI, and the ebXML initiative of UN/CEFACT and the Organization for the Advancement of Structured Information Standards (OASIS) has provided a foundation for XML-based international electronic commerce transactions.

If the enterprise does not exploit these standards, then additional expense and reduced flexibility will be incurred later.

Electronic Commerce

Substantial progress is being made in the development of standards for electronic commerce, particularly B2B commerce. XML is the common thread of many of these standards. The ebXML consortium has defined a substantial framework for ad hoc B2B conduct of business over the Internet. The processes and documents for various forms of exchanges must be defined to apply these standards. These will likely be adapted from specifications developed by other existing consortia.

The enterprise should be positioned to implement these standards quickly as supporting products become available; otherwise, the enterprise is likely to be at a competitive disadvantage as other enterprises begin to exploit this technology.

Managing Change

Business changes, and consequently system changes, are an ongoing process. Changes will be driven by market forces, by new technology, by new products, and by process innovation. Change is essential to the continued existence of the enterprise in a competitive and changing world. At the same time, change brings significant risks.

Enterprise integration improves the ability to change and the potential for streamlining operations, improving responsiveness and quality, and reducing costs. At the same time, integration and streamlining can increase the risk of change, making reliable operation of the business more dependent on the reliable operation of each of its parts.

Effective management of the business and technical changes must be in place beginning with the design of the EIA and infrastructure. Disciplines for incorporating standards, incorporating enterprise infrastructure, and complying with the EIA must be applied to the design and integration of each application.

Now we will focus on change management at the operational level—management of the change once the infrastructure is in place and the new or revised hardware, software, or application is available to be installed. This change management responsibility will be typically associated with the infrastructure management organization. It requires a knowledge of the infrastructure, the applications, and their interdependencies.

We will examine the following issues:

- Configuration management
- Defined processes

- Testing
- Business transformation
- Risk management

Configuration Management

The basic prerequisite for change control is knowing what you currently have and what is going to change. This requires the creation and maintenance of some form of configuration model. It may be as simple as a spreadsheet, but more likely, it is a database application. The configuration model should include the following along with their relationships and version dependencies:

- Network nodes and links
- Firewalls and gateways
- Computing hardware
- Systems software
- Application services
- Applications
- Documentation
- Users

The model must support transformation to new configurations. This could be as simple as creating a copy and configuring it for a future date. However, it is likely that multiple future configurations will be needed as changes are introduced over time. Often compatibility of different products will depend on their versions, and a series of changes may be required to upgrade individual products without encountering incompatibilities.

Successive configurations each should be validated for compatibility of the new or revised elements. These configurations then become the basis for a change schedule. The configurations also should provide a history of changes to assist in problem resolution.

Defined Processes

The change management organization must have defined business processes. Reliability of the network, systems, and services depends on planned, orderly, and documented implementation of changes. The primary processes are the following:

Capacity planning.   Plans for new applications or growth in existing applications must be translated into capacity plans. These plans will become the basis for installation of additional resources.

Hardware/network configuration. Changes to the network and hardware physical configurations most likely will be managed by the infrastructure organization based on capacity plans and application requirements. These changes usually will not introduce new products, but only changes in network topology and numbers of devices.

System and services software installation/upgrade. Software for operating systems and shared services generally will be within the responsibility of the infrastructure organization, but these are more likely to have interdependencies with each other and with applications, requiring additional coordination and testing.

Application deployment. A request for application deployment generally will come from the application owner supported by details provided by the application developers or technical support staff. Application deployment will require close coordination with the development organization, the application owner (business manager), and the affected end users. Application deployment will require rigorous testing prior to deployment.

Application changes. Application changes will come from the application owner with support from the application technical staff. These changes generally will require less testing, coordination, and planning, particularly with end users, because the scope of impact should be focused on particular functions.

Process improvement. As business processes are removed from applications and implemented as workflow processes, changes may be managed more directly by the associated business function organizations. At the same time, some process changes could have significant effects on infrastructure workload. It would be desirable for the change management organization to participate in a change review process to identify possible performance issues and ensure that needed capacity will be available.

These processes have interdependencies. The role of the change management organization is to identify the interdependencies in order to develop and manage coordinated schedules that will ensure the continued reliable, responsive operation of the associated systems and services.

Testing

Testing is a critical aspect of quality assurance. For infrastructure components, testing should occur in a model environment that mimics the production environment and simulates user and application activity. In order to provide an effective simulation of production, it may be necessary to configure a test system that incorporates related applications, enabling revised components to be replaced and tested individually. If possible, user inputs should be simulated so that tests are controlled and repeatable—this also reduces the cost involved with actual user participation.

For applications as well as services developed locally, a total of four phases of testing should be performed:

Unit testing. Testing of individual components of the application by application developers.

Integration testing. Testing of the application components integrated in an environment with associated software and services to validate interoperability and identify performance issues.

User acceptance testing. Testing of the application functionality based on business requirements with user involvement.

Preproduction testing. Testing in a simulated production environment with production activity levels to assess performance and determine infrastructure workload impact.

The last testing phase is much like the testing for infrastructure components. The last phase is, in both cases, under control of the infrastructure change management organization and is the basis for determining if the application can be accepted for production.

Business Transformation

Many application changes can be deployed with minimal impact on the application users. Some deployments, particularly new applications, will be the drivers of business transformation.

There are seven key elements of business transformation:

Management commitment. The management of the affected business functions must be visibly committed to the transformation and call on its employees for their support. The mood must be teamwork and nonthreatening.

Deployment plan. A plan for the transformation must define what will change for who, when, and how the transition will occur at the individual employee level. If possible, the plan should provide for a rolling change that affects a limited segment of the organization at any one time.

Policy and process changes. Changes to policies and processes must be prepared, reviewed, and discussed with employees well in advance of the deployment.

Changes to organizations, jobs, and roles.   Similarly, changes to organizations, job definitions, and roles must be determined well in advance and discussed with employees. Employee concerns should be addressed before the deployment.

Preparation of technical support.   The technical support staff, including help-desk and problem-resolution functions, must be prepared in advance with appropriate training and reference materials.

User education and training.   Users must be educated in the nature of the system change, the application functions, the user interfaces, and problem-resolution procedures so that they are reasonably comfortable using the application as soon as it is operational.

Transitional assistance.   Business and technical experts should be on call during a transitional period to assist users and operations personnel as they adapt to the new way of doing business.

If the deployment is not coordinated properly and supported for the business function community, it may cause major disruptions of the business and will foster continued opposition in the acceptance of future changes.

Risk Mitigation

A number of risks will be associated with any change to the infrastructure or applications; we will not attempt to deal with them all here. However, there are some basic principles of risk mitigation that should be observed whenever possible:

One thing at a time.   Avoid changing multiple systems at the same time. If problems emerge after changes are implemented, it is much more difficult to locate the source of the problem if there are a number of components that have been changed. In addition, if the change must be revoked, there will be less impact on the business.

Limited-scope rollout.   Do not use a big-bang approach to introduce a new application. Implement it for one segment of the organization at a time so that problems are resolved with a small group and all groups can receive an appropriate level of transitional support.

Backward compatibility.   Design changes to be backward-compatible so that the entire organization need not be transformed at the same time, and if the change is revoked, it is not necessary to redo any work already completed with the new application.

Business cycle timing.   Coordinate the change with the business cycle so that the change does not occur during peak workload periods or at times when there are critical deadlines or high-business-risk circumstances.

Change-retraction (contingency) plan. Have a plan for retraction of the change, including compensating operations, if necessary; identification of possible reentry or rework; and a checklist of everything that must be done to resume normal operations after the change is removed.

User preparedness. Prepare users to expect the change, understand the intended impact, and be prepared to report suspicious results. Users should not learn about a change after they have spent hours trying to figure out what is wrong with their local network or personal computers.

These all seem like common sense, but they are often overlooked.

Consolidating Information Systems Management

Enterprise integration relies on an information systems organization to properly manage the infrastructure and applications for reliable, responsive systems. The Internet has reversed the move of the 1990s to departmental, client-server systems and the migration away from central data-processing services. The increased complexity and risks require the skills, economies of scale, and control provided by a centralized organization.

Key functions of an information systems organization include the following:

Operations/system administration. In general, systems will be required to be operational 24 hours a day, 7 days a week to support Web access. Operations activities also include system backup and recovery services.

Infrastructure engineering. The infrastructure engineering organization is responsible for the configuration of the infrastructure and support for applications. Technical personnel may need to be on call during non-business hours to support system operations.

Production support. Support personnel will be required for a help desk, security adminstration, and resolution of more complex problems with applications. Some of these activities will require coverage 24 hours a day.

Change management. Change management was discussed earlier. This organization must validate, coordinate, and control changes to the infrastructure and applications.

Application development. Application developers will be involved in the development of new applications, changes to existing applications, adaptation of legacy systems, and the integration of COTS applications. This also will include support for development and implementation of business processes implemented with workflow management. Their special skills should be leveraged across applications for multiple business functions, and then efforts must be managed to ensure compliance with standards.

Testing.   A testing environment must be maintained for preproduction testing to assess compatibility and the performance impact of new applications and software. The same or associated environment(s) may be supported for application integration and user acceptance testing.

Standards.   A group must be responsible for the definition of infrastructure standards, compliance reviews, and the evaluation of deviation requests. Members of this group should maintain an awareness and possibly participate in the development of industry standards.

Quality improvement.   A group should be defined as responsible for quality improvement. This should include the identification of performance measures, the review of processes, the investigation of failures and defects, the analysis of overall performance, and the support for continuous process improvement.

Cost allocation.   Costs of the information systems services must be allocated to the business functions supported so that consumption of resources is evaluated appropriately against business needs. Operating statistics and other services (such as technical support) must be transformed to appropriate costs.

Internal audit.   Periodic checks must be performed to ensure compliance with standards, processes, record-keeping, and security requirements.

Some may recognize a close similarity between this organization and the traditional data-processing services organizations of the past. This is no coincidence. Many of the problems are essentially the same. The major changes are in the details and are related to security and the Internet.

Considering Critical Success Factors

Implementation of an EIA is a major undertaking. During the implementation, the technology and thus the details of the target architecture will continue to change. The effort will require upfront investment and commitment. The benefits may be of limited value until synergy of multiple applications and economies of scale begin to emerge.

There are many factors involved. Much of the effort involves technical expertise. At the same time, the effort cannot succeed without management commitment and leadership. In order to focus the leadership at a business level, the following critical success factors are suggested as objectives that will drive the successful implementation of the EIA:

Shared vision.   Top management must be committed to a vision of enterprise integration that is shared and supported by the rest of the organization. Management should identify one or more key indicators of progress toward achieving a shared vision.

Standards.   There must be a commitment to standards with a strong preference for nonproprietary industry standards to preserve vendor independence and system flexibility. The commitment to standards must be reflected in both involvement in industry standards efforts and the selection of products that are compliant with industry standards.

Service-oriented organizations.   Each business function must exhibit a service-oriented approach to fulfilling its enterprise responsibilities. Each organization must have well-defined responsibilities, functions, and processes that are applied in response to relevant events or requests. The organization is responsible and accountable for addressing the need and incorporating the services of other organizations as required.

Shared infrastructure.   The shared infrastructure must be managed centrally and eventually support all applications. The scope of the infrastructure should expand to encompass all computing and communication services that can be shared by multiple applications.

Accessible data and knowledge.   If enterprise integration is successful, then consistent, relevant data and knowledge will be accessible whenever and wherever it is needed to support business needs from top management to production operators. Data also will be communicated between systems in a timely manner without the need for human interpretation or intervention. Historical data will be preserved and accessible for accountability, performance metrics, and trend analysis.

Summary

The message of this chapter is that implementation of the EIA is first and foremost a management challenge. Top management must be committed to using the technology in a planned and orchestrated manner to achieve an integration of the activities of both people and machines. This integration is required to enable the enterprise to function as a harmonious whole in the design and integration of systems, in the improvement of business processes, in responses to business problems and opportunities, and in development of relationships with business partners and customers.

Internet technology has created a new business environment, founded on technology but propelled by business opportunities, both in new ways of doing business and in the opening of a global marketplace where political boundaries and geographic distances are no longer the key factors in the development of business relationships. In order to remain competitive, enterprises must respond to these new opportunities for international operations—both operationally and in the marketplace.

Internet technology also has created tremendous opportunity to access and exchange information and streamline business operations. The presentation of appropriate enterprise information on the Web can have a major impact on enterprise business opportunities. The ability to access and exchange appropriate data and engage the right individuals within the enterprise will improve efficiency and the quality of plans and decisions. The development of relationships over the public Internet will create new opportunities for reducing costs and marketing products, as well as opportunities for new business endeavors.

The enterprise interation architecture will support system integration and adaptation, and it will provide a foundation for deployment of the MDA. The implementation of automated business processes will enable rapid process improvement and eliminate delays. The enterprise that is adaptable, integrated, and harmonized will win in this new business environment. Others will be unable to keep up with the response to opportunities, the reductions in cost, and the improvements in quality of products and services.

We started this book with discussions of the changing technological and business environments and the business opportunities and business objectives of enterprise integration. Subsequent chapters described the general architectural approach, the requirements for shared infrastructure, the nature of business function domains, and the support of business functions with applications and an Internet-oriented architecture. Additional chapters described key technologies: messaging, workflow management, XML, components, and security. Chapter 12 built on this foundation to describe the potential for the intelligent enterprise, where a synergy of computer systems and knowledge workers opens new opportunities for the enterprise and its people to excel. In this chapter we presented the management challenge.

In many enterprises, managers are aware of some of the opportunities but do not know how to exploit the technology to realize them. They see the need for investment and the risks of ill-conceived or poorly implemented undertakings. Often they do not understand why their technical people are not defining the solutions and building the systems they need. At the same time, their technical people understand certain technologies but cannot keep up with all the new products and standards and are unable to translate the technical capabilities into business opportunities. They do not understand the enterprise priorities, and they do not know why their managers do not pursue an integration architecture, install the necessary infrastructure, and provide the necessary leadership to integrate the enterprise.

Hopefully, this chapter provides a management roadmap and this book helps bridge the gap between business objectives and technological capabilities so that managers can lead and technical people can support a coordinated pursuit of enterprise integration.

References

The following are references I found useful in the preparation of this book. Much of the material for this book came from standards documents available on the World Wide Web. Since industry standards continue to evolve, references to those documents are not included here but are provided on the Web page associated with this book. Please refer to the Web page at *www.wiley.com/compbooks/cummins* for current references.

Austin, Tom, *PKI*, John Wiley & Sons, New York, 2001.

Birbeck, Mark, Jason Diamond, Jon Duckett, Oli Gauti Gudmundsson, Pete Kobak, Evan Lenz, Steve Livingstone, Daniel Marcus, Stephen Mohr, Nikola Ozu, Jonathon Pinnock, Keith Visco, Andrew Watt, Kevin Williams, and Zoran Zaev, *Professional XML*, 2d ed., Birmingham, UK: Wrox Press, 2001.

Darnell, Rick, *HTML 4: Professional Reference Edition,* Indianapolis: Sams Publishing, 1998.

Hartman, Bret, Donald J. Flinn, and Konstantin Beznosov, *Enterprise Security with EJB and CORBA*, New York: John Wiley & Sons, 2001.

Lyons-Burke, Kathy, *Federal Agency Use of Public Key Technology for Digital Signatures and Authentication*, NIST Special Publication 800-25, Washington: National Institute of Standards and Technology, September 2000.

Maruyama, Hiroshi, Kent Tamura, and Naohiko Uramoto, *XML and Java: Developing Web Applications*, Reading, MA: Addison-Wesley, 1999.

Murhammer, Martin W., Oreun Atakan, Stefan Bretz, Larry R. Pufgh, Kazunari Suzuki, and David H. Wood, *TCP/IP Tutorial and Technical Overview,* 6th ed., Upper Saddle River, NJ: Prentice-Hall, 1998.

"NIST, Internet Security Policy: A Technical Guide," draft NIST Special Publication, National Institute of Standards and Technology, Washington, July 1997.

Parker, Tim, and Mark A. Sportack, *TCP/IP Unleashed,* Indianapolis: Sams Publishing, 2000.

Sheresh, Beth, and Doug Sheresh, *Understanding Directory Services,* Indianapolis: New Riders Publishing, 2000.

Slama, Dirk, Jason Garbis, and Perry Russell, *Enterprise CORBA,* Upper Saddle River, NJ: Prentice-Hall, 1999.

Strebe, Matthew, and Charles Perkins, *Firewalls,* Sybex, Inc., Alameda, CA, 2000.

Yeager, Nancy J., and Robert E. McGrath, *Web Server Tehnology: The Advanced Guide for World Wide Web Information Providers,* San Francisco: Morgan Kaufman Publishers, 1996.

Zahavi, Ron, *Enterprise Application Integration with CORBA: Component and Web-Based Solutions,* New York: John Wiley & Sons, 2000.

Index

CPSIA information can be obtained at www.ICGtesting.com
Printed in the USA
LVOW11s0054040813

346097LV00005B/28/A